Dear Doti,

The power is inside of you to realize all the power that has ever been needed. Perceive at the 3rd eye all that you have missed. The seat of intuition is there & should not be missed!

~[signature]

**YOUR GUIDE
to
SCIENTIFIC
SELF-REALIZATION**

YOUR GUIDE to SCIENTIFIC SELF-REALIZATION

Heal the Body, Calm the Mind, and Be Ever Joyful Through the Power of Yoga

Dr. Derek Simpson

Ascended Books

Your Guide to Scientific Self-Realization by Dr. Derek Simpson

Copyright © 2016 Dr. Derek Simpson

Editor: Amy Keslinke, MA

All rights reserved. No part of this publication may be reproduced, distributed, or transmitted in any form or by any means, including photocopying, recording, or other electronic or mechanical methods, without the prior written permission of the publisher, except in the case of brief quotations embodied in critical reviews and certain other noncommercial uses permitted by copyright law. For permission requests, write to the publisher at the address at the bottom of the page.

Scripture quotations from The Authorized (King James) Version. Rights in the Authorized Version in the United Kingdom are vested in the Crown. Reproduced by permission of the Crown's patentee, Cambridge University Press.

Scripture quotations taken from the New American Standard Bible®, Copyright © 1960, 1962, 1963, 1968, 1971, 1972, 1973, 1975, 1977, 1995 by The Lockman Foundation. Used by permission. www.Lockman.org

Includes bibliographical references
First Printing, 2017

Ascended Books
drsimpson_1@hotmail.com

Dedicated to God,
Gurus, and Saints of all Religions.
For without your inspiration
none of this would be possible.

Acknowledgments

I would like to recognize the people in my life that helped me get to this point. First, I want to thank my wife, because without her loving devotion and constant positive vibration, I may not have been so inspired to do the work.

Secondly, I would like to thank my mother, who always pushed me to strive for more; my sisters and brothers, who have supported me in all the life decisions I have made; and my stepfather for keeping us all together under one roof.

Next, I would like to thank my editor, Amy Keslinke. Without her editorial knowledge, this book would not have read as well or looked as good. It is difficult to find the "right" editor and the Divine answered my prayers perfectly with Amy's help.

There also have been others in my life that, no matter how little I saw them, were always happy to see me. These people include my best friend and best man, J.R. Wydra, and his beautiful wife, Kelly Wydra. We may not see them for years at a time, but J.R. and Kelly are always consistently awesome. The same goes for my cousin Justin Ferrell and close friends, Lisa M. Blacker, Drs. Kateri Porto and Matthew Peahl.

I also want to thank the wonderful physicians I met while in medical school. They contributed greatly to my level of consciousness, helping me to shed away the many layers of karma that were necessary for God-realization. These physicians include Dr. Kateri Porto, Dr. Matthew Peahl, Dr. Christian Carroll, Dr. Mats Gunnars, and Dr. Timothy Francis. Other family such as Scott and Asha Zimmerle were also instrumental in my research on the topic of self-realization.

Finally, the countless spiritual teachers, angels, saints, gurus, masters of self-realization, and Christ figures that have helped me to see the light in all of creation. This book is for each of you that are fighting the good fight and continue to do so in the spiritual realms.

- Dr. Derek Simpson

Contents

Preface .... *i*
Introduction .... *iii*

Chapter 1   The Journey 1
Chapter 2   Inner Peace 7
Chapter 3   Bliss 11
Chapter 4   The Minervan Man 15
Chapter 5   Self-Realization 21
Chapter 6   Meditation 29
Chapter 7   Yoga 37
Chapter 8   Samadhi 45
Chapter 9   Muscle Testing 61
Chapter 10   Intro to LOCs 81
Chapter 11   1st Dimension LOCs 99
Chapter 12   Christ Consciousness and Beyond 113
Chapter 13   2nd Dimension LOCs 137
Chapter 14   3rd Dimension LOCs 153
Chapter 15   Multidimensional LOCs 197
Chapter 16   Extradimensional LOCs 209
Chapter 17   A Siddhi Summary 273
Chapter 18   A Self-Realized Summary 287
Chapter 19   How to Get Started Meditating 297
Chapter 20   The Beginning of Self-Realization 301

Appendix A: References for the Yoga Sutras, Samadhi, and Yogic Siddhis 305
Appendix B: Self-Realization LOC Chart 308
Appendix C: Aeon Calculation and Diagram 310
Appendix D: Kriya Organizations 311
Appendix E: Types of Meditation 314

Notes 316
Selected Bibliography 337
Glossary 339
Index 349
Author Bio 359

Figures/Tables/Lists

Figure 8.1	Types of Samadhi	56
Figure 8.2	The Eleven Limbs of Yoga	57
Table 10.1	Dr. Hawkin's LOC Scale	89
Figure 10.2	Spiritual Light of the Third Eye	92
Figure 10.3A	Categories of Consciousness	94
Figure 10.3B	Categories of Consciousness (cont.)	95
Figure 12.1	Energy Flow to Cosmic Consciousness	116
Table 12.2A	A Numerical Baseline	124
Table 12.2B	A Numerical Baseline (cont.)	126
Figure 12.3	CC1 Value as an Exponent	127
Figure 12.4	The Actual Value of CC1	128
Figure 14.1	Sphere of Samadhi	156
Figure 15.1	The Interstate	198
Figure 15.2	Interstate Shape	200
Figure 16.1	Spiritual Light of the Third Eye	233
Figure 16.2	The Graphing of Eternity	243
Figure 16.3	Soul's Love in Nirvikalpa	249
Table 17.1	Master Siddhis Chart	280
List A.1	Yoga Sutras References	305
List A.2	Samadhi References	305
List A.3	Siddhi References	307
Table B.1	Self-Realization LOC Chart	308
Table B.2	Self-Realization LOC Chart (cont.)	309
Figure C.1	Aeon Calculation	310
Table C.2	Aeon Calculation Diagram	310
List D.1	Kriya Organizations	311
List E.1	Types of Meditation	314

Disclaimer

The author of this book does not dispense medical advice or prescribe the use of any technique as a form of treatment for physical or medical problems without the advice of a physician, either directly or indirectly. The reader should regularly consult a physician in matters relating to his/her health and particularly with respect to any symptoms that may require diagnosis or medical attention. The intent of the author is only to offer information of a general nature to help you in your quest for emotional wellbeing, good health, and spiritual realization. In the event you use any of the information in this book for yourself, which is your constitutional right, the author and publisher assume no responsibility for your actions.

Although the author and publisher have made every effort to ensure that the information in this book was correct at press time, the author and publisher do not assume and hereby disclaim any liability to any party for any loss, damage, or disruption caused by errors or omissions, whether such errors or omissions result from negligence, accident, or any other cause.

Many quotations have been used in reference to the traditions of spiritual teachers, gurus, saints, and self-realized masters. None of these individuals directly endorse the interpretation this book gives on the mathematical calculation of self-realization and the many levels of consciousness associated. This includes Sivananda, Yogananda, Sri Chinmoy, and any other individual that has been quoted or referenced.

Preface

To be inclusive in this book, many resources, citations, and references were used to gain the greatest understanding of the process of self-realization. Originally, I experienced all the states and hand-wrote all information down in five to six journals while overseas. Shortly after finishing I knew I had to publish the experiences, so that others could understand how to achieve the bliss-joy-love I had received.

On this path, many have given their all to understand the path to self-realization and without their added knowledge, this book would not be possible. I have included three sets of resources that are mentioned in the Appendices of the book. I felt they needed more attention, so they are specifically indexed in Appendix A. This is because the knowledge gained here is not my own. Credit in this case, should always be given, when credit is due. One is on Patanjali's *Yoga Sutras*, the second is on *samadhi*, and the third is on *siddhis*.

I have cited wherever exact quotations have been used. It has been difficult to use my own words to describe exactly the ideas conveyed by the ancient masters, so some interpretations may appear the same or similar to others. This is because the Sanskrit origin of most words used by Patanjali or other ancient writers were only interpreted by a few words in English. If you are interested in reading more on these subjects, I would suggest following up on the sources contained in Appendix A.

Wherever Patanjali's *Yoga Sutras* are mentioned, the footnote referenced in the Notes section will be specific to that *sutra* (verse). There have been many interpretations of this master's famous text, and they will all be referenced here in the beginning of the book, rather than as footnotes throughout, in order to prevent confusion towards citation and interpretation itself. Some individuals have given very simple and direct translations, while others have given more expanded ideas and opinions. This book gives a blend of both simple and expanded interpretations in order to be easily comprehended for a modern age. The translation references are included in Appendix A.1 in the back of the book after the Notes page and the Bibliography.

The references for *samadhi*, are similarly listed, as they are for the *Yoga Sutra* translations. Many masters, gurus, teachers, and swamis have commented on this term *samadhi* and their ideas have been taken into great consideration to bridge the gap between old and new interpretations. Some may or may not agree on the interpretations provided by this book, but all interpretations have been considered very carefully. Some footnotes were included if a specific master's interpretation was relevant to the book's topic.

The three views of *samadhi*, included in this book, are detailed in Chapter 8. They are the "Classical and Modern Views" and the "Expanded View." All definitions under "Classical and Modern Views of Samadhi" are from Patanjali and others who wrote direct interpretations of the Patanjali's *Yoga Sutras*. There also references to the works of Sivananda, Yogananda, Sri Chinmoy, Jnaneshvara Bharati, and anyone who expounded upon the aspects of *samadhi* during the 20th century and early 21st century. Finally, the "Expanded View of Samadhi" is from my own personal experiences in meditation mixed with ideas of the masters. The sources are included in Appendix A.2 after the *Yoga Sutra* translations and are ordered in accordance to date to show which writings came first.

Although Swami Sivananda's published works seem to be only from the very late 20th century, this master's works actually originated early in the 20th century. His work was very extensive, but also easily available for reference. This is also the same for Ramana Maharshi and Yogananda, as their book material manifested in the early- to mid-20th century.

Finally, there were many sources that talked about the paranormal powers of yogis. This is talked about in Chapter 17: A Siddhi Summary. These include (in alphabetical order according to the author's name) the references listed third in Appendix A.3.

INTRODUCTION

This book is my personal account of the spiritual experiences I had in China between 2013 to 2014, while practicing meditative yoga. I have learned much through different spiritual organizations allowing me to discover scientifically and intuitively the quantitative process of self-realization.

My first spiritual teacher (guru) was Paramahansa Yogananda from Self-Realization Fellowship (SRF). Since my work with him I have discovered that an individual can connect with more than one guru. This includes Lahiri Mahasaya, Sri Yukteswar, St. Francis of Assisi, Sivananda Saraswati, and Sri Chinmoy. All of these masters have communicated with me at one time or another and have shared their immense love and guidance.

I originally began my journey towards self-realization with the teachings from SRF, but many intermediary and final techniques and methods were discovered intuitively from deep meditation while overseas. My goal was to reach this highly-exalted state, but also to discover an even faster way for the average workingman or -woman to achieve it. I explain this story more completely in the first chapter of the book.

It is also necessary to note that there are many organizations in the world that offer spiritually evolving yogic techniques to help the world advance. The one spoken about in this book is called the *Kriya*. There are many versions of the *Kriya*, but the version that I used was originally taught by Sri Lahiri Mahasaya. This information can be discovered in his published diaries, called *Purana Purusha* by Dr. Ashoke Kumar Chatterjee. Also in the back of the book under "Kriya Organizations," are the major groups that teach *Kriya* or another soul-evolving technique that is similar.

What does it mean to become self-realized? To never have negative emotion again towards oneself or others? To always be cheery and delightful?

I believe it is to know inwardly—within yourself—that love is the highest truth. Self-realization means to become so realized within love itself, that you can say, "I love you" to anyone and truly mean it. It means to outwardly be able to transcend time and space throughout all situations with an infinite level of stillness, peace, and bliss that is beyond the comparison of normal consciousness.

The type of realization presented in this book is of the workingman's variety. Any human being on the planet, regardless of their position in life, has the opportunity to achieve realization if they work hard enough. This is the workingman's type of spiritual labor that will allow you to create an unlimited level of stillness, peace, joy, and bliss at any desired moment. This manifestation is important because we all struggle, in one way or another, maintaining the peace of mind required to traverse the storms of everyday life.

Your Guide to Scientific Self-realization is the only book of its kind. It is the first book to quantify the entire process to self-realization through muscle-testing. Each chapter is sequential in preparing you in this journey, including basic techniques that can be used, daily practices, links to other resources, and charts to help guide your ascension. This book is literally my personal journey, illustrated as I experienced it.

Quotes are also included from the saints, avatars, and gurus of all religions. Each belief system is represented to help create harmony amongst the many spiritual practices in the world. Unifying all of these beliefs is the practice of yoga. Contrary to common belief, yoga isn't just for slender, disciplined, vegetable-eating individuals, but also for the curvy, omnivorous, meat-eating, concrete-jungle fighting warriors of this world. It is for you and for every workingman or -woman that desires something greater in his/her life.

The focus of the book is on yogic meditation, but one that can be practiced at any time—while mowing the lawn, driving the car, or shuffling paper at work. This book is for both the experienced meditator or for those who are just beginning the path to inner peace through yoga.

This is also a book for those who want to understand their own level of inner peace, sustained happiness, spiritual realization and most importantly, how to reach life goals. Life goals are more easily achieved if your spiritual life is line with the Divine. The information in this book is meant to show the "measureable" way to self-realization and how to stay on the straight-and-narrow. This is literally a guidebook giving the exact numbers and levels required to reach enlightenment. It also provides a method to measure your own enlightenment, showing the precise progress in reaching the highest states of consciousness. With your own effort, you will not only help yourself, but will raise the consciousness of the world, bringing humankind to their rightful place with the Divine.

Each of the many varying belief systems is unique. To understand one completely, it is best to see how they all fit together as a unit. One religion cannot exist without the others in this physical world of equal and opposite—physical, mental, emotional, and spiritual reactions. If you are an agnostic, you are usually content in your position of not knowing everything about SPIRIT. If you are an atheist, you believe there is no 'presence' beyond self and generally fall in the category of a humanist. Being an agnostic or atheist may be considered the opposite to those who are Christian, Islamic, or Jewish, but ultimately none is lesser or greater than the others. Each belief system is really just a piece to the puzzle of existence.

This book also assumes that, whether you are an atheist, Catholic, Buddhist, or Muslim, you desire to do good for yourself and others. This assumption is presented along a large scale of what is 'good', but we will assume all fall within the general realm of morality, including the Golden Rule ('Do unto others, as you would have done unto you'), do not murder/steal/covet, and so forth. These moral guidelines are widely accepted for most people.

Some choose not to categorize themselves at all and refuse association with any label in the continuum of religious taxonomy. One part of this continuum is the Unitarian Universalist perspective, which says that all religions, faiths, and belief systems are a part of the same process in "the free and responsible search for truth and meaning."[1] All Unitarian Universalists can have any varying level of faith or belief system, but still have meditation as the core or even a part of their practice. To continue to create equality among the various religious languages, words like 'Lord' or 'God' may be used in this book, as other belief systems acknowledge these words as acceptable and equal to the

---

[1] UUA.org 1996–2017.

word 'Creator'. If one views this 'Creator' as an unexplainable vibration with the power to create at will, most people reading this book will see the innate connections of the Divine in all faith systems. My desire is to have everyone see this definition of the Divine as a benefit, not a threat, to their spiritual frame of reference, whether or not he or another individual believes it to be relative or absolute in nature. With the loss of threat comes the hope of assimilation of new knowledge, its many applications, and future spiritual evolution and acceptance.

If one subjective word was used to describe this energy or unexplainable vibration, that word would be bliss. As you ascend in "levels of consciousness," or LOC, blissful feelings will increase. The experience of bliss is what you should want to think, feel, and have when desiring to achieve a higher level of unified consciousness. It is absolutely possible, however, to achieve bliss without having a definable higher vibration. When you are guided by a belief-system, it may appear easier to achieve higher levels of vibrational consciousness because you already possess a conception of the Divine. It is not necessary, but very helpful!

The 'She' pronoun may also be used interchangeably with the 'He' pronoun to give no bias to the gender or sex of God. If God is beyond creation, then how could 'He' be limited to one sex? Do we believe that we are the only creation in the universe? Did God only create self-conscious species that are exclusively either male or female? Doesn't that appear a little limiting to an all-powerful creative SPIRIT, considering that "lower" life forms such as bacteria can reproduce asexually? These are thoughts to ponder.

If you are completely absorbed in your own belief-systems, ideas of religious unification will appear heretical. If you put God in a box, then the borders you create will continue to create division between other belief systems. Instead, if you think "outside" of the box, then you will begin to see the boundaries as a way to segregate and exclude other people and ideas. Open-mindedness is required when reading this book, otherwise the only reward will be intolerance and frustration.

One of the ways of practicing your open-mindedness while journeying through spiritual texts is to digest new religious vernacular with an impartial eye. "Blessing" is one word that is commonly used in religious circles. For example, as one ascends in LOC, realization of the 'true self' occurs allowing one to be "blessed," or be more apt to receiving "blessings." These blessings are really just feel-good vibrations that seemingly appear out of nowhere, urging the mind and consciousness of the individual to progress forward into the meditative unknown. Some religions believe that these "feel-good" vibrations come from a deity or an already self-realized human-being. Where they actually arrive from does not matter; what matters is how the blessings are achieved. Meditation, in this way, is the best opportunity to obtain these positive, energetic waves provided by your spiritual director.

Those who are considered "experts" in the field of yoga often facilitate the process of meditation. These experts are usually given the name of guru, saint, master, and avatar. They are considered to have manifested the purest vibration of the Divine. These teachers are able to transmit a pure vibration to those devotees or open-minded individuals who are willing to receive it. Some of the greatest teachers include Bhagavan Krishna (Christ of India) and Jesus Christ (Christ of the Western world). These two benevolent prophets are considered to be some of the highest sources of God's divine manifestation. There are also lesser or minor saints that have lived as a part of most cultures. They also are able to transmit a certain portion of this pure consciousness to those who have a willing and open mind.

The goal of meditation is to achieve pure conscious awareness. It is described as "being awake inside without being aware of anything except awareness itself."[2] In this way meditation is both the destination as well as the journey. However it is applied, meditation will always provide some positive benefit to those who attempt it.

What is really the best belief system then? It is the one where love, tolerance, open-mindedness, compassion, and humility reign supreme. You may not agree with another's belief system, but that doesn't mean you should be frustrated or angered by it. Seeing that meditation can be inserted as a process of religious and spiritual self-evaluation can be crucial to discovering the truth behind all of existence and being at peace with all paths to the Divine.

This book was written initially based upon pure experience; in the moment it was occurring. I personally knew very little about the intricacy of self-realization, except that I intrinsically desired a perfect

---

[2] Phelan 1979, 6.

peace and boundless joy. In the process to self-realization, I discovered that my experience was the same or similar to many of the masters of self-realization. My path is to provide you the Way in a concise, discreet, measurable, and attainable manner.

This information needs to be shared with the world so that others may know that self-realization is not limited to avatars, masters, gurus, and Christ figures of the world religions.

Now is the time for the peoples of Earth to acknowledge their oneness in the Divine. Through this oneness true harmony and peace are found. Read on, and you will see that this is the true age of ascension

CHAPTER 1

The Journey

The journey towards self-discovery is one that you will take. Sometimes the path is long and arduous with many twists and turns, seemingly unending, but a certain goal shall be achieved. Whether this end be something simple like marriage to a soul-mate, wonderful children, or the perfect job, a goal is in mind.

For you, that goal is greater than what mere physical achievements can purely satisfy. Realize too that the "goal" is not the end in itself, for after you have achieved the "goal," there will then be another goal in mind, until you have become divinely satiated. If this is the case, then the journey should really be the focus then, not the goal. But isn't the goal the thing that needs to be achieved? For, without it, wouldn't the journey seem less sweet?

It is both the journey and the goal that needs to be kept in mind. One cannot exist without the other. A goal without the journey, is like a house without a roof or a child without a parent. Each needs to be present in one form or another in order to exist. My journey was and is still like this—I desired to reach self-realization but did not realize it until I had met the teacher that would take me there.

A Desire for Peace

I had always known that my desire was to have peace that could not be shaken, no matter the circumstance. Even as a very young child, experiencing the woes of parents who could not get along, inner peace was necessary to maintain stability in my childhood.

Even after my parents divorced, the turmoil did not stop. My father, after his divorce from my mother, died not even three years later of stomach cancer, leading me to fall further into unrest. During this time, although still very young, I sought after every type of temptation to prevent myself from facing the truth of my father's passing.

These attractions did not last long because the spiritual pull on my heart was great, leading me to engross myself in a diverse blend of religious traditions. These included both Christianity and Buddhism. It was not until later, at the end of medical school, that I discovered meditative yoga and the ultimate path to freedom.

My father was a non-practicing Jehovah's Witness and my mother a Catholic. How they decided that it would be wise to have children together is beyond my rational understanding, but alas, here I am with two sisters. I remember as a toddler attending Kingdom Hall conventions and going door-to-door with my father's mother. My mother, not being as keen on the practices of the Jehovah's Witnesses, struggled to find spiritual harmony within our family unit. It was not long before my father and mother decided divorce was a better choice.

My mother did not start dating for a while so as to help us kids deal better with the divorce and the nature of our present situation. My eldest sister did not see it this way. She felt it was necessary for my mother to find love again because she knew that a loving and consistently present father figure was necessary for us. Mind you, my eldest sister was only 10 at the time, but being wise beyond her years, she decided to set up my stepfather and my mother on a date. My stepfather lived a block down the street and was always kind, courteous, and helpful. Soon, he and my mother started dating and were married within a few years.

Religiously, my stepfather didn't mind what we practiced, as he was open to most things. So, we all attended a Presbyterian church, and this church was the one in which I was baptized and raised. My mother, now not restricted by the covenants of the Jehovah's Witness religion, could be free to explore her new-age spiritual belief systems.

Around seventh grade, shortly after my father passed, I became very interested in Eastern religion and mysticism. I tried to make sense of the nature of life and death by seeking solace in the mystical meditative religions of the East. In the end, I chose to attend a Christian-based church as a Presbyterian, but also blended Buddhist philosophy into my spiritually-mixed mindset.

Throughout my undergraduate studies, I delved further and further into Christianity from a fundamentalist perspective, but found the restriction to be too great. My religious exclusivity prevented further inclusion from other religions that had perspectives of truth on the nature of creation and the Divine that were legitimate, universal, and authentic.

As soon as I realized that not just one religious viewpoint could be a genuine path to the Divine, I began to open myself further to other religious perspectives while still maintaining Jesus Christ as my ultimate spiritual teacher. Still on the search for perfect peace, I acted as I believed was Christ-like but never achieved the unshakable level of peace desired. At this time, I felt something was missing.

The Path

Near the end of my medical school education, I realized I needed the help of a teacher or "guru" to help me learn meditation. I was no longer interested in cryptic and allegorical messages found in the ancient biblical texts. I was looking for a how-to, step-by-step, scientific approach to raising my consciousness leading to the perpetual peace and joy I had been seeking.

What I could not find clearly in the Christian bible was a rational and direct approach to meditation. I had tried Buddhist meditation at a Nichiren Shoshu temple but could not connect to the constant verbal chanting and prayer. While I was four years into medical school with my first degree in chiropractic medicine, a chiropractic student I knew invited me for meditation at a group called Self-Realization Fellowship. Their meditation teacher, Paramahansa Yogananda, had passed almost 60 years before, but the organization was still thriving in United States and throughout the world.

Being skeptical, I attended the meditation and was happy to experience a service that was very similar to the traditional Presbyterian Sunday worship services, but with a strong Eastern and yogic foundational perspective. Self-Realization Fellowship offered a year of lessons that provided step-by-step instructions on how to meditate and evolve the body and brain enough so I could achieve self-realization in this lifetime.

For $0.70 a lesson, at one lesson every week for an entire year, this plan seemed like a no-brainer for me, considering I had very little experience with consistent meditation. At the end of these lessons, I could become initiated in a spiritual technique called the *Kriya*. This technique has been taught by many masters over the last two centuries, but this particular group's guru, Paramahansa Yogananda, merged both the yogic teachings of the East with those religious and spiritual values of the West.

I decided that the lessons were the perfect way for a student (so used to academic obligations) to stay motivated to practice and meditate morning and night. After the first year of following the lessons, I received a meditative, breath technique called the *Kriya* and found that my internal level of peace and happiness increased as an automatic result of the practice. I no longer needed to devise certain mindful methods of thought and positive affirmations to maintain peace; instead, peace would automatically manifest itself. At this time, I knew that my path was the right one, and if I continued at this pace, the experience of self-realization could become a reality.

During this time, I was getting married, and my wife and I were planning on traveling to China to teach English as a first-year-of-marriage experience. While I was in China, I began to experience higher levels of consciousness: having visions of the universe, becoming one with the reality of time-space, and interacting directly with ancient masters of the past.

My ability to maintain peace was easy. At this point, it had gone beyond peace and evolved into joy and finally, everlasting, ever-new bliss. This constant manifestation of bliss is what I have characterized as the quality of one who is able to reach self-realization, and the peaks of God-realization. This high level of self-realization is to be so enamored with the Divine's presence, that sometimes even walking around is quite a task! The bliss of the Divine is so intense that one can only think of joy and bliss, as no other thought can be let in. This state is the truest level of realization. If you can obtain, access, and maintain this bliss at any moment, then you have reached the highest peaks of God-realization.

This level is my own body's current state of realization. Even while I am at work as a chiropractor adjusting low backs and necks, this bliss overflows infinitely, allowing me to weather any storm. Sitting for any length of time practicing certain techniques allows the body to automatically enter an extreme state of bliss.

My journey, however, has just begun. Before I had the Divine's bliss, I knew only moments where complete peace would envelop me. Now, peace is always present. The goal has been achieved, but there is still more to do.

This book outlines that experience. It is an attempt to bring to light the scientific approach to achieving self-realization with a "measureable," but theoretical, numerical scale. It is not about fantastic visions, but a scientific, systematic, and mathematical approach to self-realization which is ultimately quantifiable and realistically attainable.

CHAPTER 2

Inner Peace

Wouldn't it be nice if there were some way of inserting a little peace into our lives when moments of strife, trial, and tribulation arise? Maybe a little peace in the mind of the guy swerving around everyone on the road. Maybe a little peace in the mind of the boss who thinks an employee is not pulling his/her own weight. Maybe we could insert a little peace into the minds of our children and every other person that we find is not offering what we think we deserve.

Everyone goes through it. We all get frustrated at life's seemingly meaningful events. These events, whether large or small, can make us believe that they stand head and shoulders above every other incident crossing our path. Maybe someone cuts us off on the road. Maybe our boss is telling us how we need to pick up the pace. Maybe our children are not the perfect angels they could be.

What if you could insert that peace into your life—right here and right now? What if you could access an infinite amount of peace that could be used to overcome any life obstacle that comes your way? The road-raging driver, the mad-minded boss, and the childish-child would seem like no more than just an act on the stage of life. This is what true peace does.

This kind of true peace doesn't come from taking a few breaths and counting to 10; it is peace that is all-encompassing. It is present and available in all of life's situations. This "true" peace is the "inner" peace that is gained through contact with the Divine in meditation and prayer. This inner peace comes straight from the "Top."

The Top is the Divine Presence, the unexplainable, high-level, feel-good vibration that exists beyond all else. Whether you call it God, Allah, Jehovah, The Universe, Vibration, Energy, Goddess, Spirit, Yahweh, Alpha and Omega, Father, or Mother does not matter. What matters is where it comes from. It comes from an infinite source that has no beginning and no end.

Whether you worry, judge another, have conflict, make assumptions, or lose appreciation for life itself, peace (in general) will always be needed to balance the scales. The surface-level variety of peace only lasts for a short time, but the kind that comes from your soul connection to the Divine is unlimited and always available.

Some say that this soul-linked inner peace comes through self-acceptance, letting go of all cares, and being in the present moment. But how does one do this? Most people on the path to inner peace go through trial-and-error until they can discover a technique, way of thinking, or spiritual practice that helps them develop the inner peace they seek.

Some people will say it is their salvation in Jesus Christ, others will say their *shahada* or complete faith in Allah brings them their ultimate peace. But what about those who have no central belief in a higher power—are they exempt from true inner peace? Proponents of a strong religious system would argue yes, because without the existence of a higher power, how could one have true spiritual inner peace in a physical body that appears to both imperfect and insufficient?

The Buddha, who reached the highest level of enlightenment, taught that a god did not exist. The Buddha said that understanding the heart instead of the focusing our attention on the heavens is the best way to find answers to our troubles and thus attain inner peace.[1]

This book will show that all paths to inner peace are correct. However, some small sects of major religions believe that killing or hurting another human life is acceptable. The only paths to true inner peace are through peaceable acts—not ones that physically, mentally, emotionally, or spiritually bring harm to yourself or another.

One of these acts, namely meditation, will be expounded upon at great lengths in this book, showing how one can achieve inner peace easily and quickly. This inner peace will lead to self-realization, but it must begin with your choice to start your meditative practice today.

---

[1] Dhammika 1996-2012.

CHAPTER 3

Bliss

Bliss is emotional transcendence.

Bliss is an enlightened state of being that is commonly confused for an emotion experienced in everyday living. It is an emotion, but it is also not an emotion. Bliss is the transcendence of all emotion. Many think that bliss is a combination of all the best emotions including joy, happiness, contentment, peace, and tranquility. It could be described in such a combined way, but ultimately this definition is not the most precise. It may appear that bliss, while commonly used in our modern language as, "perfect happiness"[1] or "supreme happiness,"[2] is "an exhilarating psychological state of pride and optimism, or even an absence of depression,"[3] bliss goes far beyond these definitions.

Bliss is used in this book to describe how good the Divine vibration feels and how it affects a person's physiological and psychological

---

[1] Collins English Dictionary 2014.
[2] Random House Kenerman Webster's College Dictionary 2010.
[3] WordNet 3.0. (n.d.).

being. When you are on the path of self-realization, constantly increasing in prayerful meditative mindfulness, bliss is a common "feeling." Bliss is given as a gift by the Divine to help motivate you on the path while you ascend on the stepladder of stillness and mindfulness. Bliss also protects you from impending harm that would have negative effects on the physical body and mental/emotional states.

If bliss is really a transcendence of all other emotions—even those emotions that describe the highest level of joy—then how is it perceived, and what is its purpose?

Bliss is given and perceived as a spiritual gift, by great power of will, or by the ultimate way of self-realization through scientific meditative techniques. Bliss can be given as a gift in the moments of suffering when all hope seems to be lost. By great willpower, an individual thinking "good" things, setting their mind ablaze with devotion towards the Divine love, can bring about a blissful way of being.

Bliss can also be manifested more completely, fully, and permanently through the use of a scientific meditative technique. Indeed, bliss is perceived and felt as an extreme happiness, but it is invariably a protection from the ills that plague us while in the physical body.

Those who live on planet Earth know that suffering is inevitable. Without suffering, you would not have a reason to seek a higher way of being. Bliss is given to help overcome that suffering and is the state of mind that all mortals hope to achieve. Bliss not only relieves the suffering, but also allows you to become and remain unattached to constant and inevitable suffering that occurs in everyday life.

The longer you are able to remain in a blissful and meditative state of mindfulness, the more likely you will remain unattached to your body's physical suffering and the woes of life. Bliss does not allow an individual to become "detached" from a particular suffering, because becoming detached suggests an occurrence by force. Bliss, being transcendent, cannot cause anything to be done by force, only by perfect transition. "Unattached" suggests that, when you are in the state of bliss, an easy transition is created between an initial "suffering," the experiencing of the "suffering," and the movement past said "suffering."

Notice that when you have manifested a perfect level of joyfulness in the body, no rude comment or physical injury has any effect on the body or mind. Bliss changes the vibrational state of the body, allowing it to experience the feeling of pain, but not allowing it to be transmitted negatively to the mind. If bliss is able to continue to overflow in the body and mind, the consciousness will then easily transcend the suffering, nullifying it to ease forward progression.

A man or woman of moderate or advanced realization can manifest this bliss every day through attention and focus to the third eye. Through this focus, the Divine's superconscious mind is perceived in all of its glory, bestowing the perceiver with the Divine Sense. With a bliss-permeated body, physical, mental, emotional, and even spiritual karma can be taken on and burned easily without additional distress to the body. This taking on of karma is the ultimate role of the Minervan man† or ascended master‡ in this current world age.

Bliss not only serves the Minervan man or ascended master in this age, but it also serves as the ultimate euphoric ecstasy. It is truly better than any drug, as it allows you to manifest the highest states of joy as a gift, willfully and spontaneously (with no effort).

Although it can come and stay for a period of time, bliss serves to provide some entertainment from the physical world that we live in. Realize that you do not come from this world. You are a divine being having an earthly experience. This world is not perfect and is full of suffering, but that suffering is only present so that you might be directed back towards the Divine. For without it, there would be no purpose in seeking what is good and righteous.

With a continuous influx of blissful, mindful engagement, true contentment and satisfaction becomes possible. You do not know true satisfaction until you have experienced the calm after the emotional storm of cathartic release. Experiencing bliss acts in the same way. It brings peace, contentment, joy, happiness, and satisfaction all at once. It is, in some ways, a combination of emotions, but ultimately, bliss

---

† Minervan man is explained more completely in Chapter 4
‡ Read more about the ascended master in Chapter 17

transcends basic "happy" emotions to the level where no suffering can prevail over the body, mind, and consciousness.

In this world, you can witness suffering at any given moment, whether it is on the TV, the computer, or in person. You could go to many extremes to attempt to escape the mass-suffering going on in the world, including eating, smoking, drinking, working too hard, working not enough, and more. In such a world, moderation is necessary. Bliss allows for true contentment to manifest and take hold in the mind. By doing so, satisfaction is guaranteed and moderation can ensue, leading to a healthy and balanced lifestyle.

Those who practice yoga are called to lead a balanced lifestyle as role models to all. Those who practice Kriya yoga, or some other spiritually evolving technique, practice moderation because they know that extremes will only serve to push away those individuals who are one-sided. Remaining in the middle allows for a wider scope of awareness among what is possible and what is not. Practicing a spiritualized yoga that incorporates a scientific technique is the fastest way to achieve the bliss described above.

Bliss is for all and to all it will eventually come.

CHAPTER 4

The Minervan Man

The Minervan man is one who embodies the workingman or -woman in their capability to achieve the highest levels of realization. The word *minerva* in Latin as a noun means "spinning, genius, skill, learning, or working."[1] *Minerva*, originally Etruscan from Proto-Indo-European *men-es-wah*, which extended from *men-s-*, means "mind" in Sanskrit or "full of mind or sense"[2].

In Roman culture, Minerva was the goddess of wisdom who was worshipped for strategic warfare, commerce, schools, and the arts, especially weaving and spinning. Minerva is considered the Roman counterpart of the goddess Athena.[3] The term *minervan* is used because it represents the word "working" in both Latin and Sanskrit, two languages that remain the basis for most others on this planet.

The workingman which is representative of humankind, not just male or female, is the average individual who will exist in future spiritual ages as a majority of fully, spiritually enlightened human

---

[1] Google Translate for "working" in Latin
[2] Wiktionary (n.d.).
[3] Wikipedia (n.d.).

beings who live on the planet. One who is a "Minervan man" will embody both an androgynous aspect inwardly and/or outwardly. This person may appear to be gender-specific as a "male" or "female" but will vibrate inwardly with the Divine aspect that sees the equality in all people and created things.

Generally, the Minervan man will be an extremely devotional being and/or a renaissance man or renaissance woman with the innate ability for spiritual ventures. Being a jack-of-all and master-of-none, he will gravitate towards a strong spiritual and meditative practice knowing that the Divine is the only real satisfaction. Outwardly, he goes about his workday attempting to be content with all that transpires in life, but inwardly desires something he cannot describe or understand.

An Earthly Evolution

As the millennia continue forward, the spiritual consciousness of the Earth will increase allowing for more and more spiritually evolved beings to populate the Earth. This expansion is possible because we are now in a spiritual upward cycle, bringing about a fuller awareness of our true nature as the Divine. We see this development everywhere. Whether we are becoming aware of new technologies, creating greater equality amongst all, or realizing that we can heal through non-physical means, this transformation is occurring.

In this current era, the existence of the Minervan man is only about 1.5% of the world's population.[†] That may not sound like very much, but this is around 100,000,000 people. So, if the Minervan man represents around 100,000,000 people, how can these individuals be recognized?

The Minervan man is one who has achieved at least *savikalpa samadhi*. For those who understand what this level represents, they say "How can this be true?" "It has to be impossible!" It is not impossible, in fact achievement of *savikalpa* can be both a transient experience and/or a permanent existence.

Savikalpa samadhi is considered the greatest minor *samadhi* or the greatest minor level of stillness achieved. This stillness is one that manifests throughout the entire body, not just the limbs, heart, or mind. For many spiritualists, yogis, and other practitioners of faith, this

---

† How I came to this percentage is mentioned later on in the chapter.

level of realization represents complete stillness in the body that can be carried easily throughout the day.†

To become a permanent resident of this state, you will need to be initiated through a Divine Superconscious Experience (DSCE).‡ This is the divine initiation provided by God and gurus to help start the upward ascension of the mind towards the infinite state of joy experienced in *nirvikalpa samadhi*;∞ this state being the highest experience of God's consciousness. Achievement of this state requires great willpower and the grace of the guru. Willpower comes in the form of intensified devotion during a prayerful/meditative practice using a spiritually evolving breath-/energy-control technique. The grace of a guru, saint, or prophet is required because, without their assistance, it is nearly impossible to achieve such a plateau of existence.

Achievement of this state transiently occurs in one major way—through group prayer or meditation. Typically, the larger the group, the better the effect. If everyone is truly of one mind, then this transient ascension occurs more readily.‡

Group Focus is Key

There are five major world religions—Hinduism, Judaism, Buddhism, Christianity, and Islam—that are practiced in today's society. However, not all of them allow *savikalpa samadhi* to occur because one-mindedness is not practiced by the entire group. Out of the five major world religions, Islam and Buddhism achieve this state most often in their group meditations.

Devout Muslims are known to pray five times per day, which allows them to be unified with their spiritual brothers and sisters more often throughout their practice. The same goes for Buddhists, but their focus during meditation is on the universe, becoming one with it, and transcending the suffering of this Earth-reality. Because both these spiritual practices are focused on maintaining stillness in meditation, stillness is what becomes manifested. If these individuals are praying in large groups, then that stillness becomes amplified into the greatest minor stillness of *savikalpa*.

---

† More on *savikalpa samadhi* is expounded upon in Chapter 14
‡ More on DSCE is expounded upon in Chapter 14
∞ More on *nirvikalpa samadhi* is expounded upon in Chapter 16

To some degree, the stillness of *savikalpa* can be carried throughout the day by these individuals, but only with great willpower. If the individual has not been completely attuned to *savikalpa* through a DSCE (Divine Superconscious Experience), then he will drop out of this level of stillness until he can become re-attuned in the group setting.

Some spiritual practices, such as Hinduism, Buddhism, and even Christianity, focus on self-realization or self-actualization as a major goal. Even these individuals as a group, despite being focused on stillness and with one goal in mind, will not achieve *savikalpa*. The religious dogma of these groups embeds itself into the minds of followers, preventing them from believing it is possible to achieve true stillness.

If you find yourself in one of these groups, break free now! This affiliation inhibits you from truly evolving. This realization is absolutely essential because the Earth is in an upward state of spiritual evolution allowing for ease of ascension.

The next question would be, why couldn't the Christians, Jews, or Hindus manifest this state of stillness as a part of their group worship? These three religions are so spread in their beliefs about who, what, when, where, why, how they should do something, that it is difficult to achieve these states during group prayer or meditation. More importantly, each of these three religions specifically do something that prevents them from going deeper in stillness.

Let's start with Christianity. I, being raised as a Christian, believed (at one time) so fervently the ideals I was taught that I would condemn others in their faith for having beliefs that conflicted with my own. For this reason alone, I came to realize something was missing in my understanding of the Divine.

Although exclusion and condemnation should never be practiced by any belief system, they often occur, as a rule, because most people on their particular paths believe that their religion is the "right" one. However, even this mindset isn't what prevents the advanced state of stillness of *savikalpa samadhi*. The major aspect that is missing from Christian worship services is scheduled silent prayer.

How often do Christians sit through a worship service where the silence experienced is at least 10 minutes or longer? I personally have attended many churches over the years, and the time of silence is usually very short. At one time, I attended a Roman Catholic church, and for the first time, I experienced an above-average amount of silence in a Christian church service. While it approached the essential well-roundedness of a church service, it still didn't reach the level of silence necessary to achieve *savikalpa*.

From what I know of Protestant and Catholic religions, the ability to practice stillness is not widely known. Because they are so widely attended, these churches have the greatest chance to create a long, silent, and devotional prayer time, but often don't because average churchgoers are not educated on the value of stillness. If the Christians were to demand it, then the church officials would have to provide time for this type of silent prayer.

Judaism is about following the letter of the law while loving God. If indeed many Jews practice the Old Testament law as provided by the Torah, then the focus for prayer may strictly be one of repetition and religion. Of course, this is not the case for all Jews, but as with Christianity, the religion is divided on what to practice and how to practice their belief system.

Jews practice stillness of the heart, usually during silent meditation. This practice is sometimes described as a "heart of stillness." Psalm 65:2 says, "to You silence is praise," and in the Babylonian Talmud says, "the pious men of old used to wait an hour and pray for an hour and then wait again for an hour."[4]

It makes sense that these "pious men of old" were spending times of silence reflecting on the Divine's presence before and after prayer towards the Divine. However, this practice, being one that comes much closer to the stillness of *savikalpa*, is not practiced as heavily as it could be among groups of Jews and especially during worship.

Judaism is a very important part of the history of religions, as it was the first of the three Abrahamic religions to appear. Abraham gave rise to both Christianity and Islam, and so serves a major role in their development. Judaism is just as necessary as other religious practices because it serves as the foundation for others to come.

---

[4] Babylonian Talmud: Tractate Berakoth 32b. v. 27.

Finally, many of the beliefs of Hinduism center on the worship of gods and goddesses. Many Hindus will say and understand that the version of the god or goddess to whom they pay homage is just one of the infinite versions of the Creator. But without a central belief system that all Hindus practice together in one mind, the stillness is not easily transferred during prayer and meditation.

Although Hinduism is one of diversity and plurality, it is not one of religious exclusion. There are many different denominations and schools within Hinduism as there are with Christianity, but there is no great animosity that exists between these Hindu belief systems. Hinduism is really just a collection of different religions that has constantly evolved over time.[5]

A Hindu's belief in the many paths that lead to the one God is a wonderful step in producing unity. However, this is the reason why many groups of followers do not achieve *savikalpa* as a group—because their beliefs are so widespread. A Hindu can easily be a part of one school of thought and just as easily follow the beliefs of another. If one Hindu is giving homage to Vishnu while another is giving praise to Shakti, then the devotion and presence of mind is generally one of difference. Hinduism is a wonderful religion and philosophy, but without the underlying one-mindedness, transient *savikalpa* is very difficult to achieve.

This is not to say one religion is better than another, for all religions are just paths to God—as God is still the one and only true Source. Even though the majority of the 100,000,000 people on Earth represent a larger part of Islam and Buddhism, there are individuals as a part of every group or practice in the world—whether it be paganism, Native American tribal religion, Christianity, Judaism, or Hinduism, that have achieved stillness transiently, permanently, and even higher. Generally, these Minervan-men and -women practice a form of scientific yoga to accelerate the evolution of the brain and body for higher realizations.

However, as the Minervan man begins to develop, basic religious dogma will become transcended naturally as the Divine presence becomes universally seen and experienced in all religions whether large or small.

---

[5] Pollock 2008.

CHAPTER 5

Self-Realization

Self-realization is the highest state of human achievement, bringing about perfect awareness and consciousness. It is the process of becoming fully aware of and directly experiencing the pure, universal nature of the Divine. With self-realization comes unspeakable rapture and continuous divine enjoyment of the Divine's presence.

This level of joy is the kind that cannot be spoken about in mere words alone, but must be realized as your truest nature. This experience is the universal identification with God's innate divinity within. The term "self-realization" can have many meanings to people all over the world depending upon what religion or belief-system they follow, as well as what they term the "ultimate" experience of God to be.

In the Western world, self-realization is relatively undefined, because Christianity, being a large part of Western society, has given only mere hints towards self-realization in parables and allegory. Self-realization in Western society is sometimes referred to as "enlightenment," "self-actualization," or "illumination" and generally has stronger psychological connotations associated with it.

In the Eastern understanding, self-realization is knowledge of the true Self beyond that of the material world. The little "Self" is the soul as a reflection of the purity of God within the physical body of the individual. This concept is particular to Hinduism and similar to Buddhism's enlightenment where one awakens to the realization of the whole Self. This Self is our pure connection to the Divine through our soul. The concept of self-realization is supremely elaborated upon in the branch of *Advaita Vedanta*, which is originally a part of Hinduism.[1] If the Self becomes unified with the Creator through prayer meditation, then it becomes the "Higher Self."[†] Sufism (the mystical, spiritual aspect of Islam) describes seven stages you will take before reaching the divine,[2,3] which forms the connection between you and your Higher Self. The highest stages of consciousness in Sufism is called *fanā'*, or annihilation of the base self in the Divine.[4]

Nirvana is the Buddhist version of self-realization. In Hinduism, it is referred to as *atma-jnana*, which literally means "knowledge of the true self (the soul) beyond physical reality."[5] Out of the five major world religions, Judaism does not directly seek to transcend physical reality to achieve self-realization, but to elevate the world as a whole, and in doing so, you will elevate yourself and your community.

In the strictest sense of the phrase, "self-realization" is the knowing that the soul within is purely divine. Being able to experience the Divine's pure consciousness as the self, in ultimate samadhi stillness, is *savikalpa samadhi*. Once your realization increases in awareness, your true nature in God-realization manifests. You will then experience not only the stillness of samadhi, but also the Divine's joy-bliss-consciousness in *nirvikalpa samadhi*. This is the purest form of self-realization.

Self-realization being a broader term includes God-realization, but there is a difference. One can realize the Self in God, but may not realize the Self as God until *nirvikalpa* manifests.

---

[1] Nakamura 1990.
[†] Check out my blog for more information on the nature of the whole "Self."
[2] Trimingham 1998, vii.
[3] Frager 1999, 96-97
[4] Harmless 2008, 164.
[5] spokensanskrit.de (n.d.).

The Nature of SPIRIT

Self-realization leading to God-realization, as a combination of all the ideas above, will be represented in this book. However, only those of the highest spiritual attainments will be explored deeply. A few presumptions must be made to understand the perspective of this book:

1. First, it is understood that the Divine or SPIRIT (God) itself never changes and is considered changeless.
2. Second, God is both a part of creation (the universe) and is its "creator." As its creator, God is outside of creation and is, by its very nature, non-dualistic. Being non-dualistic is to be beyond the nature of physical reality or duality. Thus, SPIRIT (God) cannot be defined by boundaries, only described with human relativities. Dualism is the existence of opposites, such as hard and soft, light and dark, good and evil.
3. Third, if we, as the Divine's creation, are always changing as a part of a dualistic† reality, then the actual experience of SPIRIT can exist in an infinite number of created forms.

So, how can something never change but be experienced differently without limit? SPIRIT or Source has to be the absolute. Without it, everything would be relative unto itself, meaning the "observer" or person perceives his own surroundings from his individual perspective. Nothing exists outside of that perception. However, not everything can be relative, because even the mere statement of this fact creates an absolute truth. By default, an absolute must then exist. An ultimate foundation has to be present upon which all things exist.

If SPIRIT is the absolute, and thus, had some part to play in creation then it is reasonable to believe that creation is somehow a part of SPIRIT. If SPIRIT is the only thing present, then the materials to manifest creation would have to come out of SPIRIT itself. SPIRIT, being unchanged and infinitely large, allows creation 'as a part of SPIRIT' to exist in an infinite number of ways. Likewise, one could achieve self-realization in an infinite number of ways.

Here is an analogy used for centuries to describe the connectedness of creation: A king brought a group of blind men into his palace

---

† Dualistic refers to the opposing natures of physical reality.

to describe an elephant. Comparing their notes after feeling its different parts, they found themselves in disagreement about the appearance of the animal. The king told them that each one was telling the truth but could only describe the piece that he felt and understood. Similarly, creation (blind men) experiences SPIRIT (the elephant), in many ways. Religions are all aspects of creation, which are all paths to God. Each one goes about it differently, but still arrives at the same goal of self-realization.

The Nature of Self-Realization

Many people over the course of human history have reached the peak of human potential. These individuals may be referred to as "avatars" in India or "Christs" in Western countries. Some call them saints, prophets, or self-realized masters. Others call them great teachers, who have come to Earth to remind us of our true nature in SPIRIT.

Expressing all forms as child or adult and communicating effectively with scholar or ignoramus, these avatars reveal the Divine in its infinitely many forms. One of these great self-realized masters, Paramahansa Yogananda, was a practitioner of meditative yoga. His purpose, as prophesied by his own teacher Sri Yukteswar, was to bring yoga from India to the Western countries. In doing so, he helped many people to realize their own true nature in SPIRIT through meditation.

He termed self-realization as,

> the knowing—in body, mind, and soul—that we are one with the omnipresence of God; that we do not have to pray that it come to us, that we are not merely near it at all times, but that God's omnipresence is our omnipresence; that we are just as much a part of Him now as we ever will be. All we have to do is improve our knowing.[6]

If what Yogananda says is true, we are all then on the same path towards realizing our oneness in SPIRIT (God). Although this path will take many different forms, they all will lead to the same place—self-realization. In psychology, Mortimer Adler describes self-realization as, "freedom from external coercion, including cultural

---

[6] Yogananda 1980, 34.

expectations, political and economic freedom, and the freedom from worldly attachments and desire."[7]

As Adler describes, you must remain unattached before you can know yourself as SPIRIT manifested in physical form. Yogananda is saying just this—that any human being on planet Earth is capable of achieving self-realization. Every person has an ego (individualistic personality) that needs to be dissolved to allow the soul (true character) to realize its divinity in SPIRIT.

Usually introspection, a process of self-questioning, is an initiator onto the path towards self-realization. This deep questioning will help you to discover what is required to start the process. Usually a website or book is discovered through the advice of a helpful friend (or search engine). From there, through divine providence and universal alignment you are directed to a particular path. The same occurred to you when you stumbled upon this book.

The deepest level of introspection may occur over many years or even many lifetimes. You cannot know how long you have searched in past incarnations until you have realized the necessity of God's presence in your life. As time goes on, this desire for realization only increases, as you become increasingly aware that this material world will only provide temporary pleasures and benefits. However, the real benefit comes through liberation of the soul in the fires of deep, silent meditation. In meditation, all will be revealed in the vast field of universal consciousness.

Staying on the Path

The path to self-realization is an arduous one. The individual, climbing up the steepest mental mountain paths, will experience an onslaught of ego-minded efforts to prevent further advancement. As one advances, the path becomes narrower; with many loose stones, jagged edges, and sudden drops. The Gospel of Matthew says,

> Enter through the narrow gate, for the gate is wide and the way is broad that leads to destruction, and there are many who enter through it. For the gate is small and the way is narrow that leads to life, and there are few who find it.[8]

---

[7] Adler 1958, 127.
[8] Matthew 7:13-14 NASB

If you are not careful in knowing where to step, you are sure to stumble and fall. All self-realized masters recommend meditation or sustained, silent devotional prayer as the surest way to prevent backward motion on this rocky path. Some of the "founding fathers" of self-realization include (earliest first):

Krishna	Hinduism	3228 – 3102 BCE	India
Buddha	Buddhism	c. 563 – 483 BCE	Nepal, India
Jesus the Christ	Christianity	6-4 BCE – 30-33 CE	Palestine
Swami Adi Shankara	Hinduism	788 CE – 820 CE	India

The first three are the primary authors initially interpreting self-realization. Swami Adi Shankara, one the greatest and most revered Hindu philosophers/theologians, united various philosophies within India. Essentially, the monastic order of swamis was revived because of his efforts.

Others have also expounded upon these ideas more fully within the context of a modern society, specifically within the last century. These individuals include:

Swami Vivekananda – 1863-1902
> Worship of the Impersonal God is through truth. And what is truth? That I am He. When I say that I am not Thou, it is untrue. When I say that I am separate from you, it is a lie, a terrible lie. I am one with the universe, born one.[9]

Mahatma Gandhi – 1869-1948
> What I want to achieve—and what I have been striving and pining to achieve these thirty years—is self-realization, to see God face to face, to attain Moksha. I live and move and have my being in pursuit of this goal.[10]

Ramana Maharshi – 1879-1950
> There is no seeing. Seeing is only being. The state of Self-realization, as we call it, is not attaining something new or

---

[9] Vivekananda 1993, 42.
[10] Gangrade 2004, 7.

reaching some goal which is far away, but simply being that which you always are and which you always have been. All that is needed is that you give up your realization of the not-true as true.[11]

Sivananda Saraswati – 1887-1963

Cosmic consciousness is not an accident or chance. It is the summit, accessible by a thorny path that has steep, slippery steps. I have ascended them, step by step, the hard way; but at every step I have experienced God coming into my life and lifting me easily to the next step.[12]

Paramahansa Yogananda – 1893-1952

A lazy person never finds God. An idle mind becomes the workshop of the devil. I have seen many *sannyasis* [monks] who renounced work and became nothing more than beggars. But persons who work for a living without any wish for the fruits of action, desiring the Lord alone, are true renunciants.[13]

Sri Chinmoy – 1931-2007

When once realisation dawns, the seeker enjoys freedom from the human personality and the human individuality. It is like a tiny drop of water which enters the ocean. Once it enters, it becomes the ocean. At that time, we don't see the personality of the one tiny drop or the individuality of the drop. It becomes the entire ocean.[14]

Thich Nhat Hanh – 1926-present

You are what you want to become. Why search anymore? You are a wonderful manifestation. The whole of the universe has come together to make your existence possible. There is nothing that is not you. The kingdom of God, the Pure Land, nirvana, happiness, and liberation are all you.[15]

---

[11] Maharshi 1985, 18.
[12] Sivananda 2006, 1.
[13] Yogananda 1980, 104.
[14] Chinmoy 1974, 31.
[15] Hanh 2003, 69-70.

The Dalai Lama – 1935-present
> "If in day-to-day life you lead a good life, honestly, with love, with compassion, and with less selfishness, then automatically it will lead to nirvana.[16]

Now is the time to grasp hold of that which has been provided. So many gurus and paths have been laid before the feet of the masses. You only need to choose that which resonates best with you. However, be aware of false teachings and pseudo-prophets. These types are abundant. So, how can you choose accurately? Continue to chapters 6 and 7 to explore the basics of meditation and yoga to provide foundation for true teachings. Also, in Chapter 9 you will learn to explore your emotional support system and how muscle testing will be the tool to discern your best path.

---

[16] The Dalai Lama 2006, 20.

CHAPTER 6

Meditation

Meditation is the practice of attempting to create an enhanced level of focus and wellbeing. The most common type of meditation is single-pointed concentration.[1] Concentration of any type can be performed while seated, standing, lying down (less known) or actively pursuing a particular action or goal. Zen Buddhism is a common type of active meditation that involves "living in the present," allowing for the thoughts of the mind to enter and be released just as easily, while performing the activities of daily life.

The word "meditation" is translated from the word *dhyana* from the Sanskrit root *dhyai*, meaning "contemplate" or "to meditate on."[2,3] This term, *dhyana*, was generally referred to as a type of religious contemplation commonly used in Buddhism and Hinduism. Meditation can refer to the practice of stillness, the process of strengthening and deepening the spiritual connection with the Divine,

---

[1] Lamrimpa 1995, 72.
[2] Feuerstein 2006, Issue 1.
[3] Macdonell 1893, 134.

or the superficial phenomenon that occurs when you relax into a state of calm passivity. It can be done with eyes open or closed, repeating a mantra[4] silently or verbally, or just keeping the mind free of intruding thoughts through focus on a higher sense of self.

The varying versions of meditation help to manifest a variety of benefits for individuals or for the whole of society. Meditation has increasingly become part of many religions, belief systems, and practices throughout the last three millennia, as it can also be considered concentrated prayer. Through the process of meditation, you can train your mind to create an auto-regulation of peace, joy, and bliss.

The goal of meditation is to achieve pure conscious awareness. It is described as "being awake inside without being aware of anything except awareness itself."[5] In this way meditation is both the destination as well as the journey. However it is applied, meditation will always provide some positive benefit to those who attempt it.

On the individual level, meditation can be used to discipline the mind to become more still or induce a certain level of consciousness. Attaining greater and greater levels of consciousness leads to the promotion of relaxation and the development of patience, love, compassion,[6,7] generosity, and forgiveness. However, the highest form of meditation targets a sustained, everlasting bliss[8] called *samadhi*, which is a state of enlightenment that is impervious to all of life's trials and tribulations.

For society, meditation helps anyone who can sustain even a moment's worth of stillness. Those who practice meditation with regularity have amassed such a store of bliss that the peace begins to extend beyond their own being, positively affecting the environment around them. Think of someone you know, who is always happy, cheerful, and outgoing. Do you notice, you feel better in their presence? This is because their effort to maintain their own happiness has built a storehouse of joy that is easily shared with all through their presence, words, and actions. In doing so, these individuals can affect

---

[4] Sivananda Radha Saraswati 2011.
[5] Phelan 1979, 48:1: 5-20.
[6] University of Wisconsin-Madison 2008
[7] Lutz, A 2008
[8] Lamrimpa 1992, 58-59

people on an individual level which then steadily affect society as a whole.

If you can manifest self-realization through meditation, you will then affect, by mere thought and presence alone, thousands of people you come in contact with in your lifetime. If one thousand people can reach self-realization to some degree, then millions will be affected. Society as a whole will grow and blossom into a new era of peace and harmony.

Meditators must be mindful of the thoughts they repeat in meditation because of the power that lies in attracting situations related to those thoughts. Thoughts can manifest into reality, especially when combined with emotion, whether negative such as hopelessness, fear, or anger or positive emotion such as peace, joy, and bliss.[9] The stronger the mental or emotional fixation to that particular thought or feeling, the faster it can become the predominant reality.

Real-World Manifestation of Meditation

In some religions or belief systems, meditation can be viewed as a ceaseless prayer in which thoughts are constantly revolving toward the Infinite, Divine, Creator, or Ultimate Energy of the universe. Even thoughts of devotion toward something that is higher than yourself could be considered a ceaseless prayer of meditation. These thoughts of love and connectedness are all that is truly required.

Each person and/or society has a different way of viewing the process of meditation, but all of them attempt to quiet the mind to allow the pure energy of the Divine to flow in. This unadulterated flow of energy is necessary for a human to conceive of himself as connected to the Divine. It just doesn't occur through conscious meditation, but also occurs naturally every night in sleep. The divinely conscious human being as its SPIRIT-self, or soul, contacts the Divine every night as it passes into sleep. This soul connection in sleep is one that is embodied and explained in both Judaism and Islam.[10] Sleep is widely known as a necessity for health, but few know of the state of sleep's true purpose.

Objects such as prayer/mala beads (Eastern religions), rosaries (Catholicism), or rudraksha beads (Hinduism, yogic traditions) as a

---

[9] Hicks 2006
[10] Judaism Islam 2006

necklace or bracelet are used to count the number of prayers or techniques performed while the mind is a deep state of meditation/prayer. Some also believe that these objects hold the spiritual energy of the individual, acting as a talisman against negative or invading energies during the deep state of meditation. Sometimes other objects may be used as a focus of meditation such as a crucifix, statues, or other pictorial representation of the desired deity or divine presence.

In the health field, meditation has been used to lower blood pressure[11], combat depression, and reduce anxiety. In the process of clearing the mind, tensions automatically decrease because stressors are released through an internal effort to maintain self-regulation of the stress. Through continued effort, the individual will be able to release from stressors experienced in the present at will by engaging in this auto-self-regulation.

The consistent and frequent experience of deep meditation cuts deep, habit-destroying pathways in the electrical circuitry of the brain. Gradually, detrimental habits that plague the body, mind, or spirit are more easily broken. Essentially, the brain can become rewired and perform exactly as the individual intends. This rewiring also occurs with any type of food or drug addiction, but meditation allows for the individual, not a substance, to become the master controller.

Be Open

Meditation is an opportunity for the peoples of the world to join with the One in all. This connection is necessary for the world to become unified in peace. In our present world society, there are many different ways to begin this connective process. An individual speaking of "something" that exists outside of a physically-based belief system, generally understood as the 'unexplainable', may refer to this as "energy," "vibration," or, for some, a "frequency."

To many, this "vibration" or "frequency" is unexplainable by normal modes of scientific inquiry. Those who have a strongly scientific/logical mind may have no rationale or desire to try to explain what exists beyond the conscious self. Those who are spiritually connected know that the "vibration" of meditation comes from an

---

[11] Rainforth 2008

ultimate "source," where all other vibratory elements of the universe have also originated.

For the purposes of this book, that 'energy' or 'vibration' is what will be described as SPIRIT or the Divine. SPIRIT is the "conscious stuff" that exists outside the space of creation.

Imagine that all of creation is inside a bubble. Everything within that bubble is created or manifested in a way that can be experienced through one of the five physical senses. These senses are both objective and subjective, as both logic and emotion are enacted in a human being. SPIRIT is the stuff that exists outside of this bubble in a void-like space, having no real desire or connection to that creation. But when SPIRIT has the desire to create outside of its conscious self, (assuming that SPIRIT has the capacity to create), it then becomes a creator or as used in this book, the Creator.

The capitalization of Creator denotes a "presence" or something that is outside or higher than the (ego) self. If the human race is a part of the physical world as a created "thing," then that which is outside of creation has to be at least a little higher in consciousness to create this "thing." The book follows this great assumption, which is similar to most of all major and minor world religions. Refer to the introduction of this book for a deeper explanation of this concept.

The History of Meditation

The earliest possible records relating to yoga and meditation existed between the third and fourth millennium BCE.[12,13] After this point, written records about meditation come from the Hindu traditions of Vedantism around 1500 BCE.[14] Then, between 500–600 BCE, meditation developed more completely in Buddhist India and Taoist China.[15] About a millennium later, in 653 AD, a Japanese monk brought Buddhist meditation from China back to Japan[16] and slowly Zen meditation began to surface strongly around the 13th century CE with the help of Zen master Dogen.[17]

---

[12] Payne and Feuerstein 2014, Intro.
[13] Feuerstein (n.d.).
[14] Everly 2013, 202.
[15] Everly 2013, 202.
[16] Dumoulin 2005, 5.
[17] Bielefeldt 1988, 2.

While the practice of meditation spread east and northeast of the Indus Valley region (modern-day Pakistan, Afghanistan, and northwestern parts of India), meditation slowly spread west to the Mediterranean before and after the life of Jesus Christ. A first century Jewish philosopher named Philo of Alexandria wrote about meditation as a way to gain insight directly from God.[18]

In 653 AD, Islam's practice of *dhikr* used a mantra or recitation of God's name while in group worship. This practice seemed to have started around the Sufism movement during the end of the first millennium CE.[19,20] As *dhikr* was practiced, more breath control techniques (referred to as *pranayama* in yoga) came into being in the second millennium CE in Sufism.[21,22,23]

From the 10th to the 14th, and up until the 19th centuries CE, hesychasm[24,25,26] or Eastern Christian "stillness" used the Jesus Prayer as a mantra during periods of prayer and silence. Hesychasm is a tradition of creating stillness by ceasing the senses to achieve an experiential knowledge of God. This started in Greece on Mount Athos in a monastery involving the repetition of the Jesus Prayer.[27]

Western Christian mediation differed from all other previous approaches, as it required no repetition of a mantra (phrase) and required no specific body posture. Guigo II in the 12th century CE developed a method that is still used today. This is *lectio, meditatio, oratio,* and *contemplatio*, which means *read, ponder, pray,* and *contemplate* (meditate) respectively.[28] Even Christian saints such as Teresa of Avila in the 16th century CE used this method along with Ignatius of Loyola.[29,30]

---

[18] Turner 1996, 439.
[19] Zaleski 2005, 147-149.
[20] Yadav 2007, 63.
[21] Hanif 2002.
[22] Kugle 2007, 245-246.
[23] Coward and Goa 2005, 97.
[24] Parry 1999, 91.
[25] Everly 2013, 202.
[26] Swami Rama 1989, 46, 63, 66, 69-70.
[27] Macedonian Heritage 2000-2016.
[28] Jaoudi 2010, 12.
[29] Wakefield 2006, 22-23.
[30] St. Theresa of Avila and Peers 2007.

Natives of North America also used ceremonies similar to meditation where they contemplated and provided offerings to the Great Spirit through drumming, sweat lodges, totem meditation, the Sun Dance, and vision quest.[31] Many more similar ceremonies exist depending on the tribe and area of origination.

Finally, in the 20th century CE, the yogis Swami Vivekananda and Paramahansa Yogananda introduced different forms of meditation from India.[32] Then later by yogic practitioners such as BKS Iyengar[33] and others. During the middle the 20th century CE, transcendental meditation (TM) became popular as well.

As you can see, the history of meditation precedes modern culture and is an age-old practice. It has spread throughout all major religions in the world. Even minor belief-systems have also been shown to use meditation or one-pointed prayer in one way or another to manifest a higher state of consciousness.

---

[31] Wayshowers Community Fellowship 2001-2008.
[32] Bowden 1993, 574-575, 632-633.
[33] Sjoman 1999, 39-41.

CHAPTER 7

Yoga

The Practice of Yoga

Meditation has not always been well known by the modern world and has recently been introduced by those who practice yoga starting in the early 20th century. Yoga is generally known in the West as a set of exercises that involve placing the body in various body postures called *asanas*. These *asanas* may be highly physical in nature making the body stretch into positions never thought possible. These *asanas* are more commonly used in Eastern practices for meditation and spiritual prayer.

The word yoga means "to unite," "to join," or "to add." In this unification of body and mind, practitioners not only benefit physically from the various postures performed, but also mentally, emotionally, and spiritually. In older practices, yoga could be considered an integration of body postures, prayer, and lifestyle. In this way, yoga can be best described as a way of life that leads to a balanced standard of living and state of being. Patanjali, the author of the *Yoga Sutras*, says that yoga really only begins after you have done preparation and study[1] by one who is qualified to teach. Yoga then can then become integrated to a more balanced existence through modification of the mind by controlling, stilling, and finally ceasing normal streams of thought patterns.[2]

The practice of yoga is a definite scientific process passed down through the millenniums since the age of the Indus Valley civilization between 3300-1900 BCE.[3] Yoga and its first forms of meditation may have come about before this time, but there is currently no written record of its existence. Archaeological artifacts suggest that yoga was possibly practiced during these times frames.

In the ancient practices of the Hindus, yoga is also seen as a separate school of philosophy and is included under the six main orthodox schools. In this way, yoga has been both indoctrinated and built upon the foundations of the different traditions of Hinduism. Mostly, yoga is a school of thought that emphasizes meditation as the primary path to liberation.[4]

Meditation evolved and developed through the practice of yoga in India and then eventually spread throughout the world by the end of 20th century CE. With the ubiquitous use of the internet in daily life, yoga can easily be learned on many websites, but it is best understood and applied by a hands-on yoga instructor.

The physical aspect of most yogic practice will either focus on power and strength or flow and flexibility, but in reality, most yogic practices have a combination of all of these aspects. Other aspects of yoga, such as tranquility and concentration, are common results of frequent and consistent yogic practice. Stillness, mindfulness, and intuitive insight are some other features that are not often discussed. These characteristics, more often mentally and spiritually associated, are gained through prolonged meditative efforts using the various yogic *asanas* and *pranayama* (breath-control techniques).

Pranayama is usually practiced while sitting in a particular yogic posture, such as *padmasana* (full lotus), *ardha padmasana* (half lotus) or *siddhasana* (perfect pose), and attempting to maintain it for long periods of time while utilizing a breathing technique. This description is similar to the type of yoga that I practiced to achieve the states of realization

---

[1] Patanjali's *Yoga Sutras* I.1
[2] Patanjali's *Yoga Sutras* I.2
[3] Crangle 1994, 2-7.
[4] Klostermaier 2007, 102, 117.

described in this book. When I personally began to practice yoga, I attempted various forms, including Hatha, Vinyasa, Ashtanga, and Kundalini yoga. I found my particular attraction to Raja yoga, and more specifically, Kriya yoga. Kriya yoga is essentially a part of Raja and is best practiced with the aspects of Raja described below.

Raja yoga is a meditative type yoga that involves three major aspects:[5]
- Hatha yoga, which addresses the physical health of the body.
- Meditation that helps to unite the physical body and mind with higher consciousness.
- Devotional chanting used to open the heart connecting you with the Divine's creation.

Vivekananda wrote *Raja Yoga*, originally published in 1897. In this exposition, he elaborated upon Raja yoga and its many aspects. He says that Raja yoga is:
- A science that has been examined, studied, and generalized for thousands of years.[6]
- A yoga practice which will allow one to perceive that which is considered to be subtle and supernatural.[7]
- Connected to the eight limbs of Patanjali[8] (see below).
- A lesson in how to gain the power of concentration.[9]
- Able to trains practitioners to control manifestations of *prana,* or vital body energy, through mental willpower.[10]
- The science of religion and the rationale behind why prayers and miracles work.[11]

---

[5] Selbie 2012.
[6] Vivekananda 1920, x.
[7] Vivekananda 1920, xi.
[8] Vivekananda 1920, 17.
[9] Vivekananda 1920, 43.
[10] Vivekananda 1920, Chap 3, 4, 5.
[11] Vivekananda 1920, 54.

Kriya yoga is a part of Raja yoga and is:[12,13]
- Specifically characterized by a meditative *pranayama* technique called the *Kriya*
- Used to evolve the body and brain to achieve higher consciousness.
- Intended to burn karma and reach self-realization, including, God-realization.

Both types of yoga involve Patanjali's eight-limbs of yoga: *yama, niyama, asana, pranayama, pratyahara, dharana, dhyana,* and *samadhi.* All schools of yoga that focus on lifestyle will embody these eight concepts as the core to the practice. Even the word *ashtanga,* which is a popular type of yoga, literally means eight parts or eight members.

When Kriya yoga is combined with consistent physical exercise and right living, frequent meditation, and true devotional chanting/singing, then *Kriya* has its most optimal effect. *Kriya* helps one achieve yoga's ultimate goal—pure enlightenment through self-realization.

Origin of Yoga

A yogi named Lahiri Mahasaya, who was taught and initiated by the great yogic master named Mahavatar Babaji around 1869, revived Kriya yoga in India and spread it throughout the world.[14] It reached the United States initially by Swami Vivekananda between 1895 and 1900 and then again, more prominently, by Paramahansa Yogananda between the years of 1920 and 1952. Yogananda developed and widely spread the practice of Kriya yoga through his organization called Self-Realization Fellowship based in Encinitas, CA, near San Diego. He created a church service similar to that of many traditional Protestant services, but instead used meditation, devotional singing, and inspirational readings to help guide those on the path of Kriya yoga.[15]

Since then, many yogis that have developed and taught varying types of yoga. These influential yogis include Swami Sivananda, BKS Iyengar, Indra Devi, Richard Hittleman, Swami Vishnu-devananda,

---

[12] Yogananda 2012.
[13] Ananda Sangha Worldwide 1995-2015.
[14] Chatterjee 2011, Chap 3.
[15] Yogananda 2012., Self-Realization Fellowship 2015.

Swami Satchidananda, Maharishi Mahesh Yogi, Ram Dass, Pattabhi Jois, TKV Desikachar[16] and others. These yogis were followers of individuals like Sri Ramakrishna, Vivekananda, Yogananda, Ramana Maharshi, and other great yogic practitioners that never ventured out from India save for a few.

Yoga has had quite a journey over the past 5,000 years, evolving with the most ancient of civilizations to the most modern. Yoga uses scientifically-tested body postures (*asana*) and breath control techniques (*pranayama*) to unite body and mind to achieve a higher-operating conscious awareness. With this awareness, will come peace, stillness of body and mind, emotional tranquility, and eventually, a constant blissful countenance that can be easily shared with all.

Yoga can be practiced by anyone, whether Hindu, Buddhist, Muslim, or Christian, because yoga is not in disagreement with any specific religious dogma. In all these religions and spiritual practices, the goal is the same—to achieve a Krishna-like, Buddha-like, Muhammad-like, or Christ-like level of humility and service. Often in Christianity, for example, followers commonly believe they can be like Christ, but never exactly the same as Christ. This belief is mirrored for those practitioners of Buddhism, Hinduism, and Islam.

In yoga, the goal is to reach liberation or *moksha*. This type of liberation is to realize that the human being is not only a body, but also a soul with a divinely-bestowed consciousness. This type of *moksha* cannot be merely known or conceived, it has to be realized fully in body and mind. It has to be felt wholly in the heart as love and at the third eye (the point between the eyebrows) as tension.

Practitioners of yoga must be initiated by a prophet, guru, or Christ-figure to achieve the most complete level of *moksha*. This level of liberation, is the highest form of self-realization. To go further in this process, one will be initiated by the Divine to reach a fuller level of self-realization called God-realization, which allows feeling to the fullest extent the nature of true God-given bliss. This bliss is the truest and highest goal of yoga.

---

[16] Hammond 2007.

Yoga is not just an exercise, but a practice that can be incorporated into any religion because of its equanimity and universality towards the highest goal of human evolution that helps all of humanity. As Sivananda said, "Yoga is a perfect and practical system of self-culture,"[17] as it is the most methodical way to attain perfection.

The Major Aspects of Yoga

The various parts of yoga were provided initially by Patanjali in his *Yoga Sutras*. This classic book was originally compiled around 400 CE and has been used as the basis to all yogic practice since then.

Patanjali described the yogic practice as eight different parts or limbs.[18] The first five of these limbs reveals what needs to be done in the frame of morals, hygiene (both mental and physical), exercise, and use of scientific techniques to control the body's respiration and life force. After these five are practiced in balance, harmony, and consistency over at least a decade, the last three parts can be practiced more easily, eventually leading to the eighth step of self-realization. The eight limbs are as follows:

1. *Yama*
   - Laws of life
   - 5 ethical restraints: Non-violence, truthfulness, integrity, chastity, and nonattachment
   - The "don'ts" of one's life
   - Focus on the external world

2. *Niyama*
   - Rules for living
   - 5 ethical observances: Simplicity, contentment, purification, refinement, surrender to the Divine
   - The "dos"
   - Focus on the inner self

---

[17] Sivananda 2011.
[18] Patanjali's *Yoga Sutras* II.26-II.29.

3. **Asana**
   - Discipline of the body
   - Physical body postures used to keep body disease-free and preserve vital energy

4. **Pranayama**
   - Breath/life-control technique (i.e. breathing exercises)
   - Necessary to reach self-realization or any high level of consciousness because this achievement requires a physically breathless state

5. **Pratyahara**
   - Withdrawal of the senses; interiorization
   - Occurs because of the practice of *pranayama*, proper *asana*, and balanced *yama/niyama*

6. **Dharana**
   - Steadiness of the mind through concentration
   - Necessary to achieve long periods of meditation practicing *pranayama*

7. **Dhyana**
   - Meditation; undisturbed flow of thoughts
   - Occurs as a result of sustained concentration (*dharana*) over long periods of time with frequent and consistent practice

8. **Samadhi**[19]
   - Translates to (*sama-*) settled (*-dhi*) mind
   - The highest form of Superconsciousness with perfect, one-pointed concentration with advanced stillness of the mind
   - Differs from *dhyana* in that it is unbounded, can be accessed at any time, and is expressed purely
   - Oneness with the object of meditation; no distinction between act of meditation and object

---

[19] Patanjali's *Yoga Sutras* III.3

- Does not occur by chance; requires devoted training to achieve
- With the act of entering a conscious-level *samadhi*, the mind no longer differentiates between what it is meditating on and what is doing the meditation, it just occurs
- Divided into whether an object is meditated upon *(savikalpa)* or whether no object is no longer needed *(nirvikalpa)*
- Can be conscious and unconscious—I discovered this aspect through experience and will be emphasize it in this book
- Sometimes referred to as the fourth or fifth dimension
- "Samadhi is a state in which you can stay only for a few hours, for a few days. You cannot stay in this state for more than twenty-one days. Usually after three weeks the body does not function." [20]

There are two main types of *samadhi*. One is called *jada,* and other is categorized into many forms—from minor to major—as *savikalpa* and *nirvikalpa*. *Jada* is a type of *samadhi* achieved by Hatha Yogis by performing a full *kechari mudra* and completely stopping the breath physically. By doing so, they enter into a breathless state with their life force completely suspended, remaining "alive" for any period of time. However, when they come out of this state, they have achieved no real and lasting spiritual realization. Alternatively, in the second category of true *samadhi* whether conscious or unconscious, spiritual realization will have been gained for the individual, and super-sensuous wisdom is gained for all who are present.

Samadhi is the last and ultimate step in Patanjali's eight yogic limbs to achieving self-realization and the final goal of man's physical, mental, emotional, and spiritual struggle to liberation on Earth. However, once this final state is achieved, *samadhi* will evolve. In the first type of *samadhi*, the practitioner will begin to question the experience itself, but with perseverance, will continue to experience oneness in the Divine's bliss *(savikalpa)*. The other type of *samadhi* is a true mindless state without questioning to determine one's true existence. In this *samadhi*, you are the Divine's bliss *(nirvikalpa)*. This differentiation is explained more thoroughly in the next chapter.

---

[20] Chinmoy 1974.

CHAPTER 8

Samadhi

In this next chapter, we will look at the classical, modern, and expanded views of *samadhi*. The classical and modern views address how the original author of the *Yoga Sutras*, Patanjali, wrote about yoga. The classical/modern section also includes ideas, concepts, and quotes from different teachers of yoga and meditation since 1000 A.D. The expanded view of *samadhi* is from my own personal experiences in meditation mixed with the classical and modern views. *Samadhi* is considered the goal of yoga and for those who practice Eastern meditation.

Mostly the Hindus and Buddhists claim *samadhi* is the highest form of consciousness achievable by man. I discovered that *samadhi* is achieved in various ways, even when you aren't at the highest possible level of consciousness. There are subtle minor forms achieved when you are using meditative techniques. There are also forms attained with huge out-of-body experiences, while other types of *samadhi* are infinitely peaceful, blissful, and truly transcendent.

CLASSICAL AND MODERN VIEWS OF SAMADHI

When looking at the different interpretations of *samadhi*, you will see that the classical or original view of samadhi is described by a few major terms. These are *sabjia* and *nirbija samadhi*. Most of the original information was documented by Patanjali, in his book called the *Yoga Sutras*. He was a great master in the field of the yogic arts around 400 BCE.

In the classical view of *sabjia samadhi*, both the terms *savikalpa* and *samprajñata* have also been used to describe the same state of *sabija*.[†] When you look them up in a Sanskrit dictionary, they are defined slightly differently, but have a tendency to be interchanged for the same kind of *sabija samadhi* state. The same goes for *nirbija samadhi*. The terms *nirvikalpa* and *asamprajñata* have also be used interchangeably with *nirbija*.[1,2,3]

Sabija samadhi has been described in a few different ways as: "with seed" or "with subject-object distinction." This subject-object distinction, in my personal experience, is to be completely absorbed in *pratyaya,* or the object of meditation. You are still aware of the world around you, but you are completely immersed in the object of meditation. This object may be a lamp, flame, the space between the eyebrows, the tip of the nose, a physical object, or a preferred image of your deity. The *pratyaya* that is specific for *sabija samadhi* is the understanding, intelligence, conception, or certainty that you have indeed achieved this state of samadhi. This *pratyaya* occurs in four major steps.[4] These are:

1. Savitarka
2. Savichara
3. Sananda
4. Sasmita

[†] Both *samprajñata* and *asamprajñata samadhis* are also called *savikalpa* and *nirvikalpa samadhi* respectively by those Hindus who practice the Vedas and Bhakti (devotional yoga). (Sivananda 2011 *Samprajñata Samadhi*)
[1] Patanjali's *Yoga Sutras* 1.18
[2] Patanjali's *Yoga Sutras* 1.43-1.44
[3] Patanjali's *Yoga Sutras* I.51
[4] Patanjali's *Yoga Sutras* I.17-1.18

While traversing these four states, you will intentionally determine the nature of *sabija* on a physical level in *savitarka*. You will question whether entry into this state actually occurred, as this is the first initiation into self-realization. Then you will come to question the nature of this *samadhi* state at a subtler level, probing yourself and the situation introspectively. Finally, you will achieve a mindful expansiveness leading to bliss and a greater loss of awareness of the little self—the ego.

In Patanjali's *Yoga Sutras*, *nirbija* and *asamprajñata* were determined by most theologians as being the same. I.K. Taimni showed in his book, that this was not the case. Below, I will explore this distinction further.

As *sabija* is "with seed," *nirbija* is defined as being "without seed," or "without subject-object distinction." *Nirbija* occurs without an object upon which to focus. In this *samadhi* state, no *pratyaya* exists, and you will be lead to the ultimate states *dharma megha samadhi* and *kaivalya*. At this point, you have complete liberation of consciousness.

Nirbija is accomplished in four stages, just as is the *sabija samadhi* state. These four stages include:

1. Nirvitarka
2. Nirvicara
3. Ananda
4. Asmita

Notice the first two stages are similarly named, while the last two are different then *sabija samadhi*. When you are in *nirbija*, no intention or introspection is required to be a part of this state. The bliss in this state is so overwhelming that you lose awareness of yourself, allowing for full immersion in the infinite and absolute consciousness of SPIRIT. You are no longer achieving anything while in this state. Instead, you become the state of *samadhi* through *dharma megha samadhi*, destroying the cause of suffering, leading to the ultimate level of samadhi through *kaivalya* (liberation).

In the modern view of samadhi, the definitions of both *sabija* and *nirbija* are the same as the classical view. However, I have seen these *samadhi* states more often referred to as *savikalpa* and *nirvikalpa*, respectively. Generally, *sabija* can be seen as the external or lower aspect of *samadhi*, whereas *nirbija* is the internal or higher aspect. *Sabija* will lead to *nirbija*, but once you have achieved *nirbija*, you can experience *sabija* at any time.

According to I.K. Taimni's book, *The Science of Yoga*,[5][†] *sabija samadhi* includes both *samprajñata* and *asamprajñata* together as oscillating levels of consciousness. In *sabija*, concrete meditation still exists with distinction between the mind and the object being meditated upon, but now it is known that as you meditate, your consciousness will oscillate between the four stages of *sabija* and the four stages of *nirbija*. *Samprajñata* contains the first four levels of *savitarka, savichara, sananda*, and *sasmita*. *Asamprajñata* contains *nirvitarka, nirvichara, ananda,* and *asmita*. This transitional process occurs to help attune the mind more easily for higher states of *samadhi*. If *nirbija* occurred too soon, then your body could burn out like an over-watted light bulb. In this case, it is always necessary to get the help of a true guru for further ascension.

As you transition between *samprajñata* and *asamprajñata* with successive attempts, spiritual evolutions of the body and mind will occur. This will build up God's Joy within the body and help you get use to feeling unattached to the physical body. Below is an outlined version of how that transition occurs.

Samprajñata → Asamprajñata → Samprajñata

Stages in both *samprajñata* and *asamprajñata* transition to one another during meditation; this shifting allows transcendence from *sabija* to *nirbija* with successive attempts and evolutions

- Savitarka → Nirvitarka → Savichara
- Savichara → Nirvichara → Sananda
- Ananda → Asmita
- Asmita → Nirbija Samadhi

In the modern view of samadhi, it is understood, that great joy comes when you enter into *nirbija samadhi*. Also, while in *nirbija*, you will lose

---

[5] Taimni 2010, 31-42

† Dr. Taimni was the first to clarify *asamprajñata* as a transitional state. I came to the same conclusion through muscle testing and experienced it before ever hearing about his book. His work is truly intuitive and should be considered a firsthand text when learning about Patanjali's *Yoga Sutras* and *samadhi*.

all mental disturbances during meditation. This is because the joy and bliss of *nirbija* is as deep and wide as the ocean. No distractions are felt because you never reach the end of the immersing, oceanic-like bliss that is felt here.

Finally, the expanded view of *samadhi*, is the one that I describe in this book in great detail. The classical view, from the time of Patanjali, was written in such a way, where it would have been difficult to give exact the interpretation of *samadhi*. This is because the Earth was in dark period of evolution when Patanjali's *Yoga Sutras* were written. As time progressed, different masters of yoga were able to expound further upon the nature of *samadhi* with more clarity. However, most of these expositions did not come into public view until the middle 1800's and not into global mainstream practice until the 1950's. Now, in the 21st century, the whole world is slowly coming to understand themselves as SPIRIT. *Samadhi* seems a like a far-off accomplishment to most meditators and practitioners of yoga. The masters, with the exception of few, also made it appear impossible that anyone could achieve it with the correct know-how, intention, and willpower.

EXPANDED VIEW OF SAMADHI

In the expanded view of *samadhi*, I explain the minor *samadhi* states, major *samadhi* states, the transitional states that occur between both, the blissful state of *nirbija/nirvikalpa samadhi,* and the ultimate *samadhi* state of *sahaja*. There are even states that go beyond the ultimate state and those will be explained at length as well.

Minor Samadhis

This type of *samadhi* is minor in nature and focuses upon the varying aspects of the Creator's Cosmic Consciousness. There are 16 "lesser" minor *samadhi* states and a 17th amalgamation of these 16 states. These 16 *samadhi* states include:

- Sleep, Wisdom, Righteousness
- Doing no harm, Compassion
- Religious devotion, Bliss, Meditation,
- Silence, Aum, Ascended masters,
- Creation, Universal abundance,
- Names of God, Transcendence

The seventeenth state is called *laya samadhi*. I have also termed it the "Sum Samadhi," or the greatest lesser minor *samadhi*. In *laya samadhi*, all sixteen states are focused together to create a complete picture of the Creator's Cosmic Consciousness. You will have to experience this state wholly before ascending to the next level of *sabija samadhi*. In this book, *sabija samadhi* is referred to *savikalpa samadhi*. In the last century, the term *savikalpa* is more commonly used to describe *sabija*.

Savikalpa Samadhi (*Sabija*)

My personal experience has been that this state came immediately after I achieved my first initiation into self-realization. It is the same as classical and the modern view, as it is meditation with intense focus on an object, whether physical or mental. You will usually be conscious when you are in *savikalpa*, however you may go unconscious for a period of time, as you are initiated into this state. This is necessary because the attunement required to enter this state is truly at the highest level.

Savikalpa is considered the greatest minor *samadhi* to ever exist. It is the first type of *samadhi* state where you can experience it unconsciously or consciously. Most often, people of this Earth era, will experience it consciously and in an active (*chetana*) state. In my experience, this means you can be "active" in the world, doing the duties of a householder (activities of everyday life), and still maintain it through willpower. It has also been considered *chetana* or active because the mind still exists while in *savikalpa*. Remember what we said before—*savikalpa* requires an object to be mediated to be called *savikalpa*. That is why the mind is also active in this state of *samadhi*.

As you transition through the four stages of *samprajñata—savitarka, savichara, sananda,* and *sasmita—*you go from questioning the nature of the experience itself to the investigation of the subtle activity of *savikalpa*. This leads to acceptance of the state with deep/delicate activity as bliss and then very deep/delicate activity as your awareness as SPIRIT. At the end of these four stages, wonderful happiness is felt, which will help you to ascend to the next level.

Asamprajñata Samadhi

After *samprajñata* comes *asamprajñata samadhi*. In the classical view, *asamprajñata* was considered the same as *nirbija* or *nirvikalpa samadhi*. In the modern view, *asamprajñata* was considered more of a transitional state. I view in the same way, but in the expanded view, I describe it as a separate state from *savikalpa (sabija) samadhi* entirely. It is still considered a transitional state to *nirvikalpa samadhi,* but I discovered many more aspects to its existence.

First, asamprajñata is the beginning of objectless meditation. Remember, this lack of object focus in meditation is the same as *nirvikalpa (nirbija) samadhi. Asamprajñata* is still a minor *samadhi* state, but it allows for the transition to a major *samadhi* state, which *nirvikalpa* is the ultimate embodiment of. You will still have to work through the four stages of: *nirvitarka, nirvichara, ananda,* and *asmita,* but as a transitional state, it will attune your body and mind to the awesome power of a major *samadhi* state.

With these four stages comes similar questioning and investigation as in *savikalpa (sabija) samadhi,* but now it is objectless. You begin to realize that no object is necessary and the real object is you. The subtle and delicate energy resides within and gives rise to the ease of meditation. This energy `is what allows you meditate with any level of concentration on the nature of SPIRIT. This will become more apparent once you achieve the top level of *nirvikalpa samadhi.* This is because in *nirvikalpa* you have to work very little to achieve the highest bliss at will. This is bliss is objectless because it is only a feeling that rises out of the pure awareness of the Self as SPIRIT. It becomes automatic and permanent once you transcend the transitional state of *asamprajñata* and the future major *samadhi* transitional states.

Major Samadhi States

The next state achieved after *asamprajñata* is called "The Interstate." This long-forgotten transitional realm allows for you to manifest a conscious major *samadhi* before actually achieving a full-blown *nirvikalpa samadhi* experience. This is the second transitional state before you can experience *nirvikalpa samadhi.* You will experience all of the similarities of the samadhi states before, but will have greater level of stillness in the mind and body. Also, your attachment to bodily needs and sensations will be greatly diminished.

At the very end of the Interstate, two smaller transitional states are necessary to achieve a full-blown initiation into *nirvikalpa.* These will be explained later in much more detail.

Nirvikalpa Samadhi (*Nirbija, Nirvana, Kevala Nirvikalpa*[6])

This is a conscious *samadhi* state that that does not require an object to focus upon, no *pratyaya* (object) exists in its highest form. The nature of bliss is what keeps you enamored while meditating in this state. It seemingly bubbles up out of nowhere to provide divine entertainment on the highest level of existence. This is the most advanced form of *samadhi* according to Patanjali which will lead to *dharma megha samadhi* and complete liberation of the soul from life. *Dharma megha samadhi* is the highest form of *nirvikalpa* that can be achieved leading to ease of bliss with least effort.

This type of samadhi is truly a non-dual consciousness. This means it goes beyond duality of creation into the non-duality of SPIRIT.[†] *Nirvikalpa* is the first time that you will experience non-dual consciousness in all of its fullness. This type of consciousness has been seen in great masters such as Krishna, Buddha, Jesus Christ, Yogananda and others that have lived throughout the last five millenniums.

In Buddhism, *nirvikalpa* is referred to as *nirvana*, and is described as "true emptiness," which allows you to be filled up with nothing but the SPIRIT's bliss consciousness. Bliss allows for the past, present, and future merge allowing for you to see time as the Divine perceives it. This state allows for simultaneous and infinite access to all.

Nirvikalpa is also where the mind dissolves into itself becoming "non-mind" without any seeds of desire. When immersed in the ocean of bliss, no desires arise, because "seeding" is impossible at this point. The desire for God is so great that nothing else is needed or desired.

Nirvikalpa is also called:
- <u>Sat-chit-ananda consciousness</u>: existence-consciousness-bliss
- <u>Advaita-avastharupa samadhi</u>: to be absorbed in non-dual
- <u>Achetana samadhi</u>: not active (non-mind)

---

[6] Maharshi 1989, 222.
[†] Non-duality later on in the book.

Nirvikalpa's stages can be summarized as:
- Nirvikalpa "proper": all states up to *dharma megha samadhi*
- Dharma megha samadhi: this is *anantya* which is the conscious form of the highest bliss available
- Kaivalya: *sahaja samadhi* is the next *samadhi* state after *nirvikalpa*.

Sahaja Samadhi (*Sahaja Avastha*[7], *Sahaja Nirvikalpa*[8])†

This *samadhi* state is the highest type of conscious *samadhi* that includes all aspects of the *samadhi* states that have come before occurring in a natural, spontaneous, simple, and easy way. This state is afforded to householders and those great masters that are required to live and mix in the world with full use of human faculties and activities.

Sahaja is non-dual consciousness that becomes the natural state of the yogi. It is it so aptly named *sahaja* or "natural" because where it allows you to spontaneously experience *laya, savikalpa,* and/or *nirvikalpa* at any time you choose. As your realization increases, the ability to enter into *nirvikalpa* and stay in its highest states while meditating, sitting, walking, driving, or even working around others with lower vibrational realization, will be easy and effortless. This is also continuous communion with the divine.[9] With constant communion with divine you now become a *jivanmukta,* which is one who has attained true *kaivalya* (liberation).

Sahaja's stages can be summarized as:
- Sahaja "proper"
- The Aionion State
- Complete mergence with the Divine Superconscious Experience

The above stages will be explained more completely later on in the book. For now, know that anything experienced before, once transcended, will become a permanent existence for you.

---

[7] Sivananda 2011.
[8] Maharshi 1989, 222.
† Spoken about by Ramana Maharshi, Sri Chinmoy, and Swami Chidananda
[9] Maharshi 1989, 224.

Throughout this process of self-realization, you will have opportunities to enter into *turiya samadhi*, either unconsciously or consciously as initiations (primarily) or to help you ascend between levels of consciousness.

Turiya Samadhi (*"transcendental consciousness"*)[10,11]

This is the highest form of *samadhi*, period. This transcendent form of consciousness is the only form of a major *samadhi* that is achieved at an unconscious level. This unconscious form can be completely unconscious, as if you were sleeping, or on an apparent wide-awake level. This wide-awake-type is saved only for those individuals who can, at-will, shut off awareness to their physical body, emotional, and mental state.

Turiya is an "infinite" form of *samadhi* which can be experienced in an "infinite" amount of ways. If it is unconscious, then we call it *turiya*. If it is in it conscious form, then we call it *anantya*. First, you will have to achieve it as an unconscious initiation, but then you will enter it consciously and willfully. *Turiya* is a countable state, meaning it is measured by numbers, but it is very difficult to ascend it because very few people on this Earth will experience it.

You will initially experience this state as a DSCE[†] (Divine Superconscious Experience) coming into *savikalpa samadhi*. At various times in the ascension process, you will enter *turiya*, as an initiation, in the form of a DSCE. *Turiya* will increase in frequency especially when you have passed into *sahaja samadhi*. Eventually with decades of practice in *nirvikalpa samadhi*, you may be able to consciously enter this state to directly commune with God and Avatars of the past for the benefit of all of mankind. In this way, your body, mind, and soul are completely dissolved in *Brahma* (Sanskrit word for the Creator). With this power to enter into *turiya*, you may be able to completely live without sleep/food or very little sleep/food if you can enter this state at will and stay here for definite periods of time.

If *turiya* has a strong physical effect on you it will produce a complete loss of hearing, complete stillness of the body, loss of breath, and loss of heart beat. In these moments, your consciousness will have

---

[10] Sivananda 2011.
[11] Sivananda 1998.
[†] Explained in Chapter 14 under the section on the Divine Superconscious Experience

literally left the body for a short time in an ecstatic state of communion with the Divine. Coming back from this experience, you will gain super-sensuous wisdom for all and a very powerful, all-loving, spiritually-physical aura. While in this state, whether conscious or unconscious, you will transcend all physical, mental, emotional, and spiritual sufferings while completely submersed in this state.

Turiya samadhi is considered the final goal of the path of yoga. This attainment requires long training and true devotion. Sri Chinmoy says, "Turiya is the highest state of consciousness, but there is no end, no fixed limit to the turiya consciousness. It is constantly transcending, transcending its own beyond."[12]

Sivananda continues to say that *turiya* is called the "fourth state"[13] or is also considered the fourth dimension transcending the three dimensions experienced on Earth. Sivananda, personally, speaks about this state as being his own goal.[14]

On the next page is a diagram of the states of *samadhi* as represented by this book's unique perspective.

---

[12] Chinmoy 2000, 47.
[13] Sivananda 2011.
[14] Sivananda 1946.

Figure 8.1 – Types of Samadhi

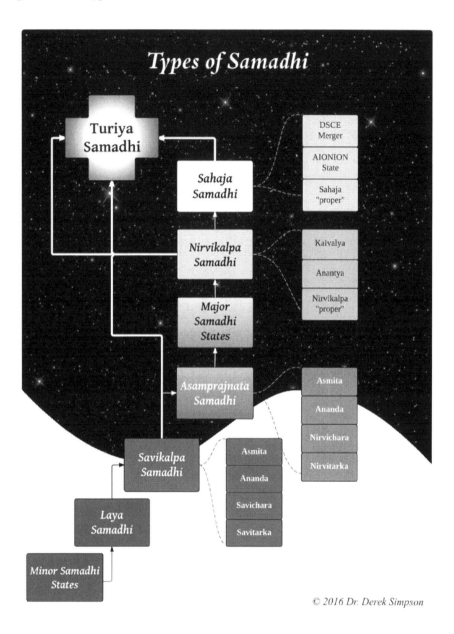

THE EXPANDED ASPECTS OF YOGA

Patanjali originally expounded upon the limbs of yoga as essential aspects to its practice. The first of the last three aspects, *samyama*, is originally a part of Patanjali's *Yoga Sutras*, but is not included as a limb of yoga. *Samyama* is included here because the last two aspects, both *anantya* and *turiya* are next steps after one achieves *samyama*.

In Patanjali's *Sutras*, each of the eight limbs follows one another in succession. It is beneficial to practice all of the eight limbs in order to allow for the next limb to develop appropriately. For instance, great concentration (*dharana*) cannot occur as completely without control of the senses (*pratyahara*). Also, proper meditation (*dhyana*) will not be achieved without first understanding how to direct concentration (*dharana*) towards one object or aspect.

Figure 8.2 – The Eleven Limbs of Yoga

The Eleven Limbs of Yoga

1. Yama
2. Niyama — Yoga "proper"
3. Asana
4. Pranayama

— Patanjali's Eight Limbs of Yoga

5. Pratyahara
6. Dharana
7. Dhyana
8. Samadhi

9. Samyama
10. Anantya — additional Limbs of Yoga
11. Turiya

© 2016 Dr. Derek Simpson

Samyama

In Patanjali's definition,[15] *samyama* is a technique that combines *dharana*, *dhyana*, and *samadhi*. It is considered mind-control over any physical, subtle (energetic), or ideational (at the level of an idea) object in the universe. *Samyama* is a finer tool to access yogic powers and higher levels of consciousness.

True knowledge and illumination comes when this three-part process becomes mastered and applied to finer states and planes of consciousness. The use and mastery of *samyama* allows the yogi to attain great *siddhis* (yogic powers) over all elements, sensations, subtle realms, universal laws, and as a result, supreme knowledge dawns on the individual.

In the expanded (this book's) definition of *samyama*, I have found that it occurs in each *samadhi* state, allowing the yogi to increase in LOC[†]. After merger with the DSCE in *sahaja samadhi,* the LOC will increase according to the Divine's will, no longer to your own individual will. The process of *samyama*, although very powerful, is *external* to the bliss state of *nirvikalpa* itself. This is because to do *samyama* over something, is to gain power over it. To continue to have power over something, *samyama* must be mastered and performed over the object at all times. However, true realization can only dawn once the yogi has decided no longer to seek this power.

Anantya

Anantya is not a level of consciousness, but a state of being. Those two statements may seem similar, but they are not. This book describes "consciousness" as a level that can be achieved. In some places, "level of consciousness" and "state of being" may be used interchangeably. However, *anantya* is also not a place or destination where you "arrive" or achieve, per se. *Anantya* in Sanskrit means "infinity" or "infinite." In this way, it is some "thing," but really a concept that can only be experienced as bliss.

When this state of being is attained, you are always achieving an infinite flow of bliss, as long as the experience is maintained. The rate of flow never slows and is always constant. Although it is at a constant

---

[15] Patanjali's *Yoga Sutras* III.4-III.6, III.16-III.49, III.53
† LOC = "Level of Consciousness" that is measured numerically described starting in Chapter 9

rate of flow, it is not to be underestimated. The flow of bliss is so overwhelming that the individual literally appears to be drunk and tottering, because the sensation is so irresistible and overpowering.

Anantya, in its complete nature, is the inclusion of everything and nothing. This state is also called *dharma megha samadhi* which is the highest form of *nirvikalpa samadhi* that can be experienced. It is achieved constantly and infinitely as it is experienced. It is complete absorption into bliss itself, allowing for no other aspect to enter. Literally, all is transcended; including time and space and all mental, emotional, and spiritual suffering that manifests there. The moment you enter in *anantya*, the greater the increase in LOC over that of *samyama* when achieved in *nirvikalpa* and *sahaja samadhi*.

After you have achieved a complete merger with the DSCE in *sahaja samadhi*, then achieving *anantya* will be the sole increase for LOC, as *samyama* will no longer allow the body and mind to increase in LOC. This is because the DSCE is similar to the state of *samyama*, but also is the environment for *anantya*. This is associated again with the Law of Ascension.[†] You cannot ascend unless you are in the highest available state.

Finally, after reaching *anantya* multiple times, you will be able to enter into this state most easily by mastering the flow of *amrita*.[‡] By activating this, you will enter *anantya* allowing for bliss to flow into your consciousness without end.

Turiya

This is the same as what was expounded above in the section on Turiya Samadhi on pp. 56–57.

Conclusion

It appears, from all that is written above, that meditation could be more of an escape from the world and its harsh realities. It should not be viewed in this way. True escape can be entered in a *turiya* state at will, without the use of any physical substance. Meditation and yoga are meant to train the conscious mind to deal with the physical, mental, emotional, and spiritual insults received while in the physical body. If

---

† The Law of Ascension is described in greater detail later on in the book.
‡ *Amrita* is the divine nectar that flows down from the area around the pineal gland, keeping the yogi eternally enraptured in the Divine's bliss.

it was an "escape" from reality, then it would be treated as a drug (prescription or illicit) or some other unnatural mind-altering tool.

The best kind of yoga is one that resonates most strongly with your temperament and constitution. It is a form of physical exercise, but it is best used as a spiritual practice to unite the body and mind with the highest form of self. Although some see it as religion, this view is inaccurate. Yogic "religion" is inclusive of not only the ideals presented in Patanjali's Eight-Limbs of Yoga, but also of a higher Creator that is in control of everything.

An atheist or agnostic could very easily connect with their "inner" self by performing the different limbs of yoga. It is not necessary to believe in a higher power to practice yoga. However, if the highest levels of self-realization are desired, then believing in a higher power is absolutely necessary. You must submit and surrender to "something" higher than yourself to achieve that which is perceived to be "unattainable."

Anyone can practice yoga. It requires consistency and discipline to maintain the frequency of practice. Morning and night are the best times and some yoga can even be practiced throughout the day while at work or other events. The only difference between the great master and the humble aspirant, is that one gave up before the goal was reached.

CHAPTER 9

Muscle Testing

Muscle testing is both a medical science and a medical art. For strict examination and diagnosis, it is a foundation for physical, kinesiological, and neurological examinations. For those interested in the progression and evolution of medicine, muscle testing has become an art that allows the examiner to dive deep into the undiscovered niches of medical awareness, allowing for direct communication with the body. Simply put, the art of muscle testing is used to ask the body the best approach to diagnosis and treatment. It has helped patients and clients release from their fears and transcend even the negative emotional nature of the consciousness itself.

For the purposes of this book, muscle testing helped open a gateway of knowledge to the infinite beyond. It helped me during deep meditation sessions to determine the numerical representations used in this book to help quantify each level of realization. It continues to allow me to ask questions that would normally be prohibited to those of a "lower" level of consciousness (LOC). As you ascend the ladder of realization, the Divine will open Its gates to you, allowing for all knowledge to be known easily and completely.

History of Muscle Testing

Muscle testing is a fairly new science, originating between 1912 and 1915 by Dr. Robert Lovett.[1,2,3,4,5] During this time, he developed manual muscle testing to help infants with polio. He created a rating system to classify the neuromuscular control of a muscle. If a muscle was strong, it was given a rating of "5" and was fully neurologically intact. If it was just slightly less than strong but still had a full range of motion, it was given a rating of "4." This is a muscle that is slightly less neurologically intact. If the person could hold the muscle up, but there was no strength in the muscle to maintain resistance against an opposing force, the muscle strength was given a "3." This rating is also given to a muscle that can move through its full range of motion against gravity. A rating of a "2" is given to a muscle that can go through the full range of motion, but not against gravity- the muscle must be facilitated by a doctor, another individual, or by an external force. The rating of "1" signifies visible contraction of the muscle, and a rating of a "0" represents total paralysis. This rating system is still used today as a mainstay to a health practitioner's neurological and muscular examinations.[6,7]

Later, in 1939, Kendall and Kendall, a married couple and both physical therapists, developed a muscular rating system that involved percentages 0-100%. They wrote a book in 1949 expounding upon tests one could use to neurologically determine the "strength" of a muscle through examination and treatment.[8] This strength could tell a doctor or healthcare practitioner whether or not the muscle was neurologically intact. Kendall and Kendall's work is the cornerstone of many books that have been written today on manual muscle testing.

---

[1] Aufsesser 1996, 13, 153-165.
[2] Florence 2005, 5.
[3] Daniels 2002, 7.
[4] Ambroz 2006.
[5] Lovett 1916, 729-733.
[6] Moses 2015.
[7] Barbano 2000, 1211.
[8] Kendall 1949.

Manual muscle testing evolved throughout the middle and later part of the 20th century as a major aspect of a doctor's neurologic test. In 1964, Dr. George Goodheart, a chiropractic physician, began to experiment with muscle testing.[9] He soon discovered that he could "apply" the kinesiological standards of the past 30 years to other medical systems that had already been in use, such as acupuncture, osteopathic organ manipulation, osteopathic lymph drainage, massage, and chiropractic/osteopathic spinal/extremity manipulation. Goodheart called this new diagnostic system, "Applied Kinesiology" (AK).

When using AK in a medical setting, a strong muscle was found to be connected to a positive response to treatment versus a weak muscle, which is usually meant to be a negative response to treatment. However, this muscular reaction can be switched depending upon what type of response is roused. In simpler terms, when you visit the doctor's office and you're asked to explain what's going on in your body, it's sometimes difficult to express what your organs, muscles, glands, etc. are feeling. It would be much easier if the doctor could consult with the muscles, allowing the body to speak for itself. This type of medicine was so successful that the originator, Dr. Goodheart, was invited to be the first chiropractor ever to work at the U.S. Olympic Medical Team in 1980 as a team physician.[46] This position brought in worldwide fame for his medical art and for the chiropractic profession as a whole.

The practice of Applied Kinesiology (AK) has branched into many forms such as Clinical Kinesiology (CK), Neuro Emotional Technique (NET), Total Body Modification (TBM), Touch for Health (TFH), Contact Reflex Analysis (CRA), and Emotional Freedom Technique (EFT). All of these types of AK medical practices utilize either basic muscle testing standards or modified muscle testing in combination with other established medical systems.

Types of Muscle Testing

Below is a small list of the different types of muscle testing that directly relate to the types of muscle testing used when I discovered the levels of consciousness associated with self-realization. They are listed on the next page chronologically by publication.

---

[9] Gin 1997, 331-7.

1. <u>Gravity Tests</u>: Dr. Robert W. Lovett,[5] Professor of Orthopedic Surgery, Harvard Medical School, 1912-1915
2. <u>Manual muscle testing (MMT)</u>: Kendall and Kendall,[8] Physical Therapists, 1949
3. <u>AK manual muscle testing</u>: George Goodheart,[10] Chiropractor, Father of Applied Kinesiology, 1964
4. <u>Indicator Muscle Testing</u>: John Diamond,[11] Psychiatrist, Behavioral Kinesiology, Psychiatry and Psychology, 1979
5. <u>Self-muscle testing</u>: Roger Callahan,[12] Psychologist, 1980s and Gary Craig,[13] Stanford Engineer, Ordained Minister, 1990s†
6. <u>Intuitive Muscle Testing</u>: Assumed start around 7,000 BCE†

The types of muscle testing seen above are the general progression in the history of kinesiology. In the early 1900s, physician Dr. Robert W. Lovett began using gravity tests to help infantile paralysis caused by polio. Then in the 1940s, physical therapists Kendall and Kendall created a book that explained, in detail, the various types of manual muscle tests. By applying a rating system to these muscle tests, scientific measurement, quantification and qualification, and diagnosis was more easily rendered.

From that point, chiropractor George Goodheart took this information and applied it to multiple medical systems, allowing for a practitioner to delve deeper into the consciousness of the body. By doing so, a dialogue could be set up between practitioner and patient, helping for more thorough treatment to be performed.

Goodheart's approach was further developed by the Australian medical doctor, Dr. John Diamond. Dr. Diamond used indicator or "straight-arm raised" muscle testing to show that people's unhealthy emotional attitudes and mental stresses had the greatest clinical effects on a person's physical wellbeing. In the 80s/90s, both Roger Callahan and Gary Craig took this information and decided to take muscle

---

[10] ICAK 2015.
[11] Diamond 1979.
[12] *In Memory of Roger Callahan* 2013.
[13] The AMT 2016.

† This testing has been used for millennia by intuitive healers. It is assumed that it started when medicinal plants were first discovered around 7,000 BCE and possibly before. It is now being expounded upon in this book as a bridge between the physical muscle testing of yesterday to the pure, intuitive muscle testing of today.

testing to the next level. This individual used his/her fingers as the mechanical levers to recreate the muscle test. However, even this physical test will be transcended, so that anyone can access the state of intuition at will.

In the course of my own education in both chiropractic and naturopathic school, I found the use of all the aforementioned types of muscle testing to be beneficial under certain circumstances. For the muscle testing used by most physical therapists, this was a no-brainer as I used it extensively in straight-laced orthopedic and neurological examination procedures.

When I learned of Dr. Goodheart's applied kinesiological concepts, I realized that this approach was what I had been looking for my whole life! It provided me with an intimate view of the patient's diseased system without having to know everything about a person's history. Although, doctors say, "80% of a person's diagnosis is through history," the muscle testing provided another level to the examination and treatment.

However, the true cause of the person's "diagnosis" may or may not be determined through history and simple examination alone. I have found that most of people's problems lie within the psyche itself and are emotionally, mentally, or spiritually rooted. These issues are connected to the subconsciousness through belief systems. For this reason, Dr. Diamond's work has greatly influenced the physicians that taught AK post-graduate seminars and consequently, myself.

Understanding the Test

I practiced MMT, AK MMT, and indicator MMT over and over again to test their validity against one another. The first two types of muscle testing are practically the same. In basic MMT, the body or muscle is placed in a position of optimal contraction. AK MMT may go a step further and utilize multiple divisions of the same muscle. The essential need for both types is determining the difference between a weak (4 out of 5 rating) and strong (5 out of 5 rating) muscle.

Indicator MMT is more challenging because the mechanical makeup of this test is more sensitive. The arm is parallel to the ground and the practitioner tests far out at the end of the arm, making it difficult for the patient to resist any force by the practitioner. Therefore, any practitioner trying to prove a point could easily fake the test. This is the real problem with this type of testing. Indicator MMT requires the practitioner to be a gentle muscle tester, and more importantly, it requires neutral intention. If you would like read more on MMT, Dr. Scott Cuthbert, a chiropractic physician, applied kinesiologist, and researcher, describes the validity and reliability of MMT in various studies.[†,14,15,16] Refer to the resources at the bottom of the page and in the Notes section at the back of the book.

In self-testing, the practitioner is the only one who is in control of the mechanical aspect of the test. In this case, not only does the mechanical apparatus have to be sound, but the chemical, emotional, mental, and spiritual aspects need to be sound as well. An individual with a pathological neurotransmitter disease such as myasthenia gravis may not be a good self-tester, as he/she can barely keep his/her eyelids open. Most other individuals should be fine, however.

If the practitioner is not mentally or emotionally sound, then he/she will be a biased tester, regardless of the form of MMT used. Spiritually, if an individual is out to harm or condemn through religious dogma or some other paradigm, the test can be swayed, as this test is meant to be strictly neurological in nature. Any deviation in intention from the practitioner can influence this test greatly.

When Dr. George Goodheart originally began testing muscles, he found that various types of body stimulation could strengthen weak muscles. This stimulation could be through massage therapy in the form of origin/ insertion, trigger point, or fascially stripping the muscle. Manipulation to the spine could also strengthen a weak muscle by taking stress off the nerve from the intervertebral foramen (where the nerve exits the spinal cord) or by relaxing tight muscles innervated by the affected nerve. Many other things could strengthen a weak muscle, and these are outlined at great length in the *Applied Kinesiology Synopsis*, 2nd Ed. by David S. Walther. Dr. Walthers says, "In most cases, the results of a test do not depend on whether the muscle is strong or weak, but how the nervous system controls the muscle."[17]

---

† If one is interested in learning more about these studies, please see the below article with Dr. Cuthbert's name cited along with a German study done by S. Hall.
[14] Hall 2008, 40-46.
[15] Cuthbert 2007, 4.
[16] Schmitt 2008, 16.

More accurately, the clinically-used terms of "strong" and "weak" are better described as "conditionally facilitated" and "conditionally inhibited," respectively. These terms signify that the nervous system controls the muscle, not the amount of power the muscle puts out.[17] A weak muscle that goes strong with a particular stimulation to the body may signify a "positive" test, meaning that particular treatment is good for the body. You could test a strong muscle (one that is functioning normally) and by stimulating the body in a certain way (through acupressure, massage, supplements under the tongue, etc.) could gain a weakening of the initially strong muscle. The weakening that occurs is considered a "positive" test. This process to discover the "positive" test is used to gain understanding of what type of treatment to provide the body for its greatest benefit.

When testing for a "yes" or "no" answer to a question that the practitioner has said either out loud or intentionally in the mind, a strong or weak muscle may be "yes" or "no" based upon how the test is calibrated. Different types of Applied Kinesiology use different ways of determining a positive test. Generally, this positive test may be the same as a "yes" answer, but not always, depending on how the question was asked.

As you can see, muscle testing is an often subjective system and often requires testing over and over to gain a statistically significant response. Some practitioners want to prove themselves and their healing ability through the muscle test. This type of practice will only end in failure. Constant testing with humility, surrender, and objectivity is necessary. My dear friend Dr. Matthew Peahl and I have talked extensively about the subject of muscle testing. He is extremely objective about his own practice and strives to maintain strictly sound standards of applied kinesological practice. Because of him, I can say that my own muscle testing and ability to determine an accurate test has developed from our constant sessions of muscle utilization and treatment.

A Muscle Testing Journey

After realizing, planning, and implementing these various types of muscle testing in my own practice, the next step was to be both precise and accurate with self-testing. Fortunately, I received training in self-

---

[17] Walthers 1988, 2.

muscle testing from a close friend named Dr. Christian Carroll before I left for a trip to China. He had used self-muscle testing consistently during his own treatment sessions and found it to be considerably accurate, but only under the consistent circumstances that were described in the previous section.

Under these circumstances, while treating specifically to raise the level of consciousness (LOC),[†] AK MMT, indicator MMT, and self-testing was all used to help determine consistency in the LOC discovered while I was teaching overseas in China. My wife, being the only individual available to test, was the muscle testing subject.

My use of muscle testing, while in China, helped me to discover a long-forgotten set of values and figures that represent the highest stages of self-realization. As will be shown in this book, muscle testing can not only be used to determine an individual's personal LOC, but it can also be used to develop intuition and other forms of psychic awareness.

The blending of hard science and esoteric practice can be a difficult one, especially when the world contains individuals at the two extremes *ad nauseam*. If you are either highly scientific or highly spiritual, realize that all perspectives and ideas must converge back unto the Whole. We as souls—a part of the one SPIRIT—must return to Source at the end of our earthly sojourn. The merger of science and spirituality must occur, otherwise it will be impossible to see universal unity, or the One in all. These same concepts are embodied in how muscle testing can be used to understand your current LOC (as shown in this book) and ascend to a higher plane of consciousness.

Indeed, I was able to raise my own LOC through intricate understanding of my LOC through muscle testing while having deep experiences in higher consciousness. I was undergoing self-realization, as based upon the writings of many self-realized masters across the major world religions and faith-systems. However, I noticed that I had gained no special powers through this process, except for the ability to bring on an unmovable body/mind bliss that could keep my consciousness in rapture for hours on end.

[†] According to Dr. Hawkins work described in Chapter 10 on the Intro to LOCs

While in this highly conscious state of true stillness called *samadhi*[†], muscle testing was still possible. The individual, being one with the consciousness of the cosmos, can muscle test "divinely" for things of the highest nature. Muscle testing is no longer limited to the physical, emotional, or mental sufferings of the individual; the spiritual natures of all beings can be accessed at will. The gurus of self-realization used this divine determination when interacting with particular individuals, whether it was to perform miracles such as bodily healing or gain knowledge of past, present, or future events related to the person. All of these actions were determined through the muscle test; they were not performed mechanically as I described here, but through the mind.

The yogi, while in any type of conscious-level *samadhi*, can still use muscle testing as a tool. One who has divinely merged with the Creator's Cosmic Consciousness through *samadhi* can access the workings of the universe. However, not all things will be revealed all at once by the yogi's desire. The question can come about, but there is no guarantee the question can be answered. The Divine will not allow the yogi to know the answers to some questions because it is not necessary for one to bring that knowledge into the world. Sometimes an intuitive answer to a question will come about. Usually, those questions are answered more easily and completely through muscle testing, since they are being provided divinely through the merged consciousness of the yogi.

It is difficult at times to determine what is and is not an "intuitive" thought. This determination takes years of practice for those who do not experience the stillness of mind that comes from meditation. Some are gifted with strong intuition, allowing them to tap into pure thought streams with ease. These are the prophets, psychics, and intuitives of this world. In order to learn how to "intuitively" test for something, a firm grasp of reality is absolutely necessary. This kind of testing requires understanding of the difference between what someone feels as a negative emotion and as a positive emotion. Negative, stressful emotion in the body means a "no" answer, and positive, peaceful emotion means a "yes" answer. To be accurate, constant testing is required. This consistency can begin with small day-to-day tasks, such as what the time is to who is calling on the phone.

---

† Expounded upon in second half of this book in Chapters 6 and 7 on Meditation and Yoga, respectively.

Once it is obvious that you can predict, with high accuracy, the truth of things, then it is reasonable to assume that you may be able to test things of a higher nature. However, even if you are testing accurately, some things cannot be known. If you are humble in your attempts and genuinely strive to only know things for the benefit of humankind, then you will be the most accurate. Universal knowledge is a gift of the Divine and should only be used for the highest purpose. If it is used for a lower purpose, it will no longer be an accurate tool. There may be other "gifts" provided for the workingman or -woman in the achievement of self-realization, but you must determine how these gifts may serve the good of the world.

The Non-Break Test

As I continued muscle testing, it was obvious that using muscles mechanically was still the most accurate tool for the measurement of one's own level of consciousness (LOC). However, just before the test itself, an instantaneous thought occurred in the back of my mind, allowing me to determine the strength of the muscle before the test was done. This intuition wasn't always accurate, but it was correct almost 90% of the time. When I was wrong, I was dead-wrong, and it proved to me that mechanical muscle testing is still necessary. Physical muscle testing is still the closest and easiest tool that you will have for measuring your own LOC while meditating deeply. Using physical muscle testing all time, while deeply meditating, will lead you to understand the "non-break" test. The non-break test is the bridge between mechanical muscle testing and using pure intuition only during the test. This concept will be explained in the next couple of pages more thoroughly.

In the non-break test, the manual component is interpreted as a feeling of what the muscle tester "feels" the answer would be. This is, however, much more difficult than it sounds and can really only be done by someone who is at least 99% accurate in their manual, indicator, and self-muscle testing. Accuracies for physicians, doctors, and healthcare practitioners are generally measured by their ability to properly treat and maintain a person's, and/or their own health.

Accuracy for the layman would be measured by how accurately one can answer a question in real time about the world or a situation. These results whether positive or negative should be measured to get a firm grasp on how "accurate" an individual's assessment really is. This sounds like pseudo-science, but all things yet to be measured with repeated randomized placebo-controlled trials will appear to be this way until a device becomes available to do such measuring. When these concepts become a part of the collective consciousness of a large group of people, it will spread more completely to the collective consciousness of the world.

It should be obvious that the body is only a physical thing manifested in a three-dimensional space, and so it is limited by these three-dimensional boundaries. If the body is used appropriately, however, it can serve a divine purpose and so too increase its own ability to become wholly attuned to the Divine will. Because of this Divine attunement, the body and its consciousness will eventually become aware of all of creation.

Since time itself, as the fourth dimension, is still only relative to the absolute nature of reality, it can be transcended, allowing for knowledge to become instantaneous. This knowledge comes at the speed of light and even faster. Knowledge, ideas, and concepts can manifest in the mind before any physical thing can move, allowing for you to transcend both time and space without moving a muscle. This manifestation of instantaneous information is called intuition.

Sivananda Saraswati, a self-realized master and founder of the Divine Life Society, says "intuition is a spiritual *anubhava*." *Anubhava* means "direct perception" in Sanskrit[18] and occurs because of the pure connection between the soul and the Divine source. Sivananda says that, through this connection, "immediate knowledge [occurs] through samadhi." He continues to say that,

> In intuition there is no reasoning process at all. Intuition transcends reason but does not contradict it. Intellect takes a man to the door of intuition and returns back. Spiritual flashes and glimpses of Truth come through intuition. Inspiration, revelation, [and] spiritual insight come through intuition.[19]

---

[18] Grimes 1996, 40.
[19] Sivananda 2011.

As I continued to self-test, I would be able to feel out whether the test would break, giving me a 'yes' answer. Despite common thought, this feeling is not in the "gut," but it is located in the heart center (fourth *chakra*). In fact, the "gut-check" type is often associated with premonitions or flashes of insight with both a spontaneous and immediate need. When you use the "non-break test,"[†] the test answer is felt in the heart center. This area is located about 2 inches above the center of your breastbone. The feeling may rise up into the throat or expand the length of the breastbone from the lower ribs as well.

A "no" answer was just the opposite. The feeling was mutual, but slightly different in the way that I could feel that the test would not break (the muscles would weaken), thus giving me 'no' answer. This feeling would occur just below the xiphoid process in the gut center (solar plexus or third *chakra*). It is difficult to describe the sensation associated with this type of muscle test, but the 'yes' answer would feel more 'open' and the 'no' answer would be feel more 'closed'. The sensation of 'open' is peaceful versus the feeling of 'closed,' which is stressful. This type of test would occur spontaneously, especially when I was in deep *samadhi* meditation.

Being in meditation allowed me to learn how to intuitively muscle test more quickly. I was able to access the psychic muscles of the brain. These "muscles" are really the overlying astral and causal counterparts of spine.[‡] The astral and causal bodies or *koshas* will be described later on in Chapters 11, 13, 14, and 16. These *koshas* directly relate to the how the consciousness will be able to access intuition of the soul. This "how and why" intuition is so immediate, but when understood, is also accurate. The gut-check (third *chakra*) intuition that everyone experiences from one time or another, is directly related to the soul's pure connection to Source. The heart-centered (fourth *chakra*) intuition is a higher form that is given by Source as a way for you to tap into your intuition at will.

[†] The "non-break test" will be explained more thoroughly in the next couple of pages.
[‡] The astral body is the energetic or subtle aspects of the physical body that make up the energy vortices called *chakras* and other overlying energy meridians that lie throughout the body. The causal body is the thought-form or particle-based reality of the body. It is literally composed of what we think of the body. The astral body is composed of what we emotionally feel about.

Heart-centered intuition is the ultimate way to test, as it requires no mechanical movement. However, it can provide the greatest amount of error if not used properly. All great masters tested the necessity of their involvement in a particular event or person in this way. They were able to feel out the necessity for an action and know whether or not it was appropriate. Their bodies were wholly attuned to the Divine will and knew immediately the appropriateness of their actions.

The Example of Jesus

I am sure that Jesus himself tested, in his divinely-merged consciousness, the necessity and timing of dying on the cross. We see in both the Gospels of Matthew and Mark that Jesus had a "sorrowful soul" while praying in the garden of Gethsemane.[20] This is because he knew that his death was to come about as a crucifixion but still continued to pray about its occurrence.

Here, Jesus acts much like a man in his own "human" sadness over things, questioning reality as it stood. Jesus had God's power to access the past, present, and future at will. Jesus was surely special, as he had the infinite power of God. This is different than the workingmen and -women[†] of this world, who may only have access to God's peace, stillness, and joy.

The types of abilities that Jesus manifested, along with those of saints and yogic masters, will be accessible for those workingmen and -women reaching self-realization in future ages. In this current age, these abilities are only available to a few because of the relative global collective level of consciousness. Relative to Jesus, he only would do what he 'tested' for. This means that Jesus, being a true Son of God, followed his heavenly Father perfectly.

In Jesus's perfected state he was able to determine who to help and who not to help. Hence, Jesus performed some miracles, but not others. This is challenging to understand, but it would give us a scientific understanding of how Jesus was all-knowing or omniscient.

In one example, Jesus healed the leper, and in doing so, he was not able to teach in that particular town because the leper had told everyone of this miracle.[21] Talking about the miracle took away from

---

[20] Matthew 26:36-46 NASB

† The workingmen and -women that will reach self-realization are referred to as the Minervan man. This is discussed in much more detail in Chapter 4.

[21] Mark 1:40-45 NASB

the event itself, although Jesus knew that the benefit to the man outweighed the risk of Jesus being hounded for his powers. In another example, Jesus depossessed a man with demons and then told him to tell all of what the Lord has done for him.[22] Jesus did not want to be looked at as God, but as one who was facilitating the Divine's power. In both of these examples, Jesus showed that humility in discernment is necessary to know, and thus, perform the greatest of acts to those who require them. This discernment can be gained more quickly by unifying mechanical muscle testing and heart-check intuition described.

If you want to learn this process of intuitive muscle testing, you must first learn how, at the very least, to self-test accurately. From this point, the non-break test will come automatically, and finally, your intuition will refine itself. You will begin to picture the muscle test in your mind and feel the direction the question is taking your consciousness. Finally, you will no longer need to picture the test, and pure intuition will take over, allowing for questions to be answered immediately and accurately. This state is the truest and purest nature of the intuitive mind.

Essential Questions for Muscle Testing

During the muscle testing procedure, there are always essential questions that will be used to help guide the practitioner to the proper path. These questions are meant to tease out boundaries that are placed against a muscle tester's ability to gather an accurate answer. Remember that muscle testing can only yield a 'yes' or 'no' answer to a question. There are no 'open-ended' answers to muscle-tested questions. There cannot be open-ended answers because the muscle test is originally a neurological switch showing whether a muscle is strong or weak; a rating of a 5 or a rating of 4, respectively. It is really that simple. Anything more complicated, and the process will become infinitely confusing for the practitioner and the layman.

The 'open-ended' answers are saved for those true self-realized masters that have absolute control over all elements and complete

---

[22] Mark 5:1-20 NASB

access to all knowledge in the universe. Muscle testing is primarily being utilized to allow the workingman or -woman achieve the highest realizations and to understand that he/she too has access to the Divine's infinite bounty.

Some questions are included below to illustrate the necessity of specificity in the question to allow for the most precise and accurate answer to be given.

"Give me a yes." "Give me a no."
Every tester needs a baseline to determine mechanically whether a break in the muscle test is a 'yes' or 'no' answer. This procedure is also essential when trying to match up the mechanical muscle testing with a non-break test. You will eventually know how a 'yes' or 'no' answer will feel in the body after performing a non-break test numerous times.

Generally, a break in the muscle test or a weak muscle signifies a 'yes' answer and a strong muscle (non-break) signifies a 'no' answer. While there are exceptions, this was the method used for the purposes of this book. Also, it makes sense that if you are trying to find a 'yes' answer, you will get many more 'no' answers in the process of discovery. In the long run during the treatment, the muscle being used will get tired more quickly if a 'no' answer is indicated by a break in the muscle test.

"Can I ask this question?"
Sometimes, when you are not allowed ask for something, it is because you are not meant to know at that certain point in time, or you are never meant to know. Those are simplest ways to describe this question. It is always best to be as direct and as clear as possible. To ask, "Can I ask this question?," is necessary because sometimes the Divine will not allow you access to certain types of information. This is mostly in the situation when you are asking about information that is for your own needs or is out to do others harm. Also, if you are too emotionally attached to a certain type of information, then you will also not be allowed to ask. These boundaries have been set up to protect you and others.

"Is it my or another's highest interest to know or receive this?"
This question is the mother lode of all questions. You can ask a question and receive an answer, but it may not be in the highest interest

of the individual to know or receive the answer. One's desire may be strong enough to want to know an answer, and therefore, he or she will receive an answer. However, the answer may not serve the highest purpose of the individual who is testing or who is being tested for.

This question is used often in practice, because sometimes a treatment can be given on request because the patient/client believes that the treatment is the best for him/her. I would say that most of the time, patients, clients, and other layman, who have no muscle testing training, generally cannot know what treatment is. While a select few are intuitive enough about their bodies, most people will over-analyze or over-generalize their conditions. Therefore, it is necessary to have muscle testers who are highly trained to eliminate bias in the testing.

Question Calibration

When you ask a question intuitively, it is usually direct and closed-ended, i.e. "Is it best for me to eat this food?" vs. "What do you think about this food for me?" The first question is direct vs. the second question which is open-ended. When you are asking a question with muscle testing for another individual or yourself, it must be very specific and direct. The wording must be perfect, otherwise the meaning will not be received well by either party. A direct question asked, in either case, is like making a statement with the same wording, i.e. "Is it best for me to eat this food?" vs. "It is best for me to eat this food." The first sentence is a direct question, and the second sentence is a statement. Only the words "it" and "is" are switched around. In this way, they essentially mean the same thing to the subconscious mind. But—here is the tricky part—in manual, indicator (straight-arm raise), or self-muscle testing, there is a manual component whereby the individual relies on a break in the muscle test to mean "yes" or an already strong muscle to stay strong for "no."

Intuitive Muscle Testing

Finally, with intuitive muscle testing, a "bad" feeling in the body (which needs to be determined by the person testing) with a direct question and statement that mean relatively the same thing, would mean a "no" answer. A "good" feeling would, consequently, mean a "yes."

It is difficult at first to understand how to recognize a "good" vs. a "bad" feeling, but usually the physical "gut" reaction is a good starting point to understand the differences. The third *chakra*, just below the ribs and above the belly button is the area where this "gut" reaction is felt. The third *chakra* is the power center in the body. It is the place where energy that is rising up in the body can either be transmuted and sent into higher energetic areas, such as the heart or third eye, to bring about greater levels of intuition. Power could also be sent down into the lower *chakras*, where the energy can be used for reproduction or basic primal needs, such as sex and aggressive behavior. The third *chakra* is also the area of choice. You choose what you want to do with the power that is being generated. This choosing ground is also the place where instantaneous intuitive responses manifest.

For example, if an assailant is running toward you about to attack, you can either send energy down your spine into your lower *chakras* to run away or you can send energy up your spine to intuitively know how to respond appropriately to the oncoming attack. This is why the third *chakra* is the center for choice and basic intuitive reactions. It is the place where I myself still receive intuitive responses to know the difference between a proper and poor choice.

When asking questions, or making statements intuitively, you need to know who or what you are addressing. If you are interested in whether or not you should take a particular route to work, it doesn't matter who you address. However, if you are asking about the highest truths, especially in regard to the another's wellbeing, important business decisions, or even life-altering decisions, then be sure to address the Divine. What does this mean? When you ask a question, generally, you will use the person's name first, and then ask the question. Sometimes the person's name will be used second, but it is essential when asking a question, in regards to higher truths, use the Divine's name first to get a correct response. A name of the Divine could be any number of names that resonate with you. Some examples include, "God," "Divine Mother," "SPIRIT," "Lord," and "Universe." When using a person's name, the question is more directed, and the answer will be clearer. For example, for higher truths you say, "Father God, is it in Dr. Derek's highest good to meditate for longer than three hours tonight?"

Even if you ask a question from a pure heart and mind, if it is not completely immersed in bliss, the ego will try to insert its opinion subtly. Being immersed in samadhi bliss is the only way to guarantee that you are operating in line with the Divine at all times. It is imperative that you use the Divine's name first; otherwise, if used last and with hesitation, the ego can insert its response, usually in opposition to the answer the Divine would provide.

Intuition vs. Muscle Testing

Intuition is the best indicator of truth, but it is hardly scientific and presents a challenge in today's society, where science reigns supreme. On the other hand, intuition is slowly becoming manifested as a viable source of truth in the collective consciousness of the world. The word intuition is a common term associated with those who are highly successful, and it is used to create anew, progressing the world forward infinitely faster than before. Intuition is not only for the successful and powerful, but also for the workingman or -woman who may be both meek and humble in her or her attempt to live a simple life.

For intuition to become commonplace, it must be tested over and over again until it becomes "statistically significant," showing a high probability or possibility that someone's intuition is accurate instead of just being random chance. If your intuition is "statistically significant," then it is proven to be both accurate and precise most of the time.

Using muscle testing to discover truths about reality is a necessary first step when attempting to develop your intuition. For the mechanically- and kinesthetically-minded individual who desires to become more intuitive, learning how to self-test is a necessary next step. I myself, being strongly scientific but intensely spiritual and metaphysical, desired a way to access an infinite amount of knowledge. After reading stories about the world-renowned psychic Edgar Cayce and the like, I realized that intuitive access is what I desired as well.

What I didn't realize was that self-realization needed to occur before I could understand how muscle testing and intuition fit together. One really begets the other in this process. The muscle testing is the physical version of the intuition. The intuition is faster and more reliable, but may only be initially accessible to those who understand its mechanism. The pure process of intuition is for all and will eventually be commonplace in future ages.

As the first chiropractor D.D. Palmer said in 1914, "When Educated and Innate Intelligences are able to converse with each other... (a possibility, which a not very distant future may disclose) we shall be able to make a correct diagnosis."[23]

---

[23] Palmer 1914, 3.

Essentially, when the rational and intuitive minds are in clear communication, the highest of truths shall be known.

The Divine has endowed each individual with an emotional direction system. The best way to discover this is to go deep into silence and discover the truth that has been given to each human being on this planet. The choice is yours. When will you decide to evolve?

CHAPTER 10

Intro to LOCs

What is a level of consciousness?

A LOC, or "level of consciousness," is a measurement of an individual's arousability and his/her ability to respond to a stimulus in the environment.[1] These levels can vary leading to either unconsciousness in a sleep state or Superconsciousness, as a yogi in meditation experiences. All of these various states, from unconsciousness to consciousness to Superconsciousness and beyond, will be explained in detail.

Unconsciousness and normal consciousness are both scientifically described in the literature, and those descriptions will be included here. The state of Superconsciousness has rarely been described accurately and has appeared in the texts of ancient scriptures such as the Bible, *Torah*, and *Bhagavad Gita*. Usually these states of consciousness are shrouded in allegory and myth and are hardly understood by the scholarly minds of this present age. Instead, these states need to be

---

[1] Kandel 2000, 901.

superconsciously intuited and tested in the fires of deep meditation. There have been few great spiritual gurus of late that have expounded upon the states of consciousness in detail. The first teachers in the United States were Swami Vivekananda and Paramahansa Yogananda. Others include the late Sri Chinmoy and his talks on the *samadhi* experience, lecturing on YouTube, through his website, and in books. Sivananda Saraswati is another divinely realized individual who created the Divine Life Society in the 1930's. Finally, Thich Nhat Hanh, a Zen Buddhist monk, has also explained these truths in his own way in accordance with the teachings of the Buddha.

Classically, *Advaita Vedanta*, a sub-school of Hindu philosophy, claims that consciousness is broken up into four "quarters," or states of being. Three of these quarters represent consciousness according to our present physical reality on Earth and in the universe. These three are waking (*vaisvanara*), dreaming (*taijasa*), and deep sleep (*pranja*).

The fourth quarter describes a state of being that is really not a state at all, but is instead a sublime, undifferentiated void, absent of characteristics and is, therefore, indefinable.[2] *Turiya* is the fourth quarter's proper name in Sanskrit, and it is generally unattainable for most individuals in this current timeframe. In this state, all things are known and experienced with a perfect, blissful consciousness. Only great masters can achieve this state willfully, but some may achieve it spontaneously as a gift from the Divine. For the workingman or -woman, the conscious form of this state, *anantya,* can be achieved, but only through great discipline, willpower, devotion, humility, and surrender.

What do the numerical values represent?

Generally, it is regarded that an individual with moral feelings of "goodness" will vibrate at a higher frequency or vibration and thus is considered "positive." An individual who is filled with sadness, fear, or anger will vibrate at a lower frequency and is considered "negative." It is known scientifically that when two vibrations of differing amplitude come together, they cancel each other out. If two waveforms of similar amplitude meet one another, the vibration created is then amplified synergistically to create an even larger or more "positive" (or "negative") vibration. In physics, this phenomenon is called

---

[2] Krishnananda 1996-2016, 10-12.

"constructive interference."[3] These "vibrations" are given off by your body cells and interact with the environment around you—causing constructive or destructive interference. You can either build someone up or break him/her down with mere thought and emotion.

The numerical values presented for each level of consciousness (LOC) start at normal, waking consciousness. Later on in Chapter 10, each LOC value will be given. These values will be explained again and elaborated upon more completely in Chapters 11–16 as well. These LOCs continue from waking consciousness, represented as a specific level of vibration. This vibration is the frequency or waveform that is given off from the smaller particles of electrons, protons, and neutrons interacting with one another inside of an atom. These atoms are of various sizes and will vibrate in different ways when they interact with one another.

When you meditate, your conscious mind elevates into Semi-Superconsciousness or Superconsciousness.[4] When this elevation occurs, your frequency ascends higher and higher, creating an increased vibrational state of the body. The electrons spinning around the nucleus of protons and the neutrons inside the nucleus of the atom become charged with a higher vibrational state, or "positive" energy so-to-speak. This "positive" increase in energy can be felt easily when you laugh heartily or when peace overcomes the body after a moment of anger or fear. All of these moments can result in temporary or permanent increases in vibration based upon the consciousness of the individual.

Some postulate that the advanced civilizations of Atlantis were so spiritually and positively elevated that their physical bodies literally vibrated into the next dimension, preventing their physical bodies from being found in the Earth's strata. This hypothesis can also be used to describe how various self-realized saints and sages throughout the ages, especially in Christianity, Hinduism, and Buddhism, were able to manifest various supernatural abilities. A few of these examples include St. Teresa of Avila, St. Francis of Assisi, Simon the Magus, and St. Joseph of Cupertino. These Christian saints were known to levitate consciously, but not necessarily at will. The same has been reported in Hinduism, Buddhism and by various other psychic mediums throughout the ages. This levitation is merely the body vibrating at an

---

[3] Michigan State University 2014.
[4] Walters 2004.

increased rate. To what level this vibration exists numerically is currently unknown, although it has been tested in the laboratory.

Levitation has been shown by researchers in animal studies[5] in 2006 and by using sound waves[6] in 2014. Although this levitation may not seem the same, all levitation will occur by some external force. This force could be sound waves or the pure vibrational consciousness of God. We cannot measure this pure consciousness with physical instruments currently, but in the future, all aspects of these universal forces will become known.

Other reports suggest that great yogis have a difficult time holding onto the physical body after a complete merger with the Divine. These masters have the ability to disappear and reappear at will. These experiences will be the ones of those becoming self-realized during the golden ages of Earth's history, but also reflect the present hypothesis of why certain civilizations may have just disappeared off the planet. Self-realization and the numbers described in this book reflect these rates of vibration and how they can help the individual achieve great yogic power and the highest states of awareness.

The numbers on the LOC scale, being monumentally huge, are not meant to be countable. They are merely given a boundary so that they can be understood, scientifically and mathematically, on a finite level. The point here is that your LOC can be calculated through muscle testing and/or intuition. However, a large set of variables is required to understand the framework of the LOCs and how they relate to the previously written descriptions of elevated states.

Many names and descriptions have been given to these LOCs to help with the ease of reading. They are meant to reflect the states already written about as a part of the various religious practices. These names have been used to help accurately describe where and at what level these states occur. The process of organizing the specificities of these levels is a scientific one. Just like when taxonomic biologists were naming the various classifications of plants, trying to create common relation among the many varieties, a spiritual taxonomy or classification must be created to make sense of the various spiritual states. The same occurs in health and medicine. Doctors LOVE abbreviations because, otherwise, their SOAP (shorthand) notes would take hours to write!

---

[5] Xie 2006, 89.
[6] Ochiai 2013.

Why should you care about these levels?

These spiritual states are the main reason that many world religions exist today. All are looking for the One, and the One is trying to help the All to remember. The ability to measure LOCs will show that anyone, in any religion, can reach the highest levels of consciousness, no matter their exact belief in God. Notice how all major world religions and most minor religions give a message of love and peace that is everlasting in one way or another. This message will be embodied in your own personal ascension with the Divine. Notice, as well, that there are numerous saints, gurus, *bodhisattvas*, avatars, or self-realized masters that have been a part of each of the religions at one point or another. Each of these masters have achieved all of these LOCs and were able to translate them through a particular teaching, which became a specific religion. All of them are really just saying the same thing, to different people, and during different periods of time to achieve the same results—self-realization. These LOCs will give you the chance to prove your meddle with the divine regardless of your background. Now, isn't that how it should be?

What is the practical application?

When you become attuned to a particular level of consciousness, various aspects and abilities are gained and can be accessed at any time. This attunement also allows you to not only access the present level of awareness, but also all past levels as well. However, as your LOC increases, all past LOCs and their various abilities become compounded upon one another into the next level achieved.

You will not have to drop lower in consciousness to activate various abilities insomuch as they will be experienced at will when need be. For example, you could tap into limitless *savikalpa samadhi* stillness while in *asamprajñata samadhi*, but not access the abundant bliss joy of *nirvikalpa samadhi*. The opposite is true, wherein *nirvikalpa* joy is abundant always with the limitless stillness of *savikalpa*.

Understanding where the consciousness lies is half the battle in the process of self-realization. Once you can perceptively understand your LOC position, you will have some idea of where you are and the possible distance that still needs to be crossed. This understanding becomes essential at the borderline between two LOCs, especially if it is the difference between a minor and major *samadhi*.

If the devotee is truly "devoted," then the excitement and conviction at these moments are monumental and help to propel the person toward his/her goal. It is so monumental because devotion is a much larger part of ascension than just pure reasoning. God wants our love, and that love comes primarily through devotion, not logical or abstract reasoning. You must be like an innocent child coming to your Divine Father's aid to achieve the unachievable while deep in meditative prayer.

Can anyone use this chart?

This LOC chart is to be used by all religions. Although the words in the chart are mostly Sanskrit, this ancient language was used even before Aramaic, which was used by Jesus the Christ. The language does not matter as much as so much as does the meaning behind it.

The ancient yogis of India were called *rishis*. These were self-realized men and women that were considered sages or saints of the post-Vedic tradition. Sometimes, they were considered "seers" like the prophets Isaiah and Jeremiah of Christianity's Old Testament. Swami Vivekananda said these individuals were "seers of thought."[7] These sages mapped out the process for self-realization using scientific meditative techniques. They also created detailed descriptions of these levels to help bring about universal awareness of self-realization. However, because India was falling into a dark age, these rishis hid this information, preventing the general populace from accessing it.

Now that the Earth and its people are coming back into awareness of the necessity of self-realization, this information is being brought out again into the light so that all may know of their divinity in God. Originally this information was available to all, but when the Dark Ages occurred, it was hidden to prevent this knowledge from being misinterpreted and ultimately misused. The Christ named Jesus came to all during the darkest period in human history to preach a message of salvation (and self-realization). However, His message was lost in translation due to the level of ignorance during the time of his life on Earth. This is exactly why we are still being challenged to understand the nature of Jesus's gospel through the myriad Christian denominations.

---

[7] Vivekananda 1897.

If people really knew that they could also be Sons and Daughters of God with an infinite amount of opportunity to get it right, in as many lives as possible, do you think there would have been as much war, strife, or suffering? No, in fact, the opposite would occur. The Divine's peace, harmony, and bliss would saturate the consciousness of the world, allowing for all to know themselves as both human and God itself. This idea is the essential message of this book: The One is in all and all is really One.

Although these ideas are paradoxical, many saints, avatars, prophets, and self-realized masters of other religions have come to preach the same message. The Divine is in all and all can come to the Divine, no matter the predicament they are in or the situations that have created themselves. All are welcome in God's kingdom.

Why is this book necessary?

This book is necessary because, as a planet, we are evolving! Many people think that the world is "going to hell in a hand basket." I would beg to differ. With the advent of socializing health care in the United States, awareness of the quality of food we eat, and the realization that multinational companies rule the collective minds of the masses, evolution is occurring!

Some Hindus believe that the world operates in a 24,000-year cycle.[8] In this cycle, the civilizations of the world ascend and descend in spiritual evolution. This evolution could explain why one could see the possibility of an enlightened civilization of Atlantis existing almost 12,000 years ago during the predicted "Golden Ages." Also, notice that 12,000 years later, human history was at one of its darkest times. During the medieval ages people were being fed to lions for entertainment, civilizations were destroyed in the name of God, and the Spanish Inquisition (Christianity) was torturing pagans in order to admit to practicing sorcery. There is a reason why those periods of time were called the "Dark" Ages—the spiritual evolution of the world was at its darkest points. Sri Yukteswar, a Kriya yogi and guru to Paramahansa Yogananda wrote a book called *The Holy Science* which talks about this cycle and how to relates to past, current, and future human histories.[9]

---

[8] Scherer 2003.
[9] Yukteswar 1990, 3–20.

Also, as a society, we are realizing that interdependence on one another, not just acting independently of one another, is the highest path. We must all help one another while still acting if we expect to help the world evolve. In the United States, as a society, we are still stuck in the 1950's with the "nuclear-type" family perspective. Life for many isn't like that anymore and may never be again. Instead, we need to look forward to how we can preserve our nation but also preserve the world, as both must work together hand-in-hand to create harmony among all people. Self-realization and understanding of how to reach these high spiritual states are the keys to solving many of society's problems.

LOC Origin

A MD, PhD by the name of Dr. David R. Hawkins, in a book called *Power vs. Force*, used muscle testing to determine various emotional states of people of all types from 1965 to 1994.[10] Dr. Hawkins used Dr. John Diamond's work[11] on truth versus falsehood to discover further uses of muscle testing with emotional, mental, and generalized spiritual states. Dr. Diamond discovered that a practitioner could ask a patient's body a question using muscle testing to determine a "yes" or "no" answer to questions the patient may not know themselves. This discovery allowed Dr. Diamond to treat the underlying emotional, mental, and spiritual causes of a person's illness without intense and long-term counseling from a psychologist or psychiatrist.

Dr. Hawkins took information he gained on states of emotions and consciousness and discovered a scale to apply these ideas to. He used a number scale from 1-1000 and applied each number to a different emotional state. Each number is actually an <u>exponent</u>. "Shame" is at the level of 20, which is actually 10^{20}, and the emotion of "pride" is at the level of 175, or 10^{175}. This applies to all emotions or states of being represented in the table. Dr. Hawkin's scale is featured in Table 10.1.

---

[10] Hawkins 1998, 14.
[11] Diamond 1979.

Table 10.1 – Dr. Hawkin's LOC scale

The number scale used is as follows:[9]

Shame	=	20		Courage	=	200
Guilt	=	30		Neutrality	=	250
Apathy	=	50		Willingness	=	310
Grief	=	75		Acceptance	=	350
Fear	=	100		Reason	=	400
Desire	=	125		Love	=	500
Anger	=	150		Joy	=	540
Pride	=	175		Peace	=	600
Enlightenment	=	700 – 1000				

Table has been reproduced with permission.

He also went further and used these numbers to calibrate the LOC of various written works, from science books to the holy scriptures of the major world religions.[12] He used 1000, or 10^{1000}, which represents the highest numerical value for the purest state of consciousness, to represent an illumined master such Jesus Christ.

Chiropractors, naturopaths, and other natural health practitioners using muscle testing can determine where a patient's LOC is during treatment using these LOC numbers. With the right level of treatment through chiropractic manipulation, craniosacral therapy, acupressure/acupuncture, supplementation, herbs, and homeopathy, an individual's LOC could easily rise to 1000. The goal in treatment is to get the LOC of the patient as high as possible in one treatment period. It was eventually determined that a doctor could treat a patient past the 1000 mark.

Dr. Timothy Francis, a chiropractic physician and a personal teacher of my own, showed the LOC could actually rise much higher than 1000. In fact, it is possible it could rise to a million ($10^{1,000,000}$), or even higher. Other doctors performing his type of treatment protocol could also achieve similar rises in LOC. The LOC would, at the very least, rise to over a 1000 and beyond easily using chiropractic, neurological belief system modifications, acupressure, and high potency homeopathy.

---

[12] Hawkins 1998, 52–57.

Currently, the highest named number in use by mathematicians is millinillion[13], which is 10^{3003}. There is even a larger number called a googolplex, which is 10^{googol}. However, the Oxford English Dictionary says this number is "not in formal mathematical use." In the LOC chart provided in at the end of this chapter, I show the numbers go far beyond 10^{1000} and 10^{googol}.

These numbers appear to be beyond comprehension, considering 10^{100} is a "googol." That is 1 with 100 zeros following it. Some physicists say that there are only 10^{80}, 10^{86}, or 10^{97} fundamental particles in the observable universe,[14,15] so to use values that are beyond a googol is going beyond the current usage of true physical measurement. However, as is explained later in this book, these numbers represent the vibrational state of your fundamental particles. These fundamental particles are known through Newtonian physics as protons, neutrons, and electrons. Smaller still are quarks, which make up protons and neutrons, and leptons, which are associated with electrons. There are still many more discovered fundamental particles not described here for sake of simplicity.[16] Realize that the LOC chart represented in this book is just a further evolution and explanation of what has already been created by Hawkins's initial research.

Beginning of this Book

The idea for this book came about when I discovered that I could ask for the numerical values for the various stages of enlightenment from Superconsciousness, Cosmic Consciousness, and up through *nirvikalpa samadhi* into *sahaja samadhi*. Remember, *samadhi* is the state of consciousness where the body becomes completely stone-still, while the consciousness of the individual becomes immersed in perfected blissfulness. This state of consciousness is the single greatest achievement for any yogi or meditator.

A dear friend of mine named Dr. Christian Carroll and I were testing each other for our own LOCs after chiropractic manipulation and nutritional testing. We discovered a new way to attune our bodies to higher LOCs, thus allowing the body to receive less physical treatment. As chiropractic physicians, we perform many adjustments

---

[13] *Names of Large Numbers.*
[14] Heile 2014.
[15] Munafo 2013.
[16] Braibant 2012, 1–3.

on one another and ourselves. It benefits us to maintain the healthiest bodies possible, while trying to receive the fewest number of adjustments. The less adjustments the better, because easier, low-force treatments have been found to consistently create more lasting cures.[†] Since we are able to muscle test and ask the body what it needs, these varying numbers of adjustments decreased over time as we attuned ourselves to higher and higher LOCs. Usually we would adjust the spine, give a supplement, stimulate an acupressure point, or massage a skin reflex to see how it affected our LOC. After each successive treatment, we would then recheck each other's LOC to find out if it had increased. Eventually, we reached values of $10^{500,000}$, $10^{1,000,000}$, and then 10^{googol}! We were astounded that these values were present, considering we weren't sure if they had been tested on anyone before. This is also because each of these values was actually an exponent!

As I was discussing my trip to China, Christian thought it necessary to help me learn how to self-test so that I could adequately treat myself while overseas. In the past, I had seen other chiropractic physicians/students like myself perform these types of self-tests thinking, "How can that be accurate?" I always doubted the power of the self-test. Personally, I felt that the most accurate test is on the patient. However, I soon proved the self-test to be highly accurate, but only under specific circumstances.[‡]

I began to self-test in treatments with patients. First I would perform normal, medical kinesiological testing and then recheck the actual finding on a patient I was treating. This way, I could recheck my finding with something I knew was accurate. As I explained before, a muscle test is like an on/off switch. It is either on or off; you cannot fake that. Even physical therapists (PTs) know if a muscle is weak or strong, because they can test properly. In this way, I was lucky to have been trained so intensely in Applied Kinesiology. Without that training, it would be difficult to prove it to others, and ultimately, myself.

See, I am VERY skeptical. I have to test, retest, retest, and retest some more until I know without a doubt that the muscle test is accurate. My patients' arms and legs get very tired because of this

---

[†] Refer to therapies like homeopathy, craniosacral, "laying of hands," and other gentle treatments. These methods have a tendency to create longer lasting remedy to those who are sensitive to them. This is because these treatment methods often work more internally with body's natural ability to heal.

[‡] Refer to the previous chapter on these details.

attention to detail! However, they always receive the highest quality of treatments because I take my time and am considerate of all muscle testing situations. Of course, I would also test something on myself and then ask another doctor to check it on me to see if I was accurate. Most of the time, it was accurate, but only under the best circumstances. This accuracy meant to me that this self-testing isn't as "full of fluff" as I originally thought.

After these many conclusions with treatment, I decided to take this a step further and test for things that were tangible, concrete, and could not change. For example, what the time was, who was calling me, finding lost items around the house, and so on. After these successful attempts, I took it yet another step further and had the intuitive idea to start measuring my own LOC while I was deep in meditation, the time when the consciousness is mostly removed from the ego and body awareness. I continued to test until I reached 10 raised to the 88,999,999th power or $10^{89,000,000}$. I discovered that at $10^{89,000,000}$, a meditating yogi could clearly see the third eye along with a centered white star, bluish-black surrounding, and golden halo. Below is an image representing this image.

Figure 10.2 – Spiritual Light of the Third Eye

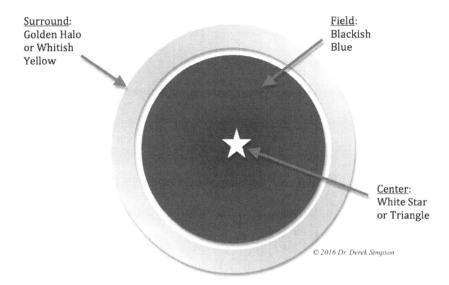

In meditation, I had always seen the blue and gold surround, but never the complete star. I was never able to surpass this LOC value, until I married to my wife, Jessie, and moved to China for a year.

One day, while meditating in China next to my sleeping wife I intuitively decided to check my LOC and muscle-tested that my LOC had ascended past $10^{89,000,000}$ to $10^{93,999,999}$! I was so excited that I thought, "I wonder if there is a way to measure for the LOCs of all the self-realized states?" What I didn't realize is that I would need to reach those levels before they could be accurately tested for... and so began my journey to self-realization.

The major LOC level categories

The first category is finitely large, while the second category is infinitely large. The concepts of "finite" numbers versus values that try to measure to infinity are loosely represented here. They are meant to represent that the process of self-realization may, in fact, be one of realizing infinity or the eternal nature of everything in creation and beyond.

The finite values of the first major classification will be explained concretely with numerical values. This first type uses the variable "CC1," which represents a value larger than a googolplex, but is necessary for ease of reading. The CC1 variable will be explained later on in Chapter 12 more completely. The second classification will be explained with another variable, called an Aeon, that represents many of the smaller variables compounded together. This is because as you ascend, the numbers will get infinitely large. It is best to represent these LOC values with variables because then it will be easily countable. This is also to show that you can measure your progress in self-realization with finite values. On the next two pages, I have included the charts that show the individual categories of consciousness and their associated LOCs.

Figure 10.3A – Categories of Consciousness

CATEGORIES of CONSCIOUSNESS

Self-named:
- Drunken Consciousness
- Perceived Nirvikalpa Samadhi
- Unconsciousness
- Subconsciousness
- Consciousness
- Semi-Superconsciousness
- Superconsciousness

Christ Consciousness:
- Christ Consciousness
- Krishna Consciousness
- Z State
- Elemental State
- Unnamed State
- Intermittent Samadhi
- Spirit State
- Minor Samadhi States
- Laya Samadhi

Cosmic Consciousness:
- Savikalpa Samadhi
- Savikalpa Samadhi Extension Experience
- Asamprajñata Samadhi
- Asamprajñata Samadhi Extension Experience
- Kundalini
- Controlled Asamprajñata Samadhi Extension Experience
- Samadhi Intensity
- Breathlessness
- Light Descension
- Void State
- Void State Breathlessness
- SPIRIT state
- Joy

SuperConsciousness — Increasing in LOC

© 2016 Dr. Derek Simpson

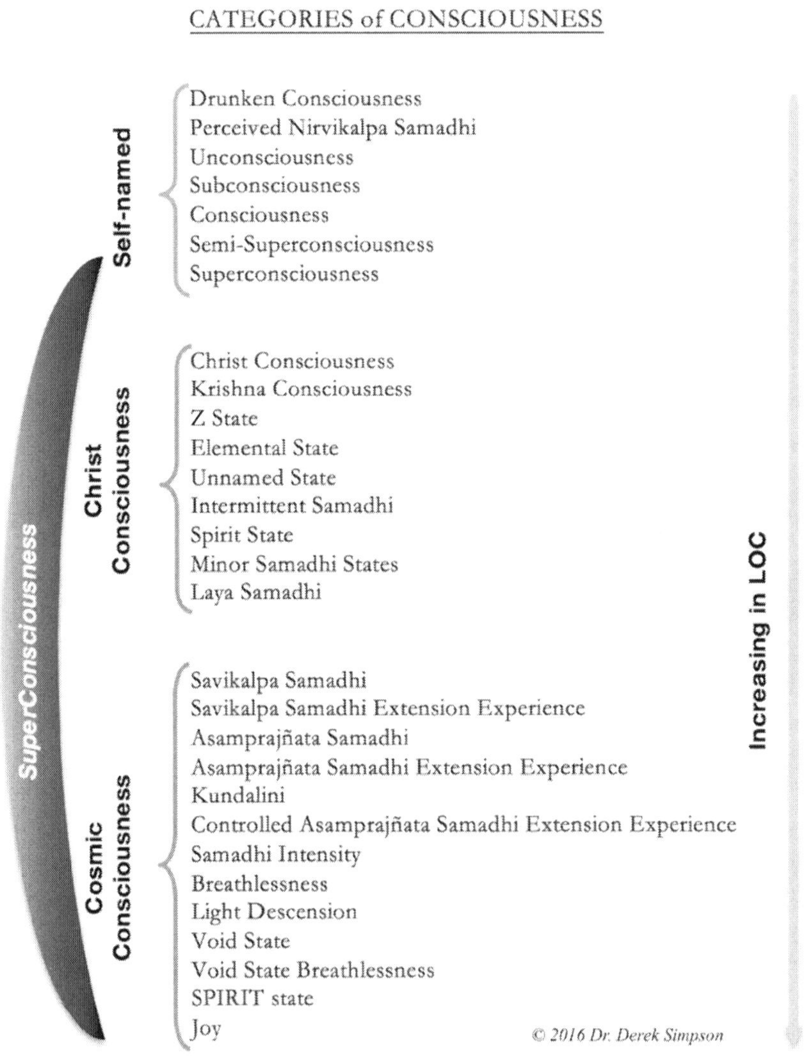

Figure 10.3B – Categories of Consciousness (cont.)

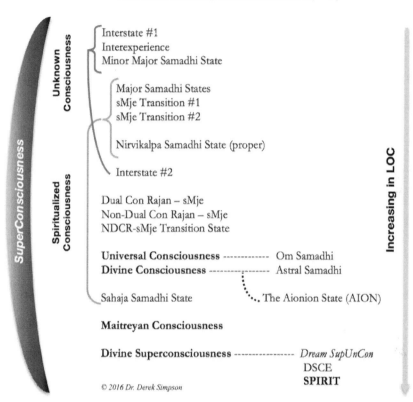

FIRST CLASSIFICATION

<u>Definition</u>: Finite levels with a concrete finality

Within the first classification there are:
- 5 dimensional realms
    - 1st, 2nd, 3rd Dimensional realms
    - Multidimensional realm
    - Extradimensional realm
- 17 major states within the 6 dimensional realms
    - This includes all bolded, non-*italicized* states under the bold-faced dimensional realms
    - Does not include The Aionion State or Maitreyan Consciousness
- 24 minor states within the 18 major states
    - All *italicized* and non-bold-faced minor states under all of the major states
    - Does not include Interstate #2 as it is the extension of Interstate #1
    - Does not include Dream SuperUnConsciousness

These will be described in ascending order from the lowest LOC value to the highest. Also, the level names will be abbreviated to enable ease of reading.

SECOND CLASSIFICATION

<u>Definition</u>: Finite levels with a loosely concrete finality

Within the second classification there are:
- 2 dimensional realms
    - Extradimensional realm
    - Uni-A-Dimensional realm
- 3 major states within the above 2 dimensional realms
    - Maitreyan Consciousness
    - The Aionion State
    - Divine Superconsciousness

*These states in the second classification span both dimensional realms

These final levels are also listed in ascending order. These states are very subtle and require a more abstract mind to understand their nature. These specific states can be seen under the subheading "Order of LOCs" after the specific categories of consciousness.

What are the categories of consciousness?

The LOC levels are not only described by the word "consciousness," but some LOC levels are grouped together by a certain category of consciousness, like Christ Consciousness or Cosmic Consciousness. The first couple of LOC levels are named similarly to their LOC level name. The first five major LOCs below Superconsciousness are self-named, while anything Superconsciousness and above can have classifications between Superconsciousness, Cosmic Consciousness, Divine Consciousness, Divine Superconsciousness, etc. Some of these names have been used for over a century now in various books on spirituality. I was able to muscle test for their connection to the LOCs presented here. Also, the term "Superconsciousness" was used to describe any LOC above Semi-Superconsciousness. This is because in the broadest sense, they are "above" consciousness.

Below is a summary of all the categories of consciousness used:

- Drunken Consciousness
- Perceived Nirvikalpa Samadhi
- Unconsciousness
- Subconsciousness
- Consciousness
- Semi-Superconsciousness
- Superconsciousness
- Christ Consciousness
- Cosmic Consciousness
- Unknown Consciousness
- Spiritualized Consciousness
- Universal Consciousness
- Divine Consciousness
- Maitreyan Consciousness
- Divine Superconsciousness

I created a chart that has all the LOC names, LOC values, # of levels per LOC, and associated categories of consciousness. This chart is shown in Appendix B. It is one of extreme complexity and will be explained thoroughly in detail throughout the next part of the book. The path to self-realization is one of great intricacy and to describe it with numbers and equations requires the same.

CHAPTER 11

1st Dimension LOCs

In this chapter, I will expound upon the specifics of the levels of consciousness (LOCs). Each LOC-containing dimension will be explained first, as they are the realms within which all the other major and minor states of being exist. There are six of these realms with twenty-one major states and twenty-five minor states. One of these states, Maitreyan Consciousness, is nearly impossible to reach for any human being who has achieved self-realization. Even some of the greatest masters are not considered a part of the Maitreyan Consciousness, nor will they ever be. The final major state is called DSCE. It is first an experience to the meditating yogi, but then will become his or her permanent existence.

The 1st Dimension represents the three-dimensional space that exists within our physical world. It is shaped like a domed cavern with many stalactites that line the top, while stalagmites line its bottom. It is a dark and damp place, stretching to almost an infinite height and width. For in its space, lies the infinitely numerous karma-bound, divinely conscious souls of creation.

The dampness in this cavern is heavy because it is representative of the karma that still needs to be burned up while in this dimension. The karma is so heavy, that it attempts to drag down the constant upward movement of the spiritually advancing mind into body consciousness. This dampness can be overcome by various techniques to help burn or cleanse the body of past-life and present-life indiscretions. However, these techniques need to be taught by one who has reached self-realization—one who can help the karma-bound body to dispel the darkness from within and without.

Karma, as described in Hinduism, is a system of causality through which beneficial actions cause beneficial effects and harmful actions cause harmful effects. These effects then create a progression of action and reaction throughout the reincarnated lives of a particular soul.[1] Reincarnation is the repetitive rebirth of a soul until it breaks the cycle by cleansing itself of all past-life and present-life karma by becoming self-realized. Once you have burned up your last bits of damp, heavy karma, your body will be covered with steam, as if it was burning moisture off an empty pot of recently boiled water. This cleansing is done through sheer power of will by breaking the physical walls of this dimension through constant attention and devotion to scientific meditation.

The LOC of Consciousness (Con) will be explained first, as this LOC is likely the easiest to understand because most of the world operates within Consciousness on a daily basis. The LOCs that exist "below" Consciousness are a part of the psychological states previously written about in history and medicine.

Also, all states-of-being within all dimensional realms or states will have a brief description based upon the most present research/literature that has been presented on it. Most information on basic LOCs come from reputable medical internet sites, as these are most accessible, and generally provide the most accurate pieces of information. After a brief description, they will be given a number for the levels contained in that state and a value for each of those levels.

CONSCIOUSNESS (Con) – Base type of consciousness

Value of Level = 1, # of Levels = 10^{3000}, Consciousness
VALUE   Value of Level = 1

---

[1] Pollock 2008, 78.

LEVEL #   # of Levels = 10^{3000}
CATEGORY   Consciousness

At the beginning of each LOC section, the three above characteristics will be listed—value, level #, and category. This is so that when you climb in consciousness, you can use this book as a guide towards your ascension.

In the self-realization LOC scale, the first major level of Consciousness (Con) included has 10^{3000} levels. Each level measures at a value of "1." The first level begins at the numerical integer of 1, and the last level is at 10^{2999}. However, the level number is represented by a round value as to make reading and comprehension easier. The same is done with all the states of being because, as you ascend to the next LOC from 10^{2999} to 10^{3000}, a shift occurs in your consciousness.

Sometimes, this shift is small and requires a special experience initiated by your own willpower, the help of a guru (spiritual teacher), or the Divine Itself. It is really unnecessary to say the exact number of levels present because, as you ascend in Consciousness to Superconsciousness and beyond, these levels represent where you are in the LOC itself. Each level becomes massively larger, and for the sake of practicality in our modern world, is uncountable for a person in any situation except for attaining self-realization. This concept will become more apparent as the various numbers of levels are revealed.

There are 3 major levels of the Consciousness LOC, according to the medical literature. They are represented by 3 letters: A, V, and P, which stand for "Alert," "response to Voice," and "response to Pain," respectively.[2] "Response to Voice," and "response to Pain" are not included in the actual LOC Consciousness measurement, as they are unnecessary for the purpose of self-realization.

Maria J. Kruse, a nurse, also elaborated upon stages of consciousness to unconsciousness by evaluating neurologically traumatized patients. These stages include confused or obtuse, somnolent, and stupor. After these stages, unconsciousness or coma occurs.[3] The Grady Coma and Glasgow Coma Scales also elaborate on the state of coma.[4] The two transition stages of "response to Voice,"

---

[2] Davey 2010, 157.
[3] Kruse 1986, 57–58.
[4] Tindall 1990.

and "response to Pain" are included as a transitional state between the LOC of Perceived Nirvikalpa Samadhi (PNrS) and Unconsciousness.

Also, the term "consciousness" refers not only to the LOC, but also to the broader category of consciousness that it belongs to. This concept will also apply to the LOCs Subconsciousness, Unconsciousness, and Drunken Consciousness. Finally, at the end of each LOC definition, the LOC name, level value, # of levels contained in the particular LOC, and category of consciousness will be given. This will hold consistent throughout all LOCs explained.

UNCONSCIOUSNESS (UnCon)

Value of Level = 1, # of Levels = 3, Unconsciousness

Unconsciousness contains three major levels. The first is induced by sleep and dreaming, and the second level is induced by fainting, alcohol, trauma, or general anesthesia. The third level is induced by coma.[4] Comatose is different than the other explanations for unconsciousness because it is due to trauma or inducement other than sleep.[5] However, comatose is a superficial or different kind of unconsciousness because it is "unnatural." In this state, you don't know whether you are really "aware" of yourself or the present situation.

Two scales have been devised to explain the comatose state. These are the Grady Coma scale and the Glasgow Coma Scale. For the sake of simplicity, the Glasgow Coma Scale will be used.

In the Glasgow Coma Scale[6,7] there are 3 sections of grading.
- 4 grades for eye opening (E)
- 6 grades for motor response (M)
- 5 grades for verbal responses (V)

Within these sections, there are 15 various gradings that attempt to give both a qualitative and quantitative understanding of this type of unconsciousness.

The medical field doesn't have the only valid perspective on levels of baseline consciousness. In fact, psychological theories of various doctors, including Sigmund Freud have also stood the test of time.

---

[5] Weyhenmeyer 2007, 177–179.

Freud's view includes a threefold view on baseline consciousness, which includes the Id, Ego, and SuperEgo.

Ego[6] is an analogous term for the first major category of normal functioning consciousness as described by Kruse[7] and others. Ego essentially mediates between the positive and negative tendencies of an individual. Even great masters use ego to describe a part of the base body-consciousness of the mind. Sivananda says, "...ego identifies itself with the body, mind, ...[and] the senses."[8] Sivananda also says, "Wherever there is ego, there are mineness, selfishness, likes and dislikes, lust, anger, greed, hypocrisy, pride, jealousy...,"[8] and any other impure, negative aspect of the mind.

Ego could also be thought of as a subjectivity of the soul. The soul in its objective nature is logical and rational, but divinely pure. Ego is really just a darkened reflection of the universal SPIRIT that resides in all beings in the universe. It acts as a negative detriment to the meditating yogi's progress towards self-realization.

The *Yoga Sutras* also describe the ego as *asmita*. *Asmita* is the process of identifying the seer with the instruments of seeing.[9] The seer is the soul and the instruments of seeing are the physical body and its physical senses. Even in the strictest sense, you cannot truly lose this negative self-projection through normal means. Gandhi says that, "many could forgo heavy meals, a full wardrobe, and fine house, and et cetera. It is the ego they cannot forgo."[10] You must release and eliminate the ego's intimidation through pure meditative contact with SPIRIT, before you can expect for the ego to lose its emotional and mental pressures.

When Freud talks about SuperEgo, he describes the part of the individual that helps to bring morals into everyday life. The "Id," as the instinctual, desiring state of being, does the opposite. SuperEgo here could be analogous to the "superconscious" mind that is manifested by the mediating yogi.

---

[6] Dickerson 2006, 47–48.
[7] Kruse 1986, 57–58.
[8] Sivananda 2011.
[9] Patanjali's *Yoga Sutras* II:6
[10] Gandhi 2002, 136.

SUBCONSCIOUSNESS (SubCon)

Value of Level = 1, # of Levels = 1, Subconsciousness

Subconsciousness is a little more difficult to describe, as many psychologists and other "mind" professionals don't have a strict definition for what the subconsciousness actually is. Even Freud himself did not have a definition for the subconsciousness because he believed it did not exist. In fact, he believed that the unconscious mind is where things like conscience, instincts, and drive exist. In other realms of understanding, the subconscious mind is where all events are stored in their entirety, along with those aspects described by Freud.

A self-realized master, known as Sri Chinmoy, commented on the subconscious mind in this way:

> In the subconscious plane everything is chaotic, unillumined, unlit and fearful. It is important in the spiritual life to clear the jungle of the subconscious plane. But how can we do it? We can do it through constant aspiration and dedication to the Light that is ever descending from above. Each individual seeker has to illumine the darkness in his subconscious world, or the subconscious will continue to stand as an obstacle to his pursuit of God-realisation.[11]

What Sri Chinmoy says is true! The subconscious mind acts a deterrent to self-realization because everything that the individual has ever experienced is stored there. During meditation is when the subconscious mind comes to the forefront. It confronts us with our deepest fears and our greatest ego-centric views. It is up to us to tame the subconscious into submission, so that we may gain access to the plane of intuition that lies in the superconscious state of meditation.

For the purpose of this book, the Subconsciousness LOC has 1 level and a value of 1, because it is so relatively undefined, and possibly, infinitely large. The subconscious mind is different to everyone and will reveal its secrets while in the deepest states of *samadhi*. Thus, I will not elaborate upon it here. Instead, I will delve much more deeply into the superconscious mind and beyond.

There is also a collective subconscious mind, and this is what contains everyone's experiences while in a physical body. These

---

[11] Chinmoy 1974, 45–46.

experiences can be accessed by trained psychics, intuitives, and those with extra-sensory perception (ESP). Those who delve into meditation can also tap into this collective subconscious mind allowing them to gain entry to information previously inaccessible by a normally "conscious" mind.

DRUNKEN CONSCIOUSNESS (DrCon)
Value of Level = 1, # of Levels = 1, Drunken Consciousness
Perceived Nirvikalpa Samadhi (NrS)
Value of Level = 1, # of Levels = 1, Drunken Consciousness
The consciousness that exists at the very lowest point of the LOC scale is referred to as Drunken Consciousness (DrCon). At this point, the individual has hit rock-bottom in his/her conscious mind.

Usually, in order to enter this consciousness, the individual consumes large amounts of alcohol, and he/she begins the descent towards Unconsciousness. However, Unconsciousness is actually higher than DrCon, because Unconsciousness is safer for the body and mind. DrCon is the body, liver, and kidneys' attempts to rid the system of the alcoholic toxin. At least in the unconscious state, the person can no longer endeavor to injure itself through liquid insult. Instead, Unconsciousness serves as a way for the body to protect itself. This type of unconsciousness is generally referred to as "passing out."

There is a subtle point in time, where the individual getting drunk on earthly wine (or some other alcoholic beverage) will "feel" as if he/she is invincible. This is referred to as "Perceived NrS" or "Perceived Nirvikalpa Samadhi" (PNrS). As alcohol consumption increases, tension is felt at the spiritual eye (point between the eyebrows), helping the individual to conjure this "perceived" state.

This PNrS reaction occurs especially with wine and less so with beer and hard alcohol. However, this state is generally not maintained, and most people in this drunken state cannot control it. The end result is that the individual may slip in and out of Unconsciousness with periods of blackouts where memory loss is inevitable. This is the body's protective mechanism, so that the individual does continue to injure the body.

Now, not everyone can achieve this state of consciousness. If your past karma or behaviors tend towards being a depressed or angry drunk, then this kind of experience will not occur for you. It is generally the happy-type of "drunk" personality that gets to experience this effervescent joy when intoxicated. However, this state is not a replacement for real joy that only true God-union brings.

It is not suggested by this book to use any illicit drug or alcohol to achieve a state of being that gives the "feeling" of joy. This is because it will never serve God, humanity, or the individual in the highest purpose. It is necessary to mention that those who seek alcohol or other drugs to receive a "high" really just want the highest states of realization. These individuals are unfortunately drawn by bad karma and *samskaras* (repetitive behaviors) that convince them that taking drugs is the best way to long-lasting happiness. It is no wonder why so many drink or do drugs in the world. What they really thirst for is the Divine's everlasting joy. If they only knew that, by deep meditation and scientific technique, this joy could be theirs evermore!

Another enlightened master, Lahiri Mahasaya, the yogi who brought Kriya yoga into the world in the early 1800's, spoke on the misconception of tantric rites.[12] Tantra is a type of meditation that was developed around the fifth century AD.[13]

It is considered by some that tantra is a fundamental spiritual science to achieve God-realization. It has influenced Hinduism, Buddhism, Jain and Sikh traditions.[14] When most think of tantra in our Western society, it is assumed that there is a strong sexual component as a part of the spiritual practice. Mahasaya says that these rites are superficial and represent a deeper virtuous practice.[15]

One practice that tantric practitioners have seemed to follow includes the consumption of alcohol as a way to bring about higher realizations. Some practitioners say that one becomes "attuned" to the alcohol, allowing him/her to remain conscious as the amount of the alcohol increases.[16]

Mahasaya says this practice of imbibing in alcohol is superficial in comparison to the real "spiritual" alcohol that is manifested. Mahasaya calls this alcohol is called "causal water"[17] or, as referenced in this book,

---

[12] Chatterjee 2011.
[13] Einoo 2009, 45.
[14] White 2000, 7.
[15] Chatterjee 2001, 279–280.
[16] Osho, 1975.
[17] Chatterjee 2001, 279–281.

amrita.† This is a sacred fluid that drips down in the back of the throat bringing on a deep *samadhi* state and a constant flow of blissful rapture. Once a person has achieved *nirvikalpa samadhi* (one of the highest achievements in self-realization), this *amrita* will drip down in the back of the throat at the call of the yogi's consciousness, allowing him or her to control the flow of bliss at any time.

Now that all these states have been explained, we will now move on to the levels that exist beyond baseline consciousness.

SEMI-SUPERCONSCIOUSNESS[18]

Value of Level = 1, # of Levels = 10^{3000} (10^{3000} to 10^{5999})
Semi-Superconsciousness
(SSupCon) – Intermediary type of Higher Consciousness
The beginning meditator can easily attain this LOC, especially if using a scientific meditative technique like the *Kriya* in Kriya yoga.

This stage is a beginning level of stillness and is usually a transitory state. As the beginner yogi starts to meditate, this stillness is presented as a gift from God and Gurus to help motivate the person to maintain a regular and frequent meditative practice.

In this state, the physical body covering, referred to as the *annamaya kosha*[19] in Vendantic (Indian-Hindu) philosophy, can be peeled back at will, if you are able to perceive the third eye. Even if you are only able to perceive a portion of the third eye, including its golden halo or blue surrounding, this is still enough to witness the astral body's covering and the cosmos that surround it. You will also perceive the causal body and its related universe, but this type of visual ability comes much later in the self-realization process. Generally, this ability will begin once you have ascended to the lesser minor samadhi states of the 3rd Dimension.

SUPERCONSCIOUSNESS

(SupCon) – Base Type of Superconsciousness

---

† Refer to Chapter 16 under the section on *nirvikalpa samadhi*.
[18] Savitri 2007.
[19] Sivananda 2011.

Value of Level SupCon = 1, # of SupCon Levels = 10^{6000}–$10^{(1E8)}$
Superconsciousness

In Sanskrit, *karana chitta* refers to the "superconscious mind,"[20] and to merge with this mind allows entrance into the base state of Superconsciousness (SupCon). This state is most often gained through deep and soulful meditation. Many avatars, gurus, and saints that have lived throughout the ages speak about the importance of this state of consciousness. Vivekananda has described this state as "perfect concentration."[179] He says, "it goes beyond the limits of reason, and comes face to face with facts which no instinct or reason can ever know."[21]

Vivekananda explains that, to follow the eight limbs of Patanjali, one will achieve samadhi or SupCon. However, later on in his book, *Raja Yoga,* he says that, "Samadhi is called the superconscious state,"[22] not that Superconsciousness is called *samadhi*. Although this might seem like semantics, other writers on levels of consciousness describe SupCon as intuition itself.[23] If this is the case, then you are able to access the superconscious mind when intuition becomes predominant. This is a common experience for those who deeply meditate on a daily basis.

One may wonder, then, if any meditator can have deeply intuitive experiences and manifest them in daily life, is that a *samadhi* state? *Samadhi* is the highest version of peace and bliss that you could experience either consciously or unconsciously. In this, you will eventually see that *samadhi* is the highest version of SupCon possible. *Samadhi* extends from being at first intermittent and then becoming present in a minor way. Next, it will become a major experience and then permanently blissful in *nirvikalpa*. Finally, in *sahaja,* it is both natural and spontaneous and then transcendent and unconscious in the *turiya* state.

---

[20] Subramuniyaswami 2000, 471.
[21] Vivekananda 1897, 34.
[22] Vivekananda 1897, 75.
[23] Durgananda (n.d.).

When you are in the baseline superconscious state, the vital functions of the body are calm and tension is felt at the third eye.†, 24 This is a common experience I personally have often, and it occurred more consistently when I gained access to the SupCon mind/state. When my body entered into *samadhi*, bliss was infinitely abundant, allowing my consciousness to transcend time and space.

As the world continues to evolve, access to intuition will occur more easily, allowing complete access to the SupCon mind. When bliss becomes easily attainable in a large majority of the population, then *samadhi* will have truly become easily available for all.

Superconsciousness, at its base level, is a generalized state that even beginning meditators can jump in and out of during deeper parts of their meditation. Intermediate to advanced meditating yogis are able to achieve it easily and maintain it during deep meditation. If you are dedicated and devoted to the Divine and your spiritual teacher, you will be able to maintain this state even while walking around performing tasks of daily life. If you are deep enough into SupCon, maintenance of this consciousness can occur easily throughout the day with right living and right thought.

It is also necessary to focus all of your energy towards the third eye while performing daily tasks. When you arrive at your evening meditation, further ascension will be made easier because you have actively attuned yourself to this state of consciousness throughout the day.† You could drop a little in LOC if your activity goes astray, as no one can completely remain in control while still under the influence of karma and astrological forces.

Though this simplified SupCon base level is unperfected, it becomes complete when you achieve unification of Cosmic Consciousness by initiation of the Divine Superconscious Experience in *savikalpa samadhi*. However, even though you can achieve the base level, you may not have achieved a *samadhi* superconscious state. *Samadhi* is a type of SupCon, but it is the perfected version of this base state.

You will see later that *samadhi* is not only a superconscious state, but also comes in many varieties from minor to major and from *savikalpa*

---

† The third eye is at the point between eyebrows, which is also called the center of intuition. This is the *anja* (sixth) *chakra* out of the seven *chakras* in the body.
24 Yogananda 1999, 39.
† This is the Law of Ascension as described later on in the book.

to *nirvikalpa* and finally to *sahaja samadhi*. The fact that there are different levels of *samadhi* means that there has to be different versions or completions of Superconsciousness itself.

Superconsciousness is gained through deep meditation and/or deep and prayerful devotion, which may lead to a transient or possible permanent experience of SupCon. Sri Chinmoy said,

> The superconscious is the possessor of direct wisdom and clear truth…. When we enter into the spiritual life with our aspiration, we can see that we are bringing the light of consciousness into our being…. At that time life's occurrences are handled consciously with the light of the soul….[25]

That "light of consciousness" is the dawning of the superconscious mindset. With this "light of consciousness" comes the intuition of the soul and direct access to the superconscious mind. Swami Kriyananda says that Superconsciousness, "…is that level of awareness that we experience when our mind is in a calm and uplifted state. It is the hidden mechanism at work behind intuition, spiritual, and physical healing, and successful problem solving."

This Superconsciousness, Sri Chinmoy explains, is the source of the soul and who we are at our highest spiritual point. Meditation will then be the most direct way to access the soul's source that remains dormant in most individuals.

Within this superconscious mind lies the power to achieve the highest realizations. Although its awareness is only a first step of many to be taken by the avid meditator, it is the gateway into the sacred places where SPIRIT lies. You must first manifest the Superconsciousness LOC through meditation or intense, devotional prayer (with the aid of a true guru) before you can access Christ Consciousness, Cosmic Consciousness, and beyond.

Accessing the superconscious mind is only one of the many hallways inside the palatial mansion of the Divine's infinite consciousness. Your entry into this sacred state of being only begins when you acknowledge the soul's power and direct connection to the Divine. It must be realized that the soul is the absolute director of all

---

[25] Chinmoy 1977, 48.

inward activities. These inward activities will lead you directly towards manifesting this state of awareness and beyond.

In this present era, the average vibrational consciousness of the world is in a generalized unperfected level of Superconsciousness. We as a human species have just come out of the darkest of all dark-ages in this current universe. Because of this, the spiritual evolution of mankind will increase at an exponential rate, allowing for awareness of all beings to come to self-realization even more quickly than in any other time period.[†]

The term Superconsciousness is also used as a broad category that encompasses the smaller LOC categories of SupCon itself and all other levels that are essentially above Semi-Superconsciousness. All experiences above Semi-Superconsciousness are included in the collective superconscious mind. Just as psychologists have expounded upon the collective unconscious, there is also a collective conscious mind, a collective subconscious mind, and a collective superconscious mind. Once you have ascended through *sahaja samadhi*, access to all experiences of each LOC state will be possible.

It has been said that, if you are able to maintain a superconscious mind permanently, then learning and memory tasks that may take years to assimilate will occur at an extremely accelerated rate. For example, those in medical programs may not need the full one to two years of initial medical training in the basic sciences to assimilate the necessary background to move on. The same could be said of lawyers, engineers, and so forth.

The necessity of not only understanding what Superconsciousness is but maintaining it absolutely in meditation and eventually in your waking hours is an initial requirement in the process towards self-realization. For this consciousness lies above normal wakefulness allowing the you to ascend as an individual consciousness eventually becoming and realizing oneself as the Infinite Ocean of SPIRIT consciousness.

---

† These concepts are elaborated upon in Sri Yukteswar's book, *The Holy Science*.

CHAPTER 12

Christ Consciousness and Beyond

CHRIST CONSCIOUSNESS (CC)
Value of Level CC = CC1, # of CC Levels = 100
Christ Consciousness

The Christ Consciousness. This is the same consciousness that Jesus Christ manifested before ascending through multiple levels of realization into the perfect consciousness of SPIRIT. Jesus the Christ is considered the Son of God in modern usage because he was the only "begotten" son sent by the Creator to save us from our sins. However, what did God really send? Was it a particular person? No, what God sent was His purely reflected consciousness into creation, whereby it could become manifest perfectly in humankind. It is available when you choose to walk a path of righteousness, humility, and unattachment.

Each human is a divinely-created "son" or "daughter" of God. The Christ Consciousness is thusly named because it represents an attainable consciousness achievable by all humankind. We are all sons and daughters of God, so this consciousness manifests as the Consciousness of the Son[1] in all. The Son Consciousness is just a synonym for the Christ Consciousness but allows for greater inclusion in all religions. This state is meant to be achievable in any religion, and the only thing that would restrict you from attainment would be your inner belief. The Christ was a human, like any other, who manifested a divinely-given consciousness that is within you and all other self-conscious beings. If you trust that, then you will realize the same.

The Christ Jesus did realize his own divinity, and this was the reason for his ascension. Of course, he was not the only one! Other "Christs" and Sons like himself, such as Krishna, Buddha, and more contemporary masters like Paramahansa Yogananda, have manifested this "Christ" consciousness at very young ages before ascending to the highest realizations described in this book. Sri Chinmoy says,

> We must realise that the Christ-Consciousness, the Buddha-Consciousness and the Krishna-Consciousness are all manifestations of the same Absolute. The Christ, the Buddha and Sri Krishna are not on isolated planes of consciousness, apart from the Absolute. On the one hand, they represent the Absolute; on the other hand, they <u>are</u> the Absolute. Here on earth they represent the Absolute, but in Heaven they actually are the Absolute.[2]

This consciousness that lies in the many Christs or Sons of God that have existed also exists in every human being. It is up to us to gain the proper vibrational foothold required to achieve this consciousness, but it is available for all.

Creation Love to Divine SPIRIT

This CC state of being is merely a beginning to the vibrational understanding required to "love all of creation." As you love all of creation through your own selfless acts of service, you will begin to see the Creator's Cosmic Consciousness little by little. Eventually, you will ascend to the LOC that exists beyond all of creation. Once you

---

[1] Chinmoy 1977.
[2] Chinmoy 1976.

experience "beyond creation," the Creator in its infinite aspects with manifest in your body. During the rise into Creator Consciousness, you will ascend into the fullest expansion of God's love, as this is necessary before you can manifest the SPIRIT alone.

In SPIRIT, there is literally an infinite amount of ways you can experience oneness with all things. This "oneness" expands into an ever-flowing bliss of *samadhi* stillness that constantly flows even with little focus to the third eye. A bliss that is so indescribable, you can only sit still, speaking no words, to marvel at its glory.

However, even this point is not the end of the experience, for you have yet to manifest God's omnipresent, omnipotent, and omniscient ability. This manifestation occurs during ascension into Divine Consciousness (described later in the book), when the highly vibrating body can manifest powerful yogic powers, such as healing and astral projection. However, these yogic powers are only given to those great world teachers who are meant to change the course of human history through their presence on Earth. The powers may also be given to those who highly desire them and work at great lengths to achieve them. For humans of the future to achieve the workingman's *samadhi*, however, these types of powers are not required.

Energy Flow

The energy flow while manifesting the CC is supremely different than that experienced before in baseline Superconsciousness (SupCon). Deeply focused meditation drives energy up the spine to evolve the consciousness. That energy is focused at the third eye to create a SupCon state. Bringing that third eye-focused energy into the heart while continuing to perform heart-centered acts of kindness and mental devotion will bring about CC. Don't forget normal meditation with the practice of techniques taught by your meditation teacher or Guru. In time, directing both the energy from the third eye and heart together towards God in devotion will manifest Cosmic (Creator's) Consciousness in time. I have created an image on the next page to illustrate this point.

Figure 12.1 – Energy Flow to Cosmic Consciousness

How is CC maintained?

In the process of maintaining the CC, you must understand the sensations felt in the body. If you can feel both the third eye and heart vibrating intensely towards all of creation in selfless service, then this consciousness will be easily kept.

Consistent meditations morning and night, along with devotion throughout the day towards the divine, is a surefire way to maintain the CC. Whenever the mind floats toward a thought other than that which is Divine, pushing it away with a thought of devotion towards the Creator in both meditation and in the daily routine is absolutely essential in maintaining both right thought and action.

The Christian bible also references this concept in 1 Thessalonians 5:17, "pray without ceasing." In this small idea lies one of keys to self-realization. To keep the mind cycling with devotion towards SPIRIT is to follow the Law of Ascension. This simple law, which is explained more thoroughly in Chapter 13 on p. 141 (under subheading "Unnamed States") and on my blog post on spiritual laws, helps to increase the ascension in LOC. This ascension occurs because thought begets action. This is a law of cause and effect explained by many masters. In the Christian bible, Jesus says in Matthew 7:12, "In everything, therefore, treat people the same way you want them to treat you, for this is the Law and the Prophets."[3]

This is the great law of karma as expounded upon by Jesus. This is where you will reap what you sow. Also, you will experience the same effect of whatever you think and do in your own life. If you do not keep your mind on the Divine, the "feeling" can be lost. This is why it is essential to practice the ideas above.[†]

Ideas for Continued Ascension

For those who are involved in practicing Kriya yoga and other meditative techniques, I have found that as you ascend into Christ Consciousness and beyond, less time will need to be spent in techniques that lead up to *Kriya*. However, they are still needed, if you cannot fully hear the sounds of the universe such as *Om*, angelic speech, etc. Techniques that would be used to increase stillness will become less used.

These techniques taught by various *Kriya* organizations are extremely powerful and should not be underestimated. My own body's ascension through the states of self-realization was not based upon the exclusive use of these adjunct techniques. However, the power of the *Kriya* alone (with the aid of one's guru/teacher) will truly help to ferry your mind to the absolute consciousness of *nirvikalpa* and *sahaja samadhi*.

The *Kriya* technique is the most powerful *pranayama* or life force control practice. It is now known openly to mankind and available through all types of organization. According to Yogananda and other masters of Kriya yoga, this type of *pranayama* (breath control) practice helps to evolve mankind's spiritual evolution. In Yogananda's book, *Autobiography of a Yogi*, he explains that mankind's spiritual climb to self-realization requires at least 1,000,000 years of disease-less evolution. Performing this scientific technique once properly in a 30-second period of time will evolve the body through one year of spiritual

---

[3] Matthew 7:12 NASB
[†] A book by Esther and Jerry Hicks, called *The Law of Attraction*, explains this concept in more detail.

unfoldment. He further wrote that if the *Kriyas* were practiced continually for 8½ hours each a day, 1000 years of spiritual evolution would occur, or, in one year, an individual would evolve 365,000 years. By this process, you could reach self-realization in 3 years.[4] Yogananda continues to say, "The Kriya shortcut of course can be taken only be deeply developed yogis, with the guidance of a guru, such yogis have carefully prepared their body and brain to withstand the power generated by intensive practice."[30]

In reality, the modern workingman or -woman may only be able meditate morning and night, allowing a maximum of an hour or less. This time frame may even be too much, but hypothetically, if you could perform *Kriyas* for at least 30 minutes twice a day, with a properly performed *Kriya* technique every 30 seconds, you could evolve 120 years per day or 43,800 years per calendar year. It would be possible to reach self-realization in one lifetime or about 23 years. In comparison to the many lifetimes you would have to live without a technique to reach self-realization, this prospect seems possible! This is the science of *pranayama* that has been given to mankind to evolve body and mind. However, there are many circumstances that may prevent a yogi from ascending so quickly.

After a long and deep meditation, some amount of stillness and peace should have been obtained. Remembering this peace throughout the day by focus to the third eye and heart is essential in maintaining the feeling that the CC provides. You have to be especially conscious of maintaining your awareness at the third eye during heavy eating or heavy sports. If you cannot keep your focus at the third eye, then you will descend from CC back to SupCon or even SSupCon.

Remember, maintaining the CC requires supreme willpower. All areas of life must be performed in moderation, otherwise constant focus to the third eye is impossible. This focus to the third eye is the fastest path to the Divine, especially while performing daily tasks, whether chores, driving, walking, working, or even exercising.

One easy way to lose the necessary energy to focus at the third eye and the heart is to have frequent sexual ejaculations. This goes for both males and females, but especially for males. Sometimes, there will be a great buildup of sperm, which will be released normally through involuntary ejaculations ("wet dreams"). It is essential for males to

---

[4] Yogananda 2012, 267.

practice tantra or a breathing technique to prevent their sperm from being released too often during sexual stimulation and/or intercourse. If you are married, this limitation will be more difficult, but it is necessary to show God that you desire the Divine alone. Maintaining this precious, life-giving energy in the body is essential when trying to burn karma and ascend from CC to Cosmic Consciousness (CosCon).

In Vajrayana Buddhism, tantric sexual practice is an aspect of the last stage of an initiate's spiritual path. The use of tantra is more easily used after realizing the void-nature of all things and thus, can attain God's bliss consciousness through specialized tantric practices.[5] Vajrayana has existed for almost 2,000 years in both India and Tibet[6], and thus, the practice of tantra has been tested thoroughly for its use in this practice. In the practice of tantra, if you attempt to maintain the sperm in the body while pleasing your partner lovingly and intimately, your own LOC will increase as a result.

How does this occur? When you provide your partner with a loving, sexual experience instead of indulging in it for yourself, it becomes a highly selfless and sacrificial act. Women are usually in this role, as, in general, men do not understand the sacrifice involved. Men have to realize that women's orgasms take a little longer to manifest, because their systems are very emotionally-based and require more affection and intimate attention. Therefore, the sacrifice for the man is great and will lead to much spiritual gain.

Women's sexual rhythms cycle with peaks, and then an orgasm or two may occur. Men's systems are wired to orgasm quickly and fully. That's it. Men go up, and then they go down. However, most of the time, this "down" for men is not the best, because sperm loss can be very draining if they have sex and ejaculate often. The same is true for females; however, their systems are subtler. If orgasms are frequent, it can be similarly draining.

If both male and female are able to cycle their peaks together (as men can peak as well), there is actually no need to orgasm as frequently. Sometimes the intimate connection through intercourse is enough to satisfy both partners' needs, which will, in turn, be used to help in ascension. If the peak is achieved without release, then the vital life-giving energy of both male and female can be transmuted into divine love for God. Also, if a man doesn't ejaculate during sexual intercourse,

---

[5] White 2000.
[6] Williams 2000, 194.

the man will be able to absorb some energy from the woman through the tip of the penis, like plugging into a wall socket.

There are times when it is OK to release the sperm. However, this ability to lose sperm without losing any energy will begin to occur in the highest stages of *nirvikalpa samadhi*. Before this, in *savikalpa* and *asamprajñata samadhi*, the loss of energy will be less with ejaculations, but it will still prevent you from maintaining the highest realizations. In *savikalpa*, you will lose the ability to become still at will. In *asamprajñata*, you may lose the ability for a short time to have deeper out-of-body experiences.

If a sexual samadhi[†] is practiced while ascending at any level with intense physical, mental, and spiritual devotion, then you can use the ejaculation as a tool for ascension. Further on in *nirvikalpa*, little if no energy is lost with sexual embrace, but this does not allow you to engage in it with reckless abandon. Moderation is still required to maintain the Divine's highest bliss. When you have reached the natural state of *sahaja samadhi*, the self-realized man or woman can help his or her partner achieve higher realizations through a "sexual samadhi" without any loss of energy whatsoever. In this way, when sperm is given to the female or vice versa, the energy is used to cause a monumental expansion in consciousness. This person being helped is then referred to as an "associate ascender."[‡]

Differences between SupCon and CC

CC is different than SupCon in the way that CC needs focus not only to the third eye, but also to the heart *chakra*. Serving mankind selflessly with love is to have the consciousness of the Christ in your body, mind, and heart. SupCon is primarily a manifestation of stillness in the body and at the third eye. CC is a manifestation of stillness in the body and at the third eye and an intense feeling of love in the heart. Some may constantly be in this state of CC but doubt their ability to achieve such a high state. Through this doubt, they prevent their bodies and consciousness from rising from CC into CosCon—their divine birthright.

[†] I originally wrote a blog post on this particular technique to explain it further. If you are interested in this article, email me, and I will send it to you.

[‡] Associate ascender is a term that will be explained more thoroughly in the book.

SupCon is produced by focusing all of your energy to the third eye while in deep meditation. However, CC can only be manifested once you are able to merge with the blackish-blue surround of the light of the third eye. This aspect I know through experience. I was able to muscle test for my LOC before and after I initially entered into CC. You may also dive into the CC over and over again and not realize that you are in the CC either momentarily or for an extended period of time. You do have the ability to see the third eye completely before entering the CC but cannot merge with it completely until you dive deep into third eye center itself.

Yogananda has said that the golden halo on the outside represents the "Holy Ghost," the blue surround is the Christ Consciousness (God in creation), and the white star is Cosmic Consciousness (God the Father).[7] This is a good qualitative description for those of you who cannot muscle test. For those who can muscle test for these LOCs, you will have an easier time of understanding their position on the self-realization scale, especially if you are unsure of how the third eye looks to you in deep meditation. If you remain skeptical, but still have a measuring tool that remains relatively accurate, with proper and clear introspection, you will discover if you have manifested CC.

This "Son" (Christ) Consciousness is the pure reflection of the "Father" (God) Consciousness in all of creation. This divinely reflected version is present in all conscious beings and truly all vibratory particles in the universe. Achieving this LOC will unify with God's omnipresence in all of creation. This is another main difference between that of CC and SupCon.

With this union of consciousness, when doing something for someone to help, with no selfish reasons or gains to be received, you may be stepping momentarily into the CC. This is similar to doing something loving for our relatives (who are sometimes hard to love) as this also stretches our superconscious minds. Another example is any professional who provides their services free of charge for the sake of wanting to improve others' lives. This selflessness is what helps people get rid of their karma[†]. These are big steps to take while ascending to or manifesting the CC.

---

[7] Yogananda 2004, 60–61.

[†] If you are interested in removing karma more quickly than ever before, then contact Dr. Simpson at his email in the back of the book.

As stillness comes more easily in the silence, the *Om* may sound without warning and without the use of a technique. Remember, you tune the ears to *Om*, not attune. *Om* is a vibrational sound that eventually will be heard without any technique and at every moment. If you can tune your mind to the vibration, like tuning a guitar string to a certain key, then the manifestation of *Om* will appear more often because the mind is more receptive to that vibration.

Om is essential to listen for when ascending in CC, because *Om* is the fabric of creation, interweaving all things together. The CC is the literal reflection of the divine SPIRIT in creation. Being able to hear *Om* unifies the mind with creation itself, enabling the Christ conscious state.[8]

This universal sound heard is a precursor to manifesting an *Om* minor *samadhi* state. This should be a common experience for all those who use techniques to hear this all-pervading sound. After mastering this, the trick would be to hear *Om* without using a technique. Such a thing requires great patience and practice. If you can hear the sound of *Om*, even with the technique, then you have tapped into the sound of the universe. Knowing this sound as pure creation itself, you will know the self as a part of the CC. Being one with the Son Consciousness will also make you sensitive to feelings of others. This is essential because, to achieve the highest levels of realization, you must see yourself as not only creation, but as the Creator Itself. When you are sensitive to the hearts of others, then you have achieved CC as well.

If you are performing all that is in the last few pages, but cannot muscle test accurately and can see the third eye partially without a specific blue surround and white star, it may be that you have ascended past this point without even knowing it. It is not necessary to have seen the third eye in its fullest *per se*, but to at least have been able to visualize the separate colors. Continue to go deeper within the colors of the third eye, as finding the true essence of these colors will lead to the Creator's Cosmic Consciousness. This may also be further ascension into CC, so don't get discouraged!

---

[8] Ananda Sangha Worldwide 1995–2015.

Other Aspects of CC

- This great state of consciousness is reached and maintained by great willpower. It is a great test of resolve for the yogi to maintain this state and ascend from it.
- This LOC is a major part of the 1st Dimension. Achieving it means greater gains later.
- The term "Christ Consciousness" (CC) not only stands for the LOC that comes directly after the Superconsciousness (SupCon) LOC, but also as a broad category of consciousness encompassing the LOCs above it. This includes the rest of the 1st Dimension and the LOCs in the 2nd Dimension.

CC1 creation

In the LOC chart itself, there is a variable used called "CC1" or "Christ Consciousness 1." This is the first numerically-valued level manifested within the Christ Consciousness itself. It begins at $10^{100,000,000}$ and ends at $10^{1E(999.9E12)}$. CC2 then begins at $10^{(1E(1E13))}$ and continues upwards like this to CC100, which is 100 CC1 levels.

The rest of the LOC chart is measured with this variable because it became apparent through muscle testing that the numbers were too large to measure with just successive numbers alone. Thus, a variable had to be created in response to a need to measure very large values. This variable stands for a vibrational idea. Although uncountable by today's standards of measurement, CC1 represents a vibrational state of being that is Christly conscious. As your body increases in LOC, so do the levels exponentially. The levels are so large, that it almost seems impossible that these "finite" levels could exist in our current realm of understanding. These levels not only describe the physical universe, but the subtle and ideational universes that lie in conjunction.

Considering the CC is what all meditators attempt to attain as a part of any meditation practice, it is one of the first major steps to obtaining self-realization. This is the reason why CC was used as a baseline for measurement.

Table 12.2A – A Numerical Baseline

A Numerical Baseline

10^1	=	10	Ten	1 followed by 1 zero	
10^2	=	100	One Hundred	1 followed by 2 zeroes	
10^3	=	1000	One Thousand	1 followed by 3 zeroes	
10^{10}	=	10,000,000,000	Ten Billion	1 followed by 10 zeroes	
10^{20}	=	1.00E+20	~ Sextillion	1 followed by 20 zeroes	
10^{30}	=	1.00E+30	Nonillion	1 followed by 30 zeroes	
10^{100}	=	1.00E+100	Googol	=	$10^{(1E2)}$
			1 followed by 100 zeroes		$10^{(10^2)}$
			ten duotrigintillion on the short scale[35]		
			ten thousand sexdecillion on the long scale[35]		
$10^{(1E6)}$	=	$10^{1\text{ Million}}$	1 followed by 1 Million zeroes		
$10^{(1E9)}$	=	$10^{1\text{ Billion}}$	1 followed by 1 Billion zeroes		
$10^{(1E12)}$	=	$10^{1\text{ Trillion}}$	1 followed by 1 Trillion zeroes		
$10^{1E(1E2)}$	=	$10^{1E(100)}$	=	10^{Googol} = Googolplex	
				$10^{10^{10^2}}$	
			1 followed by a Googol of zeroes		

On the basis of mathematical factorials, a googol = 70! which is 1x2x3x4, etc. up to 70. In a binary number system, used primarily in mathematics and digital electronics, one would need 333 bits[9] to represent googol as well. This number in exponents represents $2^{332.19281}$ as well.[10]

CC1 will stand as a numerical value for one individual level, the number level within a particular LOC, and the possible number of levels within a particular state of consciousness. So, while the LOC Christ Consciousness only has 100 CC1's, *asamprajñata samadhi* LOC has $CC1^{10}$ levels within it, while each level measures at $CC1^{100}$. As you ascend, these values continue to increase exponentially. It is hard to understand how large these numerical values are, so some reference will be given using numbers already a part of the current mathematical world. The baseline, seen above, is primarily set in the short scale[35] which is utilized in the U.S. and in modern British usage. This exponent represents how many zeros you will see after the number 1, not after the number 10.

---

[9] *Googol*. Wikipedia.
[10] *Googol*. Wikipedia.

A "googol" is seen as 1 with 100 zeros following it and when 10 is raised to a googol it becomes a "googolplex."[11,12] The difference between 10^{100} and 10^{1E100} is monumental. The difference is at least 10^{98} times greater than a googol of zeroes. Instead of 1 being followed by 100 zeros, it is followed by 10^{98} more zeroes. This may be difficult to grasp, because a googolplex is essentially an exponent raised to an exponent. Although this is a difficult mathematical concept to comprehend, other great scientists and thinkers of the 21st century have given some analogies to understand the size of a googolplex.

Carl Sagan, in the PBS science program *Cosmos: A Personal Voyage*, estimates that if you were to write a googolplex in its standard form with all its zeros, it would take more space than is available in the known universe.[13] Another analogy given by Wolgang Nitsche is genius in its own right. Nitsche literally wrote out a multivolume set of books that only contains the number googolplex. If a typical book can be printed with one million (10^6) zeros (basically 400 pages with 50 lines per page and 50 zeros per line), then there are literally 10^{94} volumes of this book available![14]

A final analogy, given by Don Page, a theoretical physicist, says that if a person can write two digits per second, then writing a googolplex would take about 1.51×10^{92} years, which is about 1.1×10^{82} times the age of the universe.[15] You can see that googolplex is, in fact, quite large, but even larger numbers exist, showing the further complexities of the universe. These complexities lie not only in the form of the physically known universe, but the subtle (astral) and ideational (causal) universes that exist overlapping this system.

Below a further numerical baseline is given to show how a googolplex is directly related to the creation of CC1.

---

[11] Kasner 1940, 23.
[12] Genevieve 1940, 566–574.
[13] Sagan 1980.
[14] Wolfgang 2013.
[15] Page 2001.

Table 12.2B – A Numerical Baseline (cont.)

A Numerical Baseline (cont.)

$10^{1E(1E2)} = 10^{1E(100)} = 10^{Googol} =$ Googolplex
$10^{10^{10^2}}$

1 followed by a Googol of zeroes
1 followed by 10 raised to 100 zeroes

$10^{1E(999.9E12)} = 10^{1E(999.9 \text{ Trillion})} =$ CC1

1 followed by 10 raised to 999.9 trillion zeroes

You can see that CC1 is larger than a googolplex. You can also see that these numbers are so big, that it is unreasonable to use them to count any physical thing in the known universe. But what about the unknown portion of the universe? How big is that really?

We may never truly know how big the universe actually is, but there are aspects about matter that are still unexplained, such as dark matter and dark energy. Both of these are most likely particle-based, although we have not been able to measure or detect these in the laboratory.

Both the existence of dark "particles" and the aspect of the unknown universe can lead you to believe that these variables such as CC1 and beyond could be used to count the physicality of the universe. Realize too that the universe is not just physical, but also energetically connected to an overlying astral universe. At the finest layer of this system is a causally-based universe structured at the level of an idea. That means that no matter what physical thing you can measure, there will always be at least 3 times more particles or "aspects" to measure.

The dark matter of the universe is the place where the purest aspect of the Divine exists. In between the matter that makes up the physical, astral, and causal universe is SPIRIT. God is literally outside of us but also within us at the same time. SPIRIT is the will that holds our own physical bodies together as well as the entire universe.

The Value of CC1

The true value of CC1 is not recognizable by our current standards of calculation and computation. This original measuring system is an extension of Dr. Hawkin's book on levels of consciousness, *Power vs. Force*. He determined that various states of emotion and realization could be discovered through muscle testing. In his book, these states are represented on a number scale of 1-1000, whereby each integer represents an exponent.[†]

The exponents are representative of emotional, mental, and spiritual states the body goes through to reach self-realization. The base of "10" used in conjunction with the exponent represents the physical body.

Figure 12.3 – CC1 Value as an Exponent

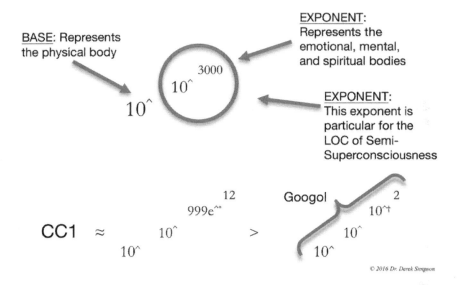

The first value seen above is representative of CC1. The second value is a googolplex. The second exponent of CC1 (denoted with an asterisk *) is "999e" which is 999 x 10. This 999e is raised to the 12th power which equals 999 trillion. The second exponent for googolplex is "10^" which is denoted with a ‡ symbol. These two second exponents show the major differences between CC1 and googolplex; denoted with a greater or less than sign ">."

[†] Theses ideas are expounded upon further in Chapter 10 Intro to LOCs

Figure 12.4 – The Actual Value of CC1

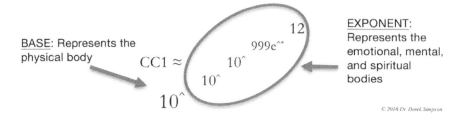

All values shown in the Self-Realization LOC scale in Appendix B are exponents. You would take the value represented in the LOC chart and then use that entire value as an exponent raised to the base of 10. This would represent the true "physical" value behind the LOCs in this book. The base of "10" is the physical body represented by countable numbers in known mathematics and the exponent is representative of the emotional, mental, and spiritual states obtained through self-realization.

If you read all of the mathematical ideas above and still cannot visualize accurately these huge values, fret not! Try to understand these few concepts about CC1:

- CC1 is much larger than a googolplex.
- CC1 is not countable by any present-day (standard) scientific method.
- CC1 represents a vibrational existence beyond the three-dimensional physical space of the known universe.
- CC1 attempts to create an initial value for the particles of the vastly unknown physical, subtle, and ideational cosmos. Beyond this still, the numbers of this LOC scale extend into the void itself where the Divine Intelligence lies undisturbed in perfect bliss consciousness, beyond all manifested creation of any of the three overlapping universes.

Collective Christ Consciousness (CCC)

As the whole world becomes elevated spiritually in the coming millennia, the Collective Christ Consciousness will develop as well. This is the collective mind reflecting the pure love of God in all of creation. Ideas of peace and harmony that float throughout the collective conscious and superconscious minds of people all over Earth will contribute to future development of the CCC. In these viewpoints are the infinite love of God permeating the collective Christ conscious mind of all those who manifest it.

The world's LOC is currently in a collective superconscious state-of-mind. This may be hard to believe, because of all that goes on in the world, but the spiritual collective whole of all minds are coming together to bring about universal peace for all of creation. This embodiment of peace is what is experienced in a mind superconsciously attuned. In future ages, the collective minds of people will ascend to the Collective Cosmic Consciousness and finally to the SPIRIT Collective Consciousness in the Golden Ages of human evolution.

Conclusion

Christ Consciousness is a spiritual state requiring a scientific mode of discovery so that all minds can understand it. This consciousness is the divinely reflected version of the Creator in all of creation.

In this creation, many "Christs" have come to give us the great message of peace and harmony about the kingdom of heaven. Whether it was the Krishna (Christ) of India, the Buddha (Christ) of Nepal, or the Christ of Nazareth. You were meant to be connected to your Divine self by accessing the kingdom of heaven which is found through deep devotion, prayer, or meditation.

All those who see themselves as a divine reflection of the Creator, as an essential co-Creator, will know themselves in this Son consciousness. God created us all in His image. We are all created, but as the physically manifested form of the Divine. God loves all His children and bestows each one of them with a divine consciousness in a physical body. We, as the Divine's children, must come back to Him in divine realization to know ourselves as SPIRIT.

KRISHNA CONSCIOUSNESS (KC)

Value of Level KC = CC1, # of KC Levels = 1000
Christ Consciousness
The next step in burning off karma is to manifest the "Krishna Consciousness" (KC). Bhagavan Sri Krishna lived between 3228 and 3102 B.C. He was another fully self-realized Christ figure that was the "savior" or "messiah" in Hinduism. The name "Krishna" is also just another name for "Christ." Our Romanized "Krishna," or *Krsna* in

Sanskrit, means "Christ." KC is not higher than CC, but merely an addition to the CC. The Christ Jesus was known to the Western world, and the Krishna Bhagavan was known to the Eastern world.

One goal of this book is to help Westerners come to the realization that all is One and One is all. To love all of creation for a Westerner would be to become one with the CC, but to love all of creation for an Easterner is to become one with the KC. Those of the East know of the Christ, and generally, fully acknowledge him as a supreme Son of God. Usually I find that those of the West, see Krishna as only a myth or a possible prophet of God. In this way, KC is to an addition to that love, so that all may find love for God's creation in its infinitely many forms.

The CC was an initiation into this state of loving God's creation. To become one with the CC is to maintain that love. Then, to further merge into that love of creation, you must ascend through the KC to continue the journey. Both are the Son Consciousness, and both are here to help all those who believe in them and this process of self-realization to ascend in their name to their own rightful place as Sons and Daughters of God.

Jesus was seen as a serious but loving man of God, and the initiation into the CC state requires serious willpower, dedication to meditation, and devotion to the Divine and spiritual teacher. Bhagavan embodied a different kind of God-like nature. He is usually depicted as an infant or young boy playing a flute.[16] This innocence is what God truly wants of us in our devotion to Him. This innocence is what is necessary to prove to Him that His Divine love and joy is all that we require. Further progression into these Christ-like states of consciousness will allow you to come closer and closer to God's ultimate gift of Love. This innocence of the KC is necessary to continue to ascend in self-realization.

You cannot ascend unless you fully believe that all are equal and all can come to God; no matter their place in life. Whether Brahmin or Untouchable, Christian or Catholic, Jew or Gentile, it does not matter. All must come to God on their own terms. To acknowledge that is to be a Hindu at its core, which is the same as being a Christian at its core.

Many are so close to achieving the KC state but cannot because they are too stuck in their own version of damnation and salvation.

---

[16] Knott 2000, 160.

You must know that all will go to God, be judged by God by their own deeds of both past lives and this present life. They will not be judged by the religious rituals and dogma created by man.

In the last 1500 years, Bhagavan Krishna has been worshipped through *bhakti*, which means devotion in Sanskrit.[17] Through attunement to the KC, you will gain understanding of innocence and necessary *bhakti* to be given to God. This state of consciousness is 100 times larger than that of the CC.

As you climb to the peak of this LOC within the cavernous 1st Dimension, you can almost see a faint glitter of moisture that is splayed across the various stalactites that line the almost infinitely large dome of this space.

Z STATE (Z)

Value of Level $Z = 10^{1E(47E12)}$, # of Z Levels = 1, Christ Consciousness
This is an intermediary state between KC and the next level. There is not much to be said about this state, except that it exists. Its purpose is currently unknown.

ELEMENTAL STATE (E)

Value of Level E = 1, # of E Levels = 579, Christ Consciousness
*The levels in E are a direct measure of stillness
This state is the last climb before you can fully burn off your physical karma. The Elemental State is in reference to the various indigenous tribes that populate the world. In these cultures, this state can be reached through various types of herbs. One that is illegal in most states is peyote. In article 32 of the Convention on Psychotropic Substances, it says that certain Native American nations can use the substance if it grows wild in the state where they live and is used religiously in their ceremonies. This herb, the peyote cactus, has been used for at least 5,700 years for special ceremonies.[18] There are other tribes that use ayahuasca, which is used by Native American shamans for its divinatory and healing effects.[19] These herbs are helpful to tribal spirituality because they allow them to elevate their consciousness

---

[17] Lockard 2008, 363.
[18] El-Seedi 2005, 238-42.
[19] Mirante 2008.

during a special ceremony or ritual in order to experience the Divine so that they can communicate with the deceased or appeal to the various spirits specific to the Native American tribe. I myself am part Native American and have known about these types of rituals since I was very young.

The Cavern Ceiling

The Elemental State butts right up against the ceiling of the cavernous space of the 1st Dimension, where it is dotted with numerous stalactites. The space continues on almost infinitely, but with numerous portal holes that lead to the next dimension. There are enough of these gateways for each of the infinite divinely-conscious souls to pass through. These portals lead to the 2nd Dimension, whereby the body will then be free of both past-life and present-life physical body karma.

After passing through, you will still be subject to the law of karma for every action, good or bad, that you perform in this life and every other henceforth. The law of karma will act more quickly because you have ascended to a "less heavy" state. This essentially makes your body lighter, and karmic law will act more quickly because of this lightness. Even thoughts themselves will manifest more quickly. It is beneficial to continue to think "happy" thoughts in order to experience the highest forms of realization and prevent unwanted forms of negative "thought" karma.

Also, astrological forces, according to the individual's sun sign, ascendant sign, moon sign, and any other planetary effects, will be negated. The individual can choose a life free of restriction to create, nearly at will, the things he/she desires. When this desire is focused on the highest good, all will become manifested as a result of this choice.

More to Do

Although the physical veil of karma and astrological force will be removed, there is still so much to do. Mental, emotional, and spiritual karma may be still present and will not be removed until you enter the natural state of *sahaja samadhi*. Sometimes your complete karmic total is released after the 1st Dimension, but this is not always the case. The good news is the first dimensional battle has been won, and at least 50% of the struggle towards self-realization has been completed. After this point, there is only 50% more to attain.

The reason for this incomplete attainment is because stillness, peace, joy, and bliss will only increase exponentially in meditation. The gains will now be much greater, even though there is an almost infinite amount of LOCs left until the devotee will be feel satisfied by his/her own accomplishment. For myself, it took less than 250 days to achieve a near infinite-like LOC, one where bliss is automatic, thoughts manifest into reality within moments, desires are no more, and the consciousness experiences only absolution. Do not be disgruntled or dismayed if you do not achieve the same results. My purpose is to inform all of the necessities to measure self-realization with both a qualitative and quantitative exactitude.

For the purpose of the Elemental State represents a universal and spiritual connection that occurs between all religions. Self-realization is not just for one type of faith, religion, or belief-system. It is for all. The Native American cultures that were originally a part of the United States and outer-lying areas near Canada and Mexico were pushed off their land because of greedy foreign militaries. Respect must be given not only to the great world religions of Hinduism, Judaism, Christianity, Islam, and Buddhism, but to all smaller practices of faith that have contributed their spiritual presence to the collective conscious whole of the Earth.

How Strong are You?

From this point on, you will have to exert enormous levels of willpower to ascend from this state and beyond. Once you have a grasp on your own ability to self-muscle test, you will understand how close you are to the top of this dimension. At the very ceiling is where the you will be able to burn the rest of your physical karma, allowing for you to ascend to the 2nd Dimension where all karma-less souls must pass.

You will be able to intuitively sense that there is a ceiling at this point that is extremely difficult to pass. You will perceive only darkness, but with a profound sense of stillness, innocence, and devotion to the Divine, you will succeed. The heaviness of the damp, karmic moisture that accumulates on each individual is great, but God has given every soul the divine right to ascend when and how he or she chooses. It is a matter of choice. You can choose to eat that jelly donut, or you can choose to eat that asparagus. You can choose to meditate, or you can choose to sleep. These decisions, although small to some, are very big to the Divine. These decisions show our depth of devotion and obedience towards God Himself.

Addictions and desires are also still very present while in this elevated state, but they are lessened as you continue to bring stillness to the mind. The process of freeing the mind of addictions is a long one and will be a constant challenge to your realization. Even when you are flying high in *samadhi* bliss, the subconscious thoughts of addictions will come back to challenge you. But once you have tasted God's ever-flowing bliss, how could anything else satisfy? When you experience God in all His fullness, He will become your addiction, and you will want more and more, always seeking Him in everything so you can continue to experience His divine presence. God-addiction is what facilitates the righteous action of the yogi.

However, the physical addictions are what make ascending past the 1st Dimension so difficult. Willpower and courage must be your ally. The LOC can drop because of these desires and addictions, especially if they take hold of the mind. The mind is the place where both good and evil fight. It is just the landscape that can be taken control of. It is up to the soldiers of righteousness to constantly win back land against the soldiers of addiction and desire. Even if the soldiers' evil win back more land than what you thought was possible, then, even in that moment, God and the Gurus are with you. Call upon them, and they will fight for you. Even the angels are right beside you, at your command, to force back the demons of undoing. God has created you as a perfect reflection of Himself, so that you may know Him as your-Self—your Ultimate Self.

Conclusion

The Elemental State is a little different, as compared to other states previously described. It is measured in stillness, a required aspect if you want to perceive the *samadhi* states in all their glory.

There are 579 levels of stillness that must be achieved before you can rise from this cavernous place. As you rise in stillness, so too do you rise in LOC in this state. Arriving at the 579th level, a minor samadhi state will be experienced. As you rise, the feeling of buoyancy will cause your consciousness to hit the upper limit of the cavern.

Once you have reached the ceiling, a transition will occur. At the 578.9^{th} level, the final bits of bodily karma will be removed, and you will ascend into a lit space. This space is not fully lit, nor is it fully dark.

Looking around at your own body, steam rises up, as if your body was too hot to maintain liquefied water. This is the karmic moisture that has been heavily laid upon your shoulders, like a lead weight preventing the upward ascension in self-realization. The goal of this state is to soar to the very top of the cave and constantly push until the light of God's love shines upon your bodily face.

If you do not achieve a karma-less state as described above, do not fret. The Divine comes when it is time and not a second before. Are there some paths of forgiveness or righteousness that need to be upheld, so that God and Guru can remove those heavy burdens? Give them up now, for now is time for your ascension.

CHAPTER 13

2nd Dimension LOCs

There are many ways to view this dimension. As you finally rise out of the darkness of the cavern, you feel immediately lighter; as there is no more karma weighing down the physical body. You would expect to see sunshine, when coming out of such a dark place, but alas, you have arrived while it is still twilight!

You have no more burden to shoulder, but only a little light can be seen of the stars burning bright. Your consciousness was originally like a seed buried in the Earth, pushing and pushing ever so slowly through the dirt, attempting to pierce through to the light of day. Finally, the seed pushed through the dirt to find more darkness, but a darkness dotted with shining orbs of bright light. Your work is far from over, but there is only a little time left before you will experience the fullest spectrum of the Divine's white light.

This realm of twilight contains dimensions that exist between and within the 578.9^{th} level to the 579th level of stillness within the Elemental State of the 1st Dimension. Once you have burned up the rest of your karma, your consciousness is transferred into the "in-between" states of the 2nd Dimension. You must continue to become karma-less before you can enter the minor samadhi states, and eventually, Cosmic Consciousness.

This 2nd Dimension has billions of smaller dimensions all piled up on top of each other. This is similar how quantum mechanics describes the existence of additional dimensions beyond the three dimensions of height, width, and depth. The spatial dimensions of physics that describe physical reality are not the same as these spiritual dimensions, which exist within the astral and causal universes. These are two universes that overlay the current physical universe in every way, except that they are expressed either by light (astral) or by particles (causal).

In these states and infinitely above them, you will still "feel" the aches and pains of the physical body, as the ego will continue to pull at your spiritually-elevated mind. As you ascend, though, your emotional consciousness will change to ultimate peace as your physical body will begin to obey your command. You may eventually achieve the breathless state of *samadhi*, but the body is still vulnerable. Be careful not to overexert yourself in any one situation, as the physical body still has its limitations.

Techniques

For all those practicing types of "pre-*Kriya*" breathing techniques, I have personally found that, as you ascend, the use of the various techniques taught by *Kriya* teachers become used less and less. Using muscle testing by way of the Higher Self, combined with intuition, these techniques were shown to not have the same effects as if you were a karma-ful being. However, these techniques are absolutely essential when climbing through the darkness of the 1st Dimension.

When in the higher dimensions, the techniques will serve to have less effect on the body, but new techniques will be intuited to help supplement this loss. If you are manifesting stillness all the time and can access it at will, then is *Hong-Sau* fully necessary at all times? I think *Hong-Sau* is an excellent way to induce stillness, but when the body desires to be still and you decide to breathe consciously, your body will give you a signal whether or not it is right.

The *Kriyas* are another example of an excellent way to burn all types of karma, but what are the other effects? Mostly, the *Kriyas* were shown to induce stillness and directly increase your LOC, if the body was stuck in one place while in these higher dimensions. You may find that simply increasing the number of hours of meditation from 1 to 2 to even 3 hours both morning and night may be necessary to access the Divine's infinite love. The more time and devotion you put in, the more likely you will achieve your rightful place at God's side, in a shorter period of time.

UNNAMED STATES (U)
Value of Level U = 10^{1E1000}, # of U Levels = $10^{71 \text{ Billion}}$
Christ Consciousness
<u>Intermittent Samadhi</u> (IS)
Value of Level IS = 1, # of IS Levels = 2.88^{1E11}, Christ Consciousness
At this time, there is not a name that exists to match the purpose of this initial state of being within the 2nd Dimension. In fact, the name itself cannot be spoken in any language that is currently on Earth.

Its primary purpose is to continue to develop the karma-less yogi in stillness and in creating open, balanced *chakras*. In this LOC, the stillness measured in the Elemental State is automatically present. This is the first state where you experience perpetual stillness. There are no relative levels to stillness; it is just constantly present in the body. This stillness even occurs while walking around performing daily tasks. Stillness helps an individual to:

- Be in more constant contact with the Divine and spiritual teachers.
- Deal with life's ups and downs more easily.
- Maintain an even higher level of stillness throughout the day, allowing the individual body to automatically ascend and evolve. This is the Law of Ascension, which is present throughout all levels of consciousness.

Law of Ascension

Basically, the Law of Ascension says to maintain your current ability, LOC, or state of consciousness as best as possible. Maintaining it, especially during your waking hours while performing daily tasks, will help the consciousness to ascend more quickly. Maintain it in every situation imaginable, and the Divine's grace will descend upon you quickly. The Law of Ascension also works more specifically within the various extension states described later on in each of the different sections on LOCs. Please refer to the end of this book in Chapter 18 for a summary on these extension states.

Measurement

This state can be measured in two different ways. In one way, it has 71 billion levels, whereby each level measures to 10^{1E1000}. These 71 billion levels are all stacked neatly next to one another in a Rubik's cube-like shape. Each one is a new ascendance in stillness and peace.

The second way one experiences the Unnamed States is through an "intermittent samadhi" or "IS" state. There are 2.88^{1E11} levels here, and each level measures at a value of 1. Another name for the intermittent samadhi is *pratyahara*, or interiorization. This is the "I that IS" always in the state of Be-ing. Meaning, *samadhi* is what puts you in the present moment with yourself, all of creation, and the Creator. In this way, love and the IS must become one during meditation so that you may know the glorious nature that can be reached during deep, silent, ever-peaceful, ever-awake-in-God consciousness.

The difficult aspect of this state is that, eventually, you will lose consciousness to the body. You may still be conscious and awake, but you will lose "awareness" of the body's physicality. This idea can create emotionally uncomfortable feelings in your mind. However, loss of consciousness of the body is closer to the Divine and is an ultimate merger.

You will come in and out of the IS, allowing you to surpass all other levels of basic stillness. You may experience sensations of the head floating above the body. Also, if the body is not ready to let go yet, then the third *chakra* may tend to pull the consciousness back down in the body, as this is generally where worry manifests itself.

If you have journeyed this far in the process of self-realization and all the signs are there, then just let go of all your cares, worries, and any other material desires. The Divine will not take anything away from you until you are ready to let go of it yourself. When the time comes to remove that material desire, it usually passes by pretty easily. Eventually, it may even come back to you! God gives all His children the desires of their hearts, as long as they choose Him first. In Psalms 37:4, it says, "Delight yourself in the Lord, and he will give you the desires of your heart."[1]

---

[1] Psalms 37:4 NASB

God has given you these physical desires as an offering, to say that I no longer want these things. I often say, "God, I give you back all my desires, they are yours. Do with them as you will." That is what the Divine wants to hear you say and mean it. God does not usually take something away unless you yearn for immediate spiritual change. You can always ask God to take it slow, but trust me when I say, it won't be that bad.

While in the Unnamed States, you may feel like you are plateauing, drifting off into nowhere. The space here is like being on a very calm sea. The consciousness is seated in a boat with no sail. The compass still points North, so there is contentment and serenity. This boating experience may even appear to be lackluster at times. The excitement of the divine chase to God may feel like it has been lost, but do not give up hope! For, if you have faith, then optimism will follow.

Riding the Unnamed midnight boat to nowhere, your consciousness allows the twilight of God to shine intermittently into the mind. This light passes in and out of existence. Traveling further into the night, the light of God will become a consistent flicker in the Spirit States of the 2nd Dimension.

SPIRIT STATES (S)

Value of Level S = CC1, # of S Levels = 47, Christ Consciousness

These states are aptly named, as they occur just before you become initiated into the Creator's Cosmic Consciousness through a Divine Superconscious Experience. These states are fairly small in comparison to the other LOC states, so they become transcended fairly easily.

There are only 47 Spirit States, and they each measure at CC1. Although CC1 is still an extremely large number, there are only 47 levels, whereas there were 100 CC1-type levels in Christ Consciousness and 1000 in Krishna Consciousness. Also in the Spirit States, the Intermittent Samadhi becomes a permanent part of your consciousness. No longer does God's light just flicker in and out. It is now a permanent fixture of light flickering inside of your mind.

Nearing the End?

At this point, you have had quite a journey! Traveling through many obstacles and hair-raising twists and turns, you emerge victorious out of the karmic dungeon, overcoming the wet, heavy, damp darkness.

This is the most difficult part of becoming self-realized. Rising out of the karmic cavern, you are finally able to perceive the Light of God shining through. It is not completely clear what is seen, but there is a lightness to the air, allowing the body to rise and go even deeper still into stillness and peace. Now that there is no weight of karma to hold your consciousness down, it can continue to rise into the 3rd Dimension. In this realm, the body and mind will individually experience all the aspects of the Creator's consciousness through the advanced stillness of the lesser minor samadhi states.

With continued devotion and meditative petitioning to the Divine above, the individual will eventually be granted access to the Creator's Cosmic Consciousness through a major samadhi experience. This accesses the Divine Superconsciousness. Through this experience, the greatest minor samadhi, *savikalpa samadhi,* is manifested, allowing for great stillness to overcome the body and mind.

From this point, ascension through the transitional state of *asamprajñata samadhi* is next with an easy move into the individual major samadhi states of the Interstate. This Interstate is a long-forgotten transitional state that helps your consciousness to accustom itself to the jump between a minor *samadhi's* stillness and a major *samadhi's* stillness.

From here, God's infinite love and bliss will be experienced in *nirvikalpa samadhi*. Accessing such wonderful bliss, you will wonder what could ever be more enticing. The final states of self-realization include *sahaja samadhi* and the incalculable state of AION. In these final states, a complete merger will occur with the Divine's bliss. Your consciousness will have unbridled access to God's bliss in every moment. For now, there is no particular time when you will be a part from God's highest experience of love. It shall always permanently be enmeshed with your consciousness.

ASCENSION TO COSMIC CONSCIOUSNESS

Ascending from body consciousness, saturated with the ego, to the Creator's Cosmic Consciousness (CosCon) is quite a challenge to overcome while living in this era. With all the unrest through violence, starvation, and constant attachment to materialism, it is obvious to see why the highest consciousness *appears* to be impossible to achieve. But with deep desire for God while using scientific meditative techniques and strong devotion, it is possible to reach God in this lifetime.

If you can muscle test accurately, providing a quantitative measurement to an already intensely qualitative process, the results could prove enlightening to the individual and the world. If you cannot muscle test, then your intuition will be tested, elevating your consciousness even further.

What is the Creator's Consciousness?

The word "cosmos" is a noun originally Latinized from of the Greek *kosmos*, which means "order, good order, or orderly arrangement." In can also refer to "ordering, arranging, or establishing" (a battle, army, government, or regime) as well. This word, when used in our modern language, refers to the universe in parts or in total. Pythagoras was the first individual to apply this word to "the universe," which could have meant "starry firmament," but it did not become popular until 1848 when it was used in a translation of Humboldt's *Kosmos*. Also, the word *kosmos* itself was used in Christian writing to refer to living a "worldly life."[2] For this book's use, *kosmos* will refer to the universe as a part or whole, depending upon context.

CosCon was a phrase coined by Richard Bucke in his book *Cosmic Consciousness: A Study in the Evolution of the Human Mind*, written in 1901. Bucke was a Canadian psychiatrist working as the medical superintendent of the Asylum for the Insane in London, Ontario, during the late 1800s. He wrote this book at the end of his life but had an experience of Cosmic Consciousness in 1872, nearly thirty years earlier. He describes it in his book and also gives some characteristics and results of the experience that he calls the "Cosmic Sense."[3] This Cosmic Sense can be identified by:

- its sudden appearance.
- a subjective experience of "inner light."
- moral elevation.
- intellectual illumination.
- a sense of immortality.
- loss of the sense of sin.

---

[2] Harper *Cosmos*.
[3] Bucke 1901, 10, 74, 79.

- loss of the fear of death.
- a gain of true happiness.

Richard Bucke's book was partially a record of his experience but also a collection of theories about why different individuals could have been considered to have a cosmic consciousness. He exerts the idea that CosCon is a higher form of consciousness than that with which ordinary man is born.[4] You can achieve this state, but it requires evolution of the mind to see a bigger picture. CosCon is literally the consciousness of the cosmos including the life and order of the universe.[5]

He also describes CosCon from the perspective of the Christian bible, saying, in Paul's language (formerly referred to as Saul who was changed on the road to Damascus), "The Saviour of man is Cosmic Consciousness…The Cosmic Sense (in whatever mind it appears) crushes the serpent's head—destroys sin, shame, the sense."[6]

If this is the case, then CosCon is not limited to the perfected masters like Jesus Christ and Bhagavan Krishna. Anyone has the possibility of attaining it, but to reach it is still very difficult.

Bucke also claimed to have learned more in that few seconds of perfect illumination, then he had learned over the previous months, or even years, of study. Although it only lasted a few seconds, the effect was ineffaceable.[7] This means that he could not have denied the existence of such an experience, nor would he deny it because it is such a pure experience of the Highest Self.

This is also my experience. Every moment of every day, I cannot deny the bliss that wells up inside of my being, allowing me to immerse myself in the ocean of bliss consciousness that is SPIRIT. To the point where even when I treating clients, I am not aware of the body, only of the bliss-joy-love that saturates my physical, mental, emotional, and spiritual selves.

Bucke goes on to say that, even when you have permanently become consciously cosmic, you cannot know everything in the universe. After this experience, you have only established an intuitional

---

[4] Bucke. 1901. p. 1
[5] Bucke. 1901. p. 3
[6] Bucke. 1901. p. 6
[7] Bucke. 1901. p. 10

mind[8], allowing for access but not complete immersion in all knowledge. This I can attest to as, initially, muscle-testing allowed me access to all types of knowledge. Now, I can use the intuition-based muscle testing of the mind to give me any truth clearly and immediately. The lesson I learned is one that I learned early on—there is no need to know everything. The need to know will come when the Divine desires it of you.

Bucke continues to attempt to connect CosCon to other religious belief systems by explaining that CosCon is even *nirvana* itself in Buddhism.[9] This idea is consistent with how the Buddhist view of *nirvana*, and it is also consistent with how future Hindu yogis would try to represent CosCon to the Western world in the 20th century. He even says that it is the "kingdom of heaven" expounded upon by Jesus the Christ and Muhammad's "Gabriel" vision read about in the *Quran*.[10]

Having been a raised in a Christian home for many years myself, I can say this is the true kingdom of heaven talked about by Jesus. However, CosCon is only the gateway by which you enter into the Divine's Kingdom. You will eventually even go beyond Cosmic Consciousness into Divine Consciousness and finally into Divine Superconsciousness. This is the ultimate reality for the highest of realizations.

Paramahansa Yogananda was one of the next individuals to write about CosCon in much depth. He has spoken about CosCon in his many publications. Yogananda was a great self-realized master, and so, his elaborations on CosCon were deeply intuited from his pure experiences in *samadhi*. CosCon is mostly explored in his book on the *Bhagavad Gita, God Talks with Arjuna*, but is also referenced in his *Autobiography of a Yogi*. Beyond that, other yogis such as Swami Sivananda from the Divine Life Society, Maharishi Mahesh Yogi, and Yogiraj Siddhanath have also spoken about CosCon.

Rising to the Challenge

There are steps you will take rising from the consciousness of the ego to that of the Creator's. This ascension is possible considering we were all once SPIRIT floating in a sea of cosmic bliss.

---

[8] Bucke. 1901. p. 18
[9] Bucke. 1901. p. 62
[10] This vision is spoken about in the *Quran* 53:4–9, *Quran* 96, and in the *Hadith of Bukhari* 1:2:48

As my journey began for myself, I had a strong internal desire to find God, but I never knew it was in the form of self-realization. Initially, I thought my path was only through the form of Jesus Christ, and then I began to discover that self-realization was much larger than just one saint or avatar. Jesus the Christ said that we will all discover the consciousness of the Christ (pure reflection of the Creator) in ourselves and in all those around us. By doing so, we would release from our karmic bonds of the physical world, ascending to seeing and experiencing our heart in all of creation. This experience is just one of the beginning steps that must be taken in finding God.

Personally, this discovery started as I accepted my role as an empath. You can have sympathy for another, but until you can really feel someone else's emotion, it will be difficult for you to expand the consciousness of your heart into all of creation. This emotion could be anywhere along the spectrum, including joy, excitement, satisfaction, and gratitude or more often, pain, frustration, anxiety, anger, and fear.

For a long time, I feared feeling these emotions, thinking they would hurt me. In some ways, they did, but I did not understand how to release them. For this reason, being an empath was initially a detriment. But as I meditated, practicing the *Kriya*, I was able to control how I felt about the emotions that channeled in, and this control was the key to expanding my consciousness even further. Now, I am no longer afraid of feeling other people. Instead, I can embrace, and help them to channel out their negative emotions.

As I began to ascend further in the first dimension through Christ and Krishna Consciousness, the Divine would provide moments of peace and serenity that would help me to push on. God knows this process to self-realization is the hardest a human could ever achieve, so encouragement is necessary; otherwise, the average workingman like myself would never attempt such towering spiritual height.[11]

As continued support is given by God and his divine helpers† the yogi is able to silence the body and mind more easily, and constant devotion can be directed towards the Divine. With the help of the *Kriya* technique to burn karma and achieve a higher-level vibration, the body becomes quieted, allowing for the Divine entrance into the body

---

[11] Yogananda 2001, 38.

† Divine helpers include: spirit guides, angels, angelic-beings, spiritual teachers, saints, perfected gurus, Christ figures, and avatars

temple. Through this process, the Creator's love pours in, initiating the devotee through the Divine Superconscious Experience.

Before you can ascend and receive the fullest experience of God's Light, you must be able to open your *chakras* sufficiently. Otherwise, the body's bulb will burn out in the receiving of the Light. The body has always had the power to open *chakras*. *Chakra* opening can be achieved through the creation of goosebumps in as many parts of the body as possible, something I discovered when I was in high school. When these goosebumps are coupled with thinking good, positive, loving thoughts, I could lift myself up physically, emotionally, and mentally. The process is called the Cosmic Energy Technique (CET).

I used this technique all the way through undergrad and into medical school. By feeling goosebumps or thrill-bumps all through the body, you can tell if your *chakras* are open or not. This is also a good way to tell if all *chakras* are balanced. You can only receive samadhi when all these centers are opened and balanced.

If *chakras* are opened and balanced, all energy meridians are generally balanced in the body as well. With this balance, you will feel simple peace and love that resonates in all the body's centers. This is especially felt in the third eye and heart. However, there isn't an overabundance of tension at the third eye when you concentrate intensely. Instead, energy is more easily distributed. This sensation can become more easily manifested if the body is free of disease.

Feel the Karmic Burn

Although physical karma has released its hold on the body, mental, emotional, and spiritual karma may still be left to burn. All forms of karma are sometimes released after ascension to the 2nd Dimension, but not always. This is where treatments of chiropractors, naturopaths, craniosacral therapists, acupuncturists, and massage therapists can be extremely helpful. They were absolutely instrumental in my body's own ascension and will be almost necessary to achieve this type of *chakra* balance. Being able to maintain open *chakras* allows an individual to advance to the most ultimate stage of superconscious stillness—*samadhi*.

However, even when you reach the highest forms of realization in *sahaja samadhi* and The Aionion State, disease can still manifest itself. Disease is just a "dis-ease" of the body, whether personal or taken on from other people. In *sahaja samadhi,* all of your personal karma and actions based upon behaviors (*samskaras*) will be completely erased. In this state of *samadhi,* you are a pure instrument of the Divine that will take on the physical, mental, emotional, and spiritual sufferings of others at the command of God. This command will usually come about unconsciously for the workingman or -woman. The soul Self will then respond in kind to this command and take on any suffering. So, although the person may not consciously "desire" to take on these particular issues, he or she will take it on involuntarily. During these times, the body may be affected physically, but your consciousness will remain unattached to the ailment. You will then supersede and dispel the disease process with the bliss consciousness provided by the Divine.

For those who have yet to burn their karma completely, various types of karma are stored in the relative astral and casual bodies, whether physical, mental, emotional, or spiritual. In Sanskrit, these overlying bodies or body coverings are referred to as *koshas*. There are five *koshas* in total that separate your "physical" existence from the Divine.

If the disease is physical, it is stored in the physical body, *annamaya kosha.* If it is emotional or energetic in nature, then it is kept in the astral or subtle body, which is composed of the *pranamaya kosha.* If it is mental disease, then it is collected in the ideational or causal body called the *manomaya kosha.* The fourth *kosha* called *jnanamaya (buddhi)* is where traumas of knowledge are accumulated. This type of suffering is influenced at the level of truth itself. Finally, disease processes can be stored in the bliss sheath called the *anandamaya kosha* or *chitta* (heart). This type of suffering is of the subtlest type and is influenced by the cause of *Purusha* as SPIRIT. The *Purusha* is considered the Higher Self, the True Self, or also called the "Son of God" by some yogis. These body coverings/bodies are described in the *Advaita Vedanta* philosophy in the *Taittiriya Upanishad* and also in Sri Yukteswar's, *The Holy Science*.[12,13,14] Spiritual karma can be stored in any of the bodies and is the hardest to dispel from the body, as it can manifest as any of the three above. Kriya yoga or some other scientific *pranayama* (breath-control) technique is best for burning all types of karma.

---

[12] Shumsky 2003, 8.
[13] Frawley 2004, 288.
[14] Yukteswar 1990, 35–36.

For those who ascend into Cosmic Consciousness, there will be no physical karma left in the *annamaya kosha*, but other types of karma may be left in the subtle/causal/truth bodies and the heart. Also, suffering may transpire in multiple ways for a cosmically conscious yogi.

Revolving thought processes are the first, most common, and fastest way to create these subtle types of sufferings. If a thought manifests in the causal body and it is permanently implanted there by a particular experience or repetitive behavior, it will turn into an emotional trauma. These subtle traumas are then stored in the astral body through the *chakra* vortices in the center of the body and in the peripheral *nadi* channels in the extremities. If the emotion repeats itself over and over again by the planted thought in the causal body, it will then appear physically in the body, causing external disease. This external disease could be a skin disorder, joint pain, muscle ache, headaches, brain fog, fatigue, and so on. Eventually, these symptoms can turn into more serious chronic conditions, like heart disease, cancer, fibromyalgia, etc.

Applied Kinesiology when coupled with chiropractic adjusting is one form of medicine that cuts the cord between the thought and emotion preventing future physical disease from occurring. In my own medical practice, while using Applied Kinesiology, I have been able to help the patient's body remove negative and harmful ideas (karma) from the causal body, preventing further damage to the subtle and physical bodies. This type of treatment is absolutely essential when you are on the path to self-realization.

There have even been reports of a great yogi named Sri Chinmoy who received treatment from chiropractors through the years while he traveled and performed in numerous sporting events.[15] Even in this yogi's subtle ability to manifest *savikalpa* and *nirvikalpa samadhi*, he needed a physical 'someone' to help facilitate optimal healing in his body. Although he was a distance runner, swimmer, and weightlifter with physical ailments, he was still able to achieve self-realization in its fullest form.[16]

Other authors, such as Normal Paulsen, a previous monk of Self-Realization Fellowship and disciple of Yogananda, have had their own interpretations of the Creator's consciousness. Paulsen's book, called the *The Christ Consciousness*, goes into depth on Christ and Cosmic

---

[15] Jackson 1996.
[16] Kilgannon 2007.

Consciousness. His own elucidation of this state and personal experiences should be taken into high consideration because of his close personal relationship with Paramahansa Yogananda. Paulsen's book would be another great reference for those wanting to read more on the Christ and Cosmic Consciousness.

Still other masters have expounded upon the truth of Cosmic Consciousness, but are rarely mentioned. Sri Aurobindo has written poems and books that explore its transcendent nature. Swami Sivananda, one of my own personal spiritual teachers, talks about CosCon in more detail, saying,

> The state of the cosmic consciousness is grand and sublime. It induces awe, supreme joy and highest, unalloyed felicity, free from pain, sorrow and fear. This state of cosmic consciousness is below the absolute consciousness or Nirguna-Brahmic Consciousness wherein the seer, sight and the things seen, or the knower, knowable and knowledge, or the subject and object become. It is doubtless a very subtle experience. It is divine experience.[17]

Many other experiences may come to the yogi before experiencing CosCon. These may include seeing all of time as one single entity—past, present, and future colliding all at once to show the finitude of God's creation and the infinitude of SPIRIT existing beyond the Creator. CosCon is the union with God's omnipresence in and beyond all of creation. Through this union, you must expand your consciousness into all of creation before you can experience the Creator's consciousness. To know His creation through the Christ Consciousness is one thing, but to know Him is to know one as the Highest Self.

Other CosCon Facts

- CosCon is a gift from God, given as you go deep into the third eye through sheer determination and willpower. *Samadhi* is then given by the guru and by the will of God when you are ready to receive it.

---

[17] Sivananda 2011.

- CosCon is manifested everywhere in the universe, in all minds and in all bodies. CosCon is the Creator's consciousness, and the Creator is the beyond creation itself.
- Yogananda says that, when one is in meditation and becomes "immovably rooted,"[18] it is a sign that one is experiencing CosCon. This can occur either in the standing position or seated.
- When you begin to merge with the Creator's consciousness, beginning to realize yourself as a part of God and not separate from God, it becomes more difficult to associated with the "I" or "Me" of the ego consciousness.
- Creativity manifests at an increasing ability as you are now merging with the Creator part of God that manifests creation at will. In this increased ability, even your brain's percent of usage will increase beyond the purported average of 10% to a possible 100% usage!

If you are maintaining the Christ Consciousness through constant service, then CosCon will come even more quickly. Any attachments, anger, or negative emotion will prevent upward movement towards the Creator's consciousness.

---

[18] Yogananda 2012, 161.

CHAPTER 14

3rd Dimension LOCs

The 3rd Dimension is the arena where the Creator will manifest Its own Superconsciousness into the mind of the yogi. This Superconsciousness is considered the Creator's Cosmic Consciousness. Once you have reached the 3rd Dimension, you will initially maintain a Christ Consciousness mindset. This is because the initial LOC found in the beginning of the 3rd Dimension is the minor *samadhi* states, which is a part of the Christ Consciousness category. These minor *samadhi* states are the way you are able to experience the Creator piece by piece before the Divine's fullest nature can be given. There are sixteen of these states in total; each one is a different aspect of the Creator's consciousness.

After these sixteen states, a sum samadhi or the *laya samadhi* occurs allowing you to experience all of the sixteen aspects of the Creator all at once. At this point, the Creator along with your spiritual teacher will choose a time and place when the Divine Superconscious Experience will be bestowed upon you through a major *samadhi*. This time cannot be muscle tested or intuited to the exact time, as this moment is the most special in the entire process of becoming self-realized. This is the moment when self-realization is actually bestowed. This is greatest gift of all gifts. This is the one thing that you have been waiting for throughout all of your incarnations. If you could know the manifestation of this experience's time and place, it would not serve its highest and most special purpose.

When you are in the 2nd Dimension, the twilight of the evening is upon you, with starlight to guide your thoughts. As the day approaches, strands of dawn's sunlight begin to pierce the consciousness of your mind. As if in slow motion, each ray that strikes the surface of the mind manifests a different aspect of Creator's consciousness. This process could take days or weeks, depending on the Divine's will. Finally, in *laya samadhi*, all seventeen rays of light shine together, giving a fuller experience of all aspects in one.

Once *laya samadhi* has been reached, the Guru can now bestow upon you God's purest Light in the form of SPIRIT or as the Divine Superconscious Experience (DSCE). As the sun breaks the dawn, your body will become covered with light as the DSCE expressed through a major *samadhi* attunes and changes the body and brain. This attunement process is essential because it prevents the body from burning out like an over-watted light bulb. The human nervous system is sensitive and requires an adjustment process so that it can continue to operate properly even after such an experience.

For a time, you will perceive the Divine's Light in all of its fullness, but only for a short while. This experience is similar to how staring into the sun without sunglasses will burn the eyes. The eyes and the body of man will be burned by the Light of God without permanent protection of continued ascendance in the LOCs. For now, you can rest comfortably in the shade of the palm tree of joy, where you can continue to experience the Creator's Superconsciousness. In the shade of this palm tree, the states of *savikalpa samadhi* and *asamprajñata samadhi* will transition the body, brain, and nerves to come to awareness of God's purest stillness and peace. These characteristics will allow you to become attuned to a major *samadhi* in the Multidimensional realm.

After this point, the Creator's superconscious mind, can be continually experienced over and over again without end. In fact, this type of Superconsciousness will evolve into the greatest state of all— Divine Superconsciousness where SPIRIT lies in absolute perfection.

MINOR SAMADHI STATES (MrS)

<u>Lesser Minor Samadhi States</u>
Value of Level MrS = 1, # of MrS Levels = 16, Christ Consciousness

<u>Laya Samadhi</u>
Value of Level LS = CC1, # of LS Levels = 1 Trillion, Christ Consciousness

These states are the lesser minor *samadhi* states. There are 17 in all. An advanced type of stillness called a minor *samadhi* characterizes this group of states. In *samadhi*, the yogi, through one-pointed concentration on the divine, is able to completely silence the mind and detach the consciousness from the body. In a lesser minor *samadhi*, the concentration, silence, and detachment are in a lesser form and are thus not complete.

Each one of the minor *samadhi* states embodies a different aspect of Creator's consciousness. Each small state is filled with a different version of the Divine's Light. Each one needs to be achieved or attuned to, resolving one into the other to achieve the highest minor *samadhi*, *savikalpa*. However, you do not need to experience all of the lesser minor *samadhi* states individually to continue to ascend to *savikalpa samadhi*. God will allow you to experience any of these states partially, entirely, quickly, or slowly based upon your needs and desires.

Initiation into this group of states occurs through willpower and the guru's help. After almost wandering aimlessly through the Unnamed and Spirit States of the 2nd Dimension, an even greater level of stillness comes to your consciousness through the aid of the Guru. No longer do you have to float on the sea of God's consciousness without a sail. Now you have a small motor that steadily pushes the body towards the everlasting light of God which is slowly breaking over the horizon in the near distance.

These states are not experienced in order and do not have to be. In actuality, they can be experienced out of order until the final lesser minor *samadhi* state, *laya samadhi*, is achieved. The Divine is not linear. It exists outside the dimension of time. A linear perspective requires the time dimension aspect to define it. The Creator, on the other hand, is more like a conglomerate point-source energy that exists outside of creation. The Creator could also be considered the substance that exists between physical matter as pure conscious energy.

These minor *samadhis* are the Divine's creation and are spherical in nature. You can experience any of the 16 lesser minor *samadhis*, but you have to be fully attuned to the vibration that is produced by all of them before the 17th lesser minor *samadhi* state, *laya samadhi*, will manifest itself. If you have already accepted one or more of the various aspects of God, as seen in the minor *samadhi* states, then those states will not be experienced because you are already attuned to them. Therefore, this process may take a few days or many lifetimes to accomplish.

The diagram on this page was created by my wife and I to show how these minor *samadhi* states can be achieved in any order during ascension.

Figure 14.1 – Sphere of Samadhi

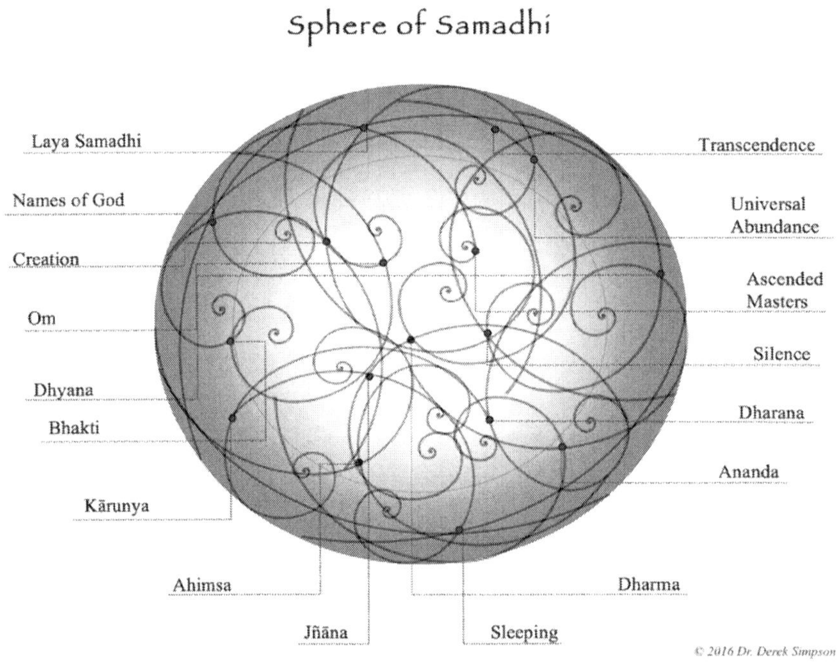

Sphere of Samadhi

- Laya Samadhi
- Names of God
- Creation
- Om
- Dhyana
- Bhakti
- Kārunya
- Ahimsa
- Jñāna
- Sleeping
- Dharma
- Ananda
- Dharana
- Silence
- Ascended Masters
- Universal Abundance
- Transcendence

© 2016 Dr. Derek Simpson

Below are the 17 minor *samadhi* states. Some are of Sanskrit origin and are translated into English to enhance understanding.[1,2]

---

[1] *List of English words of Sanskrit origin.* 2015.
[2] *Names of God.* 2015.

1. <u>Sleeping</u> —a state that can be achieved while in a wakeful state between sleep and complete consciousness.
2. <u>Jñāna</u> (Wisdom) – realization of God's wisdom

3. <u>Dharma</u> (Righteousness) – realization of God's righteousness

4. <u>Ahimsa</u> (Do no harm) – realization that no harm must come to any of God's creation

5. <u>Kārunya</u> (Compassion) – realization that compassion is necessary to serve the highest good

6. <u>Bhakti</u> (Passionate religious devotion) – realization that physical, emotional, mental, and spiritual devotion is required to God and Gurus to come to the highest bliss

7. <u>Ananda</u> (Bliss) – realization of God's bliss as a combination of peace, joy, and stillness

8. <u>Dharana</u> (One-pointed concentration/astral) – the focus is so intense at the third eye that it seems as if the eyes are glued in place. This state attunes you to the necessary concentration required for *savikalpa* and also allows you to experience an astral minor *samadhi*.

9. <u>Dhyana/Zen</u> (Meditation) – required not only in the silent morning and evenings of a person's day, but in every moment of consciousness

10. <u>Silence</u> – the deafening sound of silence is abundantly heard everywhere. Nothing is physically heard; however, great joyous knowing is apparent and abundant. This is the natural break in meditation—the nature of a *samadhi* state.

11. <u>Aum/Om</u> – the sound of *Aum* is as deafening as the silence that preceded it. The sound of an overflowing ocean rushes

into your ears, signifying that the *Om* is truly everywhere and in all creation.

12. <u>Ascended Masters</u> – the realization that all self-realized masters come from and are a part of one God and one Creator

13. <u>Creation</u> – the realization that creation and God are one in the same

14. <u>Universal Abundance</u> – the realization of the infinite abundance of everything in the universe. Everything is infinitely larger than previously known.

15. <u>Names of God</u> – the realization that the God that exists in all religions is in fact one and the same. Whether it is Yahweh, Elohim, Jehovah, Allah, Gaia, Spirit, and/or *Brahma*, they are all the Creator derived from the same SPIRIT.

16. <u>Transcendence</u> – the realization that all of creation needs to be seen as God and transcended to reach the highest planes of self-realization

17. <u>Laya Samadhi</u> (LS) – the combined experience of all other lesser minor *samadhi* states, transitioning you to the *savikalpa samadhi* state. These lesser minor *samadhi* states need to be fused together to prevent you from becoming too overwhelmed by *savikalpa*.

Laya samadhi has over a trillion levels, all which have a value of CC1. *Laya samadhi* is also referred to as the "Sum Samadhi," as it is the addition of all the other 16 lesser minor *samadhi* states. It appears on the LOC chart abbreviated as LS. It can also be known as MrS17, as it is the 17th and final state to be experienced. The experience of *laya samadhi* can happen in any length of time, at any location, anywhere—period. God likes to surprise us, and as His children, we love receiving presents!

You are now at the last step before achieving the goal of self-realization, God's purest experience of bliss and love. If you have been meditating for many years, the experience may be longer in length, allowing for many supernatural perceptions. The experience also may be short, but repeated with numerous experiences for those fast ascenders. The Divine Superconscious Experience (DSCE) may come in the standing, seated, or supine (lying down) position. The supine position may be necessary for those who are inexperienced at meditation (such as a fast ascender), but remember it is also best for relaxation which is essential for meditation. It may also come to serve as a blessing to others that witness the divine experience.

Realize that you can still drop from *laya samadhi*, so it is essential to remain ever vigilant by consistently and constantly following the eight limbs of yoga as described by Patanjali[3]—*yama* (moral conduct), *niyama* (religious observances), *asana* (proper body posture), *pranayama* (control of prana/life-control), *pratyahara* (interiorization of the mind), *dharana* (concentration) and *dhyana* (meditation), leading the eighth limb of Yoga referred to as *samadhi,* or the divine union. Delivered by your Guru, this divine union comes by God's grace alone.

DIVINE SUPERCONSCIOUS EXPERIENCE (DSCE)

This is the highest level of the major *samadhi* state. It is your divine birthright to gain access to this divine experience. If you are made in the Divine's image, then do you not also have access to the Creator's divine love and consciousness as well?

I think many humble individuals on this path to self-realization do not believe that the God's glory can be theirs. They believe in what religion teaches them, that they should be submissive toward their Creator and not demand anything. Well, I am here to tell you that God wants you to demand His love from Him. But you must do this with humility, love, service, and gentility. How do you demand with such a level of innocence? You do so through dedication to righteousness through right living, disciplined meditation, and devotion to God and His Christs and avatars.

---

[3] Patanjali's *Yoga Sutras* II.26–II.29

This is the first time that you will have a chance to access the Uni-A-Dimensional Realm of SPIRIT. This is the realm or area of consciousness that the DSCE is a part. Dream SuperUnConsciousness is also a part of this realm but is only accessed during sleep. The DSCE can be achieved willfully, but it may take many more years until this is possible.

How to Achieve the DSCE

To attain this experience, you must knock at heaven's gates with all of your might. This requires God, the guru, and the devotee (yourself). The devotee, although working at 200%, only contributes a small percentage to the upward ascension. The guru, also being of human form but fully self-realized, living at the right hand of the Father almighty, gives a similarly equal but necessary percentage. The Divine, on the other hand, has most of the say in the matter. The Creator contributes the majority of the effort required to initiate you into this level of consciousness. For this reason, it is absolutely necessary to have a guru when on the path to self-realization and to give endless devotion to the Divine above.

The guru helps to remove karma early on in the 1st Dimension and continues to light the way through the aimless waters of the 2nd Dimension. The Divine then tells the guru when you are ready to experience the awesome power of the Creator's consciousness. Through *shaktipat* or *shaktipata,* the Guru bestows the grace of pure consciousness upon the devotee by breaking the barrier to self-realization by activating the *kundalini* energy at the base of the spine.†

The Divine will not come to you in the way that you desire, but according to divine timing. Never assume that you will know how, when, and in what way it will happen. God doesn't reserve those specificities for any future-self-realized soul, as He wants to make it special and different for everyone. This experience may come in any position of the body, including while you are lying supine on your back, mind emblazoned for God's love. This particular position may be the only way you can relax the muscles deeply enough to achieve this experience, especially if you have a partially diseased musculoskeletal system or other disease process that prevents the body from fully relaxing into a perfectly straight seated posture.

---

† The *kundalini* will be explained in much greater detail in the next section.

Stages of the DSCE

When do you actually experience this Divine Superconsciousness? The first, most common arena that all people experience the DSCE is in dreams. This type of consciousness is called "Dream Super-UnConsciousness." Every night that you maintain a proper cycle of sleep, with or without dreams, the DSCE is being manifested. Every night in dreams, you become man or woman, spirit or beast—it does not matter. This is the place where all desires or fears become clear.

If the dreams are of true purity, the person will experience a higher form of the DSCE. If the subconscious mind takes over, fears can be the prime subject of the dream. However, a DSCE driven by the subconscious mind will help you to discover what parts of your consciousness still need adjusting. Also, the DSCE that includes dreams of goodness and happiness will generally lead to a complete night's rest. This sleep is essential to the well-being of the ascender.

The second most common time that you can experience a complete mergence into the DSCE is through the process of physical death. This is a time that is common to all, for no one can escape this fate. For those who are divinely realized, this time of death is predictable and can be transcended by a *mahasamadhi*. For those that live a good and moral life, this experience is joyful and occurs in the most peaceful way. For these righteous people, the shedding of the physical body or *annamaya kosha*, leads them to the astral realm, or "heaven." If you are afraid of death, it can appear frightening, causing you to kick and scream all the way out. Even those who have led an absolutely immoral life, filled with hate for oneself and others, will experience the DSCE in varying ways. This experience may not be joyful per se, but confusing to the soul leaving the body because the individual led a life opposite to their original divine design of righteousness and goodness to all.

The third way you can achieve the DSCE is through a drug-induced state of consciousness. A hallucinogen or other psychoactive drugs generally activates this state. These mind-altering substances cause various types of neurotransmitters in the brain to release, leading to an out-of-body experience. Although this appears to be the warp-drive way to the Divine and self-realization, it is not permanent and is potentially damaging to your divinely evolving brain. It is not recommended by this book to use any drug, illicit, illegal, or legal, to experience higher consciousness. The highest, fastest, and most permanent way to self-realization is through scientific meditation alone. No drug will ever give you the permanent satisfaction found in manifesting the DSCE with conscious, additive-free devotion and consistent, will-powered, scientific meditation.

A fourth way to experience the DSCE is "superunconsciously." There are numerous reports of saints who could pass into an unconscious *samadhi* (*turiya*) state involuntarily, but return consciously remembering all that happened with specific sights, smells, and sounds. These are truly inner and outer ecstatic experiences of God-realization. After waking from this state, great joy and peace emanates from these individuals who are blessed with such an experience. The saint may be unaware that it has happened but will return with a newfound awareness. This passing into the DSCE is generally regarded as an act of the Divine to help bring positive and pure SPIRIT energy into the physical body of the one manifesting the consciousness. That energy is then to be transferred into the people and environment surrounding the divinely superconscious body. In the simplest way, it acts as a blessing to all those who physically view and/or come in contact the body itself.

This type of superunconsciousness is vastly different from *jada samadhi*. A *jada samadhi* state allows you to pass into a trance state with complete loss of breath. These types of *samadhis* can be performed by highly advanced hatha yogis performing *kechari mudra*. This *mudra* allows the yogi to stop respiration breath at will and live in a life-force suspended state. However, this state does not spiritually benefit you in any way.[4,5] In the truest version of samadhi, you are able to provide "supersensuous wisdom" to all.[6] This "supersensuous" type of wisdom is of the highest and most pure forms. Supersensuous knowledge cannot be gained through a *jada samadhi*.

The fifth and final way to access a DSCE is willfully, actively, and consciously. As you transition throughout the final major samadhi states of *savikalpa*, *asamprajñata*, *nirvikalpa* and finally *sahaja*, the DSCE will be experienced at various points to initiate your consciousness. God and Gurus are the initiators at each point, as you will not be able to access the DSCE at will until much later on your journey.

---

[4] Yogananda 2001, 100.
[5] Kripalu 2004, 5–6.
[6] Sivananda 2011.

Major Milestones of Self-Realization
These milestones include:
- 25% achievement- Initiation of Self-Realization – Entry into *savikalpa samadhi*
- 50% achievement - Partial Self-realization – Entry into *asamprajñata samadhi*
- 75% achievement - Partial Self-Realization – Entry onto the Interstate #1
- 100% achievement - Full Self-Realization*[†] – Entry into a non-dual *samadhi* willfully
- Liberation/*Kaivalya***[†] – Loss of the Causal Body at SS2 (level 2 of *sahaja samadhi*)

From this point, the DSCE can continue to be experienced, but now it can be accessed at will. These experiences occur between Aeon 1 to Aeon 1,000,000.[‡]

- Partial SPIRIT mergence by an intermittent DSCE 59,999-60,000 Aeons
- Full conscious SPIRIT mergence by a controlled DSCE 500,000 Aeons
- Complete SPIRIT mergence by a permanent DSCE 888,888 Aeons

Intensities of the DSCE
During ascension to the fifth and final pathway to the DSCE, various levels of intensity are felt in a particular state of feeling or visualization. The intensities are represented arbitrarily by a 1, 2, 3, or ∞ (infinity symbol) with DSCEi-1, DSCEi-2, and so on. Initially, when you have no control over these experiences, any one of the four intensities can

---

[†] *Full Self-Realization is the same as God-Realization
**Liberation is more than God-realization. It is only saved for certain individuals during this current Earth era. This state is special and will be explain further in the section on *sahaja samadhi*.
[‡] 1 Aeon = 1 Total Sum of the entire LOC chart through *sahaja samadhi* proper. This information is talked about in the discussion on *sahaja samadhi*.

emerge giving you great auditory, visual, and out-of-body experiences. This especially occurs during initiation periods into higher LOCs or specialized experiences. The intensities are described as follows:

- DSCEi-1 = 1 aspect: Manifestation of stillness beyond a normal *sahaja samadhi*. This intensity is characterized by the flow of sweet divine nectar, or *amrita*[†]
- DSCEi-2 = 2 aspects: Visualization of the third eye, inclusive of the dark blue surround and the white orb in the center while using a *shambhavi mudra* with eyes closed. All of the above occurs in combination with the flow of divine nectar.
- DSCEi-3 = 3 aspects: Loss of awareness of the whole body occurs with an ultimate level of stillness, an extreme focus at third eye with full visualization, and flowing nectar.
- DSCEi-∞ = 3 aspects +: All of the above are manifested while eyes are open in the *shambhavi mudra* (SM). At this point in the "infinite intensity," the energy in the visual system has been completely overcome by visualization of light of the third eye. You are completely conscious and the surrounding sounds, no matter how distracting, have been overcome by the symphonic *Om* heard at the seventh *chakra* or the silence heard in *chakra* unification. This is the infinite or eighth *chakra*, representing unity between all the *chakras*. All aspects above occur, but two major stages exist within this "infinite intensity."

1. <u>1st stage</u> – The body begins to change shape, occurring especially at hands and feet.
2. <u>2nd stage</u> – Both the physical and astral worlds/cosmos begin to merge at the eyelid horizon of a half-eye-opened SM. Eventually, this mergence can lead to a spontaneous closed-eyed SM when the body has gone deeply enough into the level of consciousness.

Experiences of the DSCE

The silence, instead of symphonic *Om*, is more likely to be present in this intensity. If you continue to meditate with eyes open, you

---

† This term *amrita* is explained more completely in the section under *nirvikalpa samadhi* in Chapter 16.

will eventually be able to close the eyes and continue to maintain this state of consciousness. The closing of the eyes is not normally possible while maintaining the "infinite intensity;" however, with prolonged meditation with eyes open or half open in the *shambhavi mudra*, this LOC becomes likely.

If you think you have achieved the "infinite intensity," then you can mechanically perform a self-test to determine your current intensity and/or intuition by utilizing "states of feeling" to determine how high your consciousness has ascended. The infinite intensity is where active ascension or LOC increases will occur.

In fact, this DSCEi-∞ is similar to the extension experiences seen both in *savikalpa samadhi* and *asamprajñata samadhi*. The DSCE is also similar to how the dripping nectar appears in *nirvikalpa* and *sahaja samadhi*.† These states are all similar in the way that they help you to ascend and evolve while in a particular LOC. Each LOC has an "ascension" state, whether defined as an extension experience or not. This pattern is common within the LOC chart, as there is always an extension state that helps you to ascend to the next level.

Each of 3 numerical intensities plus the final conceptual intensity of infinity occurs in every Aeon LOC and in the first initiations of the DSCE through Aeon 1. As you increase in LOC through the DSCEi-∞, you will eventually become permanently unified in the DSCE, even during your household activities, and can choose to be in this state in any moment of your waking hours.

In the experience of the DSCE, the individual may have a sudden loss of body respiration. This leads to the breathless state, where you can consciously experience the Creator in Its fullness as SPIRIT. This loss of breath may appear frightening on the surface, but it leads to very high levels of bliss. Generally, breath will not be removed from the body unless the DSCE has been reached at its basic level. Also, the breathless state experienced is minimal at first and builds over time. This loss of breath is quite a pleasurable experience that only brings on the infinite ocean of bliss that is SPIRIT. With loss of breath will come much visual, auditory, and olfactory stimulation. These experiences will vary according to your past experience in deep meditation and future needs in realization.

---

† These extension states will be elaborated upon further in the next couple of pages in the section under *savikalpa samadhi* and then further on under the sections on *asamprajñata, nirvikalpa, sahaja samadhi* in this chapter.

The time frame of this initiation could last anywhere between seconds and hours. While you are in the DSCE, time becomes relative, meaning that a few minutes of DSCE could pass like hours or seconds depending upon the Divine's will at the moment. Realize that it is not that God is allowing you to experience His love, it is that you have now realized your ability and right to be a part of this consciousness. The vibrational LOC of the body at this point is where the next stage of attunement can begin. The time given during this initiation may be to serve other people or devotees who are surrounded by the divinely superconscious yogi.

This state has a "measurable" value to its level, but for the sake of initiation, it is measured at "infinity." The DSCE can be experienced from the point of initiation at savikalpa to the end of your physical lifespan in The Aionion State. How high your LOC has become, will depend on how intense and involved the DSCE is.

According to Hinduism and their sacred texts, there are various physical and energetic coverings that need to be unveiled before you can become fully self-realized. When you experience the DSCE, the causal body covering, the "bliss sheath" or *anandamaya (chitta) kosha,* is peeled back so that you can experience SPIRIT for a limited time.† The physical body covering, or *annamaya kosha* in the initiation of the DSCE, will become permanently casted off from the body. This allows the astral body to continue manifesting higher states of awareness in *savikalpa* and beyond. Sometimes, the astral body casing, *pranamaya kosha,* can become permanently shed first, in succession, or in combination with the physical body casing.

The physical body casing is denser and heavier than the astral body, so it stands to reason that the astral casing may be shed first. This physical body could be considered as frozen or stilled Cosmic Consciousness. If the physical body covering were indeed a stagnant version of the Creator's consciousness, then it would need to be cast off to increase the body's vibration and LOC. These shedding combinations generally occurs within a few days of each other. The differences between the sheddings are slight and hardly noticeable from one another.

Other experiences that may occur include hearing the voices of the angels with singing and laughter. The sounds can be soft and of a

---

† These concepts are in the *Advaita Vedanta* philosophy in the *Taittiriya Upanishad*.

"tinkling" nature in the most basic way. If these angelic sounds are fully auditory, words may be understood in the language most accessible to the yogi. You could even receive astral affection from the angels in the form of kisses! This can be felt like a cool blowing sensation over various parts of the face or ears.

The gurus of self-realization may also come to bless you as a part of their initiation into this newfound level of realization. It could be any number of the masters including Jesus, Krishna, Yogananda, Mahavatar Babaji, the Buddha, Gūan Yīn, and/or any other Guru/saint that is specific to your chosen path. These blessings can also be felt, but it is similar to an angel kiss, and it is difficult to distinguish between the two.

The Creator may also be directly involved in a blessing versus a physically manifested form of Creation who is doing the blessing; this including a guru, saint, angel, or being-of-Light. You must have trained your intuition and/or have muscle tested well to know the differences between these variations.

Not only self-realized masters, but also saints of all religions could be present at the initiation. Imagine this as the crowning achievement of all single achievements. To manifest the DSCE is like winning the congressional medal of honor for a soldier or the Nobel Prizes for a scientist. This is the greatest single reward any conscious being in the universe could receive. All the masters, saints, angels, and other beings of light are there to receive and welcome you into your true home of Light.

Many blessings will continue to come as you ascend. Most of these will occur in cool sensations to various parts of the body, generally the body part requiring the most amounts of help. The eyes, ears, and sensation, all being major components a human body's nervous system, will need to be attuned to the higher vibrations of the astral and causal universes. This attunement is necessary to permanently shed the causal body and fully experience SPIRIT's bliss in its entirety. These various blessings will help you to achieve those states.

The benefits of receiving such an experience is beyond words, because the bliss experienced is exactly that: a feeling that is beyond all comparison. Physically, the body gains extrasensory and intuitive awareness, but also large gains in complete sleep or rest. For every one-second fully experienced in a DSCE, the equivalent of three minutes of sleep is gained. Any extra time spent in this state that goes beyond the normal restful period of one day (which is generally 6 to 8 hours) goes towards manifesting higher-realized states of consciousness.

If an individual is very active in his or her job and working physically hard but is still able to maintain a DSCE-like awareness, then all the excess energy gained will help to provide ample energy to complete the day without getting tired. These individuals will generally have to work harder at maintaining deeper meditations morning and night if they are attempting to meditate through the night and live without sleep. Generally, only the most advanced realized masters will be able to stay up through the night, because their physical activity throughout the day is very little.

Yogavatar Lahiri Mahasaya was one of these types of yogis. He was the guru of Yogananda's guru, Swami Sri Yukteswar. Mahasaya, in many people's opinion, single-handedly spread Kriya yoga. Through him, the world now knows not only of Kriya yoga, a powerful transformative spiritual practice, but also yoga at large.

As you continue to ascend, you may have these types of experiences at random. Complete out-of-body experiences are not necessary to achieve the highest levels of *samadhi*. In the initiation of *samadhi*, it is not the guru per se that bestows the *samadhi*, but rather the Light of God. The guru is the Light, but all that is made manifest is made of Light. So, it is not the guru (the body of the guru) that gives the Light, but it is the Guru that tells or allows the Light to know that the individual body is ready to receive it. The brilliant, beautiful light of the Divine Superconsciousness is one of purity. This pure Light can only be shown to those who have been attuned or opened to it. The immediate aftermath of this state allows you to perceive all of time and space standing still. This is where the Creator's consciousness is truly felt.

Summary

In the framework of the Divine Superconscious Experience, there are different aspects to remember. It should be known that, although you are initiated into self-realization with a DSCE, it is different than the general class of *samadhi*. *Samadhi* is a general word that is used to describe Superconsciousness at its highest form coupled with perfect concentration.

Samadhi is the Sanskrit word for the DSCE but generally describes the entire classification of *samadhi* experiences. The DSCE is a name used by this book to describe the highest version of *samadhi* itself. DSCE is also the same as *anantya* (deepest conscious bliss) and *turiya* (deepest unconscious bliss). Therefore, the DSCE can be experienced both consciously and unconsciously. In this way, the DSCE is a more general classification for the highest forms of *samadhi*, whether a person is aware of the experience or not.

The word *samadhi* has been used for a long time to describe the highest goal attained when practicing meditation. When you are fully merged into the DSCE, *samadhi* is no longer something you become a part of or achieve. Once you become merged with the Absolute, the Divine Superconscious Experience becomes a Divine Superconscious Existence. The state of *samadhi* will always be present within the body, mind, and consciousness in the highest form consciously as an *anantya* DSCE or as an unconscious *turiya* DSCE.

Remember, everything is in the Divine's plan, including the possibility or likelihood that you will reach self-realization in a particular lifetime. If you show your love to the Divine, nothing will be held back.

KUNDALINI (K)

At the moment the DSCE occurs, the *kundalini* becomes activated through *shaktipat* or *shaktipata*. The guru provides this pure transmission of consciousness to break any barrier left to self-realization,[7] which comes when all efforts have finally exhausted themselves. Each experience is different and is generally very personal to the individual. When the DSCE occurs, there is no doubt that something very special has occurred. Some individuals have a complete out-of-body experience, while others may just feel immense joy.

This energy activation is essential for the highest forms of self-realization. *Kundali* or *kundli* means ring, bracelet, or coil (of a rope).[8] It is generally considered in the shape a coiled serpent in front of the coccyx, or tailbone. The *kundalini* is the residual energy of pure desire, which, before activation, can never run out.[9] It only runs out at the point of physical death. After activation, there is only a finite amount that can rise to help you ascend.

---

[7] Shivom Tirth 2005, 189.
[8] Duncan 1892, 259.
[9] Goswami 1999, 3.

When your desire becomes great enough to know God alone and nothing else, this energy becomes activated. Then, by steadfast meditation and devotion, your *kundalini* can be focused towards God to achieve the highest level of liberation or self-realization. The *kundalini* is also a part of the subtle or astral body, which is composed of energy called *prana*.[10] *Prana* flows in energy channels called *nadis* and circulate around the *chakras*.[11] The *prana* is subtle energy focused in the seven *chakras* that becomes focused towards the Divine to achieve realization.

I discovered that the *kundalini* energy pulses through the spine in a certain amount of time, once it becomes activated. The rate associated with this pulse shows how fast you are moving towards self-realization. If you have activated this energy through meditation, the pulse will occur in minutes to hours. Every time a pulse occurs and that pulsed energy has reached the seventh (crown) *chakra*, it will be used to evolve the brain further so that it can receive the next level of realization. If the *kundalini* is activated through some unnatural means, such as drugs or trauma, it may remain stagnant until your LOC is great enough to help it rise. The pulse may also rise more slowly over one or many lifetimes. The rise is a pulse, at first, occurring over a very short period of time. This will continue until it is rising constantly. At this point, the final bulk of *kundalini* energy will rise all at once, causing great spiritual experiences to occur.

The *kundalini* can also be activated naturally through "associate ascending." An "associate ascender" is an individual, generally the companion (husband/wife/partner) or devotee of the actively ascending yogi, that becomes elevated in the presence of the yogi. This elevation occurs because the vibrational state of the yogi or guru is so high that it physically transforms and attunes the body and brain of the individual or individuals in constant close proximity. This phenomenon is similar to the idea of resonance, a concept in physics where two tuning forks or objects of the same natural frequency will vibrate together, if one of the objects begins to vibrate first.

I would even go further to say that "associate ascending" is like *forced vibration*, since the "associated ascender" is generally "lower" in vibration than the yogi who is actively becoming self-realized. This "lower" vibration gets excited into a higher frequency by force. Most

---

[10] Seidman 2000, 117.
[11] Seidman. 2000, 20–22.

of the time, it is gentle, but it can be more intense, such as experiencing a sexual samadhi during a physical orgasm.

Think of a guitar string being played. The harder the string is plucked, the more the surrounding air particles and guitar sound box will be forced into resonating at the same frequency as the string, creating a louder sound. This concept is similar to how the guru provides *shaktipat* to his or her devotees to awaken self-realization. It can be done gently by the guru at the right time or forcefully with drugs or trauma. The played guitar string would be the case of *forced vibration* by spiritual means. The second, by drugs/trauma, is an example of purely physical means, and it is detriment to the process of self-realization.

In the future, many more households (families) will ascend as a group, because everyone is in close physical, mental, emotional, and spiritual proximity. For meditating adults in the same household, if children have yet to be created, a serious choice should be made to determine if a couple wants to build a family or to become self-realized sooner. This choice may be more particular for the man, because, by losing his sperm, life-force is also lost, preventing higher levels of realization. The loss of life-energy is also the same for the female, which is dependent upon the sensitivity of her own constitution. This life-force is essential to create one path or another. The physical materials may be there to create, but the actual life-giving forces are in short supply.

As you raise your energy up through the *chakras* to gain higher levels of consciousness, less energy will be available to create children. If your destiny is to create children, then your desires (and energy) are generally centered around the lower *chakras*. This is so enough life-force is there to produce the necessary energetic material to create a child. If, on the other hand, you choose to become self-realized first, then all the energy will be constantly pushed away from the first and second *chakras* (male and female organs). This energy shift doesn't make it more difficult to have children later. You will, however, have to learn to push your energy back towards the sex organs in order to have enough life-force to create life. It really all comes down to desire. Desire is what pushes the energy is one direction or another.

However, don't be fooled into thinking that having kids and then becoming self-realized will be easy! It will actually be much more difficult than becoming self-realized first! How much time do you think you will have for your meditations, if your duty is to raise your children? I am, of course, by no means suggesting not to have children, but be sure to search your heart for your true intention. There have been few great men and women that could have children, raise them, and still become fully self-realized. One was Lahiri Mahasaya and there have been others, but still they are few in number. The best part of becoming self-realized first is that it is permanent! It will never leave you! What conscious choice will you make?

Certain things allow the *kundalini* to rise more quickly, become slowed, or stop completely with continued stagnation. With the guru's help and direct permission from the Divine, you can awaken the *kundalini*. The Divine pushes the *kundalini* further if need be, and it is facilitated and nurtured by you. Once your spiritual teacher activates it, you can continually activate the *kundalini* by pulling in cosmic energy by the "Cosmic Energy Technique" (CET). This technique was described on p. 149 in Chapter 13.

Also, the rising *kundalini* can be slowed to the point of stopping when energy is being drained through too much sexual release and/or not enough good (God) foods. Foods and sexual release are the biggest factors that will affect the rise of the *kundalini*, but sleep can make it stop as well. *Kundalini* can also become stagnant because of lack of exercise, chronic disease, and poor lifestyle. But by creating stability in the body through exercise, a balanced lifestyle, and healthy eating, sluggish energy will not cause permanent damage to the physical or subtle (astral/energetic) bodies.

As mentioned previously, drugs can activate the *kundalini*, but no type of artificial substance, such as marijuana, hallucinogens, alcohol, or tobacco, will allow the *kundalini* to rise properly and naturally. There is great danger when using these substances to activate the *kundalini*; therefore, it is NOT recommended. To activate the *kundalini* without the help of a self-realized guru would be like committing spiritual suicide. The rise of the *kundalini* should be done progressively and scientifically. Without the help of a self-realized guru in this process and the Divine's intervention, you cannot expect to receive the ultimate love by the use of these deluding substances.

Once the *kundalini* has been activated properly, many wonderful sensations will become apparent in the body. These sensations are felt differently while in various LOCs, like the difference between *savikalpa* and *asamprajñata*. This is because the *kundalini* is rising at different rates, with varying amounts, located at different *chakras* in the body. These sensations may be expressed as physical, emotional, and/or mental outpourings. This process also occurs because as the debris is removed and the last remnants of trauma are cleared out. It is necessary to remove any final debris to achieve the major *samadhi* state, which is a precursor to *nirvikalpa samadhi*. These pulses will also spend a certain percentage of time in each of the *chakras*, depending on what energy center requires the most of attention at the time of the pulse. Once the pulse has reached the seventh *chakra*, it will be used immediately to evolve the brain further.

Initially, the *kundalini* will only rise in pulsing streams, one at a time, but eventually in its final ascension, it will rise as a large portion. It will have to pass through all six *chakras*, before being used by the seventh *chakra* to evolve the brain to receive God's Light. As the energy rises, it will activate *chakras* one through five, allowing you to draw upon powers of discrimination associated with each *chakra*. You will also begin to hear the sounds of each *chakra* and see its associated color.

Once this bulk arrives at the third *chakra* (solar plexus), you may experience overwhelming energy and power in the body. When the bulk arrives at the heart (dorsal, fourth) *chakra*, love will overflow in your consciousness. The same is true as the *kundalini* rises and completely activates each of the energy centers in the body. The general sensations you may have are of immense bliss and joyous celebration. In regards to gender specificity, women may feel greater experiential gains in the second *chakra*, where their reproductive systems reside, or in the fourth *chakra*; whereas men may have greater changes in energy at the first and third *chakras*.

This energy needs to rise, because it not only activates the essential energy centers in the body, but it also clears the spine of any spiritual debris that has collected over past lifetimes by the three bodies; physical, astral (subtle), and causal (ideational). A small hollow astral tube called the *sushumna* travels down the center of the spine. The clearing occurs primarily within this small space, but also affects the energy channels that are connected to it. Without this clearing, you would not be able to receive the Divine's pure Light. This Light is a necessity towards becoming self-realized. Its descension into the spine will be discussed in Chapter 14 on p. 192.

SAVIKALPA SAMADHI (SaS)

Value of Level SaS = $CC1^2$, # of SaS Levels = 133 Billion
Cosmic Consciousness

In *savikalpa*, the meditator, the process of meditation, and the object of meditation (SPIRIT as Creator) become one. The wave of the ocean that was once separated by the appearance of physical walls has now become a part of that vast ocean. When in *samadhi*, the mind is conscious of creation outside of itself. This consciousness may appear trance-like, but you are fully conscious of the bliss within and the world without.

In the initiation to SaS, your attention and life current become switched off from the physical senses allowing for the DSCE to occur, but in greater levels of stillness. As the soul becomes released from the ego in *samadhi*, your consciousness becomes aware of SPIRIT beyond creation as the Creator's Cosmic Consciousness. At this time, body-bound habits, or *samskaras*, can be destroyed. They may not be completely destroyed, however, because *samskaras* are absolutely and completely destroyed after entering the natural *samadhi* state of *sahaja*.

Once the lesser minor *samadhi* states have been achieved, including *laya samadhi*, you will become attuned to Cosmic Consciousness through the highest level of a major *samadhi*, the Divine Superconscious Experience (DSCE). The first level of *samadhi* of the Creator's Cosmic Consciousness is *savikalpa samadhi* (SaS). SaS is considered the greatest minor *samadhi* state, as it allows for the greatest level of stillness possible without the continued occurrence of out-of-body-like experiences. This is the level of stillness that is achievable while walking around, interacting with the world, performing householder duties.

Initiation into SaS

The initiation into the state of *savikalpa samadhi* by a DSCE may occur in many ways. It may occur seated, if the body is relatively undiseased, or in the supine position. Many yogis have been pictured in the lotus position; however, this position is very difficult for those who have limited flexibility in the low back and thigh muscles. These "lotus" yogis usually have been practicing the art of yoga since adolescence. It is likely that most people in the world cannot achieve this type of yogic body posture (*asana*), and it is not necessary to reach self-realization. My own body achieved self-realization through the seated-chair posture taught by my guru, Sri Yoganandaji, and the supine position.

Many sensations may be felt in this state of consciousness, including the feeling of being joyful and happy. Some have described their initial experiences in Cosmic Consciousness (CosCon) as being so joyful that to move the body would be take away from this joy. This was my exact experience, but as you progress, the bliss will become easily maintained at any moment you desire.

At this blissful point, you now feel the Creator's consciousness completely, and you begin to slowly merge with its ultimate form as SPIRIT. SPIRIT is the Creator beyond creation without the desire to create. It is the Creator in Its formless, desireless state. The body may feel both heavy and light at the same time, as nature's duality can now be experienced and manifested at the same time in the physical body. This is because becoming of one mind and body with CosCon allows you to experience the non-duality of the Divine's mind beyond creation. Remember, creation is dualistic, and the Creator is non-dualistic because It exists outside of Its creation.

Any action performed in this state for the highest good of others is expanded much greater in joy and love in your consciousness, even in the simplest form, like doing household chores. As long as the focus is on the third eye, higher realizations will continue to emerge, allowing for joy to overflow. This focus on the third eye is one way that the Law of Ascension manifests in the process of self-realization. The focus can be done during any activity and during any time of the day without limit. The limit, including to any business practice, profession, or work position, is determined by your own willpower.

At the base level of SaS, you will have to exert large amounts of willpower to maintain this LOC. You can fluctuate in and out of SaS very easily and without meaning. Also, as soon as you go to sleep, your experience of this consciousness will disappear. Therefore, it is necessary to meditate morning and night upon the Divine, if you expect to continue to ascend in LOC. This will be a common theme through the self-realization process.

However, this theme can be averted if you meditate to your most intense ability each night.† If you were to meditate with intense devotion and silence, after practicing the techniques mentioned in the next few pages for at least 2-3 hours before you go to bed, it is likely your current state of consciousness will not leave you. On the other hand, after manifesting the DSCE and SaS, you may choose to drop your discipline on the path of self-realization. By doing so, the LOC would drop very quickly.

Many realizations will come to you, providing the true nature of the Divine's existence. You will realize that your body is really full of light, particularly Divine Light. You may experience an ultra-still state frequently, which is without comparison to the previous states of stillness. You will also feel that the third eye is always emanating a high level of tension and focus. The heart *chakra* will blaze deeply and fiercely as well because the *kundalini* energy is still pulsing through the spine, helping the body to continually evolve. Desires for anything physical are small, and all of life's questions seem easily answered through deep meditation and stillness. You know that you are SPIRIT in meditation, but you cannot fully embrace this vibration as active awareness while performing daily duties.

However, realize this state of SaS is not self-realization. It is only about 25% of true self-realization. Once you are able to enter the major *samadhi* states at will, only 50% of self-realization is achieved. Only when you achieve a non-dual existence by choice will a fully self-realized existence become manifest in your body and consciousness. This type of self-realization is more specifically called God-realization.

Stages of SaS

Patanjali describes *savikalpa* in four major stages in his *Yoga Sutras*.[12] These four stages are also considered together as *samprajñata samadhi*, or *samadhi* "with difference." At this stage, you are aware of yourself as both the physical body and as a part of the Creator. These four stages

---

† Intensity here is determined not necessarily by timeframe, but by cycling your thoughts and devotion towards the Divine. The longer you can remain in complete concentration, the better your experience. This also means you shouldn't go without a full night's rest to achieve this intensity. Some of my most intense sessions of meditation have occurred before the work day in 20 minutes or less!

[12] Patanjali's *Yoga Sutras* I:17–18

come after the interiorization† of the 2nd Dimension and the deep concentration (*dharana*) attuned to in the lesser minor *samadhi* states. As you are able to resolve one stage into the other through deep meditation (*dhyana*) and non-interrupted concentration, the Creator's Cosmic Consciousness will be felt as omnipresence in *samadhi*. Patanjali further explains that attainment of the highest type of *samadhi* is "by profound, devoted mediation on (the Lord) Ishvara."[13] *Ishvara* (in Sanskrit) means the "supreme soul, ruler, or king."

The first stage is called *savitarka* (intentional). The yogi, after being initiated into the Creator's consciousness, experiences doubt about whether he or she achieved the goal of self-realization. This amazing intuitive experience is mixed with an argumentative mind saying, "Did this really just happen? Did I really just achieve the impossible?" These thoughts are constant in the mind of the yogi, as this consciousness is not like any other experienced before. Doubt is a necessary component when dealing with a new state of consciousness, especially when one lives in a scientific age in which logic and rationale must be given to everything. This stage may continue to appear even while you are ascending in *asamprajñata samadhi* and the Interstate, because it is difficult to imagine that you could reach even a portion of self-realization during this current era on Earth.

The second stage elaborated upon by Patanjali is *savichara* (introspective). This stage consists of intuitive experience mixed with discernment-guided intelligence—reasoning or contemplation towards the Divine in one of Its aspects as love, bliss, or wisdom. In the previous lesser minor *samadhis*, you were able to intuitively realize the major aspects of God while in a minor level of minor *samadhi* stillness. In *savikalpa*, those aspects can now be realized in a major level of minor *samadhi* stillness. Each of these stillness levels are necessary, as the Divine's awesome power cannot be achieved in one single moment. If this were to happen, the body's bulb would burn up in an instant. God and gurus would not allow this to occur.

The third stage is *sananda* (bliss), a special interiorization experienced by feelings of joy or definable bliss. This type of joy is what seekers of self-realization yearn for. It may occur at various moments throughout the ascension in SaS. This joy could manifest as

---

† In the 2nd Dimension this is called IS or intermittent *samadhi* which is also the same as *pratyahara*.
[13] Patanjali's *Yoga Sutras* I:23–29

the *savikalpa samadhi* extension experience described later in this chapter or intermittently to support your efforts.

The fourth stage is *sasmita* (identity). In this stage, you experience a sense of "I-ness" or individuality. You know you are now beyond creation and are merging with the consciousness of the Creator beyond creation. This intuitive experience is mixed with a pure sense of being. You know the consciousness that lies within the physical body is a part of the Creator. By this point, you also know of your physical body as creation itself. As the LOC increases, this sense of "I-ness" will help you to see that you are not only a part of the Creator, but as the Creator manifested into both a soul and physical form. In fact, you are a co-Creator on the project of the Earth and the ever-expanding universe.

Techniques in SaS

Use of scientific meditative techniques while in SaS is still extremely helpful in ascension. You may or may not be able to hear the *Om* sound fully while in the deepest states of stillness without the use of a technique. With a technique, the *Om* sound should be an obvious sound of true intensity. The third eye will become visually apparent while in these depths, but realize that Cosmic Consciousness has already been achieved. Further penetration into the third eye will continue to help you to ascend in consciousness.

The continued practice of *Kriya* and other special meditation exercises given by the guru has proven to be infinitely useful while in SaS. These yogic practices and exercises are necessary to maintain the physical tenacity of the body while in these higher-level spiritual states. The *Kriya* has never failed in evolving the body and mind towards the highest plateaus when the body requires it, but it is not necessary constant. When a minor or major samadhi is in progress, the body only desires to go deeper into that profound stillness. It would be going against the "wishes" of the body to try to perform a breathing technique when the body wants to be breathless, for example. Sometimes the body will call for the *Kriyas*, separate from the possible special techniques given with the *Kriya*. At this point, self-muscle testing and/or intuitive perception becomes necessary.

Kriyas are especially helpful when you need help in removing spiritual debris throughout the day or cannot drop into the *samadhi* state as easily as usual. The performance of the *Kriyas* will help you to continue to rise quickly in LOC.† Other techniques can be performed to elevate the LOC without moving any part of the body. This non-movement will become absolutely necessary if you desire to achieve the ultimate state of *nirvikalpa samadhi.*

You also have to be careful while in SaS, because your consciousness is now more open to all of creation. If your mind has become unified with that of the Creator, you will be open to perceiving and receiving all that is in creation. Creation is duality, and duality has both "light" and "dark" sides—light meaning "good" and dark meaning "bad" or negative. These positive and negative energies are always on a constant collision course with one another, battling for spiritual territory. Your mind is more open to these energies, but it is also more susceptible. It is best to use spiritual protection in the form of something worn on the body, like a crucifix (Yogananda wore one), *rudraksha* beads, prayer beads of any kind, or even a bracelet that is prayed or meditated with. Some stones or metals, when worn close to the body, can also have beneficial effects on warding off negative, unwanted vibrations. All levels below SaS, including the lesser minor *samadhis* are innately protected from these dark energies. This is a benefit for those who have yet ascended into the Creator's consciousness.

As the LOC of the world increases from Superconsciousness to Christ Consciousness and to Cosmic Consciousness, the third eye will be used as a way to access the highest realizations. The current LOC of the world is at $10^{29,999}$, which is at a base level for Superconsciousness. As the world delves deeper into the ages of light and human awareness, the LOC of the world will increase exponentially as a result, providing a pure environment of light and love for all peoples of the world.

SAVIKALPA SAMADHI EXTENSION EXPERIENCE (SaSee)

This is an elevated state of stillness within SaS that mimics the next level of samadhi to be experienced in *asamprajñata.* During these experiences, SPIRIT draws your consciousness into higher and higher elevated states of stillness and bliss. This is the time when your LOC can begin to increase more easily, usually at an exponential rate. Time

---

† There are other techniques that have been discovered and developed that will be mentioned in future publications and in my blogs.

during these experiences is relative and how long an experience has occurred could be easily skewed. As the LOC increases, the time required to go into a *samadhi* state will decrease, and the time frame required to achieve a relative increase in LOC will also decrease.

You may also consciously experience a breathless state while operating in relative stillness, such as while working at the computer or even watching TV. However, watching TV is not recommended, because the mind's concentration becomes challenged by the constant interruptions of sight, sound, and the body's mental and emotional reaction. This state is also much harder to achieve completely if a person's body is full of physical disease. You may be able to achieve SaS, but not achieve SaSee, because you are not continuing to live the life of a morally righteous individual. This is the same for future realizations that will be explained later in the book.

In this state of SaSee and future states that utilize LOC increases with the Law of Ascension, your discipline will be used to drive yourself to being blissful. This high-flying feeling is paramount in the ascent. Realize that bliss is not only a combination of enjoyment, pleasure, and satisfaction, but also a transcendence of all emotion. Bliss should be your pleasure when achieving higher LOCs. Use the emotional reaction that bliss provides you to drive yourself consistently toward your goal. This gives you a physical reaction to what you are experiencing. This drive tends to be very primitive and operates simply. However, if your pleasure could become wholly spiritual, then God would be all that you would choose because God's ever-flowing, ever-new bliss is the greatest spiritual, emotional, mental, and physical pleasure that any one individual could experience. Choose this pleasure of bliss, and God-realization shall be yours!

ASAMPRAJÑATA (Añ)

Level Value of Añ = $CC1^{100}$, # of Añ Levels = $\{10^{[1E(999.9E12)]}\}^{10}$
Añ1 = $[10^{1E(999.9E12)}]^1$ = SaS133B-1
Añ2 = $[10^{1E(999.9E12)}]^2$
Añ3 = $[10^{1E(999.9E12)}]^3$, etc.
Cosmic Consciousness

Patanjali describes this state as being the same as *nirvikalpa samadhi*. *Asamprajñata* (Añ) means that all differentiations of nature meld into the one SPIRIT or "to be without difference."[14] This is the more advanced of the two basic categories of *samadhi* referenced in the book by Patanjali. *Samprajñata*, the first basic category of *samadhi* according to Patanjali and a portal into more advanced states, means "to be with difference." Añ is the state in the previous section on the *savikalpa samadhi* extension experience (SaSee). Essentially, Añ, at its baseline level, is the same as SaSee at its peak. This similarity is necessary so that you do not become overwhelmed by the transition between the two LOCs.

SaS is the greatest minor *samadhi*, and Añ is the beginning transition state to major *samadhi*, and serves as a greater part of *nirvikalpa samadhi* (NrS). Patanjali was not incorrect but only elaborated on those aspects of self-realization that were meant to be seen during that time.[†] Without an understanding of how to use intuition and/or muscle testing properly, you would be without at least two definitive ways to check your current LOC status. It is not necessary to have muscle testing to determine your qualitative state, but in a scientific world, using a binary, neurologic switch such as muscle testing proves useful in gaining a quantitative perspective.

The world is in a time where science and metaphysics are beginning to understand one another and become one. With the advent of particle accelerators at Fermilab in Illinois and CERN in Switzerland, there is no surprise that physicists are proving that matter is really just empty space. With the realization that all of creation is just empty space, you will truly experience the next level of awareness in Añ.

Basics of Asamprajñata

Añ is a true absence of gross awareness, meaning there is no longer an object upon which to meditate. There are only the impressions the

---

[14] Patanjali's *Yoga Sutras* I:17–18

[†] According to Peter Peterson, Patanjali may have lived as early as second century BCE. In Hindu Astrology, as determined by Swami Sri Yukteswar in his book *The Holy Science*, this was during a time when mankind was de-evolving. How could man cope with a detailed map of the states of self-realization if he was in fact regressing spiritually as a species? This is the major reason Patanjali did not go into more depth of the specificities of levels of consciousness and also why most ancient yogic text is veiled in obscurity. Other masters could have expounded further upon these ideas, but it was not their purpose to go into such great detail. Without the evolution of muscle testing, discovering and measuring the values of each state would have been difficult.

physical objects have created in the causal thought field of the mind. Generally, many sensations experienced in this state are primarily the "out-of-body" type because the mind will become detached from the body's sensations. This will occur primarily in the vision, touch sensation, and body awareness. Your proprioception, or awareness of the body in space, will transcend, as if you were merely floating instead of walking. Some other similar sensations could be experienced. Actions performed while in the highest versions of this state will feel like you are not the body, but in fact, the etheric soul.

Because of this transient nature, you may inadvertently pull karma from others to help them evolve as well. In this state, the body and mind have no separation anxiety. Most people will have a difficult time letting go of reality. The body and mind will struggle to maintain togetherness in deeper meditation, so as to create harmony and balance between physical experience and true non-physical existence. Remind yourself often that you are made of SPIRIT! Separation of mind and body is inevitable in God-union, but it will be done gently and with respect to your own level of comfort.

So, the body can experience a diseased state without the mind being attached to pain or discomfort the body is experiencing. Many masters do remove karma consciously and willfully to help their disciples and devotees ascend. As you ascend, you may subconsciously desire to help a fellow associate ascender and pull the karma out of his or her body as a result. This may be acceptable in some instances, but it is highly unadvisable to pull karma from people consciously. It can have disastrous consequences, as your unprepared body may not be able to withstand the negative consequence of the karma being taken on. This pulling of karma can also occur by the will of the Divine, and will be used purposely toward your self-realization and tolerated well. God will never give someone more than he or she can handle.

Añ has 10 major levels associated with it. Each level has a colossal value but can be transcended if you are dedicated to the practices of meditation and ascension. As you ascend in LOC throughout the 10 levels of Añ, a number of experiences may be had. Not everyone will have the same type of experiences, but the sensation of the absence of gross (body) awareness will be common for everyone.

Other Experiences of Añ

You may feel both very large and very small at the same time—as large as the universe or as small as an atom. You may visually or intuitionally perceive, at the third eye, creation itself expanding from its initial big bang into the many different component parts as it is now and what it may become in the future. This perception does not have to be large, in the sense of galaxies, but could be as small as molecules or atoms themselves. To realize that you are a part of all of creation in every form is the fullest realization of the Christ Consciousness. Going beyond creation, you may perceive the Creator as light or any form that resonates with you.

Often, in deep *samadhi* meditation, yogis have been able to converse with different forms of the Divine as Krishna, Christ, Mother Mary, and other saints/deities special to the devotee. If you are able to perceive SPIRIT in this way, it is because your causal body is providing the visual instruments necessary to manifest the experience.

All of these visual and intuitional perceptions are a part of true existence. All opposites always occur at the same time and are never apart from each other. This is why Añ is a part of Cosmic Consciousness. The Creator has to exist beyond all things to maintain the duality between all things. This separateness is what convinces you, in deep meditation, that you can be both Divine and man at the same time. These concepts are embodied in all of mankind's greatest self-realized masters.

Jesus the Christ said
You will know that I am in My Father, and you in Me, and I in you.[15]

The Buddha, who came 500 years before Christ spoke in the same manner,
You are my children; I am your father; through me you have been released from your sufferings.... I myself having attained salvation, am a savior of others.[16]

---

[15] John 14:20 NIV
[16] Walker 2003, 121.

Sri Krishna, the Christ of India, 3000 years before Christ also knowing himself as true Divinity Itself said,

I am the goal of the wise man, and I am the way. I am the end of the path, the witness, the Lord, the sustainer. I am the place of the abode, the beginning, the friend and the refuge.[17]

It is obvious that from these quotes that these individuals were, in fact, claiming to be the Divine in the most absolute form. These enlightened Sons of God were both human and Divine, and thus, were able to maintain both the duality of creation and the non-duality of SPIRIT.

These avatars were easily able to transcend planes of existence in Añ and beyond. What they experienced is similar to what the devoted meditator will feel while in Añ, but to the greatest degree. For they were perfected masters, ones who have "ascended" in a previous lifetime, they could not become the highest version of a perfected human in that lifetime. People who "ascend" in this life may be considered fully self-realized, but not truly a master who has been perfected. They are not perfected masters like Jesus and Krishna, but an "ascended master."[†] Añ and other levels of realization in this book are of the workingman variety. The workingman's variety, remember, is to purely know yourself as bliss. To be able to toil on Earth but still know yourself as SPIRIT's bliss is the future of Earth's spiritual reality.

In this bliss, you may experience sensations of incredible energy or perfect serenity. Both sensations may occur at the same time, causing supreme bliss to rain down upon your consciousness. Slowing time itself while in these out-of-body experiences, you will perceive light as a manifestation of pure SPIRIT, oscillating in and out of existence in the infinite forms of creation. SPIRIT can only be perceived as dark particles, because "SPIRIT stuff" is technically "non-existence stuff," meaning that, before creation manifested as physical, astral, and causal cosmos, there was nothing more than the void and consciousness.

During these advanced stages of Añ, you may slip in and out of an even stiller state called *asamprajñata samadhi* extension experience (AñSee). When you advance into this stage for a period of time (usually from seconds to minutes), the LOC will begin to increase. This is similar to the previous state of SaSee, which was the advanced level of stillness present in SaS or *savikalpa samadhi*.

---

[17] Isherwood and Prabhavananda 1946.
† Can read more about the ascended master at the end of this book in Chapter 17

There may be moments of still attunement without much out-of-body experience. At these times, you will feel very "human." This is good, because the body needs to attune itself to the LOC that is being experienced. As long as you have great intuition and/or accurate muscle testing, you can determine if your LOC has decreased or if you are maintaining the current state. Without a slower adjustment period, the body would just burn up like an over-watted light bulb. Instead, God and Gurus will only provide what a body can handle.

You are able to continue to experience these sensations because you are able to actively pull the life-force (*prana*) from your extremities and centralize it in the spine. This *prana* is also called *qi* (chi) and is used extensively in describing energy flow in acupuncture meridians. This energy that moves through the various *nadis,* or energy meridians, in the body can be pulled in actively towards the spine. Doing so will actively increase your LOC. The Cosmic Energy Technique (p. 149), *Kriyas,* and other *mudras* explained throughout this book can pull this energy from the extremities and from the Divine to help fuel the body's acceleration toward self-realization.

As you progress in the Añ states, you will begin to see that eternity can be experienced in every moment because your consciousness is always living in the eternal moment. In this progression, the body has to continue to attune itself to experiencing the higher levels of God-realization. These sensations may cause pain and discomfort in the body, but your consciousness will prove that the mind controls the body. You also will overcome these sensations listed below, producing little suffering.[†]

[†] It should be noted that this book does not recommend meditating to any physical, emotional, or mental extremes. It is best to be moderate in all aspects of practicing yoga. If you are having pain in a particular position, it is best to sit in a body posture that is more relaxing and less restrictive. Living with the basic essentials, such as food and water, on a daily basis is essential to perform yoga well. Yoga is about union to the Divine through balance, NOT through extremes. In this era, you will actually advance slower if you are too extreme about your habits because you can become too fixated on the action itself and not why you are performing it. If any of the sensations are experienced above, it is recommended to have them ruled out from any other types of serious conditions that could cause permanent bodily damage, which can, and usually does, cause a serious impediment to self-realization. Always contact a licensed healthcare professional if the above sensations persist after meditating for long periods.

1. <u>Burning eyes</u> – The burning sensation is so that the eyes can receive God's Light without discomfort.
2. <u>Extremity Tingling</u> – Whether caused by loss of blood flow to an extremity is due to sitting too long or physical ailments that still require healing, Añ will reveal that these discomforts are creations of the mind, ego consciousness, and ultimately *maya*, the universal delusive force.
3. <u>Extremity Coldness</u> – This sensation is very common because the life force of the body is being drawn into the spine, up to the third eye and crown *chakra*, so that further evolution of the body and consciousness can occur.

This sensation of "extremity coldness" is still one that I experience on a daily basis, but only because I am always focusing my energy towards the upper *chakras* and away from the extremities. This coldness especially becomes accentuated when it is colder outside.

Añ has been described by other sources[18] as a *nirvikalpa* (NrS) transitional state. Although NrS is described in the *Yoga Sutras* and has been interpreted as being one and the same as NrS, it also serves as the beginning stages of NrS. The various transitions mentioned in the next few pages will show how you will build in strength and willpower, so that you may be able to withstand the awesome power of the Divine's Love in NrS.

Below are the various stages that you must be attuned to before achieving NrS. Each stage will represent physical, emotional, mental, and spiritual healings and transitions that are necessary to experience NrS in all of its fullness. All initial stages of Añ 1-10 need to be achieved first before these next stages can be measured accurately.

KUNDALINI (K)
Value of Level K = no value
Last Level = 0 seconds, K is based on a rate

---

[18] Taimni 2010, 31–42

Cosmic Consciousness
As mentioned on p. 172, this level is a measurement of the rate by which the *kundalini* energy fluxes through the spine from the coccyx to the top of the skull within a certain period time. This movement can be instantaneous or could stretch out to years or to little movement over lifetimes. The *kundalini* may continue to rise until the attainment of NrS, throughout the rest of the smaller attunements that occur after one achieves Añ 10.

rate = pulse/min (for most people active in their self-realization process)
last level = 0 seconds or pulsations become a constant flow

CONTROLLED AÑ SAMADHI EXTENSION EXP (CAñSee)
Level Value of CAñSee = time (sec/min), # of CAñSee Levels = ∞
Cosmic Consciousness
CAñSee is also a pre-major *samadhi* state or a minor major *samadhi* experience (MrsMje). This LOC is required initially so that your body and consciousness are not overwhelmed by the influx of the Creator's Light and Consciousness during an actual major *samadhi* experience. You can control, through willpower, access to this state of consciousness. The previous states of SaSee and AñSee can be experienced, but are only accessible at random times. This is currently why this state is so special and also allows you to see what type of willpower is necessary to achieve a controlled *samadhi* experience, and a minor major *samadhi* state.

    This state cannot be achieved while you are physically diseased. You can still suffer with symptoms in the body, but your LOC (or current spiritual state) is unaffected by the experiences of the body. This is vital to understand, as your consciousness may be karma-ful, allowing for astrological forces to force your body to experience disease states more fully.

    This state is also measured in time with seconds and/or minutes. The number of levels can be infinitely long, because time can continue on for infinity. However, this time is usually finite, because you can only live for so long.

SAMADHI INTENSITY (SIT)

Value of Level SIT = 1, # of SIT Levels = 100, Cosmic Consciousness
Samadhi Intensity is a rating system used for a SaSee in SaS and both the AñSee and CAñSee in Añ, as these are three minor *samadhi* experiences that can occur in their highest stages while in these two major LOCs. Levels 1-100 describe the level of stillness possible. This stillness can fluctuate wildly as you go deeper or is interrupted by outside influence. SIT can go from 3 to 29 to 57 and the back to 3 again in a couple of minutes. When interaction with the physical world occurs, this intensity will decrease again unless constant focus on the Divine can be maintained. This is a measure of your essential willpower to maintain all activities toward the Divine.

BREATHLESSNESS (B)

Value of Level B = 1, # of B Levels = 399,999, Cosmic Consciousness
Breathlessness is necessary to experience and is entered into during any type of unconscious *samadhi*. During conscious-level *samadhi* states, breathlessness will occur in segments. It will oscillate on and off while you are conscious. Experiencing *samadhi* allows you to suspend the life force leading to a state of "deathlessness." This deathlessness, brought on by breathlessness, is a necessary transition to *nirvikalpa samadhi*. You must be without breath if you expect to enter into both the Divine Superconscious Experience (DSCE) and the major *samadhi* experience (sMje) at will. This breathlessness leads to suspended animation of the body's cells, which can directly feed from the life current that is being provided by the Creator, so you can become completely sustained by the Creator's consciousness.

An article in the *London Telegraph* explains how a yogi in India named Sadhu Haridas was able to be buried for 40 days at the request of the Maharajah with no air or food and still survive.[19] In this situation, the yogi could enter the breathless state at will and thus sustain his bodily cells only on SPIRIT. This is the true dynamo that powers all things in creation. It is only by our ignorance to this great power that we choose to breathe and not live by God's bread alone. The Gospel Matthew wrote that, "Man shall not live by bread alone, but by every word that proceeds out of the mouth of God."[20]

---

[19] London Telegraph 1880, 2.
[20] Matthew 4:4 NASB

However, no one should attempt to hold his or her breath to achieve this state of consciousness. It must occur naturally and spontaneously. The breathless state requires years of meditation with the lessons of a self-realized guru teaching scientific meditation and leading the devotee safely to this state. Holding your breath will only cause great harm to your body when you are not ready for it.

The level of breathlessness that actually occurs here is very subtle. Some, including myself, have noticed that after really deep periods of meditation you have not taken a breath for a period of time. During these moments, great amounts of peace, joy, and bliss permeate the body. If your mind wanders back to the idea of breathing, well, then, breathing occurs. This is not a bad thing, but when your mind begins to wander towards the Divine again in complete focus and devotion, the respiration mechanism slows down to a stop. This stopping may only be from seconds to minutes. As anyone knows, holding your breath for a couple of minutes can be more easily done if practiced. Those who spend long periods of time in the water, like divers and the military, have to practice these types of breath-holding techniques. This is not the same as meditating and then reaching a naturally and spontaneous breathless state.

In meditation, all the energy being focused towards the upper *chakras* (especially the third eye) gets so intensely concentrated that you naturally become more breathless. The life force is not only being drawn away from the extremities but also from the core and the upper thoracic region, where the heart and lungs are located. As this energy rises towards the throat, third eye, and crown of the head, the respiration ceases for short periods of time. This is a natural part of very deep relaxation.

Again, breathlessness is not the same as shortness of breath (SOB) or other types of breathing difficulties in conditions like COPD (emphysema, chronic bronchitis), asthma, heart disease, and obesity. As a physician, who must be highly objective, I can tell you that this natural breathlessness occurs so often that it seems natural when I haven't taken a breath. It doesn't feel bad, and it doesn't take away from my function. The difference is that I am not focused on the respiration or the thought of respiration at all. In fact, I am so immersed in bliss and thoughts of the Divine that, most of the time, even while I am treating clients, this breathless state occurs. You will only know what I mean when you decide to sit, relax, and be still for long periods of time. Truly, the proof is in the pudding.

This breathlessness in *asamprajñata* measures how much breath you are respiring (both inhalation and exhalation). This breathlessness will only occur while are you in SIT and is extremely transient. It is not measured by a rate per se, except that there are different levels of respiration of breath that are not occurring. As the levels increase, the greater the level of deathlessness, and thus, breathlessness. Any levels of breathlessness that occur before SaS will be measured in seconds to minutes only. If the breathlessness has occurred longer, it is because the individual has at least gained access to SaS.

This LOC measurement is very transient and can fluctuate wildly and almost instantly based on the depth of meditation of the individual. You can go completely breathless in an instant, and with the mere thought of breathing, bring your lungs back to life.

I remember being on the path, practicing basic techniques like the *Hong-sau* and experiencing brief moments of breathlessness within the first six months. It shocked me at first, and all of the sudden, I would take a deep breath in, like I had just come up for air. In those moments, I thought, "Did I just stop breathing?" When I asked others about it, they said it was pretty normal for that to happen and said it was a result of deep conscious meditation. The deeper I went, the longer the time it happened, and the less I was afraid.

As you decide to meditate deeper and deeper, especially being on path of disciplined meditation, you will find yourself growing in leaps and bounds. This breathlessness is the beginning of that growth. As long as it is not forced and happens naturally and spontaneously, you know you are making true gains in relaxation and self-realization.

LIGHT DESCENSION (LD)

Value of Level LD = 1, # of LD Levels =7, Cosmic Consciousness

After the *kundalini* has risen, clearing out all debris impeding higher states of awareness, the "Light" of SPIRIT will begin to descend into the spinal *chakras*. As the Light descends into the spine, the seventh *chakra* and all *chakras* below will fill with light. This Light will help you to experience a fuller sense of the minor major *samadhi* leading to the occurrence of a major *samadhi*. The Light is to fill the astral spinal cord with a sustained pulse so you may achieve a major *samadhi* experience without a rough transition.

Ramana Maharshi, another man of self-realization, was said to have transitioned so quickly that he left his family and material possessions at the age of sixteen years old after a "simulated death experience" while sitting in a room of his Uncle's home. This transition was so rough that he became completely unaware of his body, to the point where insects chewed away portions of his legs and his body wasted because of not eating.[21] This is *not* the path of self-realization for the workingman and -woman in the concrete jungles of life. The transition to SPIRIT must occur slowly, otherwise you may be too scared of the repercussions on your family life, especially if there are children involved.

My wife was particularly concerned when I began to transition in this state of consciousness because there is no bliss, only lack of body awareness. You may become physically, emotionally, and mentally detached for a time, but once you reach *nirvikalpa samadhi*, the joy will overwhelm the man or woman so much that sharing it through hugging, kissing, and deeper levels of intimacy will be a primary course of action. This is especially for those couples who are affectionate!

The light will continue to travel physically through the central canal of the spinal cord, but through its astral counterpart, the *sushumna*. How long it takes for the Light to descend completely is indefinite. You can help push the LD along more quickly if you are sensitive to where the energy is in the body by practicing *Kriyas* or by pulling in cosmic energy through the Cosmic Energy Technique. *Kriyas* help to cycle energy in the spine, so this is an obvious choice to help the Light to descend.

The *Kriyas* are similar to the *kundalini* in that the cycling of energy in the spine helps to clear any debris that has been collected over lifetimes of indiscriminate living. Practicing the *Kriyas* will help to lubricate the *sushumna* to facilitate the movement of Light. *Kriyas* are also necessary because they help to bring the meditator into a breathless state, bringing the Light more easily through the spine.

Pulling in cosmic energy from the universe by the Cosmic Energy Technique will help to push the Light further down into the spine. As the cosmic energy is pulled in, it will enter through the medulla and travel down through the spine to the extremities. You have to envision that the chilling feeling you receive from pulling in cosmic energy has

---

[21] Maharshi 1989, 2–3.

to be directed downward from the medulla oblongata into the spine and through the extremities. Imagination comes in to help visualize that this cosmic energetic force is pushing its way into each of the astral *chakra* wheels and peripheral *nadi* channels. You must also express yourself as spiritually as possible, making every effort to maintain the highest consciousness. This will facilitate the movement as well.

Keeping the astral wheels of light turning constantly and in balance with one another will fully manifest the expression of that *chakra*. This expression will occur in all forms including physically, emotionally, mentally, and spiritually. Once the sixth *chakra* has fully filled with the Light, then the fifth will be next in line to receive the Light. The Light will continue down the spine until all *chakras* are burning brightly.

As a *chakra* is filled with Light, it will release a final traumatic "feeling" and become accentuated with the characteristic of that particular *chakra*. If you have had trouble speaking in any form, the fifth *chakra* may manifest physically as a verbal outpouring and then in its place will be words of purity. The fourth *chakra* is for the Christ consciousness and for the Divine's Love itself. You will know love as its purest Divine form once this *chakra* has been filled. This continues down until the first *chakra* is fully filled with Light.

Finally, after the LD is finished, the body consciousness will be less affected by mental, emotional, verbal, and physical insults. The clarity experienced in the body and mind will be of the greatest yet, for the Divine's Light now fills the bodily vessel within and without. This everlasting flow allows for the consciousness of SPIRIT to ascend in the form of stillness, peace, joy, wisdom, and bliss.

VOID STATE (V)

Value of V levels = $CC1^{100}$, # of V Levels = $CC1^5$
$V1 = CC1^1$
$V2 = CC1^2$
$V3 = CC1^3$, etc.
Cosmic Consciousness
This is the VOID, filled with a darkless dark. This is where SPIRIT lies. The perfect SPIRIT consciousness, which has split itself into the Creator, Son Consciousness, and the holy vibration *Om*, lies within this space. Really, it is not a space, but that which lies beyond the dimension itself. It is dimensionless. It is the Unifier of all dimensions, for It created them. In this VOID, nothing exists. Here, there is no

sound. Everything is silent. There is only consciousness. This consciousness is pure and simple. It has no desire but to be. Nothing else can be known, as there is "no-thing" in the VOID. The VOID is a traveling space to SPIRIT beyond the desires of the Creator. You must experience this consciousness before you can understand what lies beyond the Creator's Cosmic Consciousness.

The role of this state is to help you realize the true form of reality. The reality is that the body and the surrounding environment exists only in the mind. All that has been created comes from the dream consciousness of SPIRIT. As the soul, a piece of this SPIRIT, you are dreaming your reality here on Earth as a human being. You are dreaming your own existence.

The VOID state occurs after the LD has completely passed through all seven *chakras*. In this state, the minor major *samadhi* can be instantaneously transmitted to the yogi, allowing for deep silence. The VOID state is a part of CAñSe and a higher form of this *samadhi* experience. It isn't easy to maintain, but how can a VOID be maintained, where there is nothing to be maintained? This is the mental challenge in the attainment of this state of consciousness. Realize that this VOID is a version of non-duality. Although there is instant transmission of the *samadhi* experience, the samadhi is difficult both to obtain and maintain. If you can master this mental challenge, then SPIRIT will be closer still. There are 5 levels to the VOID state:

- V1: Darkless Dark Space, A Space of Nothingness, SPIRIT only. In this space, the VOID offers no questions and answers because there is nothing to be gained or lost in the sea of nothingness. Nothing can be physically muscle tested. This level challenges you (if you are a muscle tester) to use intuition instead of a physical muscle test to learn what lies beyond.
- V2 – V5: In these higher levels of VOID consciousness, you can intuit and/or muscle test further musings to determine what lies within or beyond this state. You become aware that the VOID state offers a protective space that is infinitely larger, allowing for SPIRIT's calm inner light to act as a barrier against all worldliness that may challenge it.

VOID STATE BREATHLESSNESS (VB)

Value of Level VB = 1, # of VB Levels = CC1⁵
Cosmic Consciousness
This is the "breathlessness" that exists within the VOID state and is similar to the breathlessness noted above. However, it is measured differently.

SPIRIT STATE (SP)

Value of Level SP = 1, # of SP Levels = 100, Cosmic Consciousness
The SPIRIT State is similar to the Spirit States experienced in the 2nd Dimension, but it occurs very quickly. *Samadhi* is possible in this state but is difficult to obtain and maintain. No levels or values are given to samadhi while in SPIRIT state. It just is present. Breathlessness levels do not exist here, as breathlessness is already present.

During both the VOID state and SPIRIT state, many cooling sensations are felt in the body because the *prana* or *qi* is being focused towards the spine and third eye. These cooling sensations are necessary if you want to receive SPIRIT's Light of Love.

JOY

Value of Level JOY = 1, # of JOY Levels = 847
Cosmic Consciousness
This is the last measureable state of Añ before you can ascend to *nirvikalpa* (NrS). You must know the Creator's Joy and experience it in all its intensity before Añ can fully become transcended. This LOC is very transient and decreases very easily without focus. It is primarily measured while in the SPIRIT state.

The goal here is to maintain the joy experienced consistently at higher levels to continue attune oneself to higher LOCs. This experience is necessary so you can receive the Creator's initiation into NrS. NrS is really just the Divine's Joy becoming incarnate and fully manifest in the body of the yogi.

This joy will occur at an almost infinite number of levels. This stage is where 75% of self-realization will manifest itself. It is the stage of consciousness that all of those on the spiritual path desire. Even if a person can experience a minor *samadhi* at some level, it will never compare to the joy of the Divine experienced in combination with *samadhi* stillness. This is what makes the major *samadhi* state so special.

ॐ

Even in these high states of consciousness, you will still feel that the Divine is playing hide and seek with you because you have yet to receive the purity and fullness of the Divine's Joy. This is the true "feeling" behind SPIRIT's consciousness. You will continue to experience this hide and seek feeling until you have received the highest form of NrS, called Ecstatic Consciousness (EC), or activation of the divine nectar, *amrita*.

However, before NrS can be fully experienced, you must traverse the Interstate, allowing for an almost infinite amount of major *samadhi* states of consciousness.

CHAPTER 15

Multidimensional LOCs

In the multidimensional realm, the major *samadhi* experience is finally achieved. Although this is not yet a major *samadhi* experience associated with *nirvikalpa samadhi*, it is one step closer towards achieving your goals of being self-realized.

The Multidimensional Realm (MD) is named this way because it contains the many dimensional exits of the Interstate, allowing for you to attune yourself easily and without too much strain on the body. This long-forgotten realm is absolutely necessary in your ascension, but it is generally passed up too quickly to notice. As soon as you ascend from this realm, you will transcend into the Extradimensional Realm, which is inclusive of both *nirvikalpa* and *sahaja samadhi*.

The Interstate will be represented as the major structural aspect of the multidimensional realm (MD). It makes up the entirety of the MD, but is still quite vast in its own complexity.

INTERSTATE (IState)

Value of Level Istate #1 = 1, # of Istate #1 Levels = 1
Unknown Consciousness

This LOC is the "inter-" state that transitions you from the minor major *samadhi* state (MrsMje) of *asamprajñata* (Añ) to *nirvikalpa* (NrS) by attuning you to almost an infinite number of major *samadhi* experiences. The goal is to continually upgrade your mind and body, so that it may receive the Divine's Love without any negative consequences.

This state is an example of a "compactified" dimension.[1] Imagine a 3D image placed upon a flat piece of paper that is then curled up into figure eight. This drawing illustrates how the three dimensions of our present physical reality could possibly have multidimensional space within this basic framework.

Figure 15.1 – The Interstate

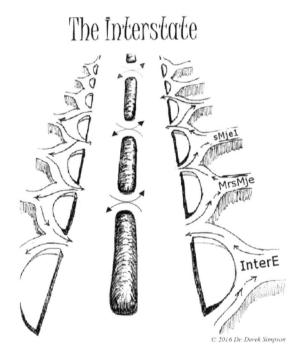

This is the original drawing of Interstate LOC in its primary form.

---

[1] Wise 2004, 32–35.

The Interstate is a level of consciousness (LOC) that is between Añ and NrS. "Inter" meaning "between" and "interstate" representing a road or highway that allows you to travel on while experiencing the various major *samadhi* states as "exit" on/off ramps.

The Interstate itself, not including the exits, is within a category of consciousness called the "Unknown Consciousness" (UCon). It is unknown because it fits in no known category and cannot be described by any language currently spoken on Earth. Angels and angelic beings facilitate movement along the Interstate, and the language used is that of their thoughts. The Interstate is purely represented by ideas as a part of the causal (ideational) cosmos. The "exits" represent the major *samadhi* experiences you will experience as a part of "Spiritualized Consciousness." During this travel, you will also begin to merge with the causal spine, or the *brahmanadi* during your travel on the Interstate, allowing for further release of the causal body.

This unknown conscious state is the literal ideational bridge that exists between the Creator's Cosmic Consciousness (CosCon) and SPIRIT's Spiritualized Consciousness (SpCon). As you get off onto one of these exits, you will enter SpCon. As you ascend to the next exit or major *samadhi* LOC, you will become a part of UCon by traveling on the main Interstate highway. Then, when getting onto the next exit, you become a part of SpCon again. Sometimes, if you are too caught up in delusion or worldly matters, you will remain attuned to the present LOC but will remain in UCon until you can refocus your energies toward the Divine. This waiting period is sometimes necessary, because you may need to remain in the material world to communicate appropriately with those of a lower LOC or level of vibration through household duties. It is also helpful to remain in the UCon if you need to attune to the present LOC. This prevents your consciousness from becoming shocked during the transition from one major *samadhi* exit to the next.

The Interstate itself has been constructed with 44.4 million dimensions to facilitate the movement of souls. The 44.4 million dimensions that exist within this Interstate are all curled upon one another in a "compactified" configuration. "Compactification" is a concept described as a part of string theory. This idea attempts to unify various theories about the multiple dimensions that exist outside of the observable four dimensions. The exact number of dimensions in the universe is currently unknown. However, the precise number has been postulated at ten, eleven, or even twenty-six.[2] The Interstate itself represents this concept and has its own configuration to help illustrate its existence within this dimension-ful universe.

The Interstate's shape is that of a giant trinity knot, one that infinitely loops back onto itself allowing for the fullest expression of the circular infinite space in which it exists. This trinity knot is also referred to as a trefoil knot in mathematical knot theory or a *triquetra*. The *triquetra* is a shape that was originally used by Germanic pagans and as a part of Celtic art in the most notable manuscripts of the Book of Kells. Both Christians and polytheists later used the symbol to represent the Trinity or as the triune deity as "Father," "Son," and "Holy Spirit." In either case, the shape of this Interstate is a continuous loop, helping you to achieve the necessary requirements in the major samadhi to achieve NrS.

Figure 15.2 – Interstate Shape

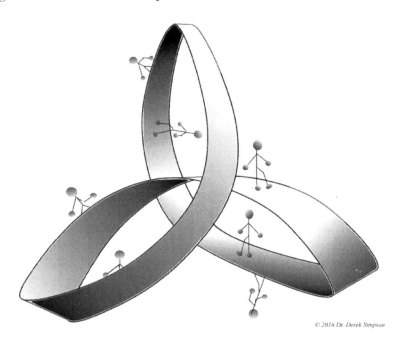

A simplified shape of the Interstate in its secondary enfoldment

---

[2] Kaku 1994.

Along this 44.4 million-dimensional space exist 100 trillion exits along both sides. Odd-numbered exits are on the "right" side and even-numbered on the "left" side. These exits are relative depending on which way you enter the Interstate and the way you decide to travel. This arrangement is meant to be paradoxical, as you are beginning to merge with the non-dual existence of SPIRIT. Each exit represents a three-dimensional space where you can experience another level of SPIRIT's infinite bliss through the samadhi major experience (sMje). Angels or angelic beings facilitate movement along this Interstate. The "44.4" value is representative of their presence along this "inter-" state of consciousness.[†]

Each "I" or soul manifestation of SPIRIT will only go as fast they are meant to go. The Istate itself is made of SPIRIT light so that the I's consciousness will travel very easily. Each "I" or individual can go in either direction on the Istate, and they can turn around to go a different direction. The I's can pass each other as individual ascension increases. Each individual consciousness traveling the Interstate can get on and off as the consciousness becomes aware of the particular exit.

This Istate stretches throughout all of creation but is contained only within this one universe.[‡] You can get an IPASS to get onto the Interstate, but God and gurus can only give it. The IPASS is the initial-pass into sMje, and after this point, you will be able to get on and get off as you please. No speed can be measured, either as a rate, integer, or limit.

In the Dark Ages, there were very few people on Earth traveling on the Istate. In the current present age of 2016 CE, there are a few more than in the past 2000 years. There is high movement and little traffic. During the peak of the golden ages of realization, the Istate is practically in rush hour, with traffic oscillating between a standstill and light speed.

Once you are able to increase your LOC high enough, your consciousness will come back onto the Interstate and travel down to

---

[†] In Doreen Virtue's work on angelic communication through numbers, the number "4" symbolically represents the presence of angels when they are speaking with us. Oddly enough, the number "4" actually looks like an angel with the left side of the "4" being its wings!

[‡] This book assumes that there is only one universe in creation with three layers—physical, subtle (astral), and ideational (causal).

the next available exit that you are becoming attuned to. This process continues until you reach the end the Interstate #1, whereby you will be initiated into NrS and the Extradimensional realm. NrS is referred to as the ultimate level of the Creator's consciousness by some realized masters. However, beyond this level lies an even higher dispensation, only reserved for souls that have a special reason for being there. This is to expound upon many mysteries or help the world to evolve as a whole.

INTEREXPERIENCE (IE)
Value of Level IE = $CC1^{72}$, # of IE Levels = 1
Unknown Consciousness
The first exit along the Interstate is called the "Interexperience," "InterE," or "IE" and is a part of the Unknown Consciousness of the Interstate. This is the first exit along the Interstate. You will develop an elevation in consciousness, thereby gaining entry onto the first exit. This initial exit is fairly simple to attain.

MINOR SAMADHI MAJOR EXPERIENCE (MrsMje)
Value of Level MrsMje = $CC1^{72}$, # of MrsMje Levels = 1
Unknown Consciousness
This is the next intermediary LOC or exit. It exists between IE and sMje proper and is also a part of the Unknown Consciousness. Both the IE and the MrsMje were states of awareness that are used to help attune your consciousness.

SAMADHI MAJOR EXPERIENCE (sMje)
Value of Level sMje = $CC1^{100}$, # of sMje Levels = $9.\overline{98}E^{10}$
sMje 1 = Exit 3 = CC1^1
sMje 2 = Exit 4 = CC1^2
sMje 3 = Exit 5 = CC1^3, etc.
Exits 3 to 1 Billion on Interstate #1
Spiritualized Consciousness
Before you can experience a major *samadhi* consciously, another "Divine Superconscious Experience," or a DSCE, must be initiated in your body. This experience could take many forms, but it will be vastly different then the minor major *samadhi* types of stillness previously experienced. The body, at the very least, will experience full-body

numbness and breathlessness with full awareness. With the expansion of this newfound awareness, you will be overcome with immense joy.

To awaken the ability to experience a conscious major *samadhi*, you must go beyond the pure desire for spiritual. You need to know that the Divine's Joy already exists in yourself and that feeling this Joy will lead to the highest states of realization. It is our submission and humility that the Creator desires. The Divine knows you have willpower; for, without it, it would be impossible to have gotten this far! It is now your love and devotion that the Divine wants. Through this, the Divine will bless you with eternal awareness of ever-new joy.

A person in this state consciously for the first time may have a hard time walking because the bliss is so potent. This may be a first experience of being drunk on God's divine wine. The body, being drawn up like a puppet suddenly frozen in time, will have the purest of all love descend upon it, taking away all pain and suffering. As it lingers you will think, "Is there anything more beautiful?" But even beyond this level of love, there is an infinite level of love to be experienced as ever-new bliss. Similar to the Christ Consciousness, this exit helps to continue the expansion of the heart with the Divine's love. The heart has to expand spiritually if you expect to handle this awesome power.

Practicing scientific meditative techniques while in a major *samadhi* state is very powerful. Any effects will be amplified exponentially, allowing your consciousness to become overwhelmed by the Divine's bliss with massive increases in LOC. You may just stop in the middle of performing your *Kriyas*, because the love is so intense that you can only think about loving God. This is a natural stopping point for the *Kriyas*. However, if the body wants to remain still, do not force it into performing a certain technique, not even the *Kriyas*. Breaking these advanced stages of stillness is detrimental to the progression of your consciousness. Pulling in cosmic energy through the medulla will also help you to achieve stillness more easily, especially if the body needs to be quieted.

Joy will begin to present itself as a feeling at the throat, as this is the love that is ascending from the heart *chakra*, developed initially in the Christ Consciousness LOC. After manifesting a conscious major samadhi experience, you can sleep and wake up again, still holding the same type of God-realization. This is the power of this state of consciousness. However, be careful during intense exercise; the body, at this point, can almost instantly relax itself, which can lead to an immediate drop in blood pressure.

I had a personal experience in China while playing an intense game of badminton against my wife. Needless to say, keeping the body calm and playing intense sports do not mix. Either allow the body to experience the intensity of the game, or exercise moderately with the physical exercises given by the Guru and yogic *asanas* (body postures). The body will use what instrument is necessary to manifest the needs and desires of the body. Whether it is the physical use of the legs, astral hearing to perceive the Holy Vibration *Om*, or causal vision to see the particles within space itself; the instruments are there for your needs.

Other sensations experienced in this state may be a slight burning sensation of the eyes. This sensation warms parts of the body so they don't burn up with the increased intensity of the Divine's Light.

As this Light, stillness, joy, and bliss descend further into the body and mind of the yogi, the body will be able to rely less and less upon physical sustenance and gross vibrational particles for food. Eating physical (earthly) food will become unnecessary for these yogis, who can choose at any time to relinquish the need for consistent meals. Sometimes, the power of *inedia* (non-eating) can be given sooner to the yogi but will appear spontaneously as you discover how to consciously enter into a state of *samyama*.† However, it is not recommended by this book to fast without previous and proper bodily training. Consulting a licensed physician on this matter is necessary before engaging in this practice. If fasting is to become a normal habit, it should be carried out consistently and frequently before one can know how to live by the Divine's Light alone.

This is the first major *samadhi* experience you will be able to attain consciously. To experience the third exit of the Interstate is to experience love itself. This exit presents the emanating love of the Trinity: Creator, Son Consciousness, and the Holy Vibration. This love spreads throughout all of creation.

---

† *Samyama* was explained thoroughly in Chapter 8 on *samadhi*. Later in Chapter 17, *samyama* will be described as a way to gain supernatural power, if it is the true desire of the yogi.

Difference Between Minor and Major Samadhi (sMje):

- Joy is overwhelmingly larger in sMje, leading to automatic bliss.
- The body is at the command of the consciousness, allowing for more physical pliability and instant alignment.
- While in a sMje, thoughts are no longer your own but you become manifested as a Divine superconscious receiver.

Essentials

You still need to maintain moderation in diet. You cannot be completely free of this physical/behavioral ego influence, whether good or bad, until you have merged completely with the Divine Superconsciousness of SPIRIT. During any kind of eating, you must maintain mindfulness while you are consciously holding a major *samadhi* experience. Otherwise, the experience will be lost.

Suffering will still manifest itself in your body. This suffering is necessary, as it will propel the consciousness toward higher and higher realizations. Participating in the physical world, while in an sMje, in its many activities, such as eating in an extreme way or watching violent TV shows/movies, will still affect the consciousness. You have to be in the Divine Consciousness before these things will start to have little effect in an indefinite amount. The category of Divine Consciousness embodies The Aionion State which is beyond *sahaja samadhi*; *sahaja* being the highest known *samadhi* state, until now. However, even in Divine Consciousness, under prolonged exposure, the mind will lose its temporary perception of God and drop back into the baseline consciousness of the state experienced. The yogi, while in a divinely conscious state, has access to all instruments of the three bodies, whether physical, astral, or causal.

SAMADHI MAJOR EXP TRANSITION STATE #1 (sMje-T1)

Value of Level sMje-T1 = $CC1^{CC1}$, # of sMje-T1 Levels = 1,000,000 Spiritualized Consciousness

This transitional state occurs between levels 999,999,999 and 1,000,000,000 sMje. Within this last level of sMje before NrS, there are 1,000,000 levels. Each level measures at $CC1^{100}$. This transition state should be attuned to fairly quickly, considering the Interexperience exit and Minor Major Samadhi exit was at $CC1^{72}$.

This state brings on the feeling of lightness and looseness of the bodily temple to the point where yogic *asanas* of difficult complexity will be performed with ease. For those yogis primarily interested in meditation, this includes *ardha padmasana* (half-lotus) and *padmasana* (full lotus).

You may also begin to the feel joy of God manifesting in the mouth. It feels like you are biting into a jelly or custard donut. It makes you feel physically and mentally really great, but leaves the mouth and body with an "ooey-gooey" feeling. This is the beginning of the dripping divine nectar *amrita*. You know you are close to the Creator and the *nirvikalpa* state when this feeling arises.

In this transitional state, the ego consciousness still attempts to drag down your elevated spiritualizing consciousness into the body. This "devil" nature will continue to try to insert delusional thoughts of violence and drama into your mind during this time. These could possibly include thoughts of grandeur with great yogic *siddhis* (powers). All great masters have been tempted by the ego in various ways. Jesus the Christ was tempted by the devil in the Gospel of Matthew.[3] The same goes for the Buddha, who was tempted by Mara, the Evil-one, which occurred moments before he achieved enlightenment.[4] There are also stories of the Sri Bhagavan Krishna, the Christ of India, being tempted in the wilderness three times[†] as well.

All these cases illustrate the same point: if you truly desire God, for God Himself, then your prize will be, at the very least, ever-new joy and the bliss of God-realization.

You can use the Cosmic Energy Technique to increase the stillness of the mind and body, inducing a more instantaneous major *samadhi* state. Meditating morning and night with the full barrage of techniques is going to be necessary to ascend in consciousness. Willpower must be at its greatest height to transcend to NrS. This Samadhi Major Experience Transitional State, although only the first, is the most difficult to attune to completely.

It is also necessary to know how to clear yourself of dark forces. Using John Livingston's work as a base will be necessary. His book,

---

[3] Matthew 4:1–11 NASB
[4] Stache-Rosen (n.d.).
† The Lord Krishna is said to have been tempted just like Jesus the Christ. However, it is noted that the "tempter" is, in fact, the "ego," which is battling for spiritual ground as you ascend in consciousness.

Adversaries Walk Among Us, is a necessary resource when trying to ascend.[5] You can also use the gurus to help you ascend, if this is all you believe in; however, there are powers beyond our control that attempt to prevent you from your ultimate goal of self-realization. Your job, as the devotee, is to give them the best fight of your life!

You must give up everything to find God. God knows every thought that you think. It is up to you, to show Him, that He is your greatest desire of all.

SAMADHI MAJOR EXP TRANSITION STATE #2 (sMje-T2)

Value of Level sMje-T2 = .9 - .99 - .999 - .9999, etc.
\# of sMje-T2 Levels = $CC1^{CC1}$
Spiritualized Consciousness
This transitional state occurs between: levels 999,999,999.9 and 999,999,999.$\overline{}$9, as the "9" repeats for $CC1^{CC1}$ times. It is easily transcended and generally forgotten about, because the first transitional state is more difficult to transcend.

At this point, you are now waiting for the Divine to provide everlasting relief from the delusion of this world. You need only to continue to remember to give up everything to the Lord of all Lords. Ask the gurus, angels, and/or spirit guides to provide spiritual relief and ease of transition. Once you let go, the Creator will provide the transition when it is at your highest good and the highest good of all those who are around you. Remember, the gift of this state is one of the fullest-types of realizations possible. It will not only change you, but all those who come in contact with this consciousness. It is not for one; it is for all.

---

[5] Livingston 2004.

CHAPTER 16

Extradimensional LOCs

The extradimensional realm includes both *nirvikalpa* and *sahaja samadhi*. These two are the highest levels of consciousness (LOCs) that can be achieved in the process of becoming self-realized.

The Extradimensional Realm is a part of reality that goes outside the normal three dimensions of length, width, and height. It is also outside of most of reality itself—whether it is physical, astral (subtle), or causal (ideational). These types of samadhis are very close to the actual existence of the Creator itself, which is external to creation. Hence, it is "extra"-dimensional.

The last realm is referred to as the "Uni-A-Dimensional" Realm. This is the "place" where SPIRIT lies in perfect bliss consciousness, without desire to create. It is achieved when you go to sleep at night or are able to access a Divine Superconscious Experience (DSCE) willfully or by the Divine's will. It is "Uni-"dimensional because it unifies both SPIRIT with the desire to create as the Creator along with its creation itself. It is "A"-dimensional because it is not in existence at all; it is totally without attachment to the nature of reality. As SPIRIT, it is not for or against creating or creation. It is just the state of being.

It exists as pure consciousness alone, one that is accessible first through the DSCE, then as *anantya* willfully in *nirvikalpa samadhi,* and finally, permanently, spontaneously, naturally, and easily in *sahaja samadhi.*

NIRVIKALPA SAMADHI (NrS)

Value of Level NrS = $CC1^{(CC1\wedge 1E100)}$, # of NrS Levels = $1E^{12}$
Spiritualized Consciousness

As mentioned before, *nirvikalpa samadhi* (NrS) is just another name for *asamprajñata* (Añ), according to some of the oldest and most revered texts on yoga. However, NrS is the end stage of this two-part transition.

NrS is classified as a state of non-dual consciousness that is truly the highest goal of yoga.[1] Although this state of non-dual consciousness is difficult to attain normally, this *samadhi* allows you to easily enter into non-duality. This is one of its major hallmarks. It is understood that NrS is the knowing of yourself as the infinite SPIRIT while also experiencing Its multitude of physical, astral, and causal creation.

The difference between *savikalpa* (SaS) and *nirvikalpa* (NrS) is that the lower self (ego) will immerse itself into the Highest Self (SPIRIT), allowing for you to become aware that the two selves are really a whole. In NrS, you go deeper, but the true reality of nature is revealed. You will truly know yourself as both SPIRIT and creation as one.[2] This understanding is what allows for real joy to manifest itself. This is the bliss consciousness of *nirvikalpa*, able to ever transcend the ups and downs of life. You will lose little to none of this bliss, especially if you remain focused.[3]

In my own current personal experience, I am able to maintain *nirvikalpa samadhi* by giving all my attention to the third eye. With this little attention, great waves of bliss engulf my consciousness. This bliss occurs most often while writing this book, watching the TV, playing a video game, walking in public, or even riding a bike! God's bliss is really in every part of creation and can be experienced by choice by the willful and devoted yogi. It can be achievable everywhere and by everyone—no exceptions.

---

[1] Patanjali's *Yoga Sutras* I.3
[2] Yogananda 2005, 86.
[3] Yogananda 2001, 101.

Attuning yourself to Añ is the 1st transition, allowing you to accustom yourself to the many parts of the Divine's Love. Then, you realize that there is still an Interstate between Añ and NrS. This Interstate helps to evolve your consciousness in the variations of major *samadhi*, or major stillness. This state has been long forgotten because many self-realized yogis are easily able to transcend the Interstate with fewer major *samadhi* experiences. This transcendence allows them to become the Creator's Love almost instantly. But for the people of this current Earth era (present day), the transition period of the Interstate is necessary to experience both the ultimate love of God and His stillness combined as one. This is the kingdom [of heaven] that the apostle Matthew talks about, "Then the King will say to those on His right, 'Come, you who are blessed of My Father, inherit the kingdom prepared for you from the foundation of the world.'"[4]

Those who inherit this divine Kingdom, express the Divine in their environment as personality, form, and action. God's character has always been a part of yourself as the soul. This piece of SPIRIT (Creator without desire to create) is inside of the physical shell of the human being. In this way, the character (soul) and personality (shell) are fusing into one entity. You are becoming less and less associated with ego and the inherited astrological forces as a result.

As mentioned before, various layers cover the body allowing the soul to express itself in a multitude of ways. These were described in the sections on Christ and Cosmic Consciousness. As you express the many forms of NrS, the bliss sheath, *anandamaya (chitta) kosha*, or the causal body covering, will slowly reveal the soul a little at a time. When this *kosha* becomes uncovered for even a small period of time, you will perceive God and SPIRIT in a state of non-duality. Once this covering is fully shed in *sahaja samadhi* (SS), you will experience supreme non-dual bliss at any time. This view of the Divine is the purest version. The pure Light of the soul shining through, a little at a time, will eventually dissolve the necessity of the causal body covering, revealing the true nature of everything.

Difference Between NrS and Interstate

The rise and fall of the LOC in NrS versus the sMje (initial major *samadhi* state) are quite different from each other. One originated on

---

[4] Matthew 25:34 NASB

the Interstate while the other is the ultimate goal of yoga. You can drop and rise within sMje but never drop within NrS levels, because sMje is like a measure of impermanence or transiency. NrS is the true level of permanence.

The Interstate represents an actual highway within NrS. Highways are fairly permanent in the physical world, and so, this permanence is directly related to its own symbolism of solid concrete and iron rebar construction. The exits of the Interstate themselves change as you continue down the Interstate in either direction. In this way, the impermanence is related to the fact that things are always changing with these various sMje exits. The consciousness can drop to the Interstate #2 but cannot drop into the Interstate #1, because this goes beyond the permanence of NrS.

Experiences of NrS

The sensations experienced in NrS are unlike any other level previously experienced. The yogi, having the divine privilege of entering this state of consciousness, will be able to manifest an infinite amount of joy at any time.

Initially, after ascending into NrS, an increased lightness and looseness will be associated easily with the body. This feeling will manifest easily with little focus and relaxation. The spine will become naturally straighter because the Divine's Joy is permanently imbedded into the very causal and astral matrices that make up the physical spinal column. With the spine being straighter, you may feel taller and in fact, more confident. This Joy provides you supreme control over the emotions, allowing you to perform any task easily and without disruption of the joy within. If there are genetic or physical traumas of the body that could not be healed by conventional medicines, NrS will be a true healing salve for you. This trauma could range from food attachments, phobias, skin disorders, or even genetic issues of color blindness or the inability to create children. There is nothing that cannot be healed by the manifestation of SPIRIT as Joy.

The speed at which you enter the stillness of *samadhi* is uncanny. The stillness will progress from the feet and hands to the jaw and head, and finally the eyes themselves will become still. Passing into the breathless state will feel like mere child's play as you ascend. You will truly feel like you can perform magic or have powers beyond that of a normal human being. Some will gain even greater sensitivity to the thoughts of others, manifesting ESP-like abilities in the expression of divine intuition.

These sensations and abilities can develop generally or more specifically, depending on your life path, needs, and personal desires. Although you have the Divine's Joy, this does not mean you do not still desire. But the desires are now guided supremely by the Divine's will, allowing the individual to operate solely on SPIRIT alone. With this direct guidance, the third eye will just explode with bliss. So enamored you will be, that you will wonder why God would not be the ultimate desire always.

When your body closes in on *kaivalya* (true liberation from the causal body), both sides of the nasal cavity become wide open so that air can easily pass through. This adaptation occurs because you are entering into the breathless state, or non-dual reality. It is accompanied by a mild pulsating feeling at the median of the nose. There are many other sensations to be experienced, but most are personal to the individual experiencing them.

To ascend in NrS is to attempt to manifest its hallmark at all times. This hallmark is unlimited joy and bliss that is almost instantly accessible. It must be sought out every day if you are to manifest the highest nature of self-realization. You can do it without taking away from the purity of Creator's consciousness. Maybe you can watch a fun, cute movie that helps to manifest a joyful state. Maybe it is OK to eat a sweet thing once in a while to help bring the consciousness up, especially when it is struggling.

If you are struggling too much as a householder, then you may not be getting the point of living in moderation. Moderation in meditation and lifestyle is necessary while you are a householder. It is obviously more difficult to reach self-realization as a householder, but if you are disciplined, the gains are incredibly faster and larger than your life as an ascetic or renunciant. Householders do not necessarily have gurus that they can turn to in the physical form to help them ascend to the next level. They need to fully rely upon their metaphysical belief in God and gurus, especially during this particular Earth era. Being a part of an organization that performs special techniques may assist to evolve the householder's body and mind. Such exercises are still necessary, but may not be performed quite as often and regularly when you have achieved *nirvikalpa samadhi*.

Another hallmark of this state includes innate protection from negative consciousness. This mostly includes metaphysical negative energies that are used by ego or delusive entities to prevent you from ascending. The joy obtained in NrS acts like divine protection against those negative energetic influences. As seen in SaS (*savikalpa*), prayers or some other protection were needed on the body to prevent negative energies from affecting the sensitive consciousness of the elevating yogi. Now, these "talismans" are no longer needed, as the joy manifested can clear those energies instantly. If you would like extra protection, talismans are best worn at night in order to prevent unwanted negative energies from flooding in to your unconscious mind while sleeping. If deep ecstatic joy is maintained for long periods of time before sleep, it is enough to keep away even the fiercest of foes. You need to understand that just because joy can be manifested, doesn't mean it is there automatically. Focus still needs to be provided to the third eye with consistent meditations to keep this joy alive.

During this state of NrS, you may still have negative habits, because you have not lost the causal body completely. This behavioral issue may prevent your ultimate realization into the non-duality of NrS. These habits are not fully removed until the causal body is shed in the second level of SS (*sahaja samadhi*). Also, the ego is still present! It is surprising that you could be so enamored by God's joy and still be affected by the ego. At this point, the soulic nucleus has such a strong pull on your consciousness that you barely feel the pull of ego. The subtlety of the *nirvikalpa* contributes to the soul's power over your consciousness.

However, do not be fooled! You are not free of ego until you have transcended NrS. At this point, the ego still rules the causal body, but the soul rules the physical and astral bodies. Ego is also present in the dream state called "Dream SuperUnConsciousness." It is "super" because you can do anything in your dreams, and it is "unconsciousness," because a person enters into it by sleep, which is the natural result of the day's own conscious actions.

INTERSTATE #2 (IState #2)
Value of Level Istate #2 = 1, # of Istate #2 Levels = 1
Spiritualized Consciousness
This is the second part of the Interstate originally described in Chapter 15. This consciousness is the "inter-" state that will continue to

transition you from NrS to SS by attuning you to almost a 100 trillion more major *samadhi* experiences. This will continually upgrade your mind and body so that it may merge with the Divine's Love, shed the causal body, and help you to know yourself as SPIRIT.

NON-DUAL/DUAL CONSCIOUS RAJAN sMje

DCR-sMje = Dual Consciousness Rajan Samadhi Major Experience
NDCR-sMje = Non-Dual Consciousness Rajan Samadhi Major Experience
Non-Dual/Dual Conscious Rajan Samadhi Major Experience (sMje)
Value of Level NDCR/DCR-sMje = $CC1^{[CC1\wedge(1E100)]}/CC1^{[CC1\wedge(1E100)]}$
# of NDCR/DCR-sMje Levels = $9.9999E^{13}$ (99.$\overline{9}$ Trillion)
sMje 1 Billion = Exit 1 Billion and 3 = $CC1^{1\ Billion}$
sMje 1 Billion and 1 = Exit 1 Billion and 4 = $CC1^{1\ Billion\ and\ 1}$
sMje 1 Billion and 2 = Exit 1 Billion and 5 = $CC1^{1\ Billion\ and\ 2}$, etc.
Exits 1 Billion and 3 to 100 Trillion on Interstate #2
Spiritualized Consciousness

Dual and non-dual consciousness describes the major *samadhi* experience in *nirvikalpa* (NrS). Duality is the oppositional difference that exists in all of creation. Creation, that is the universe and everything in it, must have a perceived difference between light and dark, good and evil, white and black for creation to exist at all. Without this difference, physical matter could be not solid, and water could not be a liquid. All would just blend together, and the forces that maintain creation would fall apart. These different forces are what allow creation to exist.

There is a non-dual counterpart of duality which exists beyond creation. That is the Creator. This non-dual perspective exists outside of the boundaries of its creation. It would be like a human being (creator) drawing a three-dimensional image on a piece of paper (creation). The human being can create the laws necessary to allow for the creation to exist. The creation has color, created by writing utensils, and has form that is initially manifested in the mind of the creator or human being. Duality is the three-dimensional image, while non-duality is the Creator (artist). These concepts are imbedded into the experience of the major samadhi states of NrS as you experience the nature of a dual and non-dual consciousness.

The major *samadhi* state of NrS is the *rajan* or "king" (in Sanskrit) of all *samadhis* experienced. It is the first state of consciousness that you can actively gain full self-realization by entering into a state of non-duality. This full self-realization is referred more specifically as God-realization. In this type of self-realization, you have realized the Creator God in all His divine glory and eternal nature. To this point, you have only been able to attain partial self-realization with ascension to major *samadhi* on the first part of Interstate. This type of *samadhi* on the first part of the Interstate is dualistic in nature.

Initially, you only experience a dual state *samadhi*, in which you are aware of yourself existing as creation but with the mind of the Creator. You are aware of both SPIRIT and the body/ego consciousness at the same time while in this state. Now, instead of seeing them as separate as in the lesser minor *samadhi* states and below, you see them all as one entity. This experience is similar to the minor major *samadhi* (MrsMje) experienced in *asamprajñata* (Añ), because Añ *samadhi* is a part of the Creator's Cosmic Consciousness (CosCon). This dual state *samadhi* or dual consciousness is permeated with joy that is always abundantly available. This joy stays with you throughout future experiences and will never leave. This dual consciousness is the baseline state that is now forever present in the yogi's mind. This baseline is not the *rajan*-type of *samadhi* that allows you to ascend between dualism and non-dualism. Joy is still present here, but it is not as intense as the *rajan*-type.

As you ascend, you can begin to develop non-dual consciousness intermittently. This consciousness is where you can experience SPIRIT in all of its fullness. In non-duality, there is no more individuality between soul and SPIRIT. The individual is, in fact, no longer an individual but is merged for a short time in a full SPIRIT-conscious awareness. In other words, you have lost complete body awareness and truly perceive and are the existence of all creation and beyond creation as a part of SPIRIT. You may know and act accordingly with wisdom that you are God,† and thus, have pure understanding. This understanding leads to some or many awakenings or awakening

---

† This statement is a difficult concept to understand. Realize that beyond the dualistic nature of the three-dimensional universe lies an infinitely vast space of non-duality. This is where SPIRIT lies. SPIRIT with the desire to create becomes the Creator. The Creator in Its vast intelligence wants to experience Itself through Itself. The only way to do this is to make smaller parts of Itself, as a part of an infinitely larger creation. This is how you can say you are not only a piece of God (the Creator), but God Itself.

experiences. But to become merged with God in the highest realization, is to truly realize completely Who, What, When, Where, Why, How, and How Much God truly is. And without the awareness of this non-dual reality, you could never really know the infinite reality of SPIRIT, because SPIRIT can reveal itself in an infinite amount of ways.

The time frame you can remain in a non-dual conscious *rajan* (NDCR) is dependent on your willpower to maintain a state of non-duality through right living and focus on God and Gurus. Generally, you can stay immersed in this non-dual consciousness for seconds, minutes, hours, days, or even for weeks at higher NrS LOCs. NDCR may not occur consistently, because, most of the time, sleep interrupts the process. But you will be able to enter NDCR easily, if you kept the consciousness as long as possible during your nightly meditations. You can usually start to enter NDCR at sMje 99 trillion at random. NDCR can occur before this at sMje 1 billion, but the chance is less likely. When you achieve sMje 99.¯9 trillion, you can begin to enter NDCR at will with conscious control.

The boundary between these two states is as subtle as the difference between absolute silence and the gentility of a humming heater. As soon as the heater stops, your mind will step one foot into NDCR, like walking through a door or stepping one foot into a shallow pool of water. This boundary could be analogous to the thinness of rice paper or the width of a hair. This edge, so imperceptible in nature, when crossed and merged in your body and consciousness, could forever remove the boundary of one world from another; from duality to non-duality. The *buddhi,* or intelligence of the soul, cuts the boundary between dimensions inside the landscape of the mind, allowing for non-duality to blur edges and lines between that of ego (*ahamkara*) and SPIRIT (*Sat*).

This blurring of the edges allows the *Om* to filter in through the silence to help you attain NDCR instantly. It is *Om* that will bring you to SPIRIT's consciousness. As you step in and out of *Om*, your LOC will rise and fall. This fluctuation occurs because you are stepping in and out of this subtle boundary between duality and non-duality.

This all occurs in 4 major steps:
1. As a being rises from DCR (dual-conscious *rajan*) to NDCR, the third eye becomes energized, and the neck very stiff. The energy rising to the third eye is so intense that the eyes must

squint. The eyes do not close completely because the soul wants to always be immersed in NDCR, as this is its ultimate reality. The world that is perceived with the physical eyes, at this moment in realization, is still one of duality.

2. In the next step, all you have to do is close your eyes in a place of silence and listen. With this listening, a tingling may be heard with the possibility of just a little white noise. As you progressively gain realization and immersion in the sound of this white noise, a soft rumbling will be heard, steadily increasing to a loud roar of rushing water. This roar of sound usually only occurs at the deepest parts of *Om* and at the peak of NDCR.

3. As you descend from the peak of NDCR, the *Om* becomes more difficult to hear, and the rumbling sound decreases to only white noise. At last, as the meditator arises from the plane of meditation, the *Om* silently disappears into the background. The *Om* patiently waits again for you to still your mind and body for just another peek into the infinite parts of the *Om* sMje.

4. Finally, as you move throughout the day, God's consciousness of love, peace, and joy stay with the body and mind as everlasting bliss in the state of DCR. It is very difficult to drop from this LOC, even temporarily, after one has achieved the peak of NDCR.

Although it is difficult for you to drop from DCR to the baseline *samadhi* state of the Interstate #2, it may still occur. Using the instruments of the physical body to perceive gross matter, you can still decrease in LOC very easily. Small amounts of impure foods may have little effect on the body and your consciousness, but eating and perceiving indiscriminately will surely lead to great decreases in LOC. You may decrease in LOC with too much loss of the sexual force through ejaculation. However, NrS can provide you with a sexual *samadhi* with an increase in LOC, if performed correctly. By continued use of the physical body instruments, you can be swept up into the delusion of the world for a short time. But even during these LOC drops, you generally come back to your spiritual senses, realizing that nothing in this material world can really provide long-lasting benefit.

You can see that an MrsMje of Añ pales in comparison to the joy experienced of a DCR-sMje, while even the DCR-sMje will pale in comparison to that of even seconds in a NDCR-sMje. In NDCR-sMje, a non-dual existence, you will melt back into the "a-existence" of SPIRIT. In this way, "a-existence" is where SPIRIT exists beyond existence or creation. A-existence is an absence of and/or an indifference toward creation itself. SPIRIT is indifferent, because It exists as pure bliss consciousness without desire. Remember, creation is a part of SPIRIT, and without SPIRIT, it would not hold its form in matter, energy, or thought. The Creator that creates creation is essential SPIRIT with desire to create. Without this desire, no physical, astral, or causal substance could exist.

A-existence is used here to help create a conceptual thought process connecting the difference between something that is within existence versus something that is beyond existence, not against existence per se. SPIRIT also has an impersonal association to that existence. This is why, commonly, self-realized masters appear to be lovingly impersonal, because they identify wholly with

If you can maintain a NDCR-sMje in the presence of others, then real SPIRIT. They see as SPIRIT does, beyond even the desire to create. changes within those bodies surrounding you will take place, because the body is now fully manifesting the presence of the Divine in its purest form. Only God can change a man's heart, whether it is manifest in a guru, saint or great teacher. NDCR has the power to change bad into good at will, if the consciousness is willing to receive the change. Therefore, NDCR is granted to only those who it is meant for. Not everyone has been born with a mind to do good all the time, but the mind can develop a will for good and thus, a will for manifesting self-realization.

Ascension in NrS is possible when you are able to contact the non-dual version of this *rajan samadhi* state through the spiritual eye. This non-dual experience is where the sMje occurs at its highest point or peak. At this point, all the energy in the *chakras* is transmitted to the spiritual eye and immediately ascends to the seventh *chakra* to help the body attune itself to higher LOCs. You can ascend while a part of a DCR-sMje, but it just occurs more slowly.

The LOC can increase while doing various types of activities. Commonly, if you write your experiences down in a journal or read a spiritually based text, the body can go in and out of the NDCR without warning. This occurs because you are becoming attuned to the thoughts of the spiritual text. All spiritually-based text, especially that of the self-realized gurus—whether it is the Bible, *Bhagavad Gita*, or other sacred texts—is all inspired text of the highest awareness of SPIRIT.

Don't be fooled, however, because reading spiritual text alone will not bring you in *nirvikalpa* and back. It generally takes years and years of dedicated and devotional, disciplined meditation to achieve *nirvikalpa*—assuming, of course, that your past lives have earned you such an existence. I am not saying this to discourage you, but realize that the peoples of the Earth are just coming into awareness that they are also divine—no matter where you come from, what color your skin, or with what gender you identify. In this way, we are equal in God's eyes and are all deserving of this great state of realization.

Posturally, the body will take on a flexed position, which also affects the stillness of the body. There is a tipping point between full flexion of the head and just subtle flexion. If you maintain a fully straight spine, the energy can flow more easily. When the head is slightly flexed forward, the energy becomes mildly impeded to the forward posture of the neck and intensifies the feeling of "stiffness" in the neck. This is not true physical stiffness in the muscle or joints, but a subtle pulling on the head that makes you feel like you are a puppet on a marionette. This is a good sensation and should be not be considered negative.

Another great activator of LOC is silence. Silence brings on the sound of *Om*, which allows you to go deeper into awareness. At this point, *Om* may be heard as white noise or a soft rumbling. You may also hear the sounds of the *chakras*. All of these are good, especially if they are heard without an *Om*-hearing technique. Hearing the *Om* in these various ways is a sign that you are beginning to perceive non-duality automatically.

Below are some important LOC milestones to achieve while ascending in NrS. Remember, at this point, the focus is on the sMje ascension. The separate value measured in NrS will increase until NrS9.9 and until sMje reaches 99.0 Trillion. At this point, NrS will continue to increase on its own until its own maximum of 1 Trillion.

sMje 55.9 Trillion – You and *Om* merge and become one.
This merger is an *Om*-NDCR-sMje, or, essentially, an *Om* (major) *samadhi*. The body will massively perceive the sound of *Om*. Every other sound is drowned out by its universal creative nature. It will blaze in your consciousness, and the sound of rushing water will be heard. Even with a little focus, the *Om* will easily blaze in the ears when no other loud noise is heard. Eventually, the sound will be heard even when there are loud noises occurring around your body. It is best if those noises occurring around you are continuous in nature, like a heater, AC unit, soft conversation, or the white noise of the passing world. This is why meditation is best done in silence, but is strived for in the noisy concrete jungles of the world.

Focusing on *Om* will help the consciousness to ascend more quickly, because this *Om samadhi* is an NDCR-type. This is an active way to obtain a portion of the NDCR *samadhi* and thus, the fullest version of a NrS NDCR *samadhi* state. Realize, at this point, your attunement status is "self-realized child of God." Don't forget this! You have to continually beat down heaven's door to gain access to the most prized possession of all. Now that you have God's joy, does it make sense to allow it to slip away? It is all up to you to continue to demand your birthright and not forget where you stand.

Through the merger with the *Om* and NDCR, you will finally begin to see eye-to-eye with the gurus of self-realization. This is not in the way that one is greater than the other, but that we all have our roles to play with definite earthly finality. Believe, and you will receive.

sMje 99 Trillion – This level equals sMje = 99,000,000,000,000.0
You will be able to access the NDCR fully, but intermittently, at the will of the Divine. The body's energy, past 99 trillion, will bound infinitely. As long as the yogi householder is practicing limited ejaculations, the energy contained within your *chakras* will allow for ascension to occur more quickly. You can use the ejaculation for a sexual *samadhi*, and thus, a subsequent increase in LOC, but this process still has to be done carefully and with control. Sexual activity is still the most important denominator in maintaining the highest realizations. Continued minimal ejaculations equal increased possibility for *moksha*, spiritual release, or liberation.

With this intense energy, you can feel very powerful and energetic, but remember to remain humble at all times. If humility is not maintained during these most crucial LOC-elevating moments, you will experience a proverbial slap in the face to remind the body of the necessity of mindful maintenance. The energy emitted from the mind while in NrS, at a higher level, is very powerful.

The Law of Attraction, described by Esther and Jerry Hicks, says that our own thoughts are physical things that can acquiesce very easily into our physical reality. These thoughts can manifest now more quickly than ever. One negative or selfish thought can lead you to experience an oncoming of bodily pain or suffering. Karma still applies to you, but it occurs almost instantly.

For example, if you have cyclical thoughts of negativity, it could result in the stubbing of a toe or the jamming of the finger. In this way, the mind is moving upstream thought-wise, against the current of positive self-realization. By doing so, you create eddy currents in the stream, leading to a stagnant or possibly injurious situation. The necessity for mindfulness now will ever increase in intensity. Slow and considerate is the surest path towards the highest realizations.

Many sensations are felt during this great rise in LOC, from duality to non-duality. These sensations are provided to help all who ascend in self-realization understand that there are many layers to this process. While you are in NrS, especially at the beginning stages, joy is abundant. However, true bliss has yet to really show its true nature. Bliss will become more apparent as you achieve the peak of NDCR. But bliss can still be felt increasingly as you dive deep in meditation. The deeper you go, the greater the experience, and the longer the endless stream of bliss runs to create an endless opportunity to create more joy. At times, you may think that you could float away at the very thought of this joy.

Another common sensation experienced is an icy-coldness of the extremities, especially if you are outside performing housework or yard work in a cold environment. The sensation occurs because life force is being drawn up into the spine. This icy-coldness is a positive sensation, and it should not be confused for anything that might be detrimental or injurious towards the physical body.

Usually the sensation is experienced when there is no obvious reason, such as a physical disease, for its. The feet may be quite covered in socks and shoes, and still, this sensation persists. In this way, the ascending consciousness of the yogi is actively drawing life force from the extremities to the spine. This is generally why many yogis enjoy the heat, as it allows them more comfort when the bodily energy is culminated centrally in the spinal column. However, it has been noted by Swami Sivananda,[5] that he enjoyed meditating more often in cold weather. I suspect this is because the cold air against the body creates a slower molecular movement, which would induce a greater level of physical stillness.

As I edit the last few chapters of this book, I am living in Montana in a sub-level apartment. Most people heat their homes up to 70°F or 75°F, but we keep our place between 55°F and 60°F in the winter. Sometimes, it can get a little cold, but I have noticed greater benefits in my relaxation. I can generally quiet the body faster and achieve the greatest level of stillness because I am forced to get used to the colder weather.

There are times, more often as you ascend, that you can feel completely normal one moment, but instantaneously go into a full NDCR in the next moment. However, without sheer silence, the rumbling of *Om* in the mind's ear would be supremely difficult to hear and thus the continuation of the NDCR *samadhi*.

The longer period of time you stay in a NDCR, the greater the experience. You may feel the body shift in and out of existence or even change form. Your arms may feel large, small, long, and short all at the same time. The feet may feel numb and cold but very light because of the extreme pull of life-force going to the third eye. This life force being pulled to the crown (seventh) *chakra* will help to re-atomize the body's cells to attune to higher and higher LOCs.

As explained before, thoughts will manifest more quickly, and in many ways, the universe will be at the command of your thoughts. As with any good spiritual scientist, these thought patterns should be tested in every way. *Om* may be so intense that the sound is like standing next to a great waterfall. You must urge your mind to ascend the consciousness higher and deeper, higher and deeper, until the NDCR can be manifested at will. In a NDCR, "deeper" is very *yin*, or feminine, and "higher" is very *yang*, or masculine. These seemingly opposite sides of the spectrum will ever blend together in the NDCR. These thoughts of "deeper" and "higher" will help you to ascend more quickly. But both are required to manifest an even more deep and joyful meditation.

---

[5] Sivananda 2006.

You will continue to ascend until you are able to enter NDCR at will; as this is what is required of true God-realization. At this point, ego still rules the causal body, but it becomes relinquished as the body enters NDCR. Once you are able to permanently enter this state, ego will no longer have any hold on the body.

sMje 99.⁻9 Trillion – This level equals sMje = 99,999,999,999,999
When you have achieved this level of *samadhi*, you will be able to willfully achieve an NDCR-sMje at any time. You may be seated in meditation or walking down the street. At this point, either one is possible. The very top of this sMje is very similar to *anantya* described in Chapter 8 on *samadhi*. *Anantya* is the conscious form of *turiya* allowing for you to become infinitely blissful while performing any activity; the bliss overflows at every moment without end. You are permanently entranced in a drunken state of conscious bliss.

Sensations felt while willfully gaining a NDCR are monumental on their own. The vibration of the third eye will take on a larger presence in the body. By opening it and gaining access to the NDCR, the sensation felt there is no longer one of tension, but as a great event to behold. This great event will help you to feel the pull of the consciousness upwards and inwards with little effort. The body will feel light and even agile in this meditative state. The state of breathing is generally one that is breathless, and the sinuses are cleared easily. Joy, *Om*, and stillness are all abundant in nature; with little focus, the neck stiffens, and—voila! Magic happens.

Divine Nectar of NrS

The measurement of each level of an NDCR-sMje is $CC1^{[CC1\wedge(1E100)]}$. The last portion of this measurement, "$1E^{100}$," is what helps to bring on this "greater sensation." Each NDCR-sMje level, which number from 1 billion to 100 trillion, can be measured from "1" to the very top of the $CC1^{[CC1\wedge(1E100)]}$.

However, when you arrive at the end of "$1E^{100}$," your consciousness is lifted into the "ecstatic state" or the Ecstatic Consciousness (EC). This is the peak of a NDCR-sMje and occurs at "$1E^{99}$." If your LOC continues to "$1E^{100}$," then you will ascend to the next whole level of NDCR-sMje.

EC, in this case, is the general term for the state of ecstasy. This is the quintessential state of NDCR-sMje in a form that includes an *Om samadhi*, astral *samadhi*, or a combination of both. Ecstasy is the same as *anantya*, as described in the previous section.

As this EC manifests, a divine nectar begins to drip down in the back of the throat, causing large waves of bliss to overcome the mind. The nectar is referred to as *amrita*. In Greek mythology, *amrita* is also known as ambrosia, the drink of the Gods. This divine wine would grant longevity or immortality to the individual who drank it.[6]

When the *amrita* begins to flow, you are at the highest LOC value of one NDCR-sMje level, occurring at $1E^{99}$. This divine drip is the same as the EC or brings on the highest version of the Ecstatic Consciousness in NrS. This divinely dripping nectar could also occur spontaneously as a part of the NDCR from sMje 1 billion upwards to sMje 99 trillion, but it occurs less often. Also, ascension is a direct occurrence of this divine drip. If you feel the drip, then the LOC will rise as a direct result. This drip will cause your jaw to move slowly and without control, because you are actively and unconsciously (without conscious awareness, although presently conscious) tasting the sweet nectar manifesting in the oral cavity. This slow, uncontrolled movement usually occurs while you are consciously performing household duties in the Ecstatic Consciousness.

This is the true nature of self-realization at its fullest. You can experience stillness, peace, joy, and bliss, but without this divine nectar, you cannot ever be truly and fully realized. This divine nectar, that is originally activated by the awakened *kundalini*,[7] drips onto the tongue, causing such joyous sensations to ring throughout your entire being. The mere activation of such a divinely bestowed gift allows for the deepest level of devotion towards SPIRIT. Through this ambrosial offering, even greater love for God will blossom through active, thoughtful, devotional prayer to the Divine.

The *amrita* is what will eventually transform the body into a permanent, living temple for SPIRIT's consciousness. Only a portion of it can really be felt in the *savikalpa samadhi* when it is originally activated. As you progress and reach the highest goal of yoga, *nirvikalpa*, this sweet nectar can be manifested at will to gain great yogic power. The nectar quenches all desires for sweet things on this planet and beyond. Nothing within the vast physical, astral, or causal cosmos could match the feeling the body receives during manifestation of the

---

[6] American Heritage Dictionary 2011.
[7] Dixon 2008, 215–219.

EC. It is the best gift to receive, as both Creator and creation are merged in complete Divine unity.

EC will be experienced continually in SS (*sahaja samadhi*) and AION but will solidify as a permanent part of your consciousness. Eventually, even this EC will transform into the DSCE, which is the highest single experience manifested in the self-realization process.

While this divine nectar drips, the ego will continue to battle in the mind for territory. This clashing occurs more often if you are a householder with worldly responsibilities, are sexually active, and have a family. This is because there is still voluntary loss of seminal fluid, and the householder has to constantly battle the change in environmental consciousness. However, even at this point, it will still remain difficult for the ego to gain any ground, as your consciousness is in a supreme state of realization. If you have a difficult time overcoming these types of battles, a combined technique using both the Cosmic Energy Technique and third eye opening can be used to help overcome this battle and win the war on ego. The cosmic energy being pulled down into the body is not energy from creation in any form. The energy that streams down into the body is pure SPIRIT consciousness.

You may eventually become fused into the NDCR and never break from it again before ascension to SS. SS is really a constant NDCR experience in infinitely many forms.

sMje 99.$\overline{9}$ Trillion+ – The highest possible level where sMje = 99,999,999,999,999.0 or sMje 99T-0.
NDCR-sMje Transition State (NDCRT)
Value of Level NDCRT = 0.9, 0.99, 0.999, etc. (99.$\overline{9}$ Trillion +)
# of NDCRT Levels = $10^{[1E(1E12)]}$
Spiritualized Consciousness
The "-0" portion of this level represents the "9" after the decimal point. It will repeat $10^{[1E(1E12)]}$ times until you reach true liberation in SS. This value is similar to CC1 at $10^{[1E(999.9E12)]}$, but the difference between the two values is still very large.

As you ascend in sMje 99T-0, the space between true liberation and the body becomes smaller and smaller as if you were reaching a limit. This limit is representative of the limit in calculus, where a value may come closer and closer to zero, but it may never actually reach zero. This process may only take a couple of days, depending on how fast the LOC has increased during your own personal ascension. Remember, ascension to SS can only happen by the Divine's will alone. It cannot be reached in any other way. Although these values are incredibly small, they are meant to show how even the smallest ascension may be impossible to cross without the Divine's help. You may assume that just because the value appears to be small, that it becomes that much easier to cross. Willpower alone is not enough to reach the highest form of SPIRIT's consciousness. It is through complete submission that you will gain access to this prized bounty.

Upon coming closer to SS, the *Om* may transform in character. You may not hear *Om* at all; a sudden vacuum silence may come into your consciousness instead. This ultimate silence is the transcendence from the sound of *Om*. *Om* is the holy vibration, described in Hinduism, as the Divine pulse that underlies the fabric of the universe. *Om* is also the holy word as written about in the book of Genesis that began creation. It is not a sound at all, but sheer silence. A silence that is so loud and consuming that it cannot be known by words, but only by the experience itself. This is a frequent experience beheld in SS.

The body will continue to have spontaneous *samadhi* events. You will pass in and out of the highest states of stillness frequently, at will, and without warning. Just little focus to the third eye will bring on massive waves of peace, bliss, and *samadhi* stillness. You could be performing any activity—teaching a class, eating a meal, or even playing a video game. You could be still, or at least relatively still, to bring on this state. The consciousness may eventually become permanently stuck in the Ecstatic Consciousness (EC). This "stuck" state allows the divine drip to permeate the body at a continual rate that will eventually lead to transcendence through a constant increase in LOC. This increase will not stop until you have become liberated. This is also a permanent breathless state. Even the thought of breathing will not cause respiration to occur. You could become permanently immersed in SPIRIT's consciousness for a time. This "stuck" state is also referred to as *anantya*.

If you expect to reach self-realization on your own, you will be sadly mistaken. The yogi, although experiencing great levels of self-realization, may still need assistance from outside sources to help progress the body and consciousness. This help may come in the form of various types of medicine: Applied Kinesiology, chiropractic, craniosacral therapy, homeopathy, acupuncture, herbs, hydrotherapy, and other forms of physical, emotional, and mental cleansings. All of these I have and still use in one form or another to release the body from its own mortal coils.

It is almost impossible to reach self-realization without the help of a guru, and much more difficult without the addition of a natural-healing health practitioner. It is essential to have a physician that cannot only treat the body, but the emotions and the mind as well. A competent and licensed physician practicing Applied Kinesiology or some other type of muscle testing can help you access your own issues consciously. This allows for you to release from your own karma on your own accord, but at an accelerated rate. The other benefit from being treated by a doctor who performs muscle testing is that this accelerated rate of healing does not have to be accompanied by an increase in suffering. The Divine makes it easier for those who work hard for themselves, for the higher good of all, and are willing to seek outside help for their own issues.

I am trained with the mind of a physician and have experimented with various treatments mentioned above for nearly two decades now. These various forms of treatment are necessary to reach self-realization, based upon the current environment of the world. The world you live in now is polluted, de-mineralized, stagnant, and rich in negativity. However, we are only progressing as a society of combined nations. This development has been occurring for the last 1500 years. At this point, the only way to go is up, up, up!

To remain unaware of all necessities while reaching self-realization is to remain ignorant to your true nature in SPIRIT. We all are directly connected and will remain this way until the end of existence itself, as we are all here to help one another toward the highest goal.

True temporary salvation is the treasure discovered in NrS, but the real truth lies in true permanent salvation found in SS.

OM SAMADHI (OmS)

Value of Level OmS = $CC1^{CC1^{\wedge}(1E100)}$, # of OmS Levels = CC1
Unified Consciousness
The *Om (Aum)*, as the original sound of the universe, was made manifest by the Creator. This creative sound permeated all of creation, allowing it to develop from the One into the many. It has been referenced in spiritual texts, such as the *Bhagavad Gita* and the Christian bible. The Hindu's bible, the *Bhagavad Gita*, says, "Uttering the

monosyllable *Aum*, the eternal word of Brahman, one who departs leaving the body [at death], he attains the Supreme Goal [God]."[8]

Om has great power in meditation and in the attainment of self-realization. Paramahansa Yogananda has commented on unique

parallels between the "Word of God" in the Christian bible and its true meaning. John the Gospel wrote, "In the beginning was the Word, and the Word was with God, and the Word was God.... All things came into being through Him, and apart from Him nothing came into being that has come into being."[9] Yogananda says that the "Word" here is *Om*, which in Hinduism is considered the Divine fabric that underlies all of creation. He further says that *Om* is also equal to the word Amen in Judeo-Christian religions, *Amin* of the Muslims, and "*Hum* of the Tibetans.[10] In this way, all religions are connected through the same creation story.

The syllable *Om* is actually a part of its own trinity, as *Om-Tat-Sat* in Vedic interpretations through the *Bhagavad Gita*. It says, "Om-Tat-Sat have been declared as symbolic representations of the Supreme Absolute Truth, from the beginning of creation... ."[11] *Om*, being the first part of this triune perspective, is the vibratory existence or the very matrix that the universe has been created upon. *Tat* is God in the aspect of Creator, able to create and manifest universal creation in all forms. *Sat* is God without desire to create, transcendental in nature and beyond all realities as pure SPIRIT. Yogananda gave the interpretation that *Om-Tat-Sat* is correlated to the Christian Trinity as the Holy Ghost, Son, and Father, respectively.[12]

---

[8] *Bhagavad Gita* 8.13
[9] John 1:1,3 NASB
[10] Yogananda 2004, 1577–78.
[11] *Bhagavad Gita* 17.23
[12] Yogananda 2004, 12.

The image on the previous page is *Om* (*Aum*) in *Devanagari* script, which is one the most commonly used writing systems in India, Nepal, and the world. It is a mystical sound of Hindu origin that is used as a mantra (repeated word) in meditation.

Om is the phonetical pronunciation of the Sanskrit word *Aum*. *Aum* is actually a combination of three separate syllables: *A-kara*, *U-kara*, and *Ma-kara*. Each of these syllables has a different meaning and is mentioned in all of the *Upanishads*, which are the collective texts in Vedic Sanskrit giving the basic religious concepts of Hinduism, Buddhism, and Jainism. *A-kara* means "form," as in objects of the Earth and of nature. *U-kara* means formless and represents water, fire, and air. *Ma-kara* is neither form nor formless.

Some equate *Ma-kara* to the dark matter of the universe that cannot be seen but can be understood conceptually as beyond reasoning itself. Sivananda says,

> 'A' represents the physical plane, 'U' represents the mental plane and astral planes, the world of spirits, all heavens, 'M' represents the deep sleep state, and all that is unknown even in your wakeful state, all that is beyond the reach of the intellect.[13]

Symbolism of Om

It is obvious that the syllable itself is steeped in symbolism, but what about the physical image itself? The large bottom curve symbolizes "A," the waking state. The middle curve is "U," the dream state, and the upper curve is "M," the state of deep sleep. The diamond at the top is *turiya*, the fourth state of consciousness, or the unconscious form of *anantya*. The semi-circle below the diamond represents *maya*, or the delusion of the physical world, which is the greatest obstacle to overcome to achieve self-realization.

If the *Om* (*Aum*) represents the existence of all creation, then it can be connected to all cultures and belief systems. When I first gazed upon *Om*, I noticed that the left side of the symbol looked like the number three. In Christianity, there is the Trinity (Father-Son-Holy Ghost), and in Hinduism, there is the *Trimurti* (Creator-Transformer-Preserver). Although the two, in essence, are not directly the same, they are similar.

---

[13] Sivananda 2011.

It is also commonly understood that the number "3" is also associated with perfected masters like Jesus Christ, Bhagavan Krishna, and Mahavatar Babaji. This three-shaped curve represents your awakening to the true reality of the Trinity, allowing you to perceive the Christ Consciousness, Cosmic Consciousness, and Divine Super-consciousness as the highest truths. These are embodied in every divinely-conscious being in the universe. In numerology, the number three also represents optimism, extreme generosity, and true charisma. These are also qualities of those perfected avatars.

The curve that goes off to the right is the one you must take to discover your path to Christ Consciousness. Then as you ascend in realization, you eventually reach the diamond-shaped reality of *turiya* by entering into the Creator's Cosmic Consciousness. However, to reach such a state of perfection, you need to traverse the veil that sits below the diamond, using all of your willpower, devotion, and surrender to gain access to this treasured gem.

Om is in its own category of consciousness called "Unified Consciousness" (UniCon). This type of consciousness is accessed when you use an *Om*-hearing technique to perceive it. You can hear this astral sound as a part of the fifth *chakra*, if your ears are tuned to its universal vibration. UniCon can be experienced even before Christ Consciousness, as it is attuned to through an *Om*-hearing technique. When you can hear the *Om* using a technique, you are in the Christ Consciousness. However, when you have stopped the technique and no longer can perceive this sound in your ears, you will have voluntarily jumped out of this consciousness. The longer you can spend in hearing the *Om*, the better chance you will become tuned in to its vibration and thus, ascend to the next highest LOC.

Eventually, when you can hear *Om* coming from everywhere and every part of creation, you will have reached UniCon. This consciousness is permanently attained once you can willfully perceive *Om* without the use of a technique. The experience will initially occur spontaneously during the 2nd and 3rd Dimensional realms, after all karma has been burned off. Then, it will begin to occur more frequently as you can achieve a major *samadhi* experience as a part of the Interstate. The fullest manifestation of *Om* will begin around sMje 55.9 Trillion, as you begin to merge with non-duality. It may occur before this or after, but this is the general LOC.

As always, the *Om* is best heard with complete silence but can be manifested if focus is intense, frequent, and dedicated. This is why meditation is best done in silence, but is strived for in the noisy, concrete wildernesses of the world.

The *Om* vibration encompasses three bodies and three cosmoses. The three bodies include the physical, astral, and causal. The three cosmoses are the physical, subtle, and ideational. If *Om* is the matrix upon which the astral universe was created, wouldn't *Om* then manifest as not only sound in the ears, but as astral light at the third eye? In this way, *Om* is experienced through hearing and vision. You could then reason that *Om* could be experienced through the other three senses in other ways—through taste, smell, and touch. In the past, I have had experiences of smelling tobacco smoke where there was none and my father's cologne when he was obviously no longer on Earth. These sensations I experienced could only be explained by the existence of astral smells that can be bestowed by those who have already passed on, attempting to get my attention.

Om can be experienced not only by the five physical senses, but also by the intuitive sixth sense gained when you meditate intensely on the third eye. There are other senses that go beyond even the sixth sense, but they will not be elaborated upon here.

It is, then, expected that *Om* will be manifested first, so that non-duality can be experienced at will. To focus on the *Om* is to bring attention to the very thought-nature of the universe. You must know *Om* first before you can know God, because the symbol of God is *Om*. Patanjali, in his *Yoga Sutras*, says, "The sacred word designating this creative source is the sound *Om*, called pranava."[14] *Pranava* means "cosmic sound" in Sanskrit. Patanjali also says in other sutras[15] that, by meditating on *Om*, you can remove all obstacles in the way of gaining self-realization. This is the direct route to the Divine described by Patanjali over 1500 years ago.

This mighty and creative vibration was sent into the universe to create. Its matrix is the very foundation upon which the three bodies and three cosmoses were built. Without this vibration, no physical, astral or causal thing could be held together. The vibration is like the energy bonding atoms together. Without that attraction existing between the two, nothing could be made manifest... in any image!

---

[14] Patanjali's *Yoga Sutras* I.27
[15] Patanjali's *Yoga Sutras* I.29

ASTRAL SAMADHI (AS)
Value of Level AS = $CC1^{1E(999.9E12)}$, # of AS Levels = 10^{100}
Divine Consciousness
The astral *samadhi* is one that begins by perceiving the light at the third eye. This process usually begins just before you ascend to Christ Consciousness, but it has to become fully manifest even when you're your eyes are fully open.

Figure 16.1 – Spiritual Light of the Third Eye

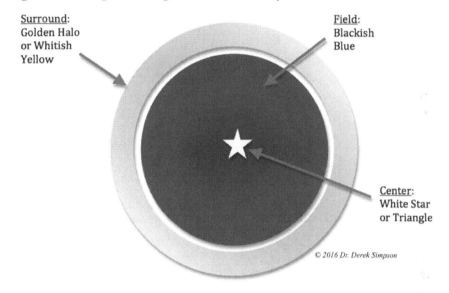

Initially, you may only see darkness at the third eye when your focus is pushed there. The intuitive visual fields have yet to be attuned to the astral light manifested at the third eye. Through frequent and increasingly intensified meditations, you will eventually perceive the light at the third eye. The initial light seen is only the outer portion of a three-part image. A whitish-golden halo is the border of this astral image. Once you can perceive this golden light and its many convolutions and provocative patterning, the blackish-blue surround will show itself. Sometimes the blackish blue will come first, but not always.

As mentioned before in Chapter 12 on the Christ Consciousness, the golden halo, blue surround, and white star are all representative of the Holy Ghost, Christ Consciousness, and Cosmic Consciousness, respectively.[16] These are divided aspects of God gleaned from the One into the many. These aspects are present and available in all beings that can attain the higher cerebral consciousness called self-realization.

This blue surround needs to be penetrated if you hope to become one with the Christ Consciousness. The blue light will come initially as a dark blue and then will transform into lighter blues. Finally, it will mix with the golden halo, creating a kaleidoscope of color.

In the center of the third eye is a white star or white orb. This white star is difficult to see at best. Do not be discouraged if you cannot initially perceive it. The necessary LOC to perceive the white star in its entirety is at $10^{89,000,000}$. This is "1" followed by 89 million zeros. The white star represents the Creator's Cosmic Consciousness. Penetrating and merging with its brilliance will lead to *savikalpa samadhi,* where you will be initiated by a divine superconscious, major samadhi experience.

An astral *samadhi* (AS) can also be experienced through the *shambhavi mudra* (SM). These positions can exist either in a natural open-eyed position, intensified and specific open-eyed positions, or with closed eyes. The SM positions are essential when ascending in LOC. These positions allow you to perceive astral light while eyes are open or closed. This is the supreme nature of AS, to experience the astral cosmos as a supreme light show in any and all of creation. As you ascend in LOC, through SS and AION, the astral *samadhi* state will begin to manifest all the time, allowing for light to explode from every object and angle and ultimately, from your own body. This type of AS really only occurs with a conscious *anantya* state that brings the infinite state of bliss consciousness. This type of state is confirmed by Jesus the Christ in the Gospel of Matthew, "…if therefore thine eye be single, thy whole body shall be full of light."[17]

Astral *samadhi* manifestations during these times will be intense. Open-eyed positions in SM will come more easily as you practice. The switch between third eye focus and binocular vision can be confusing to your mind at first, but with continual practice, this switch will become automatic. After a time, the eyes will have a tendency to stay focused at the third eye all the time, allowing the LOC to increase more rapidly and create deeper experiences.

Perception of an AS is like going to a 3D movie. You are currently in a three-dimensional world, perceiving three dimensions on a flat

---

[16] Yogananda 2004, 60–61.
[17] Matthew 6:22 KJV

screen. The extra light that comes off the object on screen to create that three-dimensionality on the screen is the same kind of light that comes off an object when perceiving astral light. An astral *samadhi* state is just being able to view that astral light with both the *samadhi* stillness and divine nectar creating the ultimate state of bliss.

Some beings can go even farther in the astral *samadhi* and project their astral bodies (while still in the conscious meditative state) to some other location on the planet or in the universe. This is called astral projection. Although extremely difficult to perform consciously, you can only perform this feat at will in SS and AION, if you are given the power to do so. You may even be able to commune with astral beings like saints, angels, and angelic beings through the third eye either intuitively or visually, but this can only occur through deep concentration, pure desire, and intense devotion towards the chosen guru/spiritual teacher.

As you ascend in the AS during NrS and SS, especially during an open-eyed SM, both the physical and astral worlds perceived will dissolve into nothingness. The blurring of these two worlds is like a *yin yang* symbol (*taiji*) in appearance lying on its side, giving way to the reality of the world. This distinction is one that is the division between *maya* (duality) from SPIRIT (non-duality). The blending of these two worlds is what convinces you the physical world is really only made up of light particles. After this blending occurs, you will go deeper into the third eye, allowing for a fuller relaxation of the extremities distally to proximally.

The blues of the astral eye will continue to become lighter, allowing for joy to increase exponentially. The golden halo will no longer be a blur of light, but an orb shining brightly in the mind's eye. This is the true nature of the astral light. When you are in the astral heaven, staring directly into the sun would never cause any damage, because you are in full use of the astral eye sense. It is not recommended by this book, however, to stare directly into the physical sun with your physical eyes, as this can cause permanent damage to the retinas. Only a yogi who has transcended into the void of SPIRIT can truly perceive this astral light without negative effects.

If the color of the spiritual eye becomes more purplish-pink, you are perceiving the truest color of SPIRIT. SPIRIT does not have form, but manifests infinitely in the many versions. These forms take place as light in the spiritual eye and generally take on the appearance of an amorphous mass. However, this mass can and will take the shape of the things that are most appealing and necessary for you to perceive.

The *Om* may play in the ears intensely or not intensely at all. In fact, it may sound like you are in a vacuum with no sound. At these points, when sound does not occur, a breathless state will manifest itself and joy will increase infinitely higher. If you are in SS, it is possible to manifest a DSCE (Divine Superconscious Experience), allowing you to merge fully for a limited period of time with SPIRIT itself.

When you are in NrS, you can perceive SPIRIT beyond creation and the infinite bliss-joy consciousness that is contained therein. But you will be able to merge completely with that consciousness all the time. The bliss experienced while in an AS and in NrS requires great concentration. This is the true drunken joy that only occurs when you are able to sip from His holy wine glass, manifesting the state of ecstasy (Ecstatic Consciousness-EC). This EC is can manifest at any time with little concentration while in SS. *Sahaja samadhi* (SS) is the natural state of realization, and so, *samadhi* can occur spontaneously, without provocation or concentration.

To achieve an open-eyed astral *samadhi* (AS) is a difficult feat to achieve. If achieved, this state creates a wonderful realization for the yogi. You will not only see heaven at the third eye, but you can see the astral heaven all around you. This is part of the "kingdom of heaven" that Jesus Christ spoke about in the New Testament of the Christian bible. You will not only experience the bliss within and without, you will perceive it through the sound of the mighty *Om* and through the eyes filled with beautiful astral light.

AS will continue to increase in intensity and beauty throughout NrS and SS. It will end its numerical ascension at the end of SS proper. This "proper" state is the baseline to SS itself. The baseline SS state is the numerical end of AS as well, so the AS will always be a part of SS, infinitely manifesting its many forms.

The astral *samadhi* state is a part of Divine Consciousness. This means that you are able to access SPIRIT in its non-dual state of existence. Although you will not be able to keep it completely, with continued effort and desire towards the highest realizations, you will be able to realize this ecstatic state continually throughout the rest of your natural life.

Differences between OmS and AS

These two *samadhis* are on the same level with one another. Once you can achieve one, the other will come easily. It is suggested to practice the type of *samadhi* that is associated with the physical sense that is less developed.

For example, men, usually, are better visual learners and should practice the *Om*, since it is associated with the ears, hearing, and listening. The opposite is generally true for a female. The female species is usually better at listening, so visualizing astral light at the third eye should be practiced more. This generality is due to male and female brains being "wired" differently. Women usually have a better-developed frontal lobe[18,19], allowing them to converse more easily in groups and communicate effectively. Males often have a more highly developed parietal lobe[20], displaying a greater ability in spatial orientation. Male and female strengths, if not completely one-sided, can be reversed or evenly balanced.

The *Om* and astral (major) *samadhis* are first manifested in their supreme states in NrS. The *Om* will commonly be manifested first, especially during this current Earth era, because the *Om* is so prevalent in our modern-day society. Whether you see *Om* in print or you hear the *Om* sound, it has firmly planted itself into the collective subconscious minds of the masses. Not many know what the word "astral" means or what it could stand for, hence the bias towards *Om*. One is not more important than the other, but they can both be experienced fully in NrS.

Because yogis from India began to teach their meditation techniques in the early 20th century, the significance of *Om* has permeated the collective subconscious minds of all those in the Western hemisphere. Of course, *Om* has been around for many millennia. It has existed in different forms and has been a main focus for many different religions. These yogis were not first to teach about it, but it was their duty to reintegrate it into modern society through spiritual organizations. On a minor level, astral and *Om* are experienced briefly in the lesser minor *samadhi* states leading up to the greatest minor *samadhi* state, *savikalpa samadhi*. You could spend a considerable

---

[18] Kuwana 2001.
[19] Witelson 2001, 27.
[20] Koscik 2009, 451–459.

amount of time in each lesser minor *samadhi* state, but ascension is generally a little quicker through these states, especially for those who desire it and want nothing but SPIRIT's consciousness alone.

SAHAJA SAMADHI (SS) and **THE AIONION STATE** (AION)

SS Value of Levels = $CC1^{(1E12)}$, # of Levels = 19
Spiritualized Consciousness
AION Value of Levels = 1 Aeon = 1 TotaLOC†
# of Levels = 999.͞9 Billion (to Infinity)
Divine Consciousness

Sahaja Samadhi. Self-realized Eternity. This is the highest dispensation for self-realization. It is a natural, spontaneous, simple, and easy consciousness that is ever-evolving out of eternal nature of SPIRIT. *Sahaja* itself means "natural" in Sanskrit. It is natural because it is a part of your nature to be completely unified with the Divine. It is also considered a spontaneous *nirvikalpa* state, available at any time. In SS, you can move throughout life totally immersed in bliss internally while performing all of life's tasks externally with ease and without mental disturbance. It is "self-realized eternity" because you can continually experience "ever-existing, ever-conscious, ever-new bliss"[21] all the time.

The consciousness of bliss is the Divine in Its purest form, existing eternally, always evolving into a new moment. In this *samadhi*, there is no separation between the soul and SPIRIT except through the physical existence of the body. *Sahaja samadhi* could also be described as the consciousness of *sat-chit-ananda*. *Sat-chit-ananda* means "truth or reality," "consciousness," and "pure happiness," respectively. You could say it is the absolute consciousness. In this way, this consciousness is the absolute nature of SPIRIT. One who attains this state exists within this perfect consciousness at all times. You are always able to access any instruments of the three bodies for the sole purpose of expressing SPIRIT in its infinite forms. Sri Chinmoy says that *sahaja samadhi* is

> by far the highest type of samadhi.[22] One gets higher joy and more illumining joy in sahaja samadhi than in nirvikalpa

---

† Referred to Appendix C for more info on a TotaLOC
[21] Yogananda 1999, 874.
[22] Chinmoy 1974, 181.

samadhi… But sahaja samadhi is spontaneous. The intensity is there, but it is so normal and spontaneous that nobody will be able to trace it.[23]

Sri Chinmoy also gives the analogy that *samadhi* is like a giant building with many floors. He says that,

> Sahaja samadhi encompasses the other samadhis—savikalpa and nirvikalpa—and it goes beyond, beyond. When one is in Sahaja Samadhi, he is the owner of the whole building… Nirvikalpa is like one height, say the thirtieth floor; it is very high, but it has only its own limited capacity… Sahaja samadhi will not be satisfied with thirtieth floor; it will be satisfied only when it touches the basement, the first floor, the second floor, all the floors. The power of sahaja samadhi is such that it can take one to any floor.[24]

This is the true satisfaction behind this level of realization. You can be wholly immersed in the joy of NrS, but working in the gross physical world. With the achievement of SS, you realize the true spherical nature of self-realization. Being able to engage in earthly activities while maintaining this supreme state is the greatest gift you could achieve in a human life.

Only those purposed as a world teacher or those meant to expound upon its mysteries for the masses are allowed to ascend into this state easily at this current time. If your desire is great enough, though, the Divine will grant you access to this limitless bounty. Also, in future ages, as the spiritual evolution of Earth continues to rise, SS will be a permanent part of many people's existence.

Most just want the supreme joy of God's consciousness in NrS. Most yogis do not dream to ascend to such heights as SS, but it is a necessary transition if you want to experience SPIRIT in the fullest as a householder. Swami Chidananda says,

> It is a rare phenomenon…. ….and the continued practice of being in a state of Nirvikalpa Samadhi that the Nirvikalpa Samadhi becomes natural to the Yogi, that it becomes

---

[23] Chinmoy 1977, 31.
[24] Chinmoy 1974, 92–93.

continued and unbroken in all the three states, namely, waking, dream and deep sleep. Thus, in the Sahaja Avastha [Sahaja Samadhi], even in the waking state, even in the midst of activity, the Yogi rests in non-dual consciousness.[25]

This is the permanent success in self-realization that is achieved when a person meditates morning and night to become completely immersed in non-dual consciousness, permanently unattached from all worldly things. This permanent nature of non-duality occurs because the your physical, mental, emotional, and spiritual karma have all been permanently cleansed.

Now there is no specific time that you need to set aside for God. God is now a part of the body and consciousness every moment of every day. There is no end to the meditation or even the incredible amount of stillness that is gained from the simple repetition of a prayer or mantra. No person in this state needs the solitude of a mountaintop to gain the eternal bliss of SPIRIT. Even the householder, living in the concrete jungles of man, can experience the constant bliss of SPIRIT.

Difference Between SS and AION

SS is subdivided into two major categories. The first is *sahaja samadhi* proper (SS proper) and the second is The Aionion State (AION). SS proper has a definitive end, because you need to become attuned to this permanent non-dual consciousness. Also, you may not have achieved full, unbridled access to either the *Om* or astral (major) *samadhis*. Generally, the astral *samadhi* will still require further attunement so that the body can continue to receive higher realizations. While in SS proper, the SS levels will be attuned to quickly, while the astral *samadhi* levels may take a bit more time. There are only 19 states to SS proper, measuring at CC1$^{(1E12)}$. These levels are fairly small, but are still necessary. If your desire is to ascend, then the adjustment period between SS proper and AION will last a very short period of time.

The second category of SS, The Aionion State, is also referred to as the "incalculable state," because ascension in AION has the potential to go for an eternity. The prefix *aion-* means "for eternity" or "age" in Greek. The *aion* spelling has been used in the Christian scripture in

---

[25] Chidananda 1999, 100.

Matthew 28:20, "... I am with you always, even to the end of the age,"[26] "age" meaning *aion* in this case. Christianity's idea for eternal life comes from *zoe* in Greek, which is a form of the prefix *aion-*.[27]

In some usages, it could also be referred to as an unbroken age or perpetuity of time.[28] Other spellings of this word, *aeon* or *eon,* could also refer to "existence" or "being."[29] The term *aeon* is also used in Gnosticism to describe the different emanations or aspects of God.[30] These various definitions and descriptions are but pieces of ideas that help to understand the whole of eternity. Those many pieces can be continually experienced while you are ascending in the AION LOC.

You can understand the differences between SS Proper and AION state by the following analogy. If you were living in Chicago, IL, or any other large city, you may get a chance to experience a skyscraper like The Willis Tower (Sears Tower). In this particular area in downtown Chicago, called the Loop, the many tall buildings will give you an idea about the transition between SS Proper and AION. When you want to go high in SS, you look up at the tallest building and say, "Wow, that looks infinitely tall. Can I really get to the top of that? Well... I can try." As you look up (performing *shambhavi mudra*) and climb higher in the elevator (of the Creator's consciousness) of the building, you soon find how easy it is to maintain such a high level of peace, joy, and bliss. You realize that "eternity" doesn't seem that eternal and self-realization seems possible. However, don't be fooled because you still need to get to the top of this building, and even further after that. Self-realization is just like that—once you get to the top of the building, there is still another to climb. Eventually, you will reach the tallest peaks and will fly like the birds under the canopy of the blue sky of God-realization.

Gaining this consciousness, you will know that SS is self-realized eternity, a never-ending experience of God-realization. Only through transcendence to that realm by physical death or through scientific meditation will you achieve and maintain this state of eternal bliss.

---

[26] Matthew 28:20 NASB
[27] Thayer and Smith 1999, s.v. "zoe."
[28] Thayer and Smith 1999, s.v. "aion."
[29] Harper (n.d.), s.v. "aeon."
[30] Encyclopaedia Brittanica Online (n.d.), s.v. "aeon."

Measurement of AION

The Aionion State will be abbreviated "AION," and when speaking about its various levels, they will be known as "Aeons." Each Aeon level is a measure of the sum total of the entire LOC chart, starting from Drunken Consciousness until the end of SS Proper. The AION LOC has an infinite amount of Aeon levels associated with it. Aeon 1 ends at the end of the first ascension through SS proper, and Aeon 2 begins at the beginning of the initial part of AION, after SS proper has ended. I have included, in Appendix C, the calculation of an Aeon with a visual representation.

As you ascend in LOC past SS proper and into AION, you can attune to an entire Aeon level at a time. This is a part of the Law of Ascension. Once you become attuned to a particular level whether in *savikalpa* or *nirvikalpa*, it will then become easier to attune to other levels as well. This is the same with Aeon levels. Although massive and seemingly uncountable by today's standards, once attuned to the vibration of an Aeon level, you then can ascend by 10's of Aeons, then 100's of Aeons, then 1000's of Aeons, and so forth. This will continue on until you get to 1,000,000 Aeons. However, in this current Earth era, it is unlikely any one individual would reach such a height. There are few that have reached these heights, and these individuals will be described at the end of this chapter.

The Graphing of Eternity

SS and its counterpart AION can be measured in a few ways. The "Incalculable" level of AION is measured by two mathematical concepts. It first can be understood conceptually as you approach the "limit" in calculus. On the next page is a graph showing these correlations.

Figure 16.2 – The Graphing of Eternity

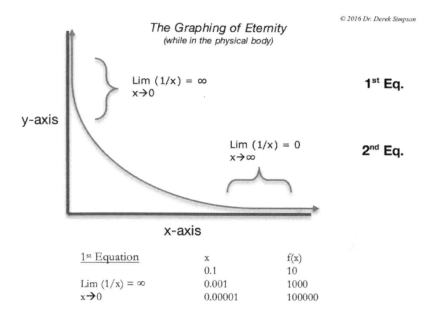

1st Equation	x	f(x)
$\lim_{x \to 0} (1/x) = \infty$	0.1	10
	0.001	1000
	0.00001	100000

x = The x value becomes progressively smaller as you ascend towards "O"neness, while your actual LOC, represented by 1/x, climbs towards ∞ or infinity.

y = 1/x or f(x) – This is the concept that as one comes closer to infinity, the distance between the SPIRIT and the soul (manifested creation) becomes progressively smaller.

Interpretation: Here is the vertical perspective. This first equation tends more towards an occult version of attaining self-realization. To become self-realized in the past, required an esoterically receptive mind to achieve what appeared to be the impossible.

2nd Equation	x	f(x)
$\lim_{x \to \infty} (1/x) = 0$	10	0.1
	1000	0.001
	100000	0.00001

x = The x value becomes progressively larger and larger as you ascend towards ∞ or infinity, while the actual LOC of the individual (1/x) climbs towards the "O"neness of SPIRIT.

y = 1/x or f(x) – This is the concept that as one comes closer to "O"neness with SPIRIT, the distance between the SPIRIT and the soul (manifested creation) becomes progressively smaller.

Interpretation: This is the horizontal perspective. With numerical values that reflect a particular level of consciousness (LOC), that impossibility of reaching eternity now becomes possible. This is because of instead of plugging in a smaller number and getting an increased "y" value (which doesn't truly reflect the increasingly smaller distance), one inputs a larger "x" value (representing LOC) and the output is a smaller distance between one's true self and God.

In either equation, the outcome 1/x or f(x) is the same. While you increase in LOC, you will either come progressively closer to "O"neness with SPIRIT or merge with infinity. Increased mergence with SPIRIT also leads to a gradual decline in the attachment to worldly things and a decreased overall effect of the ego on the soul's divine decision-making. Whether the "x" value is getting smaller (vertically ascending) or the "x" value is getting bigger (horizontally increasing), the eventual outcome is the same. This vertical ascension is the "climbing" of the mountain of self-realization. The horizontal increase is the evolution and awareness of "O"neself in all of creation.

Both equations are necessary to describe the various attunements and experiences that are required of you in self-realization. The knowing of oneself as creation first and slowly coming to the awareness that you are the eternal SPIRIT are both necessary aspects of this process. While living in a world of duality, this mergence with infinity appears to be impossible. This is a truly impossible equation that becomes possible through the realization of SPIRIT as pure bliss consciousness.

However, you will never really reach infinity while in the physical body, because to merge with infinity is to become the vast SPIRIT. The way to do this is to relinquish the physical body and pass into permanent physical death. The concept of this infinity is of the highest spiritual kind. This spiritual infinity can be experienced in an infinite number of ways, either as insurmountable bliss or this bliss with a combination of supernatural *siddhis* (yogic abilities/powers). The former is the most common way to experience this infinitude, and the latter is reserved only for the most highly realized avatars. Just know to expand the One Self into the Highest of All-Selves is the objective of this state.

Mathematical Concept of Infinity

Approaching infinity only causes frustration because it cannot be reached. In mathematics, some functions use ∞ or infinity in them. Initially, you can look at understanding the value of $1/\infty$, but you cannot actually know this value because infinity is not a number. It is just a concept. You could say that $1/\infty = 0$, but if 1 is divided by an infinite number of pieces and ends up with 0 each, then what happened to the 1? Mathematicians simply describe $1/\infty$ as "undefined."

You can approach infinity, but never really arrive at the location of infinity. You cannot really say what happens when the value approaches infinity, except that one value gets infinitely larger (x), while the other value becomes infinitely smaller (1/x). 1/x is technically going towards 0, but you cannot give an answer of zero.

Instead, a limit is used whereby:

- The LIMIT is 1/x, as x approaches infinity is 0.
- Another way to look at this is:
  LIMIT = Approaching = Infinity.

The function essentially becomes limitless.[31] The spiritual aspect of this limitless function may be easier to understand, because every individual may desire at one point or another to be "limitless" in one area of his or her life. This could be to achieve the impossible of being an Olympic-gold athlete, a high-end professional orchestral musician, or even the President of the United States.

Spiritual Concept of Infinity

Mathematicians ask the question—what happens when a value reaches infinity? This answer cannot be fully understood by theoretical math alone; it must be experienced in the fires of meditation. You must become the Infinite in the form of bliss consciousness to see infinity as it really is. As your LOC increases (x), the space between SPIRIT

---

[31] Pierce 2015.

and the soul (1/x) become progressively smaller. Eventually the soul will merge with SPIRIT in all its glory. However, this merger only occurs at the highest of realizations. These realizations are saved spontaneously for a few, worked hard for by those who supremely desire it, and actively controlled by the self-realized masters of old.

Characteristics of SS

Sahaja samadhi (SS) is a special dispensation state of realization reserved for those who truly desire it or are meant to share it with the world. It is a state where you are always experiencing an existence of non-duality. It is the highest manifested state of *nirvikalpa samadhi* or *nirvana*. Attainment of *nirvana* is used in Buddhism to describe liberation from reincarnation.[32] It is also referred to as *moksha* in Hinduism and describes the release from the cycles of rebirth.[33] Liberation cannot be achieved until the perfect, divine love of SPIRIT has been expressed in a human form. This is because living as a human is the most difficult in the universe. We experience the greatest amount of physical, mental, emotional, and spiritual diversity expressed through cycles of years and millennia.

Swami Sivananda has said that, once a yogi has reached the final and perfect state of meditation and *samadhi*, this individual is considered to be a *jivanmukta*,[34] or one who has liberated the soul. This *jivanmukta* has completed the shedding the causal body while in SS. This actually occurs in the second level of SS Proper (SS2) out of the 19 that exist.

After the ascension into SS, the *anandamaya (chitta) kosha* or "bliss sheath" is peeled back in its finality, allowing you to merge with SPIRIT while in the physical body. This is the final state for all souls who will eventually come back to God in their entirety. This sheath shall never enclose the soul again, and the causal body will be permanently removed with the emergence of the Higher Self with SPIRIT. Release of the causal body at SS2 allows you to finally burn the last negative attachment created between the connection of ego and the causal body. These attachments may burn up earlier during the ascension from the 1st to the 2nd Dimension. This is not always the

---

[32] Harvey 1990.
[33] Frazier, Jessica and Flood, G. (ed.) 2011.
[34] Sivananda 2011.

case and still may require great willpower and sacrifice to burn these negative imprints on the body.

However, this merger is not one of complete finality. You still need to ascend within the "incalculable state" and beyond to achieve the highest level of *moksha*. You cannot transcend physical death consciously until you have completely merged into SPIRIT through the DSCE (Divine Superconscious Experience). This is where yogic *siddhis* (powers) such as bilocation, complete distance healing, instant physical manifestation, assuming any form desired, and so on can be manifested by true God-realized world teachers. Not just one of these *siddhis* will manifest itself, but they, as a whole, will manifest together. In Chapter 17, *siddhis* will be discussed at length and assigned to different subtypes of self-realized persons.

Differences between SS and NrS

SS is different than NrS (*nirvikalpa*) in that you are always in the Ecstatic Consciousness (EC) with the divine nectar always dripping in SS. This is its hallmark. NrS is where you can access the EC with moderate effort and keep it with less effort. In SS, you can jump directly into the EC without any effort, and it can spontaneously occur without warning.

The divine nectar will continue to evolve into a more and more beautiful version of bliss as the LOC increases. In NrS, the divine nectar is felt as bliss and stillness. Subtle sensations are felt in the back of the throat to help signify the change occurring within. As your LOC progresses in SS proper and AION, you will begin to taste the actual sweetness of the nectar. It has a light and fragrant type of sensation attached. One that will quench even the greatest desires for sweet things. This is the fuller nature of that divine drip. The sensation of the divine drip in the back of the throat will progress to the whole of face causing intense vibrations to radiate in and around the teeth and throughout the sinus cavities.

Also, SS is the beginning of the ability to achieve an astral *samadhi* at its highest state and at will. In AION, you always perceive visual stimuli as a manifestation or emanation of astral light, and so, you are always in an astral (major) *samadhi* experience. In SS proper, you are "spiritualized," making this state in the category Spiritualized Consciousness (SpCon), but AION is "divinely" conscious (because of its eternality) making this LOC a part of the category of Divine Consciousness (DivCon). A divinely conscious individual is directly connected with their soul consciousness. This makes sense, as the soul is now released from its binding of the physical, astral, and causal bodies. This is *kaivalya*, or complete liberation leading to the absolute consciousness.

The final consciousness you will experience is "Divine Superconsciousness" or the DSCE. This is the extension state of the base samadhi level of AION, and thus, SS. You are able to experience this state during your initiation to *savikalpa samadhi* (SaS), the Interstate #1, and through the manifestation of the non-dual consciousness (NDCR-sMje) at will in *nirvikalpa samadhi* (NrS).

Divine Superconsciousness becomes more fully manifested before an LOC of 60,000 Aeons, if your willpower and desire is great enough and it serves a purpose to attune other individuals to a higher state of consciousness. After 60,000 Aeons, Divine Superconsciousness becomes manifested completely, consciously, and willfully while in seated meditation, but not while walking around. This occurrence after 60,000 Aeons still requires quite a bit of time in seated meditation but can occur with increased willpower and desire. When your LOC increases to 100,000 Aeons, the DSCE can be manifested even while performing daily duties. Other intensities to the DSCE that will be described on p. 165. Ultimately, the DSCE will continue to show itself, but in different ways as the individual continues down the path of self-realization.

Soul Love

When the causal body has finally released the soul from its bondage, the love that is manifested by the soul is now more difficult to maintain in SS. However, once the yogi is attuned to this more transient level of love, it will become easier to ascend with SS. This concept is represented in the diagram below.

Figure 16.3 – Soul's Love in Nirvikalpa

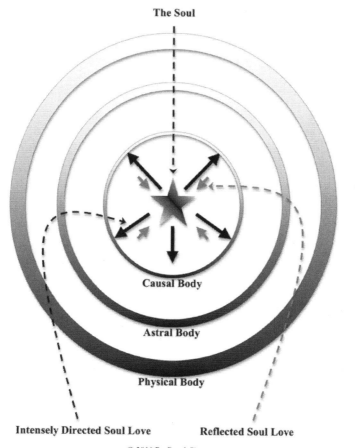

The above diagram represents soul's love in NrS and how it tries to break free of the causal body's boundary. During NrS, the soul's love is reflected very intensely off the causal body, allowing the soul to experience very intense waves of emotions from the Divine very easily as pure love. This experience is partially the reason why joy is felt so intensely in NrS and is the main hallmark of this stage of realization. When the causal body is lost in SS2, that reflected love is no more. Love becomes shared too much and lost more easily, unbalancing the cultivation performed by the yogi. This is where continual practice of meditation and devotion are absolutely needed.

In SS, you could share so much of your love while that it can become depleted. The compassionate soul desires to reach out to other lost and confused beings who desire timeless love. In the beginning stages, this loss can occur more quickly if you are not properly attuned to the present vibrational LOC. Also, time is required to attain and maintain the current LOC. This becomes increasingly more difficult for the yogi householder, because this individual is always in contact with those of a lower LOC.

Your line of work could prove to be beneficial or disastrous towards your attainment of higher LOCs. If a work environment is filled with "negative Nellies," it will be difficult to maintain an increasing vibrational state. However, the opposite is true as well. What you surround yourself with, is what you are prone to become. Remember, like attracts like when it comes to metaphysical vibration. That which you think and do, is what you attract. If you are not continually cautious of the outward display of action and do not pay attention to the inward focus on SPIRIT, you are bound to create physical suffering in the body.

Physical suffering occurs when two discordant vibrations or frequencies attempt to merge, resulting in a similar physical manifestation. The result could be headaches, physical pain the body, nausea, brain fog, and so on. Generally, the manifestation of physical suffering is associated with your weakest disposition or what the mind still suffers around intrinsically. The subconscious mind, always active during your life, stores all experiences you benefit and suffer from.

The mind is the field or the terrain where all mass consciousness exists together. Some things get brought to the foreground, while others stay in the background based upon where you place your focus. Things may be brought up by the will of a guru or God to be dealt with to help an individual to release from past indiscretions. The subconsciousness acts as an infinitely large mental storage space. Only the superconscious mind can access this storage at will for your own benefit. Once the causal body is removed, the reflected love becomes no more and an individual soul must take greater care in maintaining the love. One must still put forth effort in eating, sleeping, meditating, focusing and so forth to keep "feeling" SPIRIT. Continued indulgence in a physical body instrument, even as simple as not being "completely" in a meditative state of awareness at all times, will lead to suffering in some form or another.

Experiences of AION

As described in the beginning of this chapter, you can express SPIRIT in an infinite amount of ways while in SS. As seen with the various values of LOCs, you can be at the very baseline of SS and still experience that ever-new bliss, consciously all the time. However, there are different levels of transiency associated with each progressing Aeon LOC within The Aionion State.

The higher you ascend in AION, the greater the conversion of solid vibrational energy to completely transient energy of SPIRIT. If this particular ability is gained, the yogi could disappear or reappear at will. Many saints in India have attained such incredible powers of SPIRIT. One yogic master of India, Mahavatar Babaji, is considered the current *maitreya,* or "guardian watcher," of this current Earth epoch. His Aeon LOC has been measured beyond a googolplex of Aeons. His LOC was able to reach this peak because his supposed age is almost 2,000 years old. Some authors place the birth of Babaji at 203 CE.[35] Most accounts of this individual are transient, like the flawless master himself.

His LOC was able to rise to such an extreme level because of his extremely long hold on the physical body, becoming a true deathless guru. He is not greater than Jesus or any other Christ that has ever lived, because all come to Earth to play their part on the stage of creation. Jesus had his role to play, although physically short-lived in comparison to Babaji. Jesus's name reigns on in the hearts and minds of billions of people all over the world. To say the name of Jesus with reverence is to have an instant spiritual blessing placed upon the individual. The same is said of Mahavatar Babaji.

Jesus and Krishna have been measured at 1,000,000 Aeons, because they were considered "Christs" during their stay on Earth. Other avatars and self-realized saints are generally below this number, because their purpose was to continue to carry out the original mission that the "Christs" were sent to do. The saints of Christianity, such as St. Teresa of Avila and St. Francis of Assisi, attained very high Aeon LOCs, but other "considered" saints manifesting the stigmata and

---

[35] Govindan 2005, 55.

other miracles may have only attained Christ Consciousness.† Still other saints of India, like Giri Bala, have manifested great yogic power. She had the power of *inedia*,[36] whereby she did not need to eat to sustain herself physically. However, her own LOC was not of *sahaja samadhi*. Her desire was purely to subsist without food, not to have *nirvikalpa* bliss all the time per se. She employed a specific yogic technique that allowed her to gain a *siddhi* (power) over the need to ingest food or water. She is just one of many examples that have lived showing that the human body is really just packets of stilled, cosmically-conscious energy.

Progression of Stillness

Great significance is placed upon stillness while in meditation. As you ascend, this stillness becomes automatic and an intermittent minor *samadhi* state while in the 2nd Dimension. The stillness continues to increase, becoming a lesser minor *samadhi* state and then as a full-blown *savikalpa* samadhi, which is the greatest minor *samadhi* state. This minor *samadhi* stillness increases to a major *samadhi* stillness on the Interstate, which then merges with the joy of *nirvikalpa*. Eventually, major *samadhi* stillness is mixed with the absolute bliss consciousness of *nirvikalpa* in a state of complete permanence—this being the ultimate state of *sahaja samadhi*.

The interiorization of this stillness began permeating the yogi's consciousness with intermittent leaps to Semi-Superconsciousness and Superconsciousness during the first moments of a life in meditation. As the yogi progresses, this interiorization becomes greater and greater until the *savikalpa* state can be manifested and the Creator's stillness in Cosmic Consciousness can be kept during one's daily duties.

When interiorization manifests even more intensely as the Ecstatic Consciousness in *nirvikalpa*, the yogi is then completely taken into a pure state of drunken bliss. This occurs where you are aware of the bliss within and nothing else. You cannot even look at any other thing, for focus on any other object could prevent this bliss from reaching its peak.

---

† This is the LOC described in the very beginning of the TotaLOC as a part of 1st Dimension. This LOC comes immediately after the Superconsciousness LOC.
[36] Yogananda 2012, 505–517.

In the achievement of *sahaja samadhi*, the externalization of this interiorized ecstatic stillness can occur through continued focus to the third eye. To be able to spread the ecstatic dripping nectar to every part of the body is a part of this externalization process. This is the great hallmark of SS. The externalization will constantly upgrade each of the body's cells to receive higher forms of vibrational awareness. With externalization comes the ability to create the Ecstatic Consciousness at any moment in any situation. Here, you can truly navigate through the storms of life without any attachment to their outcomes.

How to Ascend

Ascension in SS and AION is fairly similar to all other LOCs previously described. All lifestyle practices are still necessary here. Right attitude, right behavior, right eating, and so on are all required.

There will not be a time during this ascension process when you can go back to living a life filled with "delusion." This is the normal and frequent participation in worldly activities, including watching daily TV, constant indulgence in processed foods, infrequent episodes of exercise, and most importantly, inconsistent and shortened meditation sessions. Although you will be immune to small amounts of "deluded" activities, increasing amounts of these activities will adversely affect your awareness of SPIRIT. The place of feeling is what determines how "well" you are performing. If the highest level of bliss is manifesting itself in the body at all times, with the divine nectar flowing, even when you wake up in the morning or go to sleep at night, you will know your daily activities are of the highest service to the Divine.

These concepts especially apply to the sex force. Even if you have an ejaculation or orgasm, there will be little loss in spiritual energy, if any, as all orgasms can be used to reach higher planes of reality while in SS and AION through a sexual *samadhi*. Remember, this applies to NrS as well, but to a lesser degree. Energy loss was more possible in NrS, because you still require sustaining willpower to manifest the divine nectar. Now that the divine nectar is always flowing in SS and AION, you just have to think happiness, and it flows in. This divine nectar is what supplies constant and pure SPIRIT energy to the body.

Focusing on this flow is what allows you to remain in an ecstatic state of consciousness. This is an essential breathless state that allows the body cells to remain alight with SPIRIT consciousness without having to input energy from the physical world. Any energy loss through ejaculation gives you a perceived loss of energy or awareness of SPIRIT. In this current state, the body can run on infinite energy from SPIRIT with only little physical sustenance. So, the perceived energy loss is just that—purely in the mind. It can be overcome by the release of divine *amrita*, which prevents spiritual energy loss after the physical loss of vital, energy-giving fluids.

Shambhavi mudra (SM) is another technique that helps to manifest the place of "feeling" in SS. Using SM in daily meditation practices while in SS will help to constantly achieve higher forms of awareness. When used in combination with the Cosmic Energy Technique (CET), you can ascend even higher and farther in SS and AION. These two together cause an LOC induction, activating immediate ascension, causing further increase in joy, bliss, and God perception. Realize that SPIRIT is ever-new bliss, and the perception of this bliss never ends once you merge with SS. With advanced use of SM, you will be able to blend both the physical and astral worlds, eyes wide open, allowing for heavenly light to be seen anywhere and everywhere.

You can also "practice the presence," which is a form of mental devotion and awareness that forces you to be aware of the Divine in all of your actions. This exercise is still necessary while in SS, because, if you surround yourself with minds of an extremely low LOC, you will be actively challenged to use meditative techniques to keep the bliss. I actually use this strategy in every moment of my life. Usually, it is done by practicing techniques—whether focusing on the third eye, repetition of mantras, or use of the Cosmic Energy Technique—and it is necessary to keep the evolution going, preventing the LOC from dropping or from you getting discouraged.

Practicing the presence is essential where ever you go in life. People of differing vibrations exist everywhere, and without your constant vigilance, your LOC will drop very easily. If you go to a bar and everyone is using vulgar and illicit language, then the mind will fill up on those words and automatically begin to use them. This is especially if you have ever used them yourself. Or if you are surrounded with gluttonous people, then overeating will become a normal situation because this is the energy that is being given off and absorbed. Whether you swear or overeat, the SPIRIT will remain in its fullness, but the feeling will change because the physical body instruments are being used over the instruments of the astral, causal, or soul bodies. This feeling is perceived at this point, because the body and mind are fully fused with the bliss consciousness of SPIRIT.

Practicing the presence while using mantras or thoughts of devotion are extremely helpful, because you are revolving your mind around words and ideas of the highest nature. Because your intuition is also very strong in SS, you are able to select the best mantras through the practice of intuitive muscle testing. Combine these mantras with practicing the presence, CET, and SM in meditation, and you will have a very powerful set of techniques to practice, allowing the body to evolve in every moment of every day. There is another technique which I have almost perfected, called *kechari mudra*. This *mudra* activates the release of nectar or amrita into the oral cavity. It is the most powerful technique I have discovered and is the fastest way for me to activate the highest levels of *nirvikalpa* bliss.

As ascension increases, if you are a meat-eater blood type[†] and require it for proper metabolism, your own desire for eating meat will wane as the LOC increases into NrS, SS, and especially, AION. All in all, your desire for food will decrease, as the divine nectar will serve in feeding the body's needs for physical sustenance. This will wax and wane with the seasons, but will have an overall decrease in your desire and ultimate need to eat animal protein of any kind.

Eating with the seasons is essential in maintaining proper body balance. The body has a tendency to eat a larger variety of foods in the winter (mixing is OK), and in the summer, mostly water-based foods should be consumed. This is the natural progression whether you have karma or not, have *samskaras* or not, and whether or not you have achieved self-realization.

Seasonal cycles on the Earth also have great effects on your consciousness. One particular time of each month includes a fully

---

† Refer to Dr. D'Adamo's book, *Eat Right for Your Blood Type*, for more information. This is mentioned because I myself am a blood-type O and have eaten animal meat for many years and continue to do so. The bliss maintained in my own body is as eternal as it was when I first manifested *nirvikalpa*. I will say that even in the beginning stages of *savikalpa* and *asamprajñata*, as the body was ascending, it wasn't about <u>what</u> I was eating, but <u>where</u> my consciousness was during meals themselves. If you can maintain focus towards the third eye with extreme devotion and submission towards the Divine, then anything is possible. If you limit "the way" to the Divine saying that vegetarianism or veganism is the only way, then you will be mistaken. You have to release your attachments to all physical things, allowing for the Divine to guide your actions.

visible moon. During these times, astral energy is much higher, allowing for you to feel super-charged and balanced at the same time. This is similar to self-realization, as you can be completely balanced but have all the divine energy ever desired. During the full moon, you can feel both creative and engaged. This is the peak time during the month not only for celebration, but also for you to forward yourself to bigger and better things.

Pay attention to all major holidays that have a strong pull toward your spiritual practice. These times are the best opportunities for mass increases in LOC of the individual, groups of people, and the world at large. For Christians, it may be Christmas and Easter. For Hindus, it will be *Janmashtami*, birthdays, and/or *mahasamadhis* of various gurus. Each religion has their own particular spiritual week, month, or period of time that followers celebrate to help cleanse their bodies and minds of any earthly impurity. You do not necessarily need to follow one spiritual path over another. If you can recognize the essential unity in all religions, then a celebration for a God-realized saint or avatar will prove very spiritually enlightening for those who are spiritually receptive

If you have a universally acceptable mind, your LOC has a better chance of increasing exponentially during these special days, allowing you to truly become self-realized within a shorter period of time. Ascension may occur so quickly that it could cause some mild physical suffering in your body for a shortened period of time. Nausea to headaches to other bodily symptoms may arise with this rapid attunement. Don't be afraid of these sensations, as they will pass, but if these symptoms persist over more than one day, it may be something more serious and possibly pathological. Don't confuse ascension symptoms with bodily symptoms you may ignore because you haven't eaten enough, gotten enough sleep, or maintained good exercise and proper physical hygiene. All of these factors are still required in proper ascension. Realize, too, that this type of suffering only occurs once you have attuned to The Aionion State (AION, because AION is measured in Aeons, and the jump is massively larger than normal increases in LOC.

This type of attunement can only occur if you truly desire it. You may be so overcome with bliss that further ascension is not necessary for your purposes. However, if you want to ascend to higher levels of realized bliss, being attuned to an entire Aeon is necessary. Although it may have taken you 5, 10, 15, or even 30 years to get to the peak of *nirvikalpa* and beyond, if your desire is to continue to ascend as quickly as possible, then you will attune to an entire Aeon more easily. SPIRIT knows the desires of all, and thus, grants attunement to those individuals who put forth the necessary effort.

Sensations

The feeling of divine love in the body is a wonderful sensation that can and will come to you infinitely many times while in the physical body. These divine sensations manifest themselves at the highest points of each Aeon level in SS Proper. However, this divine love is not an indication of complete liberation.

While in SS, both the "feeling" and "not feeling" are a part of the same "thing," which is SPIRIT. They are figments of creation that prevent the soul from becoming completely merged with SPIRIT. You may feel completely human one moment and supernaturally enlightened in the next. To truly experience the void of SPIRIT is to experience nothingness. How can nothingness feel like anything?

In this case, nothingness is supreme consciousness, ever-existing with an unfathomable bliss. As the physical body waxes and wanes in and out of existence through many trials of sickness and mental/emotional tribulation, the feeling of SPIRIT will come and go. It is what you can do with this type of realization that is proving. Maintain the ascension standards set above and the SPIRIT will always be in the yogi's feeling place of be-ing always.

Sahaja is not only the name of the highest *samadhi* dispensation, but it is also a certain practice of yoga. Commonly, individuals practicing Sahaja yoga will feel a cool breeze that can brush across their hands and feet while in deep meditation.[37] This sensation is indicative of the movement of *kundalini* in the body. While you are ascending, especially through the 1st, 2nd, 3rd, and multidimensional realms, "cooling" sensations can and will be experienced throughout various parts of the body. Currently, during my own meditations, these cooling sensations occur after I have meditated and quieted the physical body and mind down to absolute stillness.

These Sahaja yogic practitioners believe that cooling sensations are one of positive change, while experiencing heat in these places could

---

[37] Coney 1999.

show imbalance. The cooling sensations may occur around the ears, on the cheeks, across the face, on top of the head, and in other sensitive places that have relevance to you. These cooling sensations can be a sign of blessing from the angels, saints, gurus, or even God. These blessings are absolutely necessary when ascending on the path of self-realization. They may be felt a few times or many times. The number of times does not matter, as it could occur once or an infinite amount of times to help you know that, nearby, there is a guiding presence.

If a "heat-like" or warm flushing experience occurs while in deep meditation, then you know that there is an imbalance of some kind. These most likely occur because the physical body is what creates the heat, telling the consciousness that there is a problem. The "heated" sensations can occur at other times as well. If you are able to burn the karma of another safely, especially after performing physical healing work like massage or joint manipulation, large heat waves will be taken on into the body. This is usually reasonable, unless the healing practitioner is drained by it or it caused him/her to become ill. chiropractic medicine is a great way to help realign the musculoskeletal system to create a physically balanced body, so that the energy in the various channels of the body (*chakras* and *nadis*/meridians) can flow easily. Heat flushing can occur if there is a misalignment of the spinal joints in any way. These hot (and cool) sensations are intuitive indicators helping you to know how you are progressing down the path.

Other sensations experienced may be loss of awareness of other areas of the body. This experience may occur at the feet, for example, because life force is still being removed and sent to the spine up to the third eye for further realizations. A reason why yogis inhabit hot environments and eat nothing but vegetables, fruits, and other vegetarian foods is that the energy going to digestion for heavier foods like animal meats is not always present in a sufficient quantity. Constipation is a common occurrence for those that feel they require more meat than the average yogi, so a larger quantity of vegetables, fruits, and water are needed for these individuals to maintain proper bowel movements.

The sensitivity of the body during this ascension in AION is increased exponentially because the nature of AION is purely consciousness. When you are in baseline *nirvikalpa samadhi*, your nature

is etheric and ideational because the causal body is still ruled by ego.†
The body will reject foods that contain artificial preservatives, dyes, and other synthetic materials almost immediately. It is difficult to live in a world, surrounded by a mass assortment of seemingly delicious foodstuffs that cause pain and suffering in the individual consuming them. This is the challenge of becoming self-realized while living in a time with so many food technologies and a lack of knowledge towards their effects on the body. Taking in carbohydrates in simple form is not bad, but it can have disastrous effects on blood glucose, affecting your ability to stay awake during long periods of mediation.

As you ascend in LOC, you will be able to access various bodily aspects at will. These are the five senses of the physical body, astral vision/hearing of the subtle body, and ideational viewing of the causal body. When you manifest pure bliss consciousness in SS, the sights and sounds here are much different than at previous levels. You no longer hear the rumble of the *Om* sound, but the silence of the void (supreme silence). Initially, in the junction between NrS and SS, the sounds of *Om* begin to intermingle with the silence. This infinite silence and the finite sound of *Om* come together in the DSCE to drown out all existing noise in a symphony of dualism and non-dualism. Progressing into the pure bliss consciousness of SPIRIT, only the deafening silence is present, one that is like the vacuum of space perceived in nothingness.

The same goes for "void" vision. The light of the third eye is no longer a kaleidoscope of color seen as a part of the astral heaven or the particle-based reality of the ideational cosmos. Instead, at the spiritual eye, you perceive an amorphous mass of purple and pink with eyes closed. These colors represent the highest color frequency that goes beyond the color schema of the *chakras* or of an idyllic rainbow (of ROY G BIV‡). These colors represent SPIRIT in purity. With eyes open, through the merger of both astral light and physical reality, waves of SPIRIT are seen, existing on the surface of an infinite ocean,

---

† When you are in the highest form of *nirvikalpa samadhi*, the ecstatic state, the causal body is no longer ruled by ego. The ecstatic state, however, is very difficult to achieve all the time. Baseline *nirvikalpa samadhi* still has traces of ego and is most easily maintained after willful achievement of the ecstatic state.

‡ ROY G BIV stand for Red, Orange, Yellow, Green, Blue, Indigo, Violet. They are the colors of a physical rainbow and also the *chakras* starting from 1 up through 7

breaking on the consciousness of the yogi. You cannot know what SPIRIT really looks like, as it is made of nothing existing within a void that is of just consciousness. These colors are just one of the infinite manifestations of SPIRIT, but represent one of the highest specific color versions of SPIRIT. This is of course other than that of white light that is commonly known throughout most major and minor world religions.

Exercise Considerations

Exercise of any intense duration can be moderated easily. Because stillness is present all the time while in higher states of consciousness, willpower will need to be focused in the limbs more often to sustain more intense exercises. Increased cardiovascular exercises are not necessary per se, but keeping the physical body in shape is still essential. Each person is different and should consult with his or her physician before starting any new routines.

Any yogic *asanas* and exercises provided by the guru will serve to be very helpful. Many masters in SS do not require intense exercise. Most are commonly seen in the lotus posture, seated for days as other devotees prayed and meditated around them. This is not the case for the common workingman and -woman during this current Earth age. You must toil on the Earth while sustaining the highest God-like contact to help burn the mass karma of the world, all while advancing consciousness to the next level.

Now that the yogi has fused consciousness permanently with that of the bliss consciousness of SPIRIT in SS, the drunken *samadhi* state of bliss can occur at any moment, even during mild exercise. The most common kind of exercise that I have experienced is walking or even riding a bike, because the exercise is not very intense and allows the focused life force to be directed towards the third eye and the seventh *chakra*. Commonly for me, I would be riding down the street on a bicycle in the busy noon-hour streets of China's Jiangsu province and experiencing full-on *nirvikalpa* bliss. Trust me when I say it is not easy! If you thought you had trust issues before, try being completely immersed, attempting to balance a bike in heavy China traffic. It is a challenge at best!

Healings

At a certain point within the various levels of AION, spontaneous healing will occur in your body at will. This healing process is activated by initiations to the DSCE by a major *samadhi*, allowing access to advanced *samadhi* LOCs. Healing can also be activated consciously and willfully by the use of the Cosmic Energy Technique (CET) with directed focus to the area of disease.

Generally, if the *samadhi* state is manifested with or without the use of the CET, the spinal column, including vertebrae, spinal cord, and surrounding nerves, will be disease free. This is because of the flow of Light that has descended into the spine during the transitional state of *asamprajñata samadhi* (Añ). The healing energy of SPIRIT through the *samadhi* state and especially active use of the CET will not only heal the nerves surrounding the spinal column but also the organs that are attached to them. The common viscero-somatic (organ-muscle) or somato-visceral (muscle-organ) reflexes that cause subluxations in the spine—treated by Chiropractors and the like—will occur much less in the divine body of the individual manifesting the *sahaja* state. The same may be the case for those manifesting Añ and NrS, but it is an automatic ability in SS. The ability to heal not only yourself, but also others will continue to progress as you ascend in LOC in SS.

Siddhis

If you cannot manifest all known *siddhis* (yogic powers) through self-realization, then your enlightenment experience is for the strict purpose of bringing about knowledge for the whole world. If your desire is not for great yogic powers but to experience infinite bliss, peace, joy, wisdom, and understanding, then this will be your gifts of the SPIRIT. It is not about manifesting great power, although you may desire this experience. It is about bringing the Divine Consciousness to humanity. However, the only way to do this is through manifesting the highest levels of LOCs. You cannot perceive this infinite truth without being attuned to the LOC. Realize that you do not need to experience those states to learn about them, at least not anymore. They have all been expounded upon and made available for everyone's use in this book and by other self-realized masters in the last 2,000 years. All can now know God through scientific methods of yoga and meditation.

AION TRANSITIONAL STATES

As you ascend in LOC and are able to attune to one Aeon level at a time, quicker ascension will be possible. These transitional states are very transient and are difficult to attune to. They will be transcended in the most unusual ways, not in the normal fashion through strength of willpower and devotion. Pure surrender and humility is the only requirement. You are now in Divine Consciousness, which is one step from SPIRIT while in physical form.

AION Transitional State #1 (AT#1)

Between 59,999 – 60,000 Aeons
Value of Levels = $CC1^{(CC1\wedge(1E100))}$, # of Levels = $CC1^{(CC1\wedge(1E100))}$
Aeon Level transiency after AT#1 = 60x normal
Divine Superconsciousness

AT#1 is an extremely transient and unstable state that requires deep focus and attentiveness because you have to manifest a DSCE to even ascend while in this state. Generally, this achievement takes intense willpower while in meditation. The LOC in this transitional state fluctuates up and down wildly, greatly affected by anything that isn't focused on SPIRIT. It is as if there is a slippery slope of consciousness. You cannot run up the side of the mountain with sheer willpower, you must float up its slope in the Divine Superconscious state. You will feel like you are being sucked inside of something smaller because the body needs to attune to the new level of transiency. almost like the soul is being pulled out the small recesses of the body, merging with something much larger and deeper within.

After AT#1, the Aeons take on a new characteristic. They maintain the same type of transiency seen in the transitional state itself to help you maintain the consciousness necessary to continually ascend in God's love and bliss. In a way, it forces you to be ever mindful of the necessity of God's presence in everyday life. The transiency of this level is 60x greater than the SIT and breathlessness measured in *asamprajñata*.

Once you are able to attune completely to this level, the DSCE can now be manifested while you are seated in meditation. The DSCE cannot be carried with you throughout daily duties until the next transitional state has been reached.

The Aeon levels between AT#1 and AT#2 can be frustrating, because the focus required to ascend is monumental. You need time to attune to the consciousness in as many situations as possible before ascendance occurs. Ascending too quickly and then going out into a world of delusion can send abnormal and unnecessary shocks into the bodily system. The body needs to attune, adjust, and then ascend. This three-step process occurs over and over again, until full mergence with SPIRIT in the DSCE occurs. This is the Law of Ascension.

When you merge with the NDCR in NrS and then ascend to SS, you become permanently attuned to NDCR. Now, you have access to it at will because you have shed your final *kosha*, the bliss sheath or causal body covering. The soul is now free to truly roam in the garden of SPIRIT.

The *samadhi* experienced in *sahaja*, in its most basic form, is referred to as a Sahaja Samadhi Proper (SS proper). This is the baseline consciousness that occurs in SS and is representative of the permanent shedding of the causal body. However, you have yet to fully fuse to the infinite nature of SPIRIT. You may be able to have random, varied, and eventually, at-will experiences of the Divine Superconsciousness, but you will never fully unify with SPIRIT. If the fusion has occurred, you can no longer associate with anything of a physical nature. You would now have to exert willpower just to stay attached to the physical body. Before, you had to exert the will to stay in Divine Superconsciousness, now the opposite will occur. This LOC is generally reserved for world teachers or those truly self-realized masters, including Sri Bhagavan Krishna, Jesus Christ, Mahavatar Babaji, Yogananda, etc. There have been many named that choose to live on Earth for a period of time so that they may help to steer the mass karma of the Earth toward a positive state.

Ascension can only occur after AT#1 when the consciousness is a part of a DSCE. Here, a DSCE can be accessed while walking around. Ascension can only occur before AT#1 when accessing the intermediate level between SS proper and DSCE. This intermediate level is an extension experience similar to the CAñSe of Añ where you can access it with control, but it serves to help you ascend among the various Aeons. It is referred to as a SSee or a *sahaja samadhi* extension experience. These names have been used to help accurately describe where these states occur and at what level. This is necessary, because this process is a scientific one. All scientists go through methods of observation and analysis when discovering something new.

AION Transitional State #2 (AT#2)

Between 99,999 – 100,000 Aeons
Value of Levels = $CC1^{(CC1^{\wedge}(1E100))}$, # of Levels = 50% of an Aeon (TotaLOC)
Aeon Level Transiency after AT#2 = 60,000x normal
Divine Superconsciousness

AT#2 ends once an individual is able to achieve 100,000 Aeons, which allows you to achieve a DSCE while walking around performing household tasks. According to the number of levels in this transitional state, the TotaLOC or Aeon is now being used as a variable that not only represents the value of something but how many levels are contained within the transitional state. It should take no time to transcend these levels, considering an Aeon is colossally larger than the value of each of these levels. The transiency of the Aeons at this transitional level and after AT#2 is 1000x greater than that of the levels between 60,000 to 99,999. This also means that these Aeons are now 60,000x greater than the original Aeons found between 1 and 59,999.

However, performing an open-eyed *shambhavi mudra* may be difficult because the stimulation from the visual system can take too much away from the DSCE. The consciousness needs to be in AT#2 and steadily increasing to have enough energy to overcome the visual stimulation pouring in through the brain into the occipital cortex. Once the energy can be controlled here, ascension is easy because the eyes can experience an AS (astral *samadhi*). Instead of seeing astral light, waves of SPIRIT are perceived. This is the next step in the body's evolution—to utilize the instruments of SPIRIT to perceive Itself as a manifestation.

SPIRIT can manifest Itself in an infinite amount of ways as seen in the creation of the universe itself. However, this manifestation may be one that is most appealing or recognizable to your consciousness. Possibly, they may perceive these waves astrally, as light, or causally, as waves or particles of superether.[38] This at-will DSCE occurs to allow you access to SPIRIT in numerous ways that can be aural (sound),

---

[38] *Einstein and the Universe: A Popular Exposition of the Famous Theory* is a book by Charles Nordmann written in 1922. The word "superether" comes from this book on physics and how there is a mass of etheric particles, which overlaps the ether found in all of interstellar space. I use the term here because it is something spoken about in physics as theory, but also is known intuitively by deeply meditating yogis in the causal realm of the cosmos.

visual (sight), and tactile (touch). Touch is saved for self-realized gurus, as it shows the supreme ability to manifest SPIRIT in all of its fullness.

As you continue to ascend, the consciousness must be ever-mindful of SPIRIT and the divine drip in every moment. To manifest the divine drip is to actively increase in LOC. The benefit of AT#1 and AT#2 is that you can continue in joy without any real rise in LOC. This can be frustrating to some who want to see how high they can go. At the same time, if you are content with your current accomplishments, this situation is satisfactory. However, be cautious because if you do not continue proper meditations with increased vigilance towards SPIRIT, a decrease in your LOC is sure to occur. Fortunately, it will only drop to 100,000 Aeons and no further. Once you get beyond these transitional states, you can never drop back down again into the previous Aeon levels. You may not be in a DSCE, but you will be at the baseline Aeon in a *sahaja samadhi* at the current level of transiency.

When ascendance to 100,000 Aeons and beyond occurs (walking DSCE), you will have complete control over the *chitta (anandamaya) kosha*, leading to the ability to know anything and everything. At this point, you will have complete control over *chitta*.[39][†] This sheath can be accessed at will in SS and intermittently when you experience the DSCE throughout the 3rd Dimension, Multidimensional, and Extradimensional Realms. Being able to peel back the *chitta kosha* at will is necessary if you expect to convey, transmit, and transfer any sort of spiritual truth to those of a lower vibrational LOC without losing any energy yourself.

AION Transitional State #3 (AT#3)

Between 499,999 – 500,000 Aeons
Value of Levels = $CC1^{(CC1 \wedge CC1)}$, # of Levels = 75% of an Aeon (TotaLOC)
Aeon Level Transiency after AT#3 = $5.99E^{10}x = 59,999,999,994x$ Divine Superconsciousness
AT#3 occurs in three phases:
#3A – Normal adjustment to increased-level transiency
#3B – Similar to sMje-T2 state with repeating 9's, repeated
    $CC1^{CC1 \wedge CC1}$ times with the same transiency

---

[39] Haas 2012, 157.
† *Chitta* is perfect spiritual wisdom gained through ascension in consciousness.

#3C – DSCE cannot be accessed because a transition is taking place in the body. Physical vibration and consciousness changes greatly here. It feels like an empty space that is filled with nothing but white brightness. You can hear the SPIRIT sound of silence ringing in the ears along with visualization of the purplish-pink spiritual eye. This visualization can occur with eyes open or eyes closed. This phase has no value but presence alone. The transiency of this phase is the same as the transitional LOC itself.

This transitional state allows you a final merger into the DSCE. You may be able to experience this merger at will and while walking around; however, it cannot be maintained indefinitely as a permanent part of your consciousness. At this junction, the breathless state is now automatically present, generally sensed more conclusively with a sensation of cool air filling the nostrils.

Achieving this state will allow you supreme access to the DSCE at all times with little or no willpower. Some say that fusion into this state causes you to lose the personality of your human self and gain the true nature of your SPIRIT self. This is a worry of devotees when witnessing their guru become a permanent resident of this glorified state of consciousness. Nothing is further from the truth. Now completely a part of SPIRIT, you will lose all desire of the material world but will gain SPIRIT's bliss eternally. This allows for the deepest connection between creation and Creator.

At this level, God now becomes responsible for your actions. Through this process you are able to shed your God sheath, *Sat kosha*, the final remaining layer separating you from SPIRIT. This process can happen through death or through ascendance to this state. This mergence is also similar to how you can achieve a non-dual major *samadhi* (NDCR-sMje) in *nirvikalpa* but cannot maintain it completely as a permanent part of your consciousness until SS has been achieved.

In this state of consciousness, you are now a "born-again *siddha*." A *siddha* in yoga is generally considered an ascetic, renunciant, swami, or yogi who follows a particular spiritual practice.[40] A *siddha* may also be defined as one who has attained a *siddhi* or paranormal power.[41] These

---

[40] Zimmerman 2013.
[41] White 2012.

powers may be subtle and/or very powerful and do not necessarily define the individual.

These *siddhis* have been mentioned throughout the book; however, realize that the greatest power for all, including the perfected masters, ascended masters, and the self-realized workingman, is to manifest the Divine's bliss in any situation. This is a supernatural feat all its own. In reality, the *siddhi* in its purest form is to attain the highest identity with SPIRIT through bliss consciousness. This means to be able to become one with the DSCE, manifesting it in all situations, including sleep. The DSCE is the broader category of *anantya* and *turiya* and is the field where both of these states of mind lie. You can experience the highest conscious (*anantya*) or the highest unconscious (*turiya*) forms of bliss within the realm of the DSCE.

In this complete mergence, the ego, soul, and SPIRIT are realized as one and the same. The ego, now realized as one and the same as the "I-ness" within and the SPIRIT all around, can no longer negatively affect your consciousness. Ego may try to contact you through the medium of the mind-field, but at this point, it may only be able to annoy through the tossing of peanuts or table tennis balls.

Ego still has its affect, but just enough to make you feel off for a moment. Whether you act egoistically or spiritually does not matter, because all of your aspects are being operated together simultaneously. This is a difficult concept to grasp, but I can illustrate it for you. Do you remember when Jesus got angry and flipped over the tables in the temple? From the outside, it may appear that this anger was a result of the ego, but in fact, it was not. Jesus, being fully merged in the Absolute, could operate in any emotion, for any need, at any time, and for any purpose. The instrument of anger can be used to positively direct energy to change a particular situation. In that moment, Jesus used his divine power to spiritually convert the money-minded merchants to see the error of their ways. This is the true power of this AION merger.

When you merge with the DSCE, you can no longer measure the intensity of meditation with mere body stillness, out-of-body experiences, supreme joy, or the divine drip. Now that the body, mind, and consciousness have permanently merged into the Divine Superconsciousness of SPIRIT, the only level of intensity that is measured is how clear the thoughts have become.

The clearer and the cleaner the thoughts of the Minervan man[†], ascended, perfected master, the more quickly he or she will achieve the highest intensities of the full mergence. When you are fully merged, you feel everything in the condition of the body and consciousness of SPIRIT—without any separation. Even at this point, the devilish delusion of this material world can insert momentary thoughts of impurity, but no change in the consciousness can occur. There may seem to be some change in the demeanor of the master, whether expressing anger, indifference, or immense joy, but there is no attachment to the emotion expressed, and thus no change in the consciousness.

The true ascension into SPIRIT is all based upon the individual. How far will you go to experience and know yourself as SPIRIT? You may lose yourself in SPIRIT, only to find yourself again. This is the reality of all things—to become apart from the One, only to dissolve into Oneness again and again.

Further Measurement

When you merge with the DSCE, you can no longer measure your intensity of meditation with mere body stillness, out-of-body experiences, supreme joy, or the divine drip. Now that the body, mind, and consciousness have permanently merged into the Divine Superconsciousness of SPIRIT, the only level of intensity that is measured is how clear the thoughts have become.

AION Transitional State #4 (AT#4)

Between 999,999 – 1,000,000 Aeons
Value of Levels = $CC1^{(CC1^{\wedge}CC1)^{\wedge}CC1}$, # of Levels = 1 Aeon (TotaLOC)
Aeon Level Transiency = Christ Transiency
Divine Superconsciousness

The difference between 999,999 and 1,000,000 Aeons is like the difference between Yogananda and Jesus Christ. One was a great world teacher, inspiring millions to practice yoga as a path to permanent salvation and the other has been revered as God-incarnate, savior to the world, and respected as a true prophet in all world religions. The

---

[†] "Minervan" here represents the workingman or -woman in their climb towards self-realization. These concepts are mentioned in Chapter 4: The Minervan Man.

two may seem very similar, but their souls were purposed for different things.

Both had similar, if not the same, *siddhis* (yogic powers) that allowed them to heal at will, bilocate, and perform a full host of abilities that are only available to those world teachers that help to burn the mass karma of the world. The ascendance between the two LOC values is not necessary for the workingman, only for those who have been purposed to influence the world as a whole.

Transiency Summary:
- Normal transiency
  - Levels before AT#1
  - Aeons 1 – 59,999
- 60x normal transiency
  - Levels in AT#1
  - Aeons 60,000 – 99,999
- 60,000x normal transiency
  - Levels in AT#2
  - Aeons 100,000 – 499,999
- $5.99E^{10}x = 59,999,999,994x$ normal transiency
  - Levels in AT#3
  - Aeons 500,000 – 999,999
- The Christ Transiency
  - Levels in AT#4
  - Aeon 1,000,000

MAITREYAN CONSCIOUSNESS (MC)

This level is where few self-realized masters have ever tread. Only a few souls within the existence of the universe continually come back here during a particular epoch of time, helping humankind to evolve through its dark and golden ages.

Maitreya is a Sanskrit word used mainly in Buddhism to describe the future Buddha of Earth. It is a word that means "loving-kindness" or "friend." These *maitreyas* are the successors to the Buddha himself.[42,43] It is also believed that Zoroastrianism influenced this *maitreyan* concept. Their beliefs say the *maitreya* is one who is a "heavenly helper" or provides "universal salvation" for all.[44] Many have been given this title, and some have tried to claim it for themselves.[45] It is a name that cannot be claimed, only given by those of every religion, for the *maitreya* is a teacher, bringing peace and harmony to all religions.

In the 21st century, *maitreya* is used to describe the "world teacher." The two souls that fit this description are Jesus Christ and Mahavatar Babaji. One is the Christ of the Western world, and one is the Yogi-Christ of the Eastern world. One reportedly still lives in a physical body, while the other remains in SPIRIT. Both are here to help the world evolve to a higher plane of existence. Yogananda elaborated upon the differences on these two Christs in his book, *Autobiography of a Yogi*.

Their own LOCs are far above that of any perfected master who has come before or after. Some say that the Christ of Hinduism, known as Krishna, is the same the soul who came to the Jews, known as Jesus the Christ. This would account for the similarity in their LOCs at 1,000,000 Aeons each. However, Mahavatar Babaji, the Christ of India, is known as a savior who is helping evolve the world out of the current dark age period, even though he is still in the physical body. He is talked about in *Autobiography of a Yogi* and elsewhere; however, it is unlikely that this great master would ever show himself to the masses. Only those truly dedicated devotees and other self-realized masters are able to catch a glimpse of this divinely-created soul.

CONCLUSIONS

For each person on the path to self-realization, some things will remain the same, where others will not. Certain aspects will always be consistent, such as the characteristics of stillness, peace, joy, and bliss. They are all continually amplified as you ascend in the states of *samadhi*. Other yogis who have practiced the art of peace and joy through stillness for a lifetime may be able to gain much greater experiences while ascending in LOC. This is not the experience of the

---

[42] Horner 1975, 97.
[43] Buddha Dharma Education Association 2014.
[44] Williams 1989, 230.
[45] Wikipedia 2015.

"workingman" per se. If your ascension is quick, it is because there is great purpose in it. If the ascension is slow, then greater experiences may be had with this type of ascension.

Living in a world of duality, nothing is as it seems. One thing, however, remains the same. We are all on a journey that leads to the same place, regardless of the path you take. As the LOC increases, bliss and *samadhi* stillness will only increase exponentially in magnitude. Whether you possess great yogic powers or not should not matter. As long you can really let go of all that makes you human, while at the same time fully embracing it, you will experience the true non-duality of SPIRIT's consciousness.

Remember that the LOCs described above measure your bliss consciousness. Many may believe they will gain great powers after attaining such a high level of consciousness, but this is not the case. Only great world teachers and other self-realized avatars have access to these types of *siddhis*. It would be delusional to believe that just because you can manifest joy at any moment you can also read into the future or bilocate at will. The LOCs explained here and the techniques that were offered show a way to manifest the highest levels of bliss and *samadhi* stillness. Nothing more. It is for each person on the path to self-realization to realize what their purpose is in attaining the absolute consciousness.

In this way, self-realization is about removing the barriers of the true SPIRIT world so that the truth can shine onto this delusional dream reality. It is necessary to bring about this process in all religions and belief-systems, so that each person may understand how to reach that higher vibration and achieve true and permanent release from their earthly sufferings. It is this attainment of bliss consciousness that allows you to travel any terrain this world gives, maintaining complete blissful composure.

This self-control is maintained with moderation in meditation. This is the key to achieving the goals of those masters who came before. It is obvious their purpose was to show us that it is possible to achieve self-realization in one lifetime, if your desire is nothing else. These masters, however, lived a life of extremity. This is not the way for the future workingman and woman, living as householders, battling the trials and tribulations of a material-bound society. It is time to realize that moderation is necessary to achieve the highest levels of realization. You do not need a lonely mountaintop to ascend to the peak of

SPIRIT's consciousness. Determination, devotion, and dedication will bring on true deliverance. Ultimately, the fastest way to self-realization is to embrace ALL in moderation, with God as your center and focus.

As you harness your power of concentration and succeed at developing a meditative practice, the ego will try to either break you down or build you up. Comparisons are a common mental distraction when you are attempting to ascend up the ladder of consciousness. To compare your own meditation experiences to those of any other individual, teacher, or master is wrong, and spiritually unhealthy. Once you begin to merge with SPIRIT in meditation, you become Its instrument to carry out Its will for the evolution of the universe. As a Divine instrument, you will experience SPIRIT in the way that is special to you. The same applies to both mankind and divinely conscious souls alike.

Even the masters themselves do not think they are masters, but rather children on the stage of God's dream reality. Even after receiving his initiation into the Cosmic Consciousness through fantastical experience, Yogananda, in his book *Autobiography of a Yogi*, says to his guru, "When do I find God?" This shows that even the masters realize that the experience of SPIRIT goes on forever, always allowing the dreamer yogi to experience the many roles SPIRIT can play as yourself or others.

These roles of the divine, played on the stage of the universe, are the future of tomorrow; showing that all men and women will come to self-realization on their own terms. In the future, there will be self-realization scholars and spiritual scientists. Metaphysics and the hard sciences will no longer be at odds with one another. A scientist of one will come to realize the perfection in the science of another. Peace and harmony will reign in the hearts of man, because people of all kinds will have full, unbridled access to all ways to God. Nothing will be hidden from the masses.

The bottom line is this: it is truly the greatest gift, for you or a devotee of any religion on this path, to not only have God's joy, but also to have God in His entirety at a moment's notice. The Divine's love is enough, but you will always want to go infinitely deeper in that love. To have this love is true salvation. It is obtained in *nirvikalpa* and made permanent in *sahaja*. This state is where all things melt into one consciousness, all the time, in the everything of the yogi. There is no more matter. There is only SPIRIT.

CHAPTER 17

A Siddhi Summary

In Chapters 8, 15, and 16 it was mentioned that self-realized masters had access to yogic powers called *siddhis*.[1] These powers manifest differently, whether you are a workingman (Minervan), ascended master, or perfected master.

These *siddhis* are described as spiritual, supernatural, and sometimes, paranormal. They are obtained through long and intense practices of meditation and yoga. There are stories of individuals who would spontaneously manifest yogic power, such as the saints of Christianity, the yogis and swamis of Hinduism, the Buddhist *bodhisattvas*, and Islamic *fakirs*.

In the *Bhagavata Purana*, a scriptural text of Hinduism, eight primary *siddhis* are described. They are said to be attained by those of immense power. These include Bhagavan the Krishna, Jesus the Christ, and Mahavatar Babaji. Primary siddhis have also been achieved by lesser known saints and masters of self-realization. St. Theresa of Avila, St. Joseph of Cupertino, The Apostles of Jesus, The Buddha, Swami Adi

---

[1] *Bhagavata Purana* 11.15:3–33

Shankara, Lahiri Mahasaya, Anandamayi Ma, Neem Karoli Baba, Trailanga Swami, Yogananda, and others are included in this group.

The ten secondary powers described by Krishna are commonly experienced by those in deep meditation. There are some *siddhis* in this set that can only be attained at the highest level of self-realization. The next five minor *siddhis* are yogic powers gained through long, sustained, physical practice of yoga and meditation. Some of these abilities may be achieved with or without a *samadhi* experience and can be experienced transiently or permanently for meditators of any LOC.

The final set shown in this book was originally described by Patanjali in his *Yoga Sutras*. This four-part piece of literature briefly explains the many aspects of the physical and spiritual practices of yoga. Patanjali describes 44 *siddhis* in total. These *Yoga Sutras* were considered to be written several centuries before many of the major historical texts of Hinduism. In this way, it remains one of the first major literary sources of yogic knowledge.

Most major-known *siddhis* were included in this book, but some very minor ones may not be listed. Patanjali was considered the first to elaborate upon the various supernatural powers, but they were later emphasized in the *Bhagavata Purana*. Patanjali's list is all inclusive, but I also included the *Bhagavata's* classifications of these *siddhis*. The *siddhis* are also mentioned in the *Samkhyakarika, Tattvasamasa,* and the totality of the *Puranas*. All of these texts are derived from different schools of thought in Hinduism. This is similar to how Christianity has segregated itself into multiple denominations with different versions of the Old and New Testaments.

You do not have to be in a secluded Himalaya solitude to experience the 10 secondary and five minor powers, but it is naturally best to achieve them in the purest and safest state of scientific meditation. Some may be gifted with these abilities but not have ever meditated. These individuals have a divinely-bestowed gift that must be used for the highest purpose. Otherwise, negative karma will accumulate, causing suffering for them and others they affect. Realize too that all *siddhis* come about because of consistent, constant, and frequent concentration in the form of *samyama*.[†] However, you need to first achieve *samadhi* to understand how to combine *dharana, dhyana,* and *samadhi* together to create *samyama*, which allows you to supremely gain

---

† *Samyama* is a combination of *dharana* (concentration), *dhyana* (meditation), and *samadhi* (ultimate stillness and meditative absorption)

any power you desire. Even these powers are cravings that get in the way of the ultimate goal of yoga—liberation.

The eight primary *siddhis* are mentioned in most ancient texts of Hinduism, including the *Bhagavata Purana* and Patanjali's *Yoga Sutras*. First are the major *siddhis*, next are the secondary *siddhis* followed by the minor *siddhis* gained through meditation and yoga. Finally, the last *siddhis* mentioned are those briefly alluded to through Patanjali's work.

The first set of *siddhis* are only for supremely-realized masters and are rarely granted to lesser-realized yogis. There are few individuals that have been reported to maintain certain yogic power through a disembodied spirit, but *siddhis* are only granted to the most highly-realized souls, like Jesus the Christ and Mahavatar Babaji. Those individuals that use lesser ways to gain yogic power (whether through illicit substances or lower life forms) have not been given the greatest level of divine dispensation. These lesser ways commonly lead the yogi on a destructive path. The first three lists of siddhis mentioned below are in the *Bhagavata Purana*.

Eight Primary (Asta/Ashta/Maha) Siddhis:
1. Anima – reduction of the body to the size of an atom
2. Mahimā – expansion of one's body to envelop the universe
3. Laghimā – creation of weightlessness to the point of levitation at any height
4. Garimā – assumption of enormous weight by increasing one's personal gravity
5. Prāpti – ability to acquire any material object
6. Prākāmya – ability to see or hear anything that exists in the universe
7. Īśitā[†] (Istva, Isatva, Ishitva, Ishita) – possession of complete dominion over the elements of the natural universe

---

[†] These two *siddhis*, *Isita* and *Vasita*, tend to be switched in definition based upon the source. In the *Bhagavata Purana*, it is the opposite of the text presented in this book, but in nearly every other source I used, including a few Sanskrit dictionaries, the definitions presented above are accurate.

8. Vaśitā† (Vastva, Vasitva, Vashitva, Vashita) – power to subjugate any being

A ninth major/primary *siddhi* exists that has been described in multiple sources but has been commonly switched out with *Garimā*, the *siddhi* of infinite weight. It is:

9. (Yatra)Kāmāvasāyit(v)ā – ability to will anything into existence from anywhere one desires. This is absolute fulfillment of all one's desires.

(Yatra)Kāmāvasāyit(v)ā is the greatest of any of the *siddhis* mentioned above, as it allows for absolute dominion over the physical, subtle, and causal elements of the universe. It gives power to subjugate any being and allows for true liberation to occur. It is the "sum-siddhi" for all the yogic powers in existence.

Ten Secondary Siddhis

1. Lack of disturbance by hunger, thirst, and other bodily attachments
2. Ability to hear things far away
3. Ability to see things far away
4. Ability to move the body wherever thought goes (teleportation/astral projection)
5. Assumption of any form desired
6. Ability enter the bodies of others
7. Ability to die when one desires
8. Witnessing and participation in the pastimes of the gods
9. Ability for one's resolve to lead to perfect achievement
10. Ability for one's words become truth themselves, leading to complete fulfillment of commands

Five Minor Siddhis of Yoga and Meditation:

1. Knowledge of the past, present and future
2. Knowledge of the minds of others
3. Freedom from dualities such as hot, cold, poison, etc.

4. Testing of the effect of fire, sun, water, poison, etc. on the physical body
5. Ability to remain unconquered by others

On the next page, are the additional *siddhis* mentioned by Patanjali. He is considered the first to have recorded the various aspects of yoga.

Patanjali's 28 Siddhis
1. III.16 – Knowledge of past and future
2. III.17 – Ability to completely understand the meaning of sound coming from any living thing
3. III.18 – Knowledge of past lives
4. III.19 – Power to read another's mind
5. III.21 – Invisibility to others through sight
6. III.22 – Invisibility to others through sound and/or other senses
7. III.23 – Knowledge of the time of death of someone or oneself
8. III.24 – Ability to manifest strength of positive attitudes (friendliness, compassion, happiness)
9. III.25 – Ability to gain the strength of an elephant
10. III.26 – Ability to see subtle, hidden, or far away objects
11. III.27 – Knowledge of the arrangement and movement of the solar system
12. III.28 – Knowledge of arrangement of stars
13. III.29 – Knowledge of the laws of motion of stars in the galaxy
14. III.30 – Knowledge of the arrangement of the physical, astral, and causal bodies
15. III.31 – Ability to live without food and water
16. III.32 – Steadiness and stillness gained easily, completely, and at all times
17. III.33 – Experience of visions of the great spiritual masters
18. III.34 – Knowledge that anything can be discovered through intuition
19. III.35 – Knowledge of mind is attained through the heart

20. III.36 – Knowledge of SPIRIT beyond the duality as the Creator is gained
21. III.37 – Perception of anything can be achieved without a physical sensory organ
22. III.39 – Ability to enter into another's body
23. III.40 – Ability to levitate
24. III.41 – Ability to digest any amount of food/thing
25. III.42 – Divine power of hearing
26. III.43 – Ability to send the primary physical body to another location or to create another artificial body to be sent or used
27. III.45 – Mastery over the 5 physical elements (Earth, water, fire, air, ether = space)
28. III.46 – Mastery of the 8 *mahasiddhis*, perfection of the body, and complete immunity from any element, such as being able to pass through fire unhurt

By this point, there are 28 *siddhis* in total mentioned by Patanjali

29. III.47 – Mastery over the body leads to perfection in beauty, gracefulness, strength, and hardness
30. III.48 – Mastery over the sense organs
31. III.49 – Quickness of mind and perception is gained, mastery of complete understanding of anything at will
32. III.50 – Supreme control over everything in creation and knowledge of everything, one becomes both omnipotent and omniscient
33. III.51,53,54,55,56 – Loss of desire to supremely control everything leads to true liberation or *kaivalya* – this is the <u>ultimate</u> objective of yoga and the greatest *siddhi*

Finally, we see that there are five extra *siddhis* added with body perfection, mastery over the sense organs, quickness of mind, supreme control over everything, and true liberation.

Patanjali also says in his *Yoga Sutras*,[2] that these various "perfections" can be achieved, but should be avoided as a focus.

---

[2] Patanjali's *Yoga Sutras* III.51–III.56

Attention on them will prevent liberation from occurring. The purpose of *samadhi*, he says, is to gain *kaivalya* (liberation), not to gain *siddhis*. These yogic powers are but mere distractions from *kaivalya*, because they are a part of *maya*, or the illusion that the physical world is the true reality.

The *siddhis* mentioned above are available to different levels of self-realization. Now that they are measurable, they can also be sub-typed between three different types of realizations. The first major class of self-realized individual is the workingman/woman type, or the Minervan man described in Chapter 4. This type is available to anyone who can achieve self-realization on any level, including any LOC from *savikalpa samadhi* to *nirvikalpa samadhi* and beyond.

It is unlikely that any Minervan man would achieve higher than *nirvikalpa* in this present age, because the collective Superconsciousness of the world is at a mere $10^{29,999}$. This LOC is barely above the base number for Superconsciousness, but this LOC value can be easily attained and maintained by those individuals who are meditating with a strong, spiritually-evolving technique like the *Kriya*. It could be said that most people who are meditating, praying, or devoting themselves intensely to the SPIRIT's work are actively maintaining the collective superconscious mindset of the world. These spiritually minded individuals are the primary reason this is possible. Whether you are Muslim, Christian, Buddhist, Pagan, Jewish, or Hindu, does not matter. The collective spiritual energy emanating from a mass of worshippers, regardless of religion, who are putting their hearts and minds into the love of the Divine, will create spiritual buoyancy that keeps afloat the world's superconscious state.

The next level of realization is the ascended master. An ascended master is one who is able to manifest an LOC that is higher than *nirvikalpa samadhi*, may have a varying number of *siddhis*, and has a strong role in bringing about spiritual evolution in the world. These individuals are few and far between in this present age. There are few, if any, ascended masters who are still in the physical body today and even fewer still that may be married with or without children while in a householder position. These individuals know of their abilities, but generally take a humble stance because drawing attention to their level of realization is futile for their position as a yogi householder. Although there are many who claim this position, it is not likely one would do so. One who speaks outwardly of having salvation, does not have it, and one who has it, does not speak of salvation. This is the nature of one who is truly merged with SPIRIT.

Finally, there are the perfected masters. These are the true masters of self-realization. Originally "ascending" in a past life, these primed individuals come to this life to "manifest" as a Christ-like avatar and/or as a spiritual world teacher. Some that have already come and gone include the following (in chronological order): Bhagavan the Krishna, The Buddha, Jesus the Christ, Lahiri Mahasaya, Sri Yukteswar, Swami Sivananda, and Yogananda. The highest perfected master in physical existence is Mahavatar Babaji. He rarely shows himself to anyone because it is not needed that people see him. His divine blessing is what keeps this world from de-evolving spiritually. These individuals hold the full host of *siddhis*. They can literally move mountains at the Divine's command and live by God's bread alone.

However, being able to walk on water, exist without food and breath is not why they are here. These yogic powers are just a small benefit to their hard work and dedication over the past billion years of spiritual evolution, just for the sake of humanity. The goal of these powers is to bring about God's pure omnipotence and omnipresence in mankind. Below is a chart that shows the connections between the Minervan man, the ascended and perfected master's abilities.

Table 17.1 – Master Siddhis Chart

© 2016 Dr. Derek Simpson	Minervan	Ascended	Perfected
Description	• Willfully joyful, still, and peaceful in samadhi • Can only achieve NrS • May achieve small amount of siddhis	• Perpetually blissful, still, and peaceful in samadhi • Achieves SS and AION • Will achieve most of the siddhis and can work hard to achieve them all	• Born perpetually blissful, still, and peaceful • Achieves SS and AION at a young age • Manifests most all siddhis at a young age
Eight 1° Siddhis	Possibly 6	3, 6	ALL
Ten 2° Siddhis	1, 2, 3, 9	All except 6 and 10	ALL
Meditative Siddhis	1, 2, 3, 5	1, 2, 3, 5	ALL

On the next few pages I have described the chart in words with much more detail, so that you can understand each of these powers and which masters can manifest them.

Minervan Man Siddhis

This type of realization has a strong hold over the meditative *siddhis*, because meditation is the best and fastest way to become self-realized. Through deep and prolonged meditation, most of these powers will be realized easily as a direct result of achieving the Creator's consciousness and the eternal bliss that follows.

It is possible that the workingman will gain *Prākāmya*, or ability to see and hear all that exists in the universe (number six on the list of primary siddhis). Also, the time for a physical desire to manifest will be faster than most people, but slower than an ascended or perfected master. Physical desires that may have taken years to manifest may now only take months in duration with steady focus, determination, allowing, and release.

Ascended Master Siddhis

The ascended master will hold a permanent grasp on most of the *siddhis*. There are some here that are not included, like the ability to heal others and so forth, but those are a given and need no explanation, as all will require healing at some level.

Ascended masters will quickly elevate in self-realization, but only if they have devoted themselves fully to their appropriate spiritual path—as their destiny has already been set from previous past lives. *Siddhis* will develop most strongly in the field that the master has chosen as a career. If he or she is a healer, then healing will be a strong yogic power. If he or she is in the field of law, then he or she will hold command over truth and understanding the minds of others. Ascended masters will naturally gravitate towards a particular set of *siddhis* because of their innate desires to develop into a greater version of themselves. This does not mean that other powers won't develop, just that some have a stronger likelihood.

Within the first eight *siddhis*, only a few are possible. Becoming almost weightless (number four) is a great possibility, as one increases his or her use of *pranayamas* in conjunction with intense saturation of bliss consciousness. Realizing whatever one desires (number five) is similar to the workingman, but now physical desires that would take months, will manifest in mere weeks or days.

These manifestations always have to be prepared with attentive and directed visual and prayerful determination to decrease time frame by which the object manifests. This is because the thoughts of an ascended master are mostly occupied by SPIRIT's bliss consciousness. Therefore, it is difficult to create a desire that is greater than such an experience. However, when the need arises to create or manifest some physical item at will, the Divine will provide what is actually needed in that instant. Mere physical desires can easily be gained through bliss with focus on the desired object.

In the secondary *siddhis* described by Krishna, all yogic powers, except entering the bodies of others (number six) and orders or commands being unimpeded (number ten), are generally gained with or without effort. The powers that are gained easily include:

- #1 – Lack of disturbance by hunger, thirst, and other bodily attachments
- #2 – Ability to hear things far away
- #5 – Ability to assume any form desired
- #7 – Ability to die when one desires
- #8 – Witnessing and participation in the pastimes of the gods
- #9 – Ability of one's resolve to lead to perfect achievement

Hearing things that are far away is very common and generally is included under knowing the past and future. There are other aspects here, but these are generally the case.

Dying when one desires (number seven), for ascended masters, is a spiritual contract between Creator and creation. One may know the time and hour by which permanent physical death may occur but may or may not have control over it. If there is control, it is to prolong the inevitability of this master's passing. This life extension happens through intense desire if it is deemed necessary. In Sanskrit, this is called a *mahasamadhi* and is the last and greatest achievement that a yogi can perform before passing into the void. The powers that are gained with difficulty include:

- #3 – Ability to see things far away

- #4 – Ability to move the body wherever thought goes (teleportation/astral projection)

Seeing things that are far away (number three) is such a strong stimulation to the brain that this power is rarely gained easily. Considering the visual system is the most powerful and most complicated physical sense humans have in the body, it is also the most enticing.

If an ascended master is living during this present age, his or her role will be to live in it as a yogi householder, helping all to ascend. If you remained engrossed in the visual and sensational allure of an astral *samadhi*, would there then be any desire to remain in the physical world? This question is one that you could apply to anyone on the path of self-realization merely for the gain of great power.

The same goes for teleportation and astral projection (number four). Experiencing an astral *samadhi* is wonderful in itself, but being able to transport your body to an entirely different realm or dimension is vastly different and extremely difficult. It requires years of intense bodily and mental training. To develop this *siddhi*, you must meditate at extreme length throughout the day and night in *samadhi*, but it can prevent ascension through too much focus on the power itself. In the highest realizations, God has no form and appears often as the void of space itself.

The meditative *siddhis* are easily gained through meditation and develop as a direct result of ascension. Testing the effects of fire, sun, water, poison, etc. on the physical body (number four) is not directly needed during the present world age because there are many scientific devices and cleaning apparatuses that "test the effect" of various substances that could directly harm the physical body. However, this *siddhi's* job is to show that, even the physical body, when integrated with pure SPIRIT, is imperishable.

It is unlikely these ascended masters will come from a lifestyle of monetary wealth because living a life of humility is what creates the desire to seek a higher way of existence. When you are surrounded by supreme living comforts, there are few material struggles, impeding the consciousness from desiring disconnect from the current reality. When you have all the material comforts, why would it be necessary to want anything else? When you have materially little, much more is provided in emotional, mental, and spiritual strength.

Perfected Master Siddhis

Perfected masters can manifest all *siddhis* as needed or desired by the master and/or the Divine. Usually, a *siddhi* will be obtained because of the will of SPIRIT. The Divine does not display Her abilities haphazardly. Those siddhis of greatest yogic power only come to light when they are needed greatly by the yogi. This is the true nature of a perfected guru. Jesus did not walk on water just because he wanted to; he was divinely directed to show his apostles the meaning of absolute surrender and trust. The same goes for any other master.

Baba Lokenath, an 18th century saint, was described to have developed many *siddhis* in the same way. In Baba's case, yogic power manifested because of the extreme desire and willpower of a devotee. Sometimes, a perfected master will perform a healing or bring someone back from the dead. This is because the individual asking for it provides the necessary devotion and surrender to gain the blessing. The devotee can rouse the compassion within these yogis, allowing the Divine to work through the yogi.

The highest miracles are performed because the ego's desires no longer exist. Soul consciousness, residing in an absolutely tranquil mind, is now no longer mindful, but mindless! This leads to a mind only filled with seamless, pure bliss. In this state, God/SPIRIT controls all actions. Similarly, if SPIRIT requires a particular task of the perfected master's body medium, it will allow the consciousness to act accordingly, but not until that point. It also may not be necessary to perform and display such physical power unless given necessity to do so.

Differences Between Saints and Self-Realized Masters

A saint is one is somewhere along the continuum of the LOC scale, whether in Christ Consciousness or fully merged in *sahaja samadhi*. They are also considered a saint because miracles have occurred around the individual. These individuals can manifest a variety of yogic powers, whether consciously or unconsciously. One great example is Therese Neumann, the German catholic who manifested a full stigmata[†] for over 30 years during World War II. One can be saint, but not be fully self-realized.

---

† The stigmata is a supernatural occurrence where body sores, that correspond to the same wounds that Jesus Christ had inflicted on him during his crucifixion, appear on

Those who are a self-realized master, consciously knows himself or herself as SPIRIT. They can enter the blissful state consciously at will. They have a varying number of yogic powers, whether limited or fully developed. These individuals are considered both master and saint. In both cases, saints and masters can take on karma to suffer on the behalf of others, whether consciously or unconsciously. Both know that humility and surrender are the only ways to true peace and happiness.

---

the individual. There could be bleeding from just above the heart, feet, hands, around the top of the head, and/or from the eyes. Therese Neumann, in this case, had all of the same wounds and bled weekly from nine places.

CHAPTER 18

A Self-Realized Summary

The information included in the last few chapters may have been difficult to understand. To satisfy the teacher within and without, a summary chapter was created to further help those on the path to self-realization.

Major Points of the Major LOCs

Consciousness
This is baseline consciousness, into and from which the majority of beings are born and die. The levels that are "below" it includes: Subconsciousness, Unconsciousness, Perceived Nirvikalpa Samadhi, and Drunken Consciousness.

Superconsciousness
This state can be achieved by beginner and intermediate meditators. This state can also be permanently maintained by advanced meditators.

Christ Consciousness

This state is achieved when you love all of creation and perceive creation as yourself. You can go into and out of this state when you are superconsciously attuned and while performing altruistic acts. The CC can be maintained permanently through constant vigilance of love, superconscious meditation, proper karmic removal, and intense willpower.

Krishna Consciousness

This state is achieved by transcending the serious nature of Christ Consciousness to reach the loving, innocent, boy-like nature of Bhagavan Krishna. Once you achieve either Christ or Krishna Consciousness, you will never fall again to Superconsciousness or below.

Elemental State

Visualization of the karmic cavern's ceiling is necessary to break through into the 2nd Dimension. To release all physical karma and transcend this state, your determination and necessity for self-realization must be the driving force.

Unnamed and Spirit States

These states feel like you are floating on an endless ocean with no sail, but the compass always points North. An intermittent *samadhi* state is felt as you drift on the ocean of SPIRIT, basking in the light of a brilliant moon.

Minor Samadhi States

Here, you find an opportunity to experience sixteen of the Divine's attributes individually before the final merger into the Creator's Cosmic Consciousness. You can choose to experience these states individually or just ascend to *laya samadhi*, perceiving all of these states at once.

Savikalpa Samadhi

The first Divine Superconscious Experience (DSCE) occurs here through a major *samadhi*, initiating you into the Creator's Cosmic Consciousness. The *kundalini* is activated here and begins its ascension up the spinal *chakras*. *Savikalpa* is the greatest measure of a minor *samadhi* you can experience.

Asamprajñata Samadhi
This state is the transition required before you can merge completely into the stillness of a major *samadhi*. The *kundalini* begins to rise more rapidly, allowing for the body to become completely attuned to the Creator's consciousness. Through this spiritual merger, the body has out-of-body experiences coupled with a slow, but sure increase in God's joy.

Interstate #1
This state is usually forgotten, but allows you to experience increasingly successive levels of the stillness of a major *samadhi*. The movement of the Interstate is facilitated primarily by angelic beings. The feeling of joy also increases exponentially in this state, eventually leading to a full merger into the Divine's complete joy in *nirvikalpa samadhi*.

Nirvikalpa Samadhi
This state is inclusive of the Interstate #2, with full access to God's joy. Here, you begin to manifest the subtle differences between a dual and a non-dual reality. The *Om* and astral *samadhis* individually develop here, giving both sight and sound to God's joy-bliss-consciousness.

Sahaja Samadhi (proper)
This stage is the final and permanent merger into God's bliss consciousness. Complete loss of the causal body occurs here, freeing the soul to eternally experience SPIRIT. *Om* and astral *samadhis* combine together to create a visually-stimulating theatrical show with surround sound!

The Aionion State (AION)
This incalculable level will increase for an eternity. Transitional levels also have an increased in transiency, making it more difficult to achieve higher LOCs. The Divine Superconscious Experience (DSCE) becomes accessible at will and becomes a permanent part of your being during ascension here.

Major Aspects of the Dimensional Realms

1st Dimension
This realm is a cavern full of karma-ful beings. Superconsciousness and Christ Consciousness manifest here. Movement from here is impossible without complete removal of physical karma.

2nd Dimension
This realm is the first existing with karma-free beings. An intermittent *samadhi*-like stillness begins to manifest itself here. Movement here is possible through patience and will-power.

3rd Dimension
Minor *samadhi* states manifest here, allowing for all aspects of God to be experienced and leading to a full version of Cosmic Consciousness. The first experience of the DSCE (*anantya/turiya*) occurs here, bringing on *savikalpa samadhi*. Great transitions occur in the body through the rising of the *kundalini* in *asamprajñata samadhi*.

Multidimensional Realm
The major *samadhi* is now a major part of your experience in meditation. The major *samadhi* allows for the stillness of God to be achieved. Ascension is consistent, steady, and facilitated by legions of angelic beings.

Extradimensional Realm
Nirvikalpa samadhi manifests, giving God's Joy permanently. Full self-realization develops as you achieve a non-dual major *samadhi* experience completely and willfully within *nirvikalpa*. Astral and *Om* (major) *samadhis* become a major part of your experience. The permanent *samadhi* state of Sahaja Proper and its counterpart AION are achieved to give you an infinite playing field to ascend in LOC.

Uni-A-Dimensional Realm
This realm is where all go when they dream or have restful sleep. The DSCE appears here allowing for SPIRIT to be experienced in all its glory. This realm is the dwelling place of SPIRIT.

Major Transitional States and Realms

2nd Dimension

This realm includes the Unnamed and Spirit States. It exists within the 1st Dimension as dimensions that all wrap up on top of one another, similarly explained with quantum theory.

Laya Samadhi

This state is referred to as the Sum Samadhi, or the greatest lesser minor *samadhi* state just before *savikalpa samadhi*. Sixteen of the Divine's major aspects are experienced here together as one.

Asamprajñata Samadhi

This is a very large transitional state between *savikalpa* and *nirvikalpa*. It is a part of the Creator's consciousness and the 3rd Dimension.

Samadhi Major Experience Transition State #1 (sMje-T1)

This is the first small transition level directly before achieving *nirvikalpa samadhi*. One million levels are wrapped up inside of one level, while each level measures at $CC1^{100}$.

Samadhi Major Experience Transition State #2 (sMje-T2)

This is the second small transitional level directly before achieving *nirvikalpa samadhi* and after sMje-T1. Each level is just another repeating .9, .99, .999, .9999, whereby there are $CC1^{CC1}$ levels within this transitional state.

Law of Ascension Extension States

1st Dimension

Stillness is manifested in the meditation states mixed with seriousness, innocent love, and intense willpower.

2nd Dimension

Intermittent *samadhi* (IS) occurs in the Unnamed States. Then, the Spirit States are a further reaching of the IS into both daily activities and the minor *samadhi* states.

3rd Dimension
- Lesser Minor Samadhi State – *laya samadhi*
- Savikalpa Samadhi – self-named extension experience
- Asamprajñata Samadhi – self-named extension experience

Multidimensional Realm

There are no true extension states on the Interstate, but ascension will feel like a greater than normal amount of joy mixed with peace and blissfulness. Realize that the divine nectar has not fully manifested itself consciously and willfully. So, the fullest extent of God's joy cannot be fully felt until you have been initiated into *nirvikalpa samadhi*.

Extradimensional Realm

In *nirvikalpa samadhi*, non-dual consciousness rajan (NDCR) sMje is the extension experience. If you manifest an *Om* or astral *samadhi*, this can also act as an extension experience, increasing your LOC. *Samyama* is also another way to activate ascension. In *sahaja samadhi*, *anantya*, in combination with the astral and/or *Om samadhi*, can be used here to help ascension occur more quickly. In *sahaja*, *samyama* is no longer used for ascension. Finally, in The Aionion State, the DSCE is used to bring ascension more quickly; however, it isn't the only thing used. An astral and/or *Om samadhi* can also help speed ascension but achieving this while performing daily activities is necessary here to create the ascension process. In this state, *anantya* is used to a certain extent for ascension, but becomes less and less used as you increase in LOC. Joy will be experienced to no end, but this does not necessarily mean you will increase in LOC. How deep can you go with bliss? That will determine how your LOC increases.

Law of Ascension Aspects

- Attune, Adjust, Ascend
- Works particularly in extension states, but can occur at any time in the ascension of self-realization
- Cannot ascend unless in the highest state available
- Keeping mind cycling with devotion towards the Divine is one of the fastest ways to ascend

- Maintain what is gained in meditation as long as possible throughout the day in every activity
- Can maintain what is gained in meditation with extreme focus to the third eye
- Attunement one level at a time, then increase can occur exponentially
- Only when meditation is in every part of life, including your waking hours, sleeping hours, driving, and doing activities, does God come, because you are ready to receive the highest level of the Creator's consciousness.

Major Tricks to Ascension

- Treatment, treatment, treatment (chiropractic, naturopathic, craniosacral, massage, Reiki, etc.)
- Following the Law of Ascension to the strictest degree
- Using techniques as taught and described by various gurus and organizations
- Using other techniques, such as the *shambhavi mudra* or Cosmic Energy Technique, either separately or in combination to help facilitate your upward movement of energy
- Perform repetitive thoughts of pure devotion, always cycling devotion in your mind, especially when karma-less
- Maintain proper sleeping, eating, and exercising habits, performed in moderation with the attention <u>always</u> on the Divine

The "Don'ts" of Meditation

<u>Don't try to meditate all night long</u>

Unless you don't have work the next day, you are an insomniac, and/or you have been drinking a lot of coffee, staying up all night long is really a difficult thing and requires extreme willpower. This is especially true earlier on in the self-realization process.

I personally attempted all-night meditation the day before my own body was initiated into the joy of *nirvikalpa* and many times before. The result was extreme sleepiness and no energy for the next day. What I learned is that God will come in His own time, not by your watch and not in the way you expect.

God comes to those who challenge themselves by living life in the world, but not becoming a part of the world through participation in its many Divine-less activities. There are few that can achieve this monumental goal of an all-night meditation. It is easier, in fact, to become self-realized! Truly! Don't be surprised if meditating to the extremes makes you late for work with an angry boss and an even more angry wife! Remember guys, happy wife = happy life! ☺ The same also goes for the women attempting these types of extremes.

<u>Don't expect fantastic out-of-body experiences</u>
You, as the workingman, probably won't have HUGE out-of-body experiences in which you are consciously taken to another place and introduced to people like Jesus and the Buddha. You may experience a small portion of this experience, but it is likely you will have both full-body sensations and awareness that you are truly not the body. This awareness is commonplace and makes living in this world much more bearable for those souls who have come to Earth to achieve their dreams.

<u>Don't expect self-realization to come all at once</u>
The body is like a light bulb. If too much current and energy are allowed in with not enough to resistance to hold back the power, then—POOF—there goes the neighborhood (and the light bulb). There are stories of people who all sudden, while consciously performing life's duties, have a quick onset of realization of who and what they really are. If this is the case, then it is for the benefit of others who are surrounding that individual or it is the desire of this individual to experience it in that way. It may come on through what would appear to be a dream, but then waking suddenly out of it in full awareness of the extreme joy that has overcome the body. We are talking full raucous laughter in the middle of waking up. That is quite an alarm clock; believe you me!

The "Dos" of Meditation
- Have the belief that the process of self-realization is possible, likely, and ultimately destined

- Know, without a doubt, that all you need is what you can gain from within yourself, not from external material desires
- Know that you have all the power of the universe at your disposal to achieve your highest desires through self-realization

God has given us an opportunity to come back to the divine bliss and eternal wisdom of our original state. It is possible we may be given particular *siddhis* (yogic powers) like healing, intuition/ESP, etc., but we may not be able to bilocate and put our body in two different places at the same time. We may not be able to walk through walls or become universally large or small. We may not be able to turn water into wine at a mere thought. But if we can achieve God's bliss, then we have gain the greatest gift of all.

All of those grand yogic powers are saved for a few that have come to Earth to show the greatest version of SPIRIT's consciousness. God comes more completely and easily for the workingman while working in moderation. Especially those who really yearn for Her, God will come and bless the activities of everyday life, making those moments even more wonderful. You cannot imagine how wonderful life can be, when the Divine's bliss is tucked into every nook and cranny of existence.

CHAPTER 19

How to Get Started Meditating

I was talking to my sister one day after arriving back from China, and she asked, "Derek, how can I start bringing about peace in my life?" And of course, I said, "Start meditating today, and great things will come to you." Within the first six months of any meditator's journey, the Divine will provide great leaps and bounds in peace, joy, and bliss. The Divine wants to provide encouragement so that you do not get frustrated on the path. God knows it is difficult and will send a barrage of encouragement in the form of positive energy, angelic-beings, and whatever else will provide necessary help you.

So, I told my sister, meditation is the fastest way to gain peace and ultimately, realization, especially if you have no particular religious path in mind.

Silence

Make sure you have complete silence while meditating, as God will only speak to you fully while in the silence. The deeper the silence, the better. The sounds of universe, including the Creator Itself, can be heard and tuned to if you are focused on external noises heard by the physical ears. You must activate your astral and causal hearing through silence to hear that which is most subtle and precious.

Stillness

Sit as still as possible without moving any part of the body, including the mouth, tongue, and especially, the eyes. The eyes are especially important if you expect to manifest a still closed-eye or open-eye *shambhavi mudra*. These techniques are one the greatest keys to manifesting God consciousness.

Third Eye

Focus as intensely as possible towards the third eye with eyes closed. In this way, the *shambhavi mudra* used will help the attention on the physical body, and thus, *prana* (energy) in the body will be pushed up from the extremities into the spinal column and third eye. You cannot manifest higher realizations unless that energy is centralized further into the upper spine, including the upper thoracic spine (upper back) and cervical spine (neck).

Devotion

While focusing intensely at the third eye, revolve over and over in the mind that you love and want God more than anything else in the world. Mention that you would give all personal possessions and livelihood to God. Also, say that you want God and that you offer your life and the lives of your family members to Him and to do what He wills.

This last part may be difficult to say, but to know that we are not the body but SPIRIT, resonates with this exact idea. If God's bliss is to come into the body, it is the same as allowing God's will to use the body to Its own bidding. Here's a secret—God doesn't want your possessions, to end your life, or to end lives of others around you. God only wants YOU, the infinitely best piece of yourself, to love God over all other things. God may challenge you, but this is to be expected.

Ask the Divine to challenge you in the way that is needed, not in the way that is extreme. This extremity is really not necessary because, for the workingman or -woman, there is constant struggle on Earth to maintain peace of mind while dealing with those of a lower vibration (LOC). Once the total LOC of the world increases, peace and harmony will reign in all hearts, and self-realization will be commonplace.

Law of Ascension

Once tension is felt at the third eye, try to keep it as long as possible throughout the day while cycling the same thoughts of devotion in the mind. The tension in the third eye with thoughts of devotion is following in line with the Law of Ascension. Maintain this law and all other great things will follow. This law is one of the surest to understand while ascending.

Discipline

Spend at least 15 minutes, morning and night, meditating in silence to gain the greatest benefit. From this point, move the time frame up to 20, 30, and then 60 minutes. If you get past an hour at a time, morning and night, great gains will be had in peace, joy, and bliss.

The Guru

If the desired results are not manifesting themselves, you will need a guru to help push along the process. Many gurus and organizations provide a path to self-realization; you just need to choose what is best for you.

I personally became a part of Self-Realization Fellowship (SRF). This organization provides a sure path for the use of Kriya yoga. They also provide other spiritually advancing techniques to help the individual achieve higher levels of realization. In the process of becoming self-realized, I found other gurus, saints, and masters who taught me things while deep in meditation. It is, however, best to stick with one guru or spiritual teacher until the goal of self-realization has been attained, because the guru is the one who brings the attunement to you. The Divine signals the guru, telling him or her that the devotee (you) are ready.

Even after you have been initiated, the guru will continue to provide attunement as you are ready. This process might take days, weeks, months, years, and even lifetimes. But if you have already gotten this far, what is a little longer?

Special Techniques of Meditation Organizations

The techniques that have been taught by various yogi masters during the last three centuries are of the highest. Whether this be *Kriya* or other supportive techniques, they should be used throughout the self-realization process. Those who have learned these techniques should not second-guess their power to change a meditative situation for the better. You will always be surprised by what the gurus can do through constant devotion to the techniques, even while you are experiencing a *samadhi* state.

I think that many who practice these techniques are very humble and do not believe that they are a true child of God, yet they have been given some of the most powerful techniques in the universe! Your destiny is in your own hands. Do with it what you will, but know that self-realization is waiting for you right around the corner.

It is not that the techniques are not absolutely necessary after you have burned all your karma, it is that they are optimal to practice! They create in the body the very best vibrational situation and thus increase the possibility for self-realization. You have been given a great gift. Don't ever give up hope.

Finally, remember that meditation for the sake of meditation is like eating, when you are not hungry. Without the fire of devotion, the meditative food one will take in serves a purpose of meditative mediocrity. One must understand their position on this LOC scale, otherwise the superconscious food gained will feed only further unenlightened gluttony.

CHAPTER 20

The Beginning to Self-Realization

Steps to Self-Realization

- God – The Imperishable One is the only thing that can give the thumbs-up for your ascension.

- Gurus – It is nearly impossible to reach self-realization without the Guru's love, help, and spiritual initiations into the Creator's Consciousness and beyond.

- Spiritually Evolving Technique – You need the *Kriya* or a breath technique like the *Kriya* to help spiritually evolve the brain and body to reach self-realization. Like an over-watted lightbulb, the brain would have a spiritual melt-down, similar to Fukushima, if it was not ready for God's awesome power.

- Great Devotion – You must pour out your heart yearning for God if you expect to reach the infinite multitudes. Women generally have it, and men often have to work tirelessly to gain it.

- <u>Balance, Balance, Balance</u> — Balance in lifestyle, eating, exercise, hobbies, sexual activity, and in work habits is required in every part of life's activities.

- <u>Discipline, Discipline, Discipline</u> — If you had to choose one aspect to practice day in and day out, no matter what life throws you, it should be meditation itself. Practice it day and night, and you will be singing God's praises, and God will be singing yours!

- <u>Practice, Practice, Practice</u> — Practice makes perfect? In this case, it does. Perfection is the realization that you are God with the manifestation of His perfect bliss in your imperfect human body.

- <u>Surrender</u> — When all else fails (this will occur often), just surrender everything to SPIRIT.

- <u>Never Give Up</u>! — Come hell or high water, you must endure!

Final Thoughts

As the world evolves in the 21st century and beyond, this self-realized situation will become commonplace, and the world will no longer live in darkness. Some individuals currently in the world are fully self-realized, yet have not shown themselves. They serve the Divine's purpose by just silently vibrating their love into the world. There are also some married couples in the world in which one partner or both have been initiated into *asamprajñata samadhi* but have not have achieved any further.

Now that this information on self-realization has become available as a part of the collective Superconsciousness everywhere (and written on paper), more and more humans will reach self-realization. This message will spread goodwill to all who will hear it. Referencing this book and others that are written like it, they will see that what they are experiencing is of the highest truth.

We, as beings of the One, Unmanifested Absolute, are always constantly creating anew. We will bring to light ideas of the same in different ways. The idea, feeling, or concept is there, but the words, language, or symbols to describe it, in an attempt to define "a thing," may be drastically different. If your body, voice, or mind is meant to bring to light that which has been forgotten, does that mean that the words that you use are truly original? Or is it, in reality, a part of all that is possible and has already been seen by a SPIRIT always in the making?

To know yourself as nothing is to first know yourself as something. The men and women of past generations believe themselves to be humble and unworthy of receiving a high honor as self-realization. It is obvious that this is not the case if we are all truly divine sons and daughters of God. You must believe you can receive it before anything can progress forward. You must know yourself first as everything, always expanding out into the vast field of physical-subtle-ideational space, before you can see yourself as the void-nothingness that is the true consciousness behind all things created and uncreated. You cannot think you are nothing, when also you think you are God's gift to mankind. To believe you are nothing is to be truly a perfected master.

There will be a time when mere mortal men, women, and children are elevated to the realization of God's consciousness. Forgetting the body, you will remember the divinity that is buried deeply within. That which was once apart will now be together, never to be lost again to the delusion of physical reality. The universe and beyond will be Your stage on which to act and play as You will, creating as You so choose for the pure joy of creation itself.

"Be ye therefore perfect, even as your Father which is in heaven is perfect."[1]

---

[1] Matthew 5:48 KJV

Appendix A

List A.1 – Yoga Sutras References

1. BonGiovanni. The Yoga Sutras of Patanjali. The Threads of Union. Accessed: 02.18.16
   http://www.sacred-texts.com/hin/yogasutr.htm
2. Hartranft, Chip. 2003. *The Yoga-Sutra of Patanjali: Sanskrit-English Translation and Glossary*. PDF version.
3. Ronald Steiner and Team. International Infopage for Ashtanga Yoga. Accessed: 02.18.16
   http://www.ashtangayoga.info/source-texts/yoga-sutra-patanjali/chapter-1/
4. Shearer, Alistair. 1982. *The Yoga Sutras of Patanjali*. Random House.
5. Swami Jnaneshvara Bharati. (n.d.) *Yoga Sutras of Patanjali: The 196 Sutras*. Swamiji.com. Accessed: 02.18.16
   http://www.swamij.com/yoga-sutras-list.htm
6. Swami Venkatesananda. 1975. Electronic Ed 2008. *Enlightened Living: A New Interpretative Translation of the Yoga Sutra of Maharsi Patanjali*. The Chiltern Yoga Trust, Cape Province, South Africa. Accessed: 02.18.16
   http://www.swamivenkatesananda.org/clientuploads/publications_online/Enlightened%20Living%20by%20Swami%20Venkatesananda.pdf
7. Swami Vivekananda. 1920. *Raja Yoga*. Brentano's.
8. Yoga Sutra Study. 2015. Wordpress and Atahualpa Site. Accessed: 02.18.16 http://yogasutrastudy.info/yoga-sutra-translations/

List A.2 – Samadhi References

1. Patanjali. ~400 CE. *The Yoga Sutras*. Aphorism III.3. (One of the first standard texts on *samadhi*)
2. Chatterjee, Ashoke Kumar. 2011.* *Purana Purusha. Yogiraj Sri Shama Churn Lahiree. A Complete Biography*. Yogiraj Publications. *This particular book was written during the late 1800's in the form of diary entries by Lahiri Mahasaya himself.

3. Vivekananda, Swami. 1920. *Raja Yoga*. Brentano's. pp. 17, 34, 118
4. Taimni, I.K. 1961, 2010. *The Science of Yoga*. The Theosophical Publishing House.
5. Sri Chinmoy. 1974. *Earth's Cry Meets Heaven's Smile, Part 2*. Sri Chinmoy Library. Agni Press. Accessed: 02.18.16
http://www.srichinmoylibrary.com/earth-cry-meets-heaven-smile-2/could-you-explain-the-difference-between-samadhi-and-self
6. Sri Chinmoy. 1974. *The Summits of God-Life: Samadhi and Siddhi*. Agni Press. Sri Chinmoy Library. Accessed: 02.18.16
http://www.srichinmoylibrary.com/sgl
7. Shearer, Alistair. 1982. *The Yoga Sutras of Patanjali*. Random House.
8. Maharshi, Ramana. 1989. *Be as you are. The Teachings of Sri Ramana Maharshi*. Edited by: David Godman. pp. 222-233
9. Swami Sivananda. 1998. *Mind – its Mysteries and Control*. The Divine Life Society. Accessed: 02.18.16
http://www.dlshq.org/download/mind.htm
10. Swami Chidananda. 1999. *The Philosophy, Psychology and Practice of Yoga*. The Divine Life Society.
11. Zimmerman, Mark. 1999-2001. *Encyclopedia of the Self*. Definition: Samadhi.
http://selfknowledge.com/109718.htm
12. Maehle, Gregor. 2007. *Ashtanga Yoga: Practice and Philosophy*. New World Library
13. Swami Sivananda. 2011. *Guide to Samadhi*. The Divine Life Society. Accessed: 02.18.16
http://www.sivanandaonline.org/public_html/?cmd=displaysection&section_id=927&format=html
14. Swami Sivananda. 2011. *Samprajñata Samadhi*. The Divine Life Society. Accessed: 03.24.15
http://www.sivanandaonline.org/public_html/?cmd=displaysection&section_id=932
15. Swami Sivananda. 2011. *Samprajñata Samadhi*. Accessed: 02.18.16
http://www.sivanandaonline.org/public_html/?cmd=displaysection&section_id=932
16. Swami Sivananda. 2011. *Experiences of the Four Stages*. The Divine Life Society

http://sivanandaonline.org/public_html/?cmd=displaysection&section_id=751
17. Yogananda, Paramahansa. 2012. *Autobiography of a Yogi*. Los Angeles: Self-Realization Fellowship.
18. PlaneTalk. 2014. *Patanjali's Ten Types of Samadhi*. Accessed: 02.18.16
https://dondeg.wordpress.com/2014/05/28/patanjalis-ten-types-of-samadhi/
19. Swami Jnaneshvara Bharati. (n.d.) *Integrating 50+ Varieties of Yoga Meditation*. Swamiji.com. Accessed: 02.18.16
http://www.swamij.com/meditationtypes.htm#categories

List A.3 – Siddhi References

1. *Bhagavata Purana*. 11.15: 3-33
2. Daniélou, Alain. 1987. *While the Gods Play: Shaiva Oracles and Predictions on the Cycles of History and the Destiny of Mankind*. Inner Traditions. Chap 6.
3. Swami Krishnananda. 2015. *Glossary of Sanskrit Terms*. The Divine Life Society. Accessed: 02.23.16 http://www.swami-krishnananda.org/glossary.html
4. Swami Krishnananda. 2015. *Glossary of Sanskrit Terms*. The Divine Life Society. Accessed: 02.23.16 http://www.swami-krishnananda.org/glossary/glossary_ijkl.html
5. Jayadev, Tyagi. 1995-2016. *The Danger of Siddhis (Yogic Powers)*. Ananda Sangha Worldwide. Accessed: 02.23.16
http://www.ananda.org/ask/the-danger-of-siddhis-yogic-powers/
6. Swami Jnaneshvara Bharati. (n.d.) *Yoga Sutras of Patanjali: The 196 Sutras*. Swamiji.com Accessed: 12.03.15
http://www.swamij.com/yoga-sutras-list.htm
7. spokensanskrit.de (online Sanskrit dictionary) Accessed: 12.08.15
http://www.spokensanskrit.de/
8. Sharma, Ram Karan. (ed.) 1993. *Researches in Indian and Buddhist Philosophy: Essays in Honour of Professor Alex Wayman*. Motilal Banarsidass. Chap. 16
9. Taimni, I.K. 1961, 2010. *The Science of Yoga*. The Theosophical Publishing House

Appendix B

Table B.1 – Self-Realization LOC Chart

Self-Realization LOC Scale
© 2016 Dr. Derek Simpson

NAME	ABBREV	VALUE of Levels	# of LEVELS	CONS CATEGORY
1st Dimension				
Drunken Consciousness	DrCon	1	1	DrCon
Perceived NrS	PNrS	1	1	DrCon
Unconciousness	UnCon	1	3	UnCon
Subconciousness	SubCon	1	1	SubCon
Consciousness	Con	1	up to 10^{3000}	Con
Semi-Superconsciousness	SSupcon	1	$10^{3000} - 10^{6000}$	SSupercon
Superconsciousness	SupCon	1	$10^{6000} - 10^{(1E8)}$	Supercon
Christ Consciousness	CC	$10^{[1E(999.9E12)]}$	100	CC
Krishna Consciousness	KC	CC1	1000	CC
Z State	Z	$10^{[1E(47E12)]}$	1	CC
Elemental State	E	1	579	CC
2nd Dimension				
Unnamed State	U	10^{1E1000}	10^{71} Billion	CC
Intermittent Samadhi	IS	1	2.88^{1E11}	CC
Spirit State	S	CC1	47	CC
3rd Dimension				
Minor Samadhi State	MrS	1	16	CC
Laya Samadhi	LS	CC1	1 Trillion - 10^{1E12}	CC
Savikalpa Samadhi State	SaS	$CC1^2$	133 Billion - 1.33^{1E11}	CosCon
Savikalpa Samadhi Ext	SaSee	N/A	N/A	CosCon
Asamprajñata Samadhi	Añ	$CC1^{100}$	$CC1^{10}$	CosCon
			$Añ1 = \{CC1\}^1$	CosCon
			$Añ2 = \{CC2\}^2$	CosCon
			$Añ3 = \{CC3\}^3$, etc.	CosCon
Asamprajñata Samadhi Ext	AñSee	N/A	N/A	CosCon
Kundalini (rise/pulse)	K#m	pulse per min	last level = 0 seconds	CosCon
Controlled Añ Samadhi Exp	CAñSee	time (sec/min)	∞	CosCon
Samadhi Intensity	SIT	1	100	CosCon
Breathlessness	B	1	399,999	CosCon
Light Descension	LD	1	7	CosCon
Void State	V	$CC1^{100}$	$CC1^5$	CosCon
			$V1 = \{CC1\}^1$	CosCon
			$V2 = \{CC1\}^2$	CosCon
			$V3 = \{CC1\}^3$, etc.	CosCon
Void State Breathlessness	VB	1	CC1	CosCon
SPIRIT State	SP	1	100	CosCon
Joy	Joy	1	847	CosCon

Table B.2 – Self-Realization LOC Chart (cont.)

Self-Realization LOC Scale
© 2016 Dr. Derek Simpson

NAME	ABBREV	VALUE of Levels	# of LEVELS	CONS CATEGORY
Multidimensional Realm				
Interstate #1	IS#1	1	1	UCon
Interexperience	InterE	$CC1\wedge72$	1st Exit	UCon
Minor Major Samadhi State	MrsMje	$CC1\wedge72$	2nd Exit	UCon
Major Samadhi States	sMje	$CC1\wedge100$	3rd - 99.9 millionth exit	SpCon
sMje Transition #1	sMje-T1	$CC1\wedge CC1$	$CC1\wedge1E6$	SpCon
sMje Transition #2	sMje-T2	0.9 repeating	$CC1\wedge CC1$	SpCon
Extradimensional Realm				
Nirvikalpa Samadhi State (Proper)	NrS	$CC1\wedge(CC1\wedge1E100)$	1 trillion	SpCon
Interstate #2	IS#2	1	1	UCon
Dual Con Rajan - sMje	DCR-sMje	$CC1\wedge(CC1\wedge1E100)$	1 billion - 100 trillion exits	SpCon
Non-Dual Con Rajan - sMje	NDCR-sMje	$CC1\wedge(CC1\wedge1E100)$	1 billion - 100 trillion exits	SpCon
NDCR-sMje Transition State	NDCRT	0.9 repeating	$10\wedge[1E(1E12)]$	SpCon
OM Samadhi	OS	$CC1\wedge(CC1\wedge1E100)$	$CC1$	UniCon
Astral Samadhi	AS	$CC1\wedge[1E(999.9E12)]$	$10\wedge100$	DivCon
Sahaja Samadhi State (Proper)	SS_p	$CC1\wedge(1E12)$	19	SpCon
The AIONION State (INCALCULABLE LEVEL)	AION/Aeon	Aeon 1 = TotalLOC 1	$9.\overline{9}E11$ to ∞	DivCon
Maitreyan Consciousness				MCon
Maitreyas of current Earth Epoch:				MCon
Jesus Christ and Mahavatar Babaji				MCon
Uni-A-dimensional Realm				DivSupCon

SPIRIT

Divine Superconsciousness
Ever-perfect blissful consciousness
Dream SuperUnConsciousness

Appendix C

Figure C.1 – Aeon Calculation
1st Ascension to AION = 1 Aeon = 1 TotaLOC
1 TotaLOC = (D1 + D2 + D3 + MD + NrS + IState #2 + OmS + AS + SS Proper)

Table C.2 – Aeon Calculation Diagram

Dimension	Level	Consciousness	Broader Consciousness
	DrCon, UnCon, SubCon	Self-named	Self-named
	Con	Self-named	Consciousness
	SSupCon	Self-named	Consciousness
1st Dimension	SupCon	Superconsciousness	Superconsciousness
	CC, KC	Superconsciousness	Superconsciousness
	Z, Elemental	Superconsciousness	Superconsciousness
	Unnamed States	Superconsciousness	Superconsciousness
2nd Dimension	Sp States	Superconsciousness	Superconsciousness
	MrS	Superconsciousness	Superconsciousness
3rd Dimension	SaS	Cosmic Consciousness	Superconsciousness
	Añ	Cosmic Consciousness	Superconsciousness
	Añ Transitions	Cosmic Consciousness	Superconsciousness
Multidimensional Realm	Interstate #1	Unknown Consciousness	Superconsciousness
	NrS	Spiritualized Consciousness	Superconsciousness
	Interstate #2	Unknown Consciousness	Superconsciousness
Extradimensional Realm	Om Samadhi	Universal Consciousness	Superconsciousness
	Astral Samadhi	Divine Consciousness	Superconsciousness
	SS	Spiritualized Consciousness	Superconsciousness
	AION	Divine Consciousness	Superconsciousness
	MC	Maitreyan Consciousness	Superconsciousness
Uni-A-Dimensional Realm	Dream SuperUnCon	Divine Superconsciousness	Superconsciousness
	DSCE	Divine Superconsciousness	Superconsciousness
	SPIRIT	Divine Superconsciousness	Superconsciousness

1 Aeon spans from Broader Consciousness at the top down through the Superconsciousness entries.

Appendix D

List D.1 – Kriya Organizations

Lahiri Mahasaya – The first person or organization to disseminate Kriya yoga was Lahiri Mahasaya. He first received *Kriya* from Mahavatar Babaji in 1861 and began teaching it shortly after in Varanasi, India. Through his 35 years of teaching, many disciples branched off into different organizations, teaching scientific meditation by use of Kriya yoga. It started in India but then spread to the United States through Paramahansa Yogananda. The *Purana Purusha* is a book that has collected Lahiri Mahasaya's diaries into one source. It does provide a definition of how to perform the *Kriya*, but it is not step-by-step, as it was a personal recording of Lahiri Mahasaya's day-to-day experiences. His description is the original form of how *Kriya* is to be performed.

Shibendu Lahiri – He is the great grandson of Lahiri Mahasaya. He runs no organization or institution but teaches his great grandfather's original legacy all over the world. He was initiated into the original *Kriya* process in the age-old Rishi tradition of India—from father to son.
website: http://www.Kriyayogalahiri.com

Paramahansa Yogananda –
Self-Realization Fellowship/Yogoda Satsanga Society – This yogi was the disciple of one of Lahiri Mahasaya's disciples named Swami Sri Yukteswar. Yogananda disseminated Kriya yoga lessons through his organization called Self-Realization Fellowship, based out of Los Angeles, CA, and its sister group in India called Yogoda Satsanga Society. It is suggested to read *Autobiography of a Yogi* to get a feel of this guru and his teachings.
website: http://www.yogananda-srf.org
website: http://www.yssofindia.org

Swami Kriyananda – Ananda Sangha Worldwide – He was a direct disciple of Yogananda and split off from Self-Realization Fellowship. It is suggested to read *The Path* by Crystal Clarity Publishers to get an understanding of this Kriya yoga teacher and the Ananda group.
website: http://www.ananda.org

Roy Eugene Davis – Center for Spiritual Awareness – Mr. Davis is a direct disciple of Yogananda and was an appointed minister. He is the founder and director of this spiritual organization. This group honors all authentic enlightenment traditions. His group teaches meditation with Kriya yoga to discover your innate and natural relationship with the Infinite.
website: http://csa-davis.org

Paramahansa Hariharananda –
Kriya Yoga International Organizations – He received a first *Kriya* initiation from Swami Sri Yukteswar, a second *Kriya* initiation from Yogananda, his third *Kriya* initiation from Swami Satyananda Giri, and finally, his fourth, fifth, and sixth *Kriya* initiations from Sri Bhupendranath Sanyal Mahasaya, who was said to be a direct disciple of Lahiri Mahasaya. Check out Wikipedia to read more up on this individual.
website: http://www.Kriya.org

Marshall Govindan – Babaji's Kriya Yoga – He was initiated into Kriya yoga by S.A.A. Ramaiah, who claims to be a direct disciple of Babaji. In Govindan's books, he also claims to have meditated with Babaji in his cave for several months in the 1950s, learning the secrets of Kriya yoga. Marshall Govindan is the president of Babaji's Kriya yoga and Publications, Inc. and the President of Babaji's Kriya Yoga Order of Acharyas.
website: http://www.babajisKriyayoga.net

Swami Shankarananda Giri –
Kriya Yoga and Swami Shankarananda Giri – He was a disciple of Swami Narayana Giri. Swami Narayana was a direct disciple of Sri Yukteswar Giri. He has meditation centers all over world, and mostly near Chicago in North America.
website: https://www.Kriya-yoga.com

Swami Nityananda Giri – This yogi received *Kriya* initiation from his guru Swami Shankarananda Giri, who was a disciple of Swami Narayana Giri. Swami Narayana was a direct disciple of Sri Yukteswar Giri. Swami Nityananda received his doctorate in cytogenetics and is out of the norm for ordained swamis because most lead a life free of worldly attachment.
website: http://www.nityanandagiriKriyayoga.com

Appendix E

List E.1 – Types of Meditation

Breath Meditation – Focusing on the breath is similar to any other mindful meditation or technique-based practice. It all requires constant concentration and awareness of the body.

Christian Meditation – This type of meditation was talked about extensively in Chapter 6 in the section on the history of meditation. In modern times, very few periods of silence are used in Christian church worship. However, Metta or a devotional-type meditation is used during worship band services.

Devotional (Metta) Meditation – Metta meditation can be described in different ways. Most commonly, you can sit in meditation and focus on gracious and loving thoughts towards the Divine. There is another practice, though, which most don't think about. Metta meditation is specific to religions, mostly Christians, that don't have a sustained and lengthy silent time in their worship. In contemporary Christian worship, rock music is used to develop devotional love towards Christ and the Creator. This practice is very necessary when establishing your relationship with the Divine and your path to self-realization.

Guided Meditation – This type of meditation, surprisingly, I do myself while writing or focusing on computer tasks. Even as I write this book, I am listening to some trip-hop music with a gentle female voice singing. This is not the classic form of guided meditation, but it is something I am attracted to. Often, slow trip-hop music uses beats that are similar to a beating heart. This is why I enjoy it so much, since it activates my heart *chakra* and brings great waves of love. Most guided meditation is either done through a conscious scan of the body, inducing relaxation, an individual's voice, soft environmental music, or binaural beats. Current research seems to be focused around binaural beats.

Mantra Meditation – Often called *Om* meditation, this practice uses a Sanskrit syllable or phrase. The most popular include *Om*, *Rama*, *Om namah shivaya*, and *Om mani padme hum*. These are to be verbally or mentally produced while seated or walking in silence. The goal of this type of meditation is to attune yourself to the syllable that you are chanting. As the chanting increases, so does your devotion. Devotion is the key to this practice, as it will spiritualize the symbol, allowing it to act at the deepest levels.

Meditative Martial Arts – Qigong and Tai Chi are the two main practices of this type of meditation. Both are cultivations of life-energy, but Tai Chi is more dynamic than Qigong. Both are used in healing the body, but Qigong's emphasis is greater. However, nearly all martial arts are meditative to a degree. Some include silencing the mind more than others. While I was traveling in China, Tai Chi could be seen practiced on the streets at night in the bigger cities.

Mindfulness Meditation – Mindfulness is similar to both Zen, Vipassana, and most other types of meditation. Being mindful of the thoughts is paramount when attempting to achieve inner peace, a still mind, and further ascension in consciousness. Without this simple technique, anyone could be easily overcome by his or her own ego.

Self-Enquiry Meditation – This style is very specific to Ramana Maharshi. He practiced self-enquiry meditations during the 20th century in India. Asking the question "Who I am?" leads you to discover why you do the things you do. It is a relentless path to self-realization, but it is quicker than most because it breaks down the barriers the ego builds as you attempt to still the mind. By eliminating the barriers, more of the Divine can pour Its love into your body, leaving you eternally satisfied.

Transcendental Meditation (TM) – TM was made widely popular by Maharishi Mahesh Yogi in the 60's and 70's because the Beatles, the Beach Boys, and other celebrities became his devotees. In TM, mantras are used. These are primarily the names of Hindu deities given based upon your gender and age. This particular practice has many peer-reviewed articles as well, showing that meditation using this yogic technique will bring about great spiritual well-being. I want to point out that, generally, all yogic meditation has the same effect on the body. TM happened to be the first group that began measuring it. This research is extremely valuable because it shows how just sitting in silence for short periods of time (20 minutes) is essential to your physical, emotional, mental, and spiritual well-being.

Vipassana – This meditation began originally with the Theravada Buddhists. It focuses on the thoughts and feelings you are experiencing and the true nature behind their occurrence. Mindful breathing is also incorporated, which helps to control concentration while stilling the mind. There are at least 10 official centers and 8 non-centers for this type of meditation in the United States.

Yogic Meditation – This type of meditation is the one referenced in this book. Whether you are practicing a physical pose (*asana*), focusing at the third eye, or performing a breath-control technique like the *Kriya*, you are doing yogic meditation. In reality, all meditation comes from India, as this has been considered its birthplace. No matter what you call it, you are doing yoga!

Zen Buddhist Meditation (*Zazen*) – This type of meditation is associated with Japanese and Chinese cultures. *Zazen* meditation is often done in seated posture, whether you are cross-legged or in a chair. It includes a type of walking meditation that has grown in popularity in the last half of the 20th century. This type of meditation can be practiced easily while at home or at work.

Notes

Introduction
1. UUA.org. 1996-2017. *What We Believe.* Unitarian Universalist Association http://www.uua.org/beliefs/what-we-believe

Chapter 2 – Inner Peace
1. Dhammika, Ven. S. 1996-2012. *Good Questions Good Answers. Do Buddhists Believe in God?* Buddha Dharma Education Association. Accessed: 12.03.15 http://www.buddhanet.net/ans73.htm

Chapter 3 – Bliss
1. *Collins English Dictionary. Complete and Unabridged.* 2014. 12th Edition s.v. "bliss." Accessed: 03.06.16 http://www.thefreedictionary.com/bliss
2. *Random House Kernerman Webster's College Dictionary.* 2010. s.v. "bliss." Accessed: 03.06.16 http://www.thefreedictionary.com/bliss
3. WordNet 3.0, Farlex clipart collection. s.v. "bliss." Accessed: 03.06.16 http://www.thefreedictionary.com/bliss

Chapter 4 – The Minervan Man
1. Google. Google Translate for "working" in Latin. Accessed: 11.1.14 https://translate.google.com/?ie=UTF-8&hl=en&client=tw-ob#auto/la/working
2. *Minerva.* Wiktionary. en.m.wiktionary.org http://en.m.wiktionary.org/wiki/Minerva
3. *Minerva.* Wikipedia. Accessed: 11.1.14 http://en.m.wikipedia.org/wiki/Minerva
4. Babylonian Talmud: Tractate Berakoth 32b. v. 27. http://halakhah.com/berakoth/berakoth_32.html
5. Pollock, Robert. 2008. *Word Religions: Beliefs and Traditions from Around the Globe.* Fall River Press. p. 76.

Chapter 5 – Self-Realization

1. Nakamura, Hajime. 1989. *A History of Early Vedanta Philosophy: Part One*. Delhi: Motilal Banarsidass Publishers Private Limited.
2. Trimingham, J. Spencer. 1998. *The Sufi Orders in Islam*. Oxford University Press. p. vii
3. Frager, Robert. 1999. *Heart, Self, and Soul: The Sufi Psychology of Growth, Balance, and Harmony*. Quest Books. pp. 96–97
4. Harmless, William. 2008. *Mystics*. New York: Oxford University Press. p. 164.
5. spokensanskrit.de (online Sanskrit dictionary) (n.d.) Entry: "atmajnana" Accessed: 05.20.15 http://www.spokensanskrit.de/index.php?script=HK&beginning=0+&tinput=atmajnana&trans=Translate&direction=AU
6. Yogananda, Paramahansa. 1980. *Sayings of Paramahansa Yogananda*. Los Angeles, CA: Self-Realization Fellowship. p. 34.
7. Adler, Mortimer. 1958. *The Idea of Freedom: A Dialetical Examination of the Conceptions of Freedom. Vol. 1.* Doubleday. p. 127
8. Matthew 7:13-14 NASB
9. Vivekananda, Swami. 1993. *Living at the Source. Yoga Teachings of Vivekananda*. Shambhala Publications, Inc. p. 42
10. Gangrade, K.D. 2004. *Moral Lessons from Gandhi's Autobiography and Other Essays*. New Delhi: Concept Publishing Co. p. 7
11. Maharshi, Ramana. 1985. *Be as you are. The Teachings of Sri Ramana Maharshi*. Edited by David Godman. Sri Ramanasramam. p. 18
12. Sivananda, Swami. 2006. *Sivananda. Biography of a Modern Sage. Life and Works of Swami Sivananda*. The Divine Life Society. p. 1
13. Yogananda, Paramahansa. 1980. *Sayings of Paramahansa Yogananda*. Self-Realization Fellowship. p. 104
14. Chinmoy, Sri. 1974. *The Summits of God-Life: Samadhi and Siddhi. Question: What is the difference between samadhi and God-realisation?* Agni Press. Accessed: 12/03/14 http://www.srichinmoylibrary.com/sgl-55
15. Hanh, Thich Nhat. 2003. *No Death, No Fear: Comforting Wisdom for Life*. Riverhead Press. pp. 69–70.
16. The Dalai Lama. 2006. *Kindness, Clarity, and Insight*. Dalai Lama. Snow Lion Publications. p. 20.

Chapter 6 – Meditation

1. Gen. Lamrimpa. 1995. *Calming the Mind: Tibetan Buddhist Teachings on Cultivating Quiescence.* 2nd Edition. Snow Lion Publications. p. 72
2. Feuerstein, George. 2006. *Yoga and Meditation (Dhyana).* Moksha Journal. Issue 1. Accessed: 01.14.16 http://www.santosha.com/moksha/meditation1.html
3. Macdonell, A.A. 1893. *An Sanskrit-English Dictionary: Being a Practical Handbook with Transliteration, Accentuation and Etymological Analysis Throughout.* London: Longmans, Green, and Co. p. 134.
4. Saraswati, Sivananda Radha. 2011. *Mantras. Words of Power.* Timeless Books. 3rd Ed.
5. Phelan, Michael. 1979. *Transcendental Meditation. A Revitalization of the American Civil Religion.* Archives de sciences sociales des religions. July–Sept. 48:1 5–20. p. 6. Accessed: 01.08.16 http://www.persee.fr/doc/assr_0335-5985_1979_num_48_1_2186
6. University of Wisconsin-Madison. 2008. *Compassion Meditation Changes the Brain.* Science Daily. March 27. Accessed: 12.05.15 http://www.sciencedaily.com/releases/2008/03/080326204236.htm
7. Lutz, A., et al. 2008. *Regulation of Neural Circuity of Emotion by Compassions Meditation: Effects of Meditative Expertise.* PLoS ONE 3(3): e1897. Accessed: 03.09.16. http://journals.plos.org/plosone/article?id=10.1371/journal.pone.0001897
8. Gen. Lamrimpa. 1995. *Calming the Mind.* Snow Lion Publications. pp. 58–59
9. Hicks, Esther and Jerry. 2006. *The Law of Attraction. The Basics of the Teachings of Abraham.* Hay House.
10. Judaism Islam. 2006. *What happens to our soul when we sleep?* Discover similarities between Judaism and Islam. Accessed: 11.28.14. http://www.judaism-islam.com/what-happens-to-our-soul-while-we-sleep/
11. Rainforth, M., et al. 2008. *Stress Reduction Programs in Patients with Elevated Blood Pressure: A Systematic Review and Meta-Analysis.* Current Hypertension Reports. Accessed: 12.05.15 http://link.springer.com/article/10.1007/s11906-007-0094-3
12. Payne, Larry and Feuerstein, G. 2014. *Yoga for Dummies.* John-Wiley & Sons, Inc. 3rd Ed. Hoboken, NJ. Chap. Intro

13. Feuerstein, Georg. *A Short History of Yoga.* Accessed: 01.08.16 http://www.swamij.com/history-yoga.htm
14. Everly, George S., Lating, J.M. 2013. *A clinical guide to the treatment of human stress response.* Springer. 3rd Ed. p. 202.
15. Everly 2013, 202.
16. Dumoulin, Henrich. 2005. *Zen Buddhism: A History: Japan.* Vol. 2. World Wisdom. p. 5
17. Bielefeldt, Carl. 1988. *Dogen's Manuals of Zen Meditation.* University of California Press. p. 2
18. Turner, Francis J. (ed) 1996. *Social Work Treatment: Interlocking Theoretical Approaches.* 4th ed. The Free Press. p. 439
19. Zaleski, Philip. and Zaleski, C. 2005. *Prayer: a history.* Houghton-Mifflin Company. pp. 147–149.
20. Yadav, Rama S., Mandal, B.N. 2007. *Global Encyclopedia of Education.* Global Vision Publishing House. p. 63
21. Hanif, N. 2002. *Biographical Encyclopaedia of Sufis: Central Asian & Middle East.* Sarup & Sons: New Delhi.
22. Kugle, Scott. 2007. *Sufis and Saints' Bodies: Mysticism, Corporeality, and Sacred Power in Islam.* The University of North Carolina Press. pp. 245–246
23. Coward, Harold G. and Goa, D.J. 2005. *Mantra: Hearing the Divine in India and America.* Motilal Banarsidass Publishers. p. 97.
24. Parry, Ken. (ed) 1999. *The Blackwell Dictionary of Eastern Christianity.* Malden, MA. Wiley-Blackwell Publishing. p. 91
25. Everly 2013, 202.
26. Rama, Swami. 1989. *Meditation in Christianity.* The Himalayan International Institute of Yoga Science and Philosophy of the USA. Honesdale, PA. pp. 46, 63, 66, 69–70.
27. Macedonian Heritage. *The History of Mount Athos.* 2000-2016. Accessed: 01.01.16 http://www.macedonian-heritage.gr/Athos/General/History.html
28. Jaoudi, Maria. 2010. *Medieval and Renaissance Spirituality: Discovering the Treasures of the Great Masters.* Paulist Press: NY/NJ. p. 12
29. Wakefield, James L. 2006. *Sacred Listening: Discovering the Spiritual Exercises of Ignatius Loyola.* Baker Books. pp. 22–23
30. St. Theresa of Avila and Peers, E. A. (ed). 2007. *Interior Castle.* Dover Thrift Editions
31. Native American Traditions. 2001-2008. Wayshowers Community Fellowship. Accessed: 01.14.16

http://www.wayshowerscommunityfellowship.org/native_american_tradition.htm
32. Bowden, Henry W. 1993. *Dictionary of American Religious Biography*. Greenwood Publishing Group. 2nd Ed. pp. 574–575, 632–633
33. Sjoman, N.E. 1999. *The Yoga Tradition of the Mysore Palace*. 2nd ed. New Delhi, India: Abhinav Publications. pp. 39–41

Chapter 7 – Yoga

1. Patanjali's *Yoga Sutras* I.1
2. Patanjali's *Yoga Sutras* I.2
3. Crangle, Edward Fitzpatrick. 1994. *The Origin and Development of Early Indian Contemplative Practices*. Wiesbaden: Harrassowitz Verlag. pp. 2–7
4. Klostermaier, Klaus K. 2007. *Hinduism: A Beginner's Guide*. Oxford: Oneworld Publications. pp. 102, 117
5. Selbie, J. (Puru). 2012. *The Paths of Raja Yoga and Kriya Yoga*. Ananda Sangha Worldwide. Accessed: 05/20/15 http://www.ananda.org/ask/the-paths-of-raja-yoga-and-Kriya-yoga
6. Vivekananda, Swami. 1920. *Raja Yoga*. Brentano's. p. x.
7. Vivekananda 1920, p. xi.
8. Vivekananda 1920, p. 17.
9. Vivekananda 1920, p. 43.
10. Vivekananda 1920, Chap 3, 4, 5.
11. Vivekananda 1920, p. 54.
12. Yogananda, Paramahansa. 2012. *Autobiography of a Yogi*. Los Angeles: Self-Realization Fellowship.
13. Ananda Sangha Worldwide. 1995–2015. *The Technique of Kriya Yoga*. Accessed: 03.09.16 http://www.ananda.org/Kriya-yoga/what-is-Kriya-yoga/the-technique-of-Kriya-yoga/
14. Chatterjee, Ashoke Kumar. 2011. *Purana Purusha. Yogiraj Sri Shama Churn Lahiree. A Complete Biography*. Yogiraj Publications. Chap 3.
15. Yogananda, Paramahansa. 2012. *Autobiography of a Yogi*. Los Angeles: Self-Realization Fellowship and Self-Realization Fellowship. 2015. Accessed: 03.09.16 https://www.yogananda-srf.org
16. Hammond, H. 2007. *Yoga Pioneers*. Yoga Journal. Accessed: 12.08.15 http://www.yogajournal.com/article/history-of-yoga/yogas-trip-america/

17. Sivananda, Swami. 2011. *The Science of Yoga*. The Divine Life Society. Accessed: 12.13.15 http://www.sivanandaonline.org/public_html/?cmd=displaysection&section_id=957
18. Patanjali's *Yoga Sutras* II.26-II.29
19. Patanjali's *Yoga Sutras* III.3
20. Chinmoy, Sri. 1974. *Earth's Cry Meets Heaven's Smile, Part 2.* Question: Could you explain the difference between samadhi and self-realization? I know they are not the same theoretically, but I don't see why they're not. Agni Press. Accessed: 12.03.15 http://www.srichinmoylibrary.com/ecmh-235

Chapter 8 – Samadhi

1. Patanjali's *Yoga Sutras* I.18
2. Patanjali's *Yoga Sutras* I.43–I.44
3. Patanjali's *Yoga Sutras* I.51
4. Patanjali's *Yoga Sutras* I.17–1.18
5. Taimni, I.K. 1961, 2010. *The Science of Yoga*. The Theosophical Publishing House. pp. 31–42
6. Maharshi, Ramana. 1989. *Be as you are*. Edited by: David Godman. p. 222
7. Sivananda, Swami. 2011. *Guide to Samadhi*. The Divine Life Society. http://www.sivanandaonline.org/public_html/?cmd=displaysection&section_id=927
8. Maharshi, Ramana. 1989. *Be as you are*. Edited by: David Godman. p. 222
9. Maharshi, Ramana. 1989. *Be as you are*. Edited by: David Godman. p. 224
10. Sivananda, Swami. 2011. *Guide to Samadhi*. The Divine Life Society. http://www.sivanandaonline.org/public_html/?cmd=displaysection&section_id=927
11. Sivananda, Swami. 1998. *Mind and Its Control*. The Divine Life Society. http://www.dlshq.org/download/mind.htm#_VPID_4
12. Chinmoy, Sri. 2000. *The Wisdom of Sri Chinmoy*. p. 47
13. Sivananda, Swami. 2011. *Experiences of the Four Stages*. The Divine Life Society. http://www.sivanandaonline.org/public_html/?cmd=displaysection&section_id=751

14. Sivananda, Swami. 1946. *Sivananda Gita*. The Divine Life Society. http://sivanandaonline.org/public_html/?cmd=displaysection&section_id=962
15. Patanjali's *Yoga Sutras* III.4–III.6, III.16–III.49, III.53

Chapter 9 – Muscle Testing

1. Aufsesser, P., et al. 1996. *A Critical Examination of Selected Hand-Held Dynamometers to Assess Isometric Muscle Strength*. Adapted Physical Activity Quarterly. Pp. 13, 153–165. Human Kinetics Publishers, Inc. Accessed: 06.05.15 http://www.humankinetics.com/acucustom/sitename/Documents/DocumentItem/12754.pdf
2. Florence PK, et al. 2005. *Muscles. Testing and Function*. Lippincott, Williams and Wilkins, Baltimore. p. 5.
3. Daniels L, Worthingham K. 2002. *Muscle Testing. Techniques of Manual Examination*. Philadelphia, PA: W.B. Saunders Co. p. 7.
4. Ambroz, A., et al. 2006. *Strength Testing in Pain Management*. Practical Pain Management. Accessed: 07.15.15 http://www.practicalpainmanagement.com/resources/diagnostic-tests/strength-testing-pain-assessment
5. Lovett, R.W. and Martin, E.G. 1916. *Certain Aspects of Infantile Paralysis with a Description of a Method of Muscle Testing*. JAMA. LXVI(10):729-733. Accessed: 05.04.16. http://jama.jamanetwork.com/article.aspx?articleid=436726
6. Moses, S. 2015. *Motor Exam*. Family Practice Notebook, LLC. Accessed: 06.6.15 http://www.fpnotebook.com/Neuro/Exam/MtrExm.htm
7. Barbano RL. 2000. *Handbook of Manual Muscle Testing. Neurology*, 54(5):1211.
8. Kendall, H.O. Kendall, F.P. 1949. *Muscles: Testing and Function*. The Williams and Wilkins Co. 1st Ed.
9. Gin R.H., Green B.N. 1997. *George Goodheart, Jr., D.C., and A History of Applied Kinesiology*. J Manipulative Physiol Ther. Jun;20(5):331–7. Accessed: 11.24.15 http://www.ncbi.nlm.nih.gov/pubmed/9200049
10. *What is AK?* 2015. ICAK-USA. Accessed: 05.04.16 http://www.icakusa.com/what-is-icak-usa

11. Diamond, J. 1979. *Behavioral Kinesiology*. New York: Harper & Row.
12. *In Memory of Roger Callahan*. Nov 5 2013. Accessed: 05.04.16
    http://www.rogercallahan.com/memories/
13. TheAMT.com. 2016. *History of EFT & Tapping: Guide to the Tapping Techniques*. Accessed: 05.04.16
    http://theamt.com/history_of_tapping.htm
14. Hall, S., et al. 2008. *A review of literature in applied and specialized kinesiology*. Forsch Komplementmed; 15:40–46. Accessed: 05.04.16
    http://www.ncbi.nlm.nih.gov/pubmed/19156969
15. Cuthbert, S.C. and Goodheart, G.J. 2007. *On the reliability and validity of manual muscle testing: a literature review*. Chiropractic & Osteopathy;15:4. Accessed: 05.04.16
    http://www.ncbi.nlm.nih.gov/pubmed/17341308
16. Schmitt, W.H. and Cuthbert, S.J. 2008. *Common errors and clinical guidelines for manual muscle testing: "the arm test" and other inaccurate procedures*. Chiropr Osteopat. Dec 19;16:16. Accessed: 05.04.16
    http://www.ncbi.nlm.nih.gov/pubmed/19099575
17. Walthers, D.S. 1988. *Applied Kinesiology Synopsis*. 2nd Ed. p. 2
18. Grimes, John A. 1996. *A Concise Dictionary of Indian Philosophy: Sanskrit Terms Defined in English*. State University of New York Press; Revised Ed. p. 40
19. Sivananda, Swami. 2011. Divine Life Society. *Instructions of Samadhi*. Accessed: 11.24.15
    www.sivanandaonline.org/public_html/?cmd=displaysection&section_id=1228
20. Matthew 26:36–46 NASB
21. Mark 1:40–45 NASB
22. Mark 5:1–20 NASB
23. Palmer, D.D. 1914. *The Chiropractor*. Los Angeles: Press of Beacon Light Publishing Company. p. 3

Chapter 10 – Intro to LOCs

1. Kandel, E.R., et al. 2000. *Principles of Neural Science*. New York: McGraw-Hill. p. 901
2. Krishnananda, Swami. 1996-2016. *The Mandukya Upanishad*. The Divine Life Society. pp. 10–12. Accessed: 04.21.16
   http://www.swami-krishnananda.org/index.html

3. Michigan State University. 2014. *Waves and Vibrations*. Accessed: 07.27.14 www.msu.edu/~murph250/topics/Waves1.htm
4. Walters, D.J. 2004. *Intuition for Starters*. (sample chapter) Crystal Clarity Publishers. Accessed: 07.27.14. www.crystalclarity.com/content.php?type=sample&code=BIS
5. Xie, WJ., et al. 2006. *Acoustic Method for levitation of small living animals*. Appl. Phys. Lett. 89, 214102. Accessed: 05.04.16. http://scitation.aip.org/content/aip/journal/apl/89/21/10.1063/1.2396893
6. Ochiai, Y., et al. 2013. *Three-dimensional Mid-air Acoustic Manipulation by Ultrasonic Phased Arrays*. arXiv:1312.4006v1. Accessed: 05.04.16 http://arxiv.org/abs/1312.4006
7. Vivekananda, Swami. 1897. *The Complete Works of Swami Vivekananda*. Vol. 3. Lectures from Colombo to Almora. The Work Before Us. The Vyjayanti Press, Madras. http://www.vivekananda.net
8. Scherer, N. *Cycles of Precession*. 2003. From CycleofTime website. Accessed: 04.03.15 www.bibliotecapleyades.net/esp_precession.htm
9. Yukteswar, Sri. 1990. *The Holy Science*. Self-Realization Fellowship. Los Angeles, CA. pp. 3-20
10. Hawkins, D.R. 1998. *Power versus Force: An Anatomy of Consciousness*. Hay House, Inc. Carlsbad, CA. p. 14
11. Diamond, J. 1979. *Behavioral Kinesiology*. New York: HarperCollins Publishers.
12. Hawkins, D.R. 1998. *Power versus Force: An Anatomy of Consciousness*. Hay House, Inc. Carlsbad, CA. pp. 52–57
13. Wikipedia. *Names of Large Numbers*. Accessed: 06.15.15.https://en.m.wikipedia.org/wiki/Names_of_large_numbers
14. Heile, F. 2014. *Is the Total Number of Particles in the Universe Stable Over Long Periods of Time?* Huffington Post. Accessed: 11.24.15 http://www.huffingtonpost.com/quora/is-the-total-number-of-pa_b_4987369.html
15. Munafo, R. 2013. *Nortable Properties of Specific Numbers*. July 24. Accessed: 07.27.14 http://mrob.com/pub/math/numbers-19.html

16. Braibant, S. Giacomelli, G. Spurio, M. 2012. *Particles and Fundamental Interactions: An Introduction to Particle Physics*. 2nd ed. Springer pp. 1–3

Chapter 11 – 1st Dimension LOCs
1. Pollock, Robert. 2008. *World Religions: Beliefs and Traditions from Around the Globe*. Fall River Press. p. 78
2. Edited by P. Davey. 2010. *Medicine at a Glance*. Blackwell Publishing. 3rd ed. p. 157.
3. Kruse, M.J. 1986. *Nursing the Neurological and Neurotrauma Patient*. Totowa, N.J: Rowman & Allanheld. pp. 57-58.
4. Tindall SC. *Level of Consciousness*. In: Walker HK, Hall WD, Hurst JW, editors. 1990. *Clinical Methods: The History, Physical, and Laboratory Examinations*. 3rd edition. Boston: Butterworth Publishers; Chapter 57. Accessed: 05.04.16 http://www.ncbi.nlm.nih.gov/books/NBK380/
5. Weyhenmeyer, James A., Gallman, E.A. 2007. *Rapid Review Neuroscience 1st Ed*. Mosby Elsevier. pp. 177–179.
6. Dickerson, Leon. 2006. *Freudian Concepts of Id, Ego, and Superego Applied to Chemical and Other Addictions: Introducing Twelve-Step Programs as the Superego*. iUniverse, Inc. pp. 47–48
7. Kruse, M.J. 1986. *Nursing the Neurological and Neurotrauma Patient*. Totowa, N.J: Rowman & Allanheld. pp. 57–58.
8. Sivananda, Swami. 2011. *What is the Ego?* The Divine Life Society. sivanandaonline.org Accessed: 11.30.14. http://www.sivanandaonline.org/public_html/?cmd=displaysection&section_id=817
9. Patanjali's *Yoga Sutras* II:6
10. Gandhi, Mahatma. 2002. Author: Jackson, T.L. *Moments of Clarity, Vol. 2 Discovering Ourselves in the Stories, Experience, and Wisdom*. Xlibris. p. 136.
11. Chinmoy, Sri. 1974. *Mind-Confusion and Heart-Illumination: Part I. The subconscious mind and psychological analysis*. From: Question: What is the role of the Subconscious in the spiritual life? Sri Chinmoy. Agni Press. pp. 45–46. Accessed: 05.04.16 http://www.srichinmoylibrary.com/mchi-23
12. Chatterjee, Ashoke Kumar. 2011. *Purana Purusha. Yogiraj Sri Shama Churn Lahiree. A Complete Biography*. Yogiraj Publications. Chap. 3

13. Einoo, S. (ed.) 2009. *Genesis and Development of Tantrism.* University of Tokyo. p. 45
14. White, D. G. (ed.) 2000. *Tantra in Practice.* Princeton University Press. p. 7
15. Chatterjee, Ashoke Kumar. 2011. *Purana Purusha. Yogiraj Sri Shama Churn Lahiree. A Complete Biography.* Yogiraj Publications. pp. 279–280
16. Osho. 1975. *Yoga: A New Direction.* Chap. 6. OSHO International Foundation. http://www.osho.com
17. Chatterjee, Ashoke Kumar. 2011. *Purana Purusha. Yogiraj Sri Shama Churn Lahiree. A Complete Biography.* Yogiraj Publications. pp. 279–281
18. Savitri, Nayaswami. 2007. *Are Dreams Important?* Ananda Sangha Worldwide. Accessed: 11.24.14. http://www.ananda.org/clarity-magazine/2007/09/yogananda-dream-god-sleep/
19. Sivananda, Swami. 2011. *Atman is Distinct from the Pancha Koshas.* The Divine Life Society. Accessed: 07.28.14. www.sivanandaonline.org/public_html/?cmd=displaysection&section_id=748
20. Subramuniyaswami, Satguru Sivaya. 2000. *Loving Ganesha: Hinduism's Endearing Elephant-Faced God.* Himalayan Academy Publications. 2nd Ed. p. 471
21. Vivekananda, Swami. 1897. *Raja Yoga.* Weed-Parsons Printing Company. pg. 34
22. Vivekananda, Swami. 1897. *Raja Yoga.* Weed-Parsons Printing Company. pg. 75
23. Durgananda, Swami. (n.d.) *Meditation, Subconscious Minds and Intuition.* Sivananda Yoga Vendanta Centres in Europe. Accessed: 05.04.16. http://www.sivananda.eu/fileadmin/user_upload/inspiration/swami_durgananda/Meditation-Subconscious-Mind-and-Intuition.pdf
24. Yogananda, Paramahansa. 1999. *GTWA: The Bhagavad Gita.* Vol. I Self-Realization Fellowship. p. 39
25. Chinmoy, Sri. 1977. *Miracles, emanations, and dreams.* Question: Are our lives run by the dark sex forces of the subconscious? Sri Chinmoy. Sri Chinmoy Library. Agni Press, p. 48 http://www.srichinmoylibrary.com/med-47

Chapter 12 – Christ Consciousness and Beyond

1. Chinmoy, Sri. 1977. *A Twentieth-Century Seeker*. Question: When people think of the Christ at Christmas time, is it the Christ Consciousness that they are thinking of or is it something else? Agni Press. Accessed: 07.28.14
http://www.srichinmoylibrary.com/tcs-43
2. Chinmoy, Sri. 1976. *Sri Chinmoy Speaks, Part 4*. Question: Is it possible to distinguish between Jesus the man and what is referred to as the "Christ-Consciousness"? Sri Chinmoy Library. Agni Press. http://www.srichinmoylibrary.com/scs-101
3. Matthew 7:12 NASB
4. Yogananda, Paramahansa. 2012. *Autobiography of a Yogi*. Chapter 26, p. 267
5. White, D.G. 2000. *Tantra in Practice*. Princeton University Press.
6. Williams, Paul, et al. 2000. *Buddhist Thought: A complete introduction to the Indian tradition*. 2nd ed. Routledge. p. 194.
7. Yogananda, Paramahansa. *The Second Coming of Christ: The Resurrection of the Christ Within You. Vol. 1*. 2004. pp. 60–61.
8. Ananda Sangha Worldwide. 1995-2015. *Aum Technique*. par. 3. Accessed: 11.13.15. http://www.ananda.org/meditation/meditation-support/meditation-techniques/aum-technique/
9. *Googol*. Wikipedia. Accessed: 08.22.14
https://en.wikipedia.org/wiki/Googol
10. *Googol*. Wikipedia. Accessed: 08.22.14
https://en.wikipedia.org/wiki/Googol
11. Kasner, Edward and Newman, J.R. 1940. *Mathematics and the Imagination*. New York: Simon and Schuster. p. 23
12. Genevieve, G. 1940. *Histoire comparée des numérations écrites* (in French). Paris: Flammarion. pp. 566-574. Chapter "Les grands nombres en numération parlée (État actuel de la question)," i.e. *The large numbers in oral numeration (Present state of the question)."* Accessed from Wikipedia on *Long and Short Scales*: 08.21.14
13. Sagan, C., Druyan, A., and Soter, S. 1980. *Cosmos: A Personal Voyage, Episode 9: "The Lives of the Stars."* Carl Sagan. PBS Science Program.
14. Wolfgang, N.H. *Googolplex Written Out*. Nitsche. Stanford, CA. Aug 2013. Accessed: 05.04.16 www.googolplexwrittenout.com
15. Page, D. 2001. *How to Get to a Googolplex*. Frank Pilhofer is author of this website and this concept by Don Page, Theoretical

physicist at Theoretical Physics Institute, Edmonto. Accessed: 05.04.16 www.fpx.de/fp/Fun/Googolplex/GetAGoogol.html
16. Knott, Kim. 2000. *Hinduism: A Very Short Introduction.* Oxford University Press, USA. p. 160.
17. Lockard, Craig A. 2008. *Societies, Networks, and Transitions. A Global History. Vol. 1 to 1500.* Houghton Mifflin Company: Boston NY. p. 363.
18. El-Seedi, H.R., et al. 2005. *Prehistoric peyote use: alkaloid analysis and radiocarbon dating of archaeological specimens of Lophophora from Texas.* J Ethnopharmacol. Oct 3;101(1–3):238–42. Accessed: 05.04.16 http://www.ncbi.nlm.nih.gov/pubmed/15990261
19. Mirante, Daniel. 2008. *Overviews Shamanism. On the Origin of Ayahuasca.* Aug 31. Accessed: 08.02.2014 http://www.ayahuasca.com/ayahuasca-overviews/on-the-origins-of-ayahuasca/

Chapter 13 – 2nd Dimension LOCs

1. Psalms 37:4 NASB
2. Dictionary.com. s.v. "cosmos." Online Etymology Dictionary. Douglas Harper, Historian. Accessed: 01.07.16 http://dictionary.reference.com/browse/cosmos
3. Bucke, R.M. 1901. *Cosmic Consciousness: A Study in the Evolution of the Human Mind.* E.P. Dutton and Company, Inc. pp. 10, 74, 79
4. Bucke. 1901. p. 1
5. Bucke. 1901. p. 3
6. Bucke. 1901. p. 6
7. Bucke. 1901. p. 10
8. Bucke. 1901. p. 18
9. Bucke. 1901. p. 62
10. *Quran* 53:4–9, *Quran* 96, *Hadith of Bukhari* 1:2:48
11. Yogananda, Paramahansa. 2001. *God Talks with Arjuna: The Bhagavad Gita.* Vol. 1. p. 38
12. Shumsky, Susan G. 2003. *Exploring Chakras: Awaken Your Untapped Energy.* Career Press. New Page Books. Chap 8.
13. Frawley, David. 2004. Yoga and the Sacred Fire: Self-Realization and Planetary Transformation. Lotus Press, USA. p. 288
14. Sri Yukteswar Giri, Swami. 1990. *The Holy Science.* Self-Realization Fellowship. pp. 35–36

15. Jackson, D. 1996. *Bless You, Sir, May I Jog Another?* Outside Magazine. October. Accessed: 08.15.15. http://www.outsideonline.com/1840086/bless-you-sir-may-i-jog-another
16. Kilgannon, Corey. 2007. *Sri Chinmoy, Athletic Spiritual Leader, Dies at 76*. The New York Times. Oct 13. Accessed: 22 August 2015. http://www.nytimes.com/2007/10/13/nyregion/13chinmoy.html?_r=0
17. Sivananda, Swami. 2011. *Samadhi*. The Divine Life Society. Accessed 04.12.15 http://sivanandaonline.org/public_html/?cmd=displaysection&section_id=1034
18. Yogananda, Paramahansa. 2012. *Autobiography of a Yogi*. p. 161

Chapter 14 – 3rd Dimension LOCs

1. *List of English words of Sanskrit origin*. 2015. Wikipedia. Accessed: 07.15.15 http://en.wikipedia.org/wiki/List_of_English_words_of_Sanskrit_origin
2. *Names of God*. 2015. Wikipedia. Accessed: 05.15.15 http://en.wikipedia.org/wiki/Names_of_God
3. Patanjali's *Yoga Sutras* II.26–II.29
4. Yogananda, Paramahansa. 2001. *God Talks with Arjuna: The Bhagavad Gita*. Vol. 1. p. 100
5. Swami Kripalu. 2004. *The Science of Meditation*. Foundation for Natural Meditation. Chapter 6. pp. 5–6 Accessed: 07.13.15 http://www.naturalmeditation.net/Design/science_meditation.html
6. Sivananda, Swami. 2011. *Instructions on Samadhi*. The Divine Life Society. Accessed: 07.13.15 http://www.sivanandaonline.org/public_html/?cmd=displaysection&section_id=1228
7. Shivom Tirth, Swami. 2005. *The Second Dawn: Revival of Shaktipat Knowledge*. Swami Shivom Tirth Ashram. New York. p. 189
8. Forbes, Duncan. 1892. *A Smaller Hindustani and English Dictionary*. entry: *kundli*. W.H. Allen & Co. London. p. 259
9. Goswami, Shyam Sundar. 1999. Layayoga: *The Definitive Guide to the Chakras and Kundalini*. Inner Traditions. Chap. 3
10. Seidman, Maruti. 2000. Balancing the Chakras. North Atlantic Books. Berkeley, CA. p. 117
11. Seidman 2000, 20–22.

12. Patanjali's *Yoga Sutras* I:17–18
13. Patanjali's *Yoga Sutras* I:23–29
14. Patanjali's *Yoga Sutras* I:17–18
15. John 14:20 NASB
16. Walker III, Ethan. 2003. *The Mystic Christ*. Devi Press. Norman, OK. p. 121
17. Translated by Christopher Isherwood and Swami Prabhavananda. 1946. Excerpt from *The Song of God; Bhagavad Gita*. Vedanta Press. Vedanta Place, Hollywood, CA
18. Taimni, I.K. 1961, 2010. *The Science of Yoga*. The Theosophical Publishing House. pp. 31–42
19. London Telegraph. 1880. *Buried for Forty Days: Wonderful Performances of the Indian Fakirs*. August 22. p. 2
20. Matthew 4:4 NASB
21. Maharshi, Ramana. 1989. *Be as you are. The Teachings of Sri Ramana Maharshi*. Edited by: David Godman. Arkana Penguin Books. pp. 2–3

Chapter 15 – Multidimensional LOCs

1. Wise, Norton M. (ed.) 2004. *Growing Explanations. Historical Perspectives on Recent Science*. Duke University Press. Durham and London. pp. 32–35
2. Kaku, Michio. 1994. *Hyperspace: A Scientific Odyssey Through the 10th Dimension*. Part II. Unification in Ten Dimensions. Oxford University Press.
3. Matthew 4:1–11 NASB
4. Stache-Rosen, Valentina. (n.d.) *The Temptation of Buddha: A preliminary comparison of some Chinese versions in the life of the Buddha*. Accessed: 08.09.14. http://himalaya.socanth.cam.ac.uk/collections/journals/bot/pdf/bot_12_01_01.pdf
5. Livingston, J.G. 2004. *Adversaries Walk Among Us. A Guide to the Origin, Nature, and Removal of Demons and Spirits*. Lost Coast Press.
6. 1 Thessalonians 5:2 NASB

Chapter 16 – Extradimensional LOCs

1. Patanjali's *Yoga Sutras* I.3
2. Yogananda, Paramahansa. 2005. *Cosmic Chants*. Self-Realization Fellowship. 6th Ed. p. 86

3. Yogananda, Paramahansa. 2001. *God Talks with Arjuna: The Bhagavad Gita.* Vol. 1. p. 101
4. Gospel of Matthew 25:34 NASB
5. Sivananda, Swami. 2006. *Sivananda. Biography of a Modern Sage. Life and Works of Swami Sivananda.* The Divine Life Society.
6. American Heritage Dictionary of the English Language, 2011. s.v. "ambrosia." Fifth Edition.
7. Dixon, Jana. 2008. *Biology of Kundalini: Exploring the Fire of Life.* Lulu Publishing. pp. 215–219
8. *Bhagavad Gita* 8.13
9. John 1:1,3 NASB
10. Yogananda, Paramahansa. 2004. *The Second Coming of Christ: Resurrection of the Christ Within You. Vol. I.* pp. 1577–78
11. *Bhagavad Gita* 17.23
12. Yogananda, Paramahansa. 2004. *The Second Coming of Christ: Resurrection of the Christ Within You. Vol. II.* p. 12
13. Sivananda, Swami. 2011. *Meditation on Om.* The Divine Life Society. Accessed: 04.29.16
http://sivanandaonline.org/public_html/?cmd=displaysection&section_id=1439
14. Patanjali's *Yoga Sutras* I.27
15. Patanjali's *Yoga Sutras* I.29
16. Yogananda, Paramahansa. 2004. The Second Coming of Christ: The Resurrection of the Christ Within You. Vol. 1. p. 60–61.
17. Matthew 6:22 KJV
18. Kuwana, E. 2001. *Women have more frontal lobe neurons than men.* Neuroscience for Kids. Dec. 7th Accessed: 4.25.15
https://faculty.washington.edu/chudler/wome.html
19. Witelson, S.F., et al. 2001. *Sex difference in the numerical density of neurons in the pyramidal layers of human prefrontal cortex: a stereologic study.* Soc. Neurosci. Abstr., Vol. 27, Program No. 80.18.
20. Koscik, Tim, et al. 2009. *Sex Differences in Parietal Lobe Morphology: Relationship to Mental Rotation Performance.* Brain and cognition. 69.3 pp. 451–459. April. Accessed: 4.29.16
http://www.ncbi.nlm.nih.gov/pmc/articles/PMC2680714/
21. Yogananda, Paramahansa. 1999. *God Talks with Arjuna. The Bhagavad Gita. Vol II.* Yogoda Satsanga Society of India. p. 874
22. Chinmoy, Sri. *Earth's Cry Meets Heaven's Smile, Part 2.* Could you explain the difference between Samadhi and self-realization? I

know they are the same theoretically, but I don't see why they're not. Sri Chinmoy. Sri Chinmoy Library. Agni Press. 1974. p. 181. Accessed: 01.02.16
http://www.srichinmoy.org/resources/library/questions_answers/samadhi
23. Chinmoy, Sri. 1977. *Miracles, Emanations, and Dreams.* Question: Does one get the same joy in sahaja samadhi as in nirvikalpa samadhi? Sri Chinmoy Library. Agni Press. 1-4 p. 31 Accessed: 10.29.15 http://www.srichinmoylibrary.com/med-25
24. Chinmoy, Sri. 1974. *The Summits of God-Life: Samadhi and Siddhi.* Question: If a Master is in sahaja samadhi all the time, which is the highest form of samadhi, is it a sort of conscious descent when he goes into nirvikalpa samadhi? Sri Chinmoy Library. Agni Press. pp. 92-93. Accessed: 09.13.16
http://www.srichinmoylibrary.com/scrolling/1390094#node-1390095
25. Chidananda, Swami. 1999. *The Philosophy, Psychology, and Practice of Yoga.* The Divine Life Trust Society. p. 100
26. Matthew 28:20 NASB
27. Thayer and Smith. 1999. *Greek Lexicon Entry for Zoe.* The NAS New Testament Greek Lexicon. Accessed: 4.29.16
http://www.biblestudytools.com/lexicons/greek/nas/zoe.html
28. Thayer and Smith. 1999. *Greek Lexicon Entry for Aion.* The NAS New Testament Greek Lexicon. Accessed: 4.29.16
http://www.biblestudytools.com/lexicons/greek/nas/aion.html
29. Dictionary.com. (n.d.) *aeon.* Online Etymology Dictionary. Douglas Harper (Historian). Accessed: 04.29.16
30. Encyclopædia Britannica Online. (n.d.) s.v. "aeon." Accessed 04.29.16. http://www.britannica.com/topic/aeon
31. Pierce, Rod. 2015. *Limits (An Introduction).* Math Is Fun. Aug. 25th. Accessed: 03.03.15
http://www.mathsisfun.com/calculus/limits.html
32. Harvey, Peter. 1990. *An Introduction to Buddhism: Teaching, history, and practices.* Cambridge University Press.
33. Frazier, Jessica and Flood, G. (ed.) 2011. *The Continuum Companion to Hindu Studies.* Continuum International Publishing Group. London, New York
34. Sivananda, Swami. 2011. *Instructions on Samadhi.* The Divine Life Society. Accessed 08.01.14

www.sivanandaonline.org/public_html/?cmd=displaysection&section_id=1228
35. Govindan, Marshall. 2005. *Babaji and the 18 Siddha Kriya Yoga Tradition*. 8th edition, p. 55, Babaji's Kriya Yoga and Publications, St Etienne de Bolton, Quebec, Canada, and Ramaiah, Yogi S.A.A., Kriya Magazine, 1953,2 Arulananda Street, San Thome, Madras, 60004, India
36. Yogananda, Paramahansa. 2012. *Autobiography of a Yogi*. Self-Realization Fellowship. Chapter 46: The Woman Who Never Eats, pp. 505-517
37. Judith Coney. 1999. *Sahaja Yoga: Socializing Processes in a South Asian New Religious Movement*. Curzon Press. Great Britain.
38. Nordmann, Charles. 1922. *Einstein and the Universe: a popular exposition of the famous theory*. Henry Holt and Co. p. 212.
39. Haas, Nibodhi. 2012. *Health and Consciousness: Through Ayurveda and Yoga*. Mata Amritanandamayi Mission Trust. p. 157.
40. Zimmerman, Marion. 2013. *A Short Introduction: The Tamil Siddhas and the Siddha Medicine of Tamil Nadu*. GRIN Verlag.
41. White, D.G. and Wujastyk, D. 2012. *Yoga in Practice*. Princeton: Princeton University Press.
42. Horner, IB. (trans.) 1975. *The Minor Anthologies of the Pali canon. part III: Buddhavaṁsa (Chronicle of Buddhas) and Cariyāpiṭaka (Basket of Conduct)*. London and Boston: The Pali Text Society. p. 97. vv. 18–20 cited in Early Buddhist Art of China and Central Asia. Volume 3. 2010. Koninklijke Brill NV, Leiden, The Netherlands by Marylin Martin Rhie
43. Buddha Dharma Education Association. 2014. *Suttanta Pitaka: Khuddaka Nikāya: 14. Buddhavamsa-History of the Buddhas. Guide to Tipiṭaka*. Tullera, NSW, Australia: Buddha Dharma Education Association. Accessed: 12.2.15 http://www.buddhanet.net/budvamsa.htm
44. Williams, Paul. 1989. *Mahāyāna Buddhism: The Doctrinal Foundations*. London and New York: Routledge. p. 230
45. Wikipedia. 2015. *List of Buddha Claimants*. Accessed: 3.3.15 https://en.wikipedia.org/wiki/List_of_Buddha_claimants

Chapter 17 – A Siddhi Summary
1. *Bhagavata Purana.* 11.15: 3–33
2. Patanjali's *Yoga Sutras* III.51–III.5

Chapter 20 – The Beginning to Self-Realization
1. Matthew 5:48 KJV

Bibliography

1. Knott, Kim. 2000. *Hinduism: A Very Short Introduction*. Oxford University Press, USA.
2. Flood, Gavin. 2005. *The Blackwell Companion to Hinduism*. Wiley-Blackwell Publishing.
3. Pollock, Robert. 2008. *World Religions*. New York, NY: Fall River Press. p. 88
4. Cousins, L.S. 1996. *The Dating of a Historical Buddha: a review article*. Journal of the Royal Asiatic Society (3)6(1): 57–63.
5. Hill, Jonathan. 2006. *Zondervan Handbook to the History of the Christianity*. Lion Publishing Plc. Oxford, England. pp. 10, 20.
6. Isaeva, Natalia 1993. *Shankara and Indian Philosophy*. Albany: State University of New York Press (SUNY).
7. Alistair Shearer. 1982. *The Yoga Sutras of Patanjali*. Random House. pp. 56, 107
8. Alistair Shearer. 1982. *The Yoga Sutras of Patanjali*. Random House. p 114. "On Samadhi"
9. Swami Vivekananda. 1920. *Raja Yoga*. Brentano's. pp. 17, 34, 118. "On samadhi"
10. Sivananda, S. 1998. *Mind. Its Mysteries and Control*. The Divine Life Society. "On samadhi" Accessed: 05.06.16 http://www.dlshq.org/download/mind.htm
11. Matchett, Freda. 2003. *The Puranas*. Chap. 6. p 139 in Flood, Gavin (Ed) *Blackwell companion to Hinduism*. Blackwell Publishing.
12. Mitra, Smita. 2004. *Krishna*. Outlook Magazine. Sept 13 Accessed: 11.27.15 http://www.outlookindia.com/article/krishna-b-july-21-3228-bc/225095
13. Mahesh C. Mangalick. 2014. *SEVA to Realize the SELF: Selfless Service*. Hamilton Books, Rowman and Littlefield. p. 20
14. Nicholas Costa. 2013. *Adam to Apophis: Asteroids, Millenarianism and Climate Change*. D'Aleman Publishing. p. 257
15. Saligram Bhat. (Ed) 2008. *Kashmiri Scholars Contribution to Knowledge and World Peace*. New Delhi. S.B. Nangia. A.P.H. Publishing Corporation. p. 276

16. Dasa, Satyaraja. 2012. *The Agni and The Ectasy. Collected Essays of Steven J. Rosen.* Arktos Media, Ltd. p. 151
17. Paulsen, Norman. 2002. *The Christ Consciousness.* Solar Logos Foundation.
18. *Webster's New Universal Unabridged Dictionary.* 2003. Barnes and Noble.
19. Yukteswar, Sri. 1990. *The Holy Science.* Self-Realization Fellowship. Los Angeles, CA
20. Dienstmann, Giovanni. 2015. *Live and Dare: Master Your Mind, Master Your Life.* Accessed: 03.03.16 http://liveanddare.com/types-of-meditation/
21. Peterson, Peter. 1885. *The Auchityalamkara of Kshemendra: With a Note on the Date of Patanjali, and an Inscription from Kotah.* Education Society's Press, Byculla.
22. *Bhagavad Gita*
23. Walthers, D.S. 1988. *Applied Kinesiology Synopsis.* 2nd Ed
24. Goenka, S.N. 2001. *Vipassana Meditation.* Dhamma.org Accessed: 03.03.16 https://www.dhamma.org/en-US/locations/directory#US
25. Vogl, Albert A. 1994. *Therese Neumann: Mystic and Stigmatist (1898-1962).* TAN Books. 1st Edition.

Glossary

Advaita Vedanta is a school of Hindu philosophy and religious practice. It is one of the oldest philosophies in Hinduism and emphasizes *moksha* or complete liberation through self-realization.

amrita is a divine nectar that is stimulated though achievement of the highest state of *nirvikalpa samadhi*. It is secreted by the pituitary gland primarily through practice of *kechari mudra*.

anantya literally means, "infinity" or "infinite;" this is the conscious form of *turiya samadhi* and is achieved at the highest stages of *nirvikalpa samadhi*. It is where *amrita* flows abundantly and bliss is like an endless ocean, fully submersive, in the mind of the yogi creating the Ecstatic Consciousness (EC).

Applied Kinesiology is a medical art created and developed by a chiropractor named Dr. George Goodheart. He blended all medical fields into one practice by using muscle testing (kinesiology) to determine which technique was best to use for the client's dysfunction, at the moment of treatment.

asanas are body postures used in yoga to elicit a certain response—whether physical, emotional, mental, or spiritual.

ascended masters are men or women who have at least achieved *sahaja samadhi* or higher. They may have a varying number of yogic powers that help to alleviate the world's suffering through the burning of karma.

astral body is an encasing or *kosha* that is one of three major body layers that surround the soul. The astral body is energetic in nature, surrounds the physical body, and is often seen as colored light.

Aum *See* Om

avatar *See* perfected master

Babaji *See* Mahavatar Babaji

Bhagavad Gita is a Sanskrit scripture, representing concepts of yogic practices involving karma, devotion, and liberation.

Bhagavan Krishna is sometimes referred to as the "Christ" of India. He lived 3000 years before the birth of Christianity and is often worshipped as a deity, as the Son of God, a divine hero, or as the Supreme Power.

Buddhism is a religion that came out of the worship and practices of Siddhartha Gautama, who was also known as Lord Buddha.

causal body is a *kosha* or body layer that is composed of thoughts and ideas. It the third major and most subtle layer of the three that encase the soul.

chakras are energy vortices that number seven in total, where *prana* or life-energy flows. Each energy center lies straight in the midline of the body, from the tip of the coccyx upwards to the crown of the head. Each one is a part of the energetic or astral body and is used to express the soul through emotion and color.

Chinmoy, Sri was a great self-realized master who lived during the late 20th century. He is the embodiment of one who lived a modern life as a weightlifter, athlete, artist, author, poet, and musician but was also able to achieve the highest level of self-realization at will.

chiropractic is a century-old medical art that helps one to achieve higher levels of consciousness (LOCs) by stimulating the neuro-emotional physiology of the body through the manipulation of spinal joints and acupuncture meridian systems.

chitta means "heart" in Sanskrit. It is often considered the center of the Self by some masters but is also referred to as the *anandamaya kosha* or bliss sheath. This layer represents the final layer between the causal body and soul's bliss.

Christ Consciousness is an LOC accessible by anyone who can see love in all of creation and know creation as oneself. It is named after Jesus the Christ because one needs to be Christ-like to achieve this conscious level.

Cosmic Consciousness is the Creator's consciousness, which is achieved through a Divine Superconsciousness Experience or a *turiya samadhi* with initiation into self-realization.

Cosmic Energy Technique is a technique to help heal the body, calm the mind, ascend in consciousness, and direct energy to do the same for others.

craniosacral therapy is a type of gentle, hands-on bodywork that manipulates the joints of the cranium (skull) and the pelvis to release pain and dysfunction to increase body health and performance.

Divine Superconscious Experience is another name for *turiya samadhi*. It is experienced at varying points throughout the process of self-realization but is most commonly experienced as initiation into self-realization.

duality is the nature of opposites. This is defined reality guarded by three-dimensional boundaries and discovered by the five senses.

ecstasy (state of) *See* anantya and amrita

eleven limbs of yoga are particular to this book. In Patanjali's *Yoga Sutras*, he describes eight limbs of yoga including: *yama, niyama, pranayama, pratyahara, asana, dharana, dhyana,* and *samadhi*. In addition to the eight, there are three previously unknown limbs. These are: *samyama, anantya,* and *turiya*.

ego is the "I"ness in creation, which serves as a deterrent to self-realization. Ego is body-centric, selfish, and acts upon desires created by the subconscious mind, past karmas, and *samskaras*.

Elemental State is a state that shows the unification in all religions, especially those native to the Americas.

enlightenment *See* self-realization

George Goodheart was the creator and main developer of Applied Kinesiology. This muscle testing-based system allows the practitioner to discover the best medical technique for the client, in the moment it is needed.

God-realization is where realization of the Self becomes the realization of God; this state of being is manifested at the highest achievement of *nirvikalpa samadhi*. It is achieved through expert-level meditation, *pranayama*, devotion, and surrender.

guru literally means, "dispeller of darkness." Gurus are spiritual masters, avatars, and Christ figures helping individuals to burn karma, enlighten through Self-knowledge, and stimulate one's desire to achieve the highest goal of humanity—self-realization.

Higher Self is also called the *Purusha*. It is the soul plus the Creator. This is the relationship one makes in the achievement of a non-dual *nirvikalpa samadhi* state, consequently leading to God-realization.

Hinduism is the major religion of India. It was developed mostly from the *Vedas* and is considered the oldest religion in the world. *Moksha* or liberation is the primary goal of this religion. Yoga is one the six major schools of philosophy within the religion itself and is derived from the *Vedas* as well.

homeopathy is treatment with small doses of natural substances that, in a normally healthy person, would cause symptoms of a particular disease process. In this case, "like treats like."

I.K. Taimni was a professor in chemistry and an influential scholar who wrote an extremely accurate interpretation of Patanjali's *Yoga Sutras* in the mid 20th century.

intuition is knowledge gained directly from the soul, and ultimately, the Creator. It can be accessed through intense focus and used at will through deep meditation.

inedia is the yogic *siddhi* (power) of non-eating. It is achievable by both saints and self-realized masters alike. With this power, one lives without eating food that is grown on planet Earth. One, instead, lives by spiritual ether and water vapor or God's bliss.

inner peace is an internal serenity that is broken with great difficulty. It is achieved through frequent meditation, devotion to the Divine, and living in physical and spiritual moderation.

Interstate, the is a long-forgotten state of consciousness that is controlled by angels for the benefit of yogis who ascend past *asamprajñata samadhi*. It is the first place where a major *samadhi* is experienced and achieved.

Ishvara is a name for the supreme soul/king/lord of the universe.

Janmashtami is a holiday in Hinduism to celebrate the birth Bhagavan Krishna, a yogi Hindu Christ from around 3200 BCE.

jivanmukta is the name of one who has achieved true liberation through achievement of *sahaja samadhi*.

kaivalya is a Sanskrit word for spiritual "liberation" or self-realization.

karma is a concept in Hinduism that recognizes that every action in a past or present life will create good or bad results in present or future lives. Good actions lead to positive results, and bad actions lead to negative results.

Kendall and Kendall were physical therapists who first started using a muscle testing rating system for medical diagnosis and treatment in the 1940's.

koshas are also called "sheaths" or body coverings. They range from being physical, energetic, idea-based, and finally, of spiritual quality. Accessing and shedding these sheaths will lead an individual to both self- and God-realization.

Krishna *See* Bhagavan Krishna

Krishna Consciousness is the LOC that represents the loving and child-like embodiment of the Christ Consciousness.

Kriya is a *pranayama* technique. It was passed from Mahavatar Babaji to Lahiri Mahasaya. To practice it is to help burn karma and drive one's consciousness to self-realization and the Divine. At its basic practice, it will bring great peace, harmony, and joy to those who use it frequently.

Kriya yoga is the yoga given to Lahiri Mahasaya from Mahavatar Babaji. The goal in this yoga is to spiritually evolve mankind through a technique called the *Kriya*.

Kriyananda, Swami was a swami inducted by Yogananda himself and was originally a part of Self-Realization Fellowship. Later on, he started his own organization called Ananda Sangha Worldwide, whose goal is to also spread the teachings of Kriya yoga.

kundalini is a form of primal energy, referred to as *shakti*, located at the base of the spine. Activating it can lead to self-realization, if done properly by one's spiritual master or guru.

Lahiri Mahasaya is a spiritual master from the 1800's who brought Kriya yoga to the world. He was known as God-realized master who manifested a complete set of yogic powers while raising a large family.

level of consciousness (LOC) in medical literature, is either Consciousness, Subconsciousness, or Unconsciousness. In this book, it can also be any level that goes beyond normal consciousness, into the Superconscious, Christ Conscious, Cosmic Conscious, Divine Conscious, and Divine Superconscious realms.

life force *See* prana

mahasamadhi is where a person can consciously leave his or her body at the moment of death. This is the last and greatest *samadhi* that a master can perform. This ability can occur for those who have at least achieved *savikalpa samadhi*.

Mahavatar Babaji is the deathless avatar Christ who gave Lahiri Mahasaya, Kriya yoga, to spread throughout the world.

maitreya in Buddhism, is a word that describes an "enlightened being," that comes to Earth to share a gospel of truth and light. It refers to the succession of different "buddhas" that came after the first, as a successive line of reincarnation. In this book, it represents the highest world teachers in existence, such as Jesus the Christ and Mahavatar Babaji.

maya in Indian philosophies, is the delusional Earth reality that creates bondage preventing us from spiritually evolving. It is also the reality which we interact using our five senses.

meditation is considered focused concentration and ceaseless prayer on a particular object. It is more advanced then prayer because the goal is to free the mind from distractions and become unified with the Higher Self.

Minervan man is the workingman or -woman who achieves self-realization while living in the modern world. This level of self-realization is at *savikalpa samadhi* or above.

mudras are various body positions, whether done by the hands, eyes, or tongue, that bring about greater levels of concentration, awareness, and realization.

muscle testing is a medical-based practice that allows the practitioner to determine an appropriate treatment through musculoskeletal and neurological examination. It comes in many forms, whether by specific muscles, non-specific tests, self-testing, or testing the muscle of the mind through intuition.

nadis are energetic meridians (channels) where the *chakras* receive or send energy to and from the extremities and other parts of the physical and astral bodies.

naturopathy is a type of complementary and alternative medicine that is emphasized as primary health care in the US. It uses various types of therapies to stimulate the body's natural ability to heal itself. These therapies can include botanicals/herbs, physical modalities, hydrotherapy, spinal manipulation, homeopathy, drug prescription, lifestyle modification, nutraceuticals, and acupuncture.

nirvana is also referred to as *nirvikalpa samadhi* or *nirbija samadhi*. It is the Buddhist term given to the liberation of the body and mind from the process of rebirth.

non-duality is the reality (or non-reality) beyond the existence of opposites or duality. This is where God (the Creator) "lives" in Its uncreated, unmanifested SPIRIT form as absolute a-existence.

Om (Aum) is the vibratory "fabric" that underlies all of creation. Yogananda related *Om* to being similar to the Holy Ghost in Christianity. *Om* is the universal sound, which, when unified with sound and spiritual awareness, allows one to become realized in the highest states of consciousness. *Om* is one the major keys to self-realization.

Paramahansa Yogananda is a guru, spiritual master, and primary creator of the organization Self-Realization Fellowship. He lived during the beginning of the 20th century and is considered the person who developed and spread the teachings of yoga in the United States (and the Western world).

Patanjali is an Indian philosopher who lived around 2500 years ago. He compiled the *Yoga Sutras*, which is the basis for practice of modern yoga and meditation.

perfected masters are individuals who can enter *turiya samadhi*, at will, with no effort. They manifest any number of *siddhis* (yogic power) at the desire/command of the Divine. Their LOC is well above *sahaja samadhi*, into the Aionion State, where they are literally merged with SPIRIT Itself. This includes Jesus the Christ, Mahavatar Babaji, Lahiri Mahasaya, and others.

prana is life-force that circulates in *chakras* and energy meridians of the body giving it life. It is found in animate and inanimate objects. It can also be considered *qi* or *ki*.

pranayama as the name entails, is to restrain or control the flow of *prana*, or life-force, in the body. This is a breath-control technique to help evolve the body and brain to higher LOCs and thus achieve self-realization.

pratyaya is the object of meditation—one that is focused upon in *savikalpa samadhi*, but non-existent in *nirvikalpa samadhi*.

Purusha is the Higher Self or the soul plus the Creator.

qi *See* prana

quantum mechanics is a branch of physics that has given rise to other theories describing dimensions existing beyond the normal three of length, width, and height.

Raja yoga also called "royal" yoga or the "king" yoga, is equated with the yoga of Patanjali's *Yoga Sutras*. The goal is to unify the Higher Self with the SPIRIT Self in God-realization.

Ramana Maharshi is a great spiritual master, who lived during the mid 20th century. He reached self-realization suddenly and left his family at 16 years old to mediate in the mountains of India.

reincarnation is the cycle of rebirth that occurs as a result of one's desires not being fulfilled. It also occurs to work off past karmas and debts. It is a principal tenet of Hinduism, Buddhism, Jainism, and Sikhism. This idea was also held by some Greek historical figures such as Pythagoras, Socrates, and Plato. It is considered a part of Judaism, Taoism, Native American cultures, Islam, and early Christianity.

samadhi, asamprajñata is considered the same as *nirvikalpa samadhi* but has been discovered as a transitional state between *savikalpa samadhi* and *nirvikalpa samadhi*.

samadhi, intermittent is *pratyahara* or true interiorization experienced in the 2nd Dimension LOCs and beyond.

samadhi, major are states of *samadhi* experienced during a first, relatively unknown, transition state called the Interstate. The major *samadhi* experience then extends as a description of even *turiya samadhi* itself.

samadhi, minor are states of *samadhi* experienced by using a technique to hear *Om*. They also extend up to the greatest minor *samadhi* state, *savikalpa*.

samadhi, Om is a state of absolute stillness and perfected consciousness that lies in the vibratory manifestation of *Om*. It can be a minor or major *samadhi* experience.

samadhi, nirvikalpa is a state of major *samadhi* (at its highest point) where one can achieve true bliss consciousness and become fully self-realized through God-realization.

samadhi, rajan, major is the non-dual *samadhi* experience of *nirvikalpa samadhi*. It is the "king" (*rajan*) of the major *samadhis* in *nirvikalpa*.

samadhi, savikalpa is the greatest minor *samadhi* state. Experiencing *savikalpa*, one has become self-realized—but only partially.

samadhi, sahaja is a type of *samadhi* that is "higher" than *nirvikalpa* and is manifested spontaneously and easily. This is where all karma and *samskaras* are burned, allowing for complete liberation or *kaivalya* to occur.

samadhi, turiya is the highest form of *samadhi* and is performed unconsciously. If this state is easily achieved while walking around, performing tasks of daily living, then one has become a perfected master—a completed Son of God.

samskaras are impressions that are imprinted on us after actions are performed. They can be good or bad, but all them need to be released to achieve complete liberation in *sahaja samadhi*.

samyama is the combination of *dharana* (concentration), *dhyana* (meditation), and *samadhi*. One of the prerequisites for gaining yogic power is to being able to perform *samyama* wholly and completely.

Sat-Tat-Om is the Trinity as described by Yogananda as SPIRIT (Unmanifested God), God (as Creator), and vibratory existence (Holy Ghost), respectively.

Sat-Chit-Ananda are three words representing SPIRIT (truth/reality), consciousness, and bliss (true happiness), respectively. This state of being can only be achieved in *nirvikalpa* and *sahaja samadhi*, where it can occur spontaneously and easily.

self/soul *See* Higher Self

self-realization is an all-encompassing term representing basic self-realization and God-realization. It is achieved in *savikalpa samadhi* through the advanced practice of meditation, *pranayama*, and yoga.

sexual samadhi is a type of *samadhi* only achievable if one is married or in a life-long, faithful relationship. Through commitment comes the ability to use the sexual force to ascend higher in LOCs to reach self-realization and ultimately God-realization.

shaktipat is a type of energetic initiation, where the guru or spiritual teacher/master activates and then breaks the seal of the *kundalini* energy in the base of the spine. This begins the process to self-realization, which can be very quick to very slow.

siddha is an individual who has achieved the highest degree of spiritual perfection and enlightenment. These *siddhas* are given special yogic powers (*siddhis*) at birth or during their life on Earth.

siddhis are yogic powers or abilities that are afforded to those individuals who are meant to use them. They are given to the Minervan man, ascended masters, and perfected masters in different varieties and forms.

SPIRIT is God (the Creator) as the Unmanifested Absolute; one that is without form, without the desire to create, and in a reality of a-existence.

spiritual eye *See* third eye

string theory was derived from quantum theory and quantum mechanics. It postulates dimensions that go beyond the normal three dimensions of length, width, and height.

Sufism is the mystical aspect of Islam. It serves to transcend the physical boundaries of religious law, to achieve perfection, and embrace the divine presence within.

Superconsciousness is a LOC that exists above normal baseline consciousness. This state can be accessed more easily in deeper meditation. It is a LOC, category of consciousness, and a broader classification describing any state above baseline consciousness.

Swami Sivananda was a true spiritual master who lived from the latter part of the 19th century into the mid 20th century. He started the

Divine Life Society in India and like Yogananda, his teachings permeate the practice of modern yoga in this present age.

Swami Vivekananda was considered the first yogi to lecture about yoga in the United States (and the Western world).

Swami Sri Yukteswar was the guru to Yogananda and disciple of Lahiri Mahasaya. He was a true spiritual master as well; one who lived as a householder (living as the workingman), but manifested perfection in the body, mind, and spirit.

third eye is also referred to as the spiritual eye, the *anja* (6th) *chakra*, or the Christ center by Yogananda. By opening the third eye, one can access intuition more easily and reach self-realization in a shorter time frame.

Trinity, the in Christianity is signified by Father (God), Son (Jesus Christ), and Holy Ghost (Holy Spirit). In other religions, the Trinity is like the *Trimurti* in Hinduism. This is *Brahma* (God), Vishnu (Preserver), and Shiva (Destroyer/Regenerator). Another triune recognized in yoga is *Om-Tat-Sat*. This is basic vibratory existence, God as Creator, and God as SPIRIT, respectively.

Upanishads are a part of the four Vedas, which form essential summaries of the Hindu doctrine.

Vedas are the four scriptures of Hinduism. The school of yoga and its basic philosophies and practices are found in these texts.

yoga is derived from the Vedas. It is a philosophy that has become a way of living for many people around the globe. It can be used for exercise and stretching or used to gain access to the intuitive mind through the use of its meditative arts, *pranayamas*, *mudras*, and body postures known as *asanas*. All these practices will eventually lead to self-realization through continued practice and devotion.

Yoga Sutras *See under* Patanjali

Index

1

1st Dimension LOCs · 99, 290

2

2nd Dimension LOCs · 138, 154, 290

3

3rd Dimension LOCs · 153, 290

A

acupuncture · 227
Advaita Vedanta · 82, 148
   self-realization, concept of · 22
   Vedantism · 33
agnostic · v, 60
ahamkara · *See* ego
ahimsa · 157
Aionion State, The · 289
   comparison to *sahaja samadhi* · 240
   definition of · 240
   experiences of · 251
   graphing of eternity, the · 242
   LOC transiency, increase in · 262
   measurement of · 242
   TotalLOC measurement · 238, 264
   transitional states · 262
A-kara · 230
ambrosia · *See amrita*
amrita · 59, 107, 195, 206, 227, 254, 255, 259
   DSCE associated · 164
   Ecstatic Consciousness, measurement of · 225
   householder roles · 226
   in *nirvikalpa samadhi* · 225, 236, 252
   in *sahaja samadhi* · 247, 253
   in *savikalpa samadhi* · 225
ananda · 157
Anandamayi Ma · 274
anantya · *See under samadhi, turiya*
Applied Kinesiology · 91, 149, 227, 228
asamprajñata samadhi · 48, 179, 261, 262, 289
   breathlessness · 188, 189, 190
   concept of · 181
   definition of · 50, 180
   DSCE associated · 165
   experiences of · 183
   extension experience · 184, 187
   Joy, LOC of · 194
   Kriya, use of · 191
   kundalini · 190
   light descension · 190, 191
   mentioned · 85, 302
   nirvikalpa samadhi, as · 186
   Samadhi Intensity · 188
   sensations of · 185
   SPIRIT State · 194
   stages of · 184
   VOID State breathlessness · 194
   VOID State, levels of · 193
asanas · 204
   ardha padmasana · 38, 206
   padmasana · 38, 206
   siddhasana · 38
ascended masters · 13, 184
   definition of · 279
   maximum LOC of · 279
associate ascension · *See under kundalini*
astral universe · 125, 126, 232
astrology · 132, 181
atheist · v, 60
Atlantis · 83
Aurobindo, Sri · 150

B

Baba, Neem Karoli · 274
Babaji, Mahavatar · 40, 231, 251, 263, 280

as the *maitreya* · 270
Babylonian Talmud: Tractate Berakoth 32b. v. 27 · 19
Bala, Giri · 252
belief system · vii
Bhagavad Gita 17.23 · 229
Bhagavad Gita 8.13 · 229
Bhagavata Purana · 274
  three major lists of *siddhis* · 275
bhakti · 157
Bharati, Jnaneshvara
  Yoga Sutras · ii
Blessing · vi
bliss · vi, 4
Bliss · 13
  definition of · 11, 12
Book of Kells · 200
brahmanadi · 199
breathless state · 43, 44, 138, 165, 178, 180, 188, 191
Buddha · 8, 114, 269, 273, 280
  non-duality · 183
buddhi · 217
Buddhism · 17, 20, 22, 52, 230, 246
  bodhisattvas, powers of · 273
  maitreya · 269
  meditation history · 33
  Nichiren Shoshu · 3
  nirvana · 22, 145
  tantra · 106
  Vajrayana (tantra) · 119

C

calculus · 242
  infinity, mathematical concept of · 245
  infinity, spiritual concept of · 245
  limit, the · 242, 245
causal universe · 125
CC1
  as an exponent · 127
  definition of · 123
  googolplex comparison · 126
  numerical baseline · 124
  summary · 128
  value of · 126
  value of, actual · 128
CERN · 181
chakras · 120, 149, 170, 258, 259
  ascension in 2nd Dimension · 139

ascension to Cosmic Consciousness · 147
breathless state · 189
choice in creation of children · 171
Cosmic Energy Technique · 147
descension of LOC · 140
disease clearing · 192
eighth center · 164
fifth center · 231
fourth center in major *samadhi* · 203
fourth center in *savikalpa samadhi* · 176
kundalini sensations · 173
light descension · 190
opening sensations of · 147
pull of energy from extremities · 186
seventh center · 219, 260
seventh center in DSCE · 164
seventh center in *nirvikalpa samadhi* · 223
third eye · 92, 175, 179, 219, 226, 232, 233, 260
Chidananda, Swami, on *sahaja samadhi* · 239
China · 4
Chinmoy, Sri · 104
  Christ Consciousness · 114
  sahaja samadhi · 238
  samadhi · 82
  samadhi building analogy · 239
  self-realization · 27
  Superconsciousness · 110
  time frame in *samadhi* · 44
  treatment for the body · 149
  turiya samadhi · 55
  Yoga Sutras · ii
chiropractic · 227
Chiropractic · 261, 293
Christ consciousness · 183
Christ Consciousness · 231, 252, 288
  1 Thessalonians 5:17 · 116
  ascension ideas · 118
  ascension techniques · 117
  astral *samadhi* · 233
  CC1 variable · *See entry* CC1
  Chinmoy, Sri · 114
  comparison to Superconsciousness · 120
  Creator (Cosmic) Consciousness · 114
  energy flow of · 115
  maintenance of · 116
  Matthew 7:12 · 117

Om and ascension · 122
  other "Christs" · 114, 129
  other aspects · 122
  personal experience · 117
  sex and ascension · 118, 119, 120
  sexual samadhi · 120
  third eye · 233, 234
Christ, Jesus · 130, 231, 251, 263, 268, 280
  as the *maitreya* · 270
  Cosmic Consciousness · 144
  kingdom of heaven, the · 145
  non-duality · 183
  power of anger · 267
  temptation of · 206
  third eye · 234
  unity in consciousness · 146
Christianity · 18
  Apostles of Jesus · 273
  Francis of Assisi, Saint · 83, 251
  Guigo II · 34
  Ignatius of Loyola, Saint · 34
  Joseph of Cupertino, Saint · 83, 273
  meditation · 34
  Neumann, Therese · 284
  powers of saints · 273
  Simon the Magus · 83
  Teresa of Avila, Saint · 34, 83, 251, 273
Collective Christ Consciousness · 128
Collective Cosmic Consciousness · 129
collective subconscious mind · 104, 237
compactified dimensions · 198, 199
congressional medal of honor · 167
Consciousness LOC · 100, 287
  coma scales · 101
  Kruse, Maria · 101
  major levels of · 101
cosmic consciousness · 193
Cosmic Consciousness · 121, 155, 179, 183, 231
  ascension into · 149
  ascension to · 142
  Aurobindo, Sri · 150
  Bucke, Richard, *Cosmic Consciousness* · 143, 144
  Bucke, Richard, the "Cosmic Sense" · 143
  chakra opening · 147
  definition of · 143
  divine helpers · 146
  experiences of · 175
  Gabriel's vision · 145
  Humboldt, Alexander von, *Kosmos* · 143
  increases in brain power · 151
  kingdom of heaven, the · 145
  other aspects · 150
  Paulsen, Norman, *The Christ Consciousness* · 149
  personal experiences of · 146
  Pythagoras · 143
  Sivanada, Swami · 150
  third eye · 233
  Yogananda, Paramahansa, *Autobiography of a Yogi* · 145
  Yogananda, Paramahansa, *God Talks with Arjuna* · 145
Cosmic Energy Technique · 185, 191, 226, 293
  definition of · 147
  for healing · 261
  kundalini, activation of · 172
  major *samadhi*, use in · 203
  major *samadhi*, while in · 206
  sahaja samadhi, use in · 254, 255
craniosacral therapy · 227
Creator · *See* God

D

D'Adamo, Peter, *Eat Right for Your Blood Type* · 255
Dalai Lama · 28
Dass, Ram · 41
dharma · 157
dharma megha samadhi · 47, 59
dhyana · 29
Divine Superconscious Experience · 17, 18, 159, 188, 209, 234, 263
  achievement of · 160
  angelic voices · 166
  Creator's blessings · 167
  experiences of · 164, 165
  final merger · 266
  guru's blessings · 167
  healing for · 261
  intensities of · 163
  merger with SPIRIT in *sahaja samadhi* · 236
  stages of · 161, 162, 163
Dogen · 33
Dream SuperUnConsciousness · 214
Drunken Consciousness · 105
  Perceived Nirvikalpa Samadhi · 105

dualism
  URL · 23
duality · 23, 179, 215, 216, 235

E

ecstasy, state of · See *amrita* in *nirvikalpa samadhi*
Ecstatic Consciousness · See *amrita*
ego · 25, 78
  ahamkara · 217
  asmita · 103
  attachments in *samadhi* · 259
  definition of · 103
  descension of LOC · 206
  Gandhi · 103
  in *nirvikalpa samadhi* · 214
Elemental State · 288
  addictions · 134
  ayahuasca and ascension · 131
  definition of · 131
  descension in LOC · 134
  description of · 132
  karma, law of · 132
  personal experience of · 133
  peyote and ascension · 131
  purpose of · 133
  removal of karma · 134
  willpower and ascension · 133
Eleven Limbs of Yoga · 57
enlightenment · See self-realization
Extradimensional LOCs · 209, 290

F

Fermilab · 181
forced vibration · 170, 171
Freud, Sigmund · 103, 104

G

Gandhi · 26
  ego · 103
Gnosticism · 241
God · 20
  definition of · v, 8
  desires of the heart · 140
  SPIRIT as bliss · 144
SPIRIT, as defined as · 23, 24, 33, 115, 126, 145, 193, 201, 209, 211, 216, **219**, 235, 259, 264, 303
  URL · 22
God-realization · 4
Golden Age · 129, 201, 269
Golden Rule · v
googol · 125
  googolplex · 125
  Nitsche, Wolfgang · 125
  Page, Don · 125
  Sagan, Carl, *Cosmos A Personal Voyage* · 125
guru · vii

H

Haridas, Sadhu · 188
Hawkins, David · 88
heart of stillness · 19
Hicks, Esther and Jerry, *The Law of Attraction* · 222
Higher Self · 138, 148, 246
  URL · 22
Hinduism · 20, 22, 166, 230, 246
  atma-jnana · 22
  Bala, Giri · 252
  Bhagavata Purana · 273
  cycle of ages · 87
  definition of · 20
  swamis, powers of · 273
  tantra · 106
  Trimurti, the · 230
homeopathy · 227
Hong-sau
  personal experience of · 190
Hong-Sau · 138
householder · 213
hydrotherapy · 227

I

Indus Valley region · 34, 38
inedia · 204
inner peace · 2, 4, **8**, 9
Interstate, the · 51, 199, 211, 289
  angelic facilitation · 199, 201
  compactified dimensions · 199
  definition of · 198
  Interstate, second-half · 214, 218

Minor Samadhi Major Experience · 202
shape of · 200
Ishvara · 177
Islam · 17, 20, 31
   amin · 229
   dhikr · 34
   fakirs, powers of · 273
   Muhammad · 145
   Quran · 145
   religious practice · 17
   See Sufism for more info ·
Iyengar, BKS · 35

J

jada samadhi · 162
Jainism · 106, 230
Janmashtami · 256
Jesus Christ · vii
   Christ Consciousness · 113
   levels of consciousness · 86, 89
   muscle testing · 73
   self-realization and salvation · 86
jivanmukta · 246
jñāna · 157
John 1:1,3 NASB · 229
Judaism · 19, 31
   Philo of Alexandria · 34
   self-realization, concept of · 22

K

kaivalya · 213, 248
karma · 13, 100, 117, 132, 231, 260, 269, 300
   instant transmission in *nirvikalpa samadhi* · 222
   last release of · 246
   physical release in 2nd Dimension · 147
   pulling karma · 182
   removal of · 149, 160
   spiritual types · 148
   storage locations · 148
   storage of disease processes · 149
kārunya · 157
Kendall and Kendall · 64
kingdom of heaven, the · 211, 236
koshas

anandamaya (chitta) · 166, 211, 265
anandamaya (chitta), shedding of · 246
annamaya kosha · 107
bliss sheath · 263
causal body, shedding of · 246
God sheath · 266
intuition of the soul · 72
locations of karmic storage · 148
removal of bliss sheath · 166
removal of body coverings in DSCE · 166
sahaja samadhi, access to · 211
self-realization initiation · 161
Krishna Consciousness LOC · 129, 288
Krishna, Bhagavan · vii, 114, 129, 131, 231, 251, 263, 270, 280
   Cosmic Consciousness · 144
   non-duality · 184
   siddhis, ten secondary · 274
   temptation of · 206
Kriya · iii, 40, 107, 117, 146, 178, 185, 191
   ascension in LOC · 279
   definition of · 117
   experiences of · 138
   lessons for · 4
   meditaton, for · 299
   removal of karma · 138, 146
   science of · 118
Kriya yoga · 14, 39, 40, 107, 117, 148, 168
   definition of · 40
   Raja yoga · 39
Kriyananda, Swami, on Superconsciousness · 110
kundalini · 160, 169, 176, 190
   activation through lifestyle · 172
   amrita, activation of · 225
   anatomical parts of · 170
   asamprajñata, as a part of · 187
   associate ascension · 120, 170, 182
   Cosmic Energy Technique, usage of · 172
   definition of · 169
   kriya, use of · 191
   movement in *chakras* · 173
   movement of · 172
   rate of · 170
   Sahaja yoga, in · 257
   sensations of · 173
   shaktipat · 160, 169, 171

L

Law of Ascension · 59, 116, 175, 180, 263, 293, 299
   aspects of · 292
   definition of · 139
   extension states · 291
   URL · 59
laya samadhi · 50, 291
levels of consciousness · vi
   ascension in · 179, 256, 293
   ascension of Christians · 256
   ascension of Hindus and yogis · 256
   categories of consciousness · 93, 97
   Christ Transiency · 268
   classification of consciousness · 96
   definition of · 81
   descension of · 176
   mentioned · 61, 63
   muscle testing · 68
   numerical values of · 83
   origin of · 88
   potential of · 85
   practical application · 85
   treatment to raise · 90
   values of · 90
   world LOC · 279
Livingston, John, *Adversaries Walk Among Us* · 206
Lokenath, Baba · 284

M

Maharshi, Ramana · ii
   self-realization · 191
   the Self · 26
mahasamadhi · 161, 256, 282
Mahasaya, Lahiri · 40, 106, 168, 172, 274, 280
   Kriya · iii
   Purana Purusha (the book) · iii
   tantra · 106
maitreya · 251, 269, 270
major *samadhi* · 51
Ma-kara · 230
mantra
   dhikr · 34
   Jesus Prayer · 34
   power of mind · 31
Matthew 25:34 NASB · 211
Matthew 28:20 NASB · 241
Matthew 4:4 NASB · 188
Matthew 5:48 KJV · 303, 335
Matthew 7:13-14 NASB · 25
maya · 230, 235
meditation · 59, 255
   application of · 31
   auto-regulation of mind · 30
   clearing dark forces · 206
   goal of · vii, 5, 30
   healthcare, in · 32
   hesychasm · 34
   history of · 33
   how to get started · 297
   moderation in · 213, 271, 293
   necessity of · 175
   nirvikalpa samadhi, pathway to · 220
   overall progression of stillness · 252
   personal experiences in cold weather · 223
   religious unification · 32
   samadhi for spiritual communication · 183
   samadhi is highest goal · 30
   savikalpa samadhi, achievement of · 17
   Superconsciousness · 83
Meditation
   definition of · 29
   Zen Buddhism · 29
minerva · 15
Minervan man · 13, 20, 118, 268
   definition of · 15, 16
   maximum LOC of · 279
Minor Samadhi States · 49, 155, 288
   laya samadhi · 158
   lesser minor *samadhi* states · 156
moderation · 14
moksha · 41, 246, 247
Mortimer Adler · 24
mudras · 185
   kechari mudra · 44, 162, 255
   shambhavi mudra · 165, 234, 241, 254, 255, 264, 293
   third eye · 189, 298
Multidimensional LOCs · 197, 198, 290
   definition of · 197
muscle testing · 65, 181
   Applied Kinesiology · 63, 65
   ascension of LOC · 185
   Callahan, Roger · 64
   chakras · 72, **76**, 77
   Craig, Gary · 64
   Cuthbert, Scott · 66
   definition of · 61

Diamond, John · 64, 88
for accelerated healing · 228
Francis, Timothy · 89
Goodheart, George · 63, 64, 66
history of · 62
indicator testing · 65
intuitive testing · 69, 74, **76**, 78
Kendall and Kendall · 62, 64
levels of consciousness · 91
Lovett, Robert · 62, 64
neurological basis of · 67
non-break test · 70
Palmer, D.D. · 78
question calibration · 76
questions for · 74
self-testing · 66, 67
third eye LOC · 121
types of · 63
Walthers, David · 66
Muslim · *See Islam*

N

nadis · 170, 185, 258
Native American practices · 35
nirbija samadhi · 47
nirvana · 52, 246
nirvikalpa samadhi · 17, 58, 202, 248, 260, 289
    achievement of · 179
    amrita · 107
    as *sahaja samadhi* · 246
    ascension in LOC · 219
    breathless state · 188
    comparison of *savikalpa samadhi* · 210
    comparison of the Interstate · 211
    comparison to *sahaja samadhi* · 238
    definition of · 52, 210
    DSCE associated · 165
    duality vs. non-duality · 215
    experiences of · 212
    hallmark of · 213, 214
    love, character of · 249
    mentioned · 44, 51, 54, 59, 85, 181, 242, 257
    nature of · 258
    nature of joy in relationships · 191
    personal experiences of · 210
    postures for achievement · 220
    present habits · 214
    sensations of · 222
    sex and energy gains · 120
    sexual *samadhi* · 218
    stages of · 53
    true healing · 212
Nobel Prize · 167
non-duality · 210, 215, 217, **219**, 235, 240
    URL · 52
numerology · 231

O

Om · 117, 192, 220, 236, 237, 259
    Christ Consciousness · 122
    concept of · 231, 232
    definition of · 227
    five physical senses · 232
    in astral *samadhi* · 236
    in major *samadhi* · 204
    in nirvikalpa samadhi · 217
    in sahaja samadhi · 227
    in savikalpa samadhi · 178
    male/female differences · 237
    Minor Samadhi States · 157
    Om samadhi, major-type, merger with · 221
    Om samadhi, minor-type · 122
    Om technique · 122, 231
    personal experiences of · 232
    pranava · 232
    symphonic-type · 164

P

paganism · 20
Patanjali · i
    asamprajñata samadhi · 180
    eight limbs of yoga · 40, 42, 57, 60, 159
    savikalpa samadhi · 177
    Yoga Sutras · i, 37, 42, 47, 57, 176, 232
    Yoga Sutras references · i
    Yoga Sutras, siddhis in · 274
Paulsen, Norman · 149
peace · *See* inner peace
perfected masters · 184, 280
prana · 39, 170, 185
pranayama · 34, 38
    removal of karma · 148
pratyaya · 46
prayer · *See* meditation
Psalm 65:2 · 19

Psalms 37:4 · 140
Purana Purusha (the book) · See Mahasaya, Lahiri
Puranas · 274
Purusha · 148

Q

qi · See prana
quantum mechanics · 138
Quran · See under Islam

R

Ramakrishna · 41
reincarnation · 246
    kundalini associated · 173
Roman Catholic church · 19

S

sabjia samadhi · 46
sahaja samadhi · 58, 289
    "practicing the presence" · 254, 255
    characteristics of · 246
    comparison to AION · 240
    comparison to nirvikalpa samadhi · 247
    definition of · 53, 238, 257, 263
    DSCE associated · 165
    exercise considerations · 260
    hallmark of · 247
    karma · 132
    lifestyle for ascension · 253
    love, character of · 250
    mentioned · 54, 59, 174, 236
    See Aionion State, The, for more info · 240
    sexual samadhi · 120
    stages of · 53
Sahaja samadhi
    sat-chit-ananda, as · 238
sahaja yoga
    healing sensations of oneself or others · 258
Sahaja yoga · 257
salvation · 228, 272
samadhi · 45, 69, 90, 174, 227
    amrita · 107
    application of · 148

asamprajñata · 180
breathless state · 188
classical view · 46
concept of · 140
Cosmic Energy Technique, use of · 261
definition of · 43, 168, 169
early attainment of · 194
exercise, during · 260
expanded view · 49
initiation of Cosmic Consciousness · 150
Jada samadhi · 44
light descension · 190
major-type as DSCE · 159
major-type, first occurrence · 197
mentioned · 49, 72, 104, 115, 134, 138, 274, 300
minor-type · 155
modern view · 47, 48
muscle testing · 69
out-of-body experiences · 168
references · i
sexual samadhi · 120
Superconsciousness · 108
views of · ii, 45, 46
Yogananda, Paramahansa · 145
Samadhi
    concept of · 44
Samadhi Intensity · 190
samadhi, astral · 233, 236, 237, 240, 247
    ascension techniques · 234
    comparison with Om samadhi · 237
    concept of · 235
    shambhavi mudra · 234
    third eye focus · 233
samadhi, intermittent · 140
    as pratyahara · 140
samadhi, major-type · 202, 203, 231, 261
    essentials for maintenance · 205
    heart expansion · 203
    minor and major samadhi differences · 205
    non-eating habits · 204
    personal experiences of · 204
    sensations of · 204
    transition state #1 · 205
    transition state #2 · 207
    true potency of bliss · See
samadhi, Om · 231, 237
    comparison with astral samadhi · 237
    definition of · 228, 230
    Om-Tat-Sat · 229

symbolism of · 230
samadhi, rajan, major-type · 215, 216
    four steps from duality to non-duality
        · 217
    transition state · 226
samadhi, turiya · 54, 55, 82, 169, 230, 267
    anantya · 53, 54, 57, **58**, 59, 82, 169,
        210, 224, 225, 227, 230, 234, 267
    mentioned · 57, 59
Samkhyakarika · 274
samprajñata · 181
samprajñata samadhi · 48
samskaras · 106, 148, 255
    destruction of · 174
samyama · 57, 204, 274
    definition of · 58
savikalpa samadhi · 18, 20, 210, 248, 288
    breathless state · 190
    definition of · 50, 174, 181
    DSCE associated · 165
    experiences of · 176
    extension experience · 179, 184
    initiation to · 174
    major stages of · 176, 177, 178
    mentioned · 44, 54, 85, 242
    openness to the universe · 179
    sensations of · 180
    sex and energy loss · 120
    state of Minervan man · 16
    technique usage in · 178
    third eye penetration · 234
Savikalpa samadhi · 16
self · *See* Higher Self
self-realization · iv, 4, 5, 22, 255
    comparison of saints and self-realized
        masters · 284
    concept of · 31, 303
    definition of · iv, 22
    founding fathers of · 26
    goal of · 5
    graphing of eternity, the · 243
    highest dispensation of · 238
    holistic nature of · 239
    major milestones of · 163
    nature of disease · 147
    necessity of a guru · 228
    personal experiences of initiation ·
        191
    personal journey of · iii, vii, 1
    stages of · 176
    treatment for · 227
    true nature of · 225
Self-realization

definition of · 21
Self-Realization
    concept of · 24
Self-Realization Fellowship · iii, 3, 40
Semi-Superconsciousness LOC · 107
sexual samadhi · 253
    activation of *kundalini* · 171
    ascension in LOC · 221
    in *nirvikalpa samadhi* · 218
shahada · 8
shaktipat · *See under kundalini*
Shankara, Swami Adi · 26, 274
siddha · 266
siddhis · 58, 115, 206, 212, 244, 247, 252,
    261, 266, 267, 269, 271, 273, 295
    10 secondary types · 276
    44 types totaled in Patanjali's *Yoga*
        Sutras · 274, 277
    achievable through *samayama* · 274
    drug use for power · 275
    eight primary *(asta/ashta/maha)* types
        · 273, 275
    five minor types of yoga and
        meditation · 274, 276
    greatest power of all · 278
    how to achieve · 278
    levitation · 84
    powers of ascended masters · 280,
        281, 282, 283
    powers of perfected masters · 280,
        284
    powers of the Minervan man · 280
    powers of the Minervan man · 281
    references · i
    ten secondary powers · 274
Sikhism · 106
Sivananda · 40, 71, 82
Sivananda, Swami · ii, 280
    concept of a *jivanmukta* · 246
    Cosmic Consciousness · 27, 150
    definition of *Om* · 230
    ego · 103
    meditation in cold weather · 223
    supersensuous wisdom · 162
    Yoga Sutras · ii
SPIRIT Collective Consciousness · 129
Spirit States · 141, 288
spiritual protection · 31
stillness · 16, 17, 260, 298
    progress of · 252
string theory · 199
Subconsciousness LOC · 104
    Sri Chinmoy · 104

suffering · 12, 14, 250
Sufism · 22, 34
   fanā' · 22
Superconsciousness LOC · 81, 108, 287
   application of · 111
   Chinmoy, Sri · 110
   definition of · 111
   Kriyananda, Swami · 110
   maintenance of · 109
   perfection of · 109
   Vivekananda and *samadhi* · 108
sushumna · 173, 191

T

Taimni, I.K. · 47
   samprajñata and *asamprajñata* · 48
   The Science of Yoga · 48
tantra · 119
Taoism · 33
Tattvasamasa · 274
Thich Nhat Hanh · 27, 82
third eye · 13, 107, 115, 254, 259
   Christ Consciousness activation · 115
   description of · 121
Trailanga Swami · 274
Transcendental Meditation · 35
Trinity, the · 230
triquetra (trinity knot) · 200

U

U-kara · 230
unattachment · 12
Unconsciousness LOC · 102
   coma scales · 102
   Freud, Sigmund · 102
   Sivananda, Swami · 103
Uni-A-Dimensional LOCs · 290
Unitarian Universalist · v
Unnamed States · 139, 288
   benefits of stillness · 139
   final removal of karma · 141
   sensations of · 140
Upanishads · 230

V

Vivekananda, Swami · 35, 40, 82, 86

Raja yoga (the book) · 39
Raja Yoga (the book) · 108
self-realization · 26
Superconsciousness · 108

W

world LOC · 179

Y

yin yang · 235
yoga · 20, 59, 60
   asanas · 38
   ashtanga · 40
   definition of · iv, 37
   goal of · 41
   highest goal of · 210
   history of · 38
   origin of · 40
   schools of · 38
Yoga
   concept of · 41
   general · 37
   goal of · 42
Yoga Sutras · *See under* Patanjali
Yogananda, Paramahansa · 35, 40, 82, 87, 114, 175, 263, 268, 274, 280
   Autobiography of a Yogi · 270
   Kriya technique · 117
   mentioned · ii, iii, 3, 168, 179
   nature of a master · 272
   physical aspect of Cosmic Consciousness · 151
   power of *Om* · 229
   renunciation · 27
   self-realization · 24
   SRF lessons · 4
   third eye · 121
   Trinity, the · 229
   Yoga Sutras · ii
yogic powers · *See siddhis*
Yukteswar, Sri · 24, 87, 168, 280
   koshas · 148

Z

Z State · 131
Zen Buddhism · 33

Author Bio

Dr. Derek Simpson is a dual licensed physician of both chiropractic and naturopathic medicine currently practicing in Washington State. His focus is on family practice, internal medicine, and education while writing on self-realization, metaphysics, and spirituality.

You can connect with him through his email listed below.

Hope to hear from you soon!

Ascended Books
drsimpson_1@hotmail.com

Made in the USA
Middletown, DE
06 October 2022